THE
MOLDOVANS

STUDIES OF NATIONALITIES

Wayne S. Vucinich, General Editor

The Crimean Tatars
  Alan Fisher

The Volga Tatars: A Profile in National Resilience
  Azade-Ayşe Rorlich

The Making of the Georgian Nation
  Ronald Grigor Suny

*The Modern Uzbeks: From the Fourteenth Century to the Present:
A Cultural History*
  Edward A. Allworth

Estonia and the Estonians, second edition
  Toivo U. Raun

The Azerbaijani Turks: Power and Identity under Russian Rule
  Audrey L. Altstadt

The Kazakhs, second edition
  Martha Brill Olcott

The Latvians: A Short History
  Andrejs Plakans

The Moldovans: Romania, Russia, and the Politics of Culture
  Charles King

THE MOLDOVANS

Romania, Russia,
and the
Politics of Culture

Charles King

HOOVER INSTITUTION PRESS
Stanford University
Stanford, California

www-hoover.stanford.edu

Hoover Institution Press Publication No. 472

Copyright © 2000 by the Board of Trustees of the
  Leland Stanford Junior University

First printing, 1999

Manufactured in the United States of America

04 03 02 01 00 99   9 8 7 6 5 4 3 2 1

The paper used in this publication meets the minimum requirements of American National Standard for Information Sciences—Permanence of Paper for Printed Library Materials, ANSI Z39.48-1984. ⊗

Library of Congress Cataloging-in-Publication Data
King, Charles.
    The Moldovans : Romania, Russia, and the politics of culture / Charles King.
        p.   cm. — (Studies of nationalities)
    Includes bibliographical references and index.
    ISBN 0-8179-9791-1 (alk. paper).
    ISBN 0-8179-9792-X (pbk. : alk. paper)
    1. Moldova—History.   I. Title.   II. Series.
DK509.54.K56   1999
947.6—dc21   99-41906
                                                          CIP

Design by P. Kelley Baker

For my parents and Miss Pearlie

Contents

List of Illustrations   ix

List of Tables   xi

Abbreviations   xiii

Foreword   xv

Preface   xix

Acknowledgments   xxiii

Introduction: The Physical Setting   xxvii

1   Contested Territories, Contentious Identities   1

PART ONE
BESSARABIA BETWEEN
ROMANIA AND RUSSIA

2   From Principality to Province   11

3   Greater Romania and the Bessarabian
         Question   36

4   Forging a Soviet Moldovan Nation   63

PART TWO
MOLDOVA AS A SOVIET
REPUBLIC

5   A Stipulated Nation   91

6   Language and Ethnic Mobilization under
     Perestroika   120

PART THREE
INDEPENDENCE AND
CONFLICT

7   Politics, Identity, and Reform after the Soviet
     Union   145

8   The Multiethnic Republic   168

9   The Transnistrian Conundrum   178

10   The Gagauz   209

11   A Negotiable Nationalism   224

     Notes   231

     Glossary   269

     Bibliography   273

     Index   295

Illustrations

Photographs

Boğdan Saray, Istanbul	19
Dimitrie Cantemir	20
"Moldovan Bloc" in Sfatul Ţării, 1918	34
"The Rape of Bessarabia," 1924	45
Women of Bulboca village, Bessarabia, 1924	47
King Carol II in Bessarabia, 1935	50
Nicolae Titulescu, 1933	53
Pavel Chior	67
Moldovan Scientific Committee, 1930	71
Moldovan schoolchildren, 1989	122
Declaration of independence, 1991	152
Mircea Snegur	156
Petru Lucinschi, 1996	163
Moldovan and Transnistrian forces, 1992	182
"For the Motherland!"	188
Cossacks in Transnistria, 1992	193
Igor Smirnov, 1993	196
Alexander Lebed', 1993	199

Ilie Ilaşcu on trial, 1993   207
Stepan Topal, 1993   216

Maps
Map 1. Romanian Lands before 1812   xxvi
Map 2. Greater Romania, Soviet Moldova,
                and after, 1918 to the Present   xxvii
Map 3. Republic of Moldova   xxviii

Tables

Table 1   Bessarabian Population in the
            Nineteenth Century   24

Table 2   Ethnic Romanians in Greater
            Romania, 1930   46

Table 3   MASSR Population, 1926 and 1936   54

Table 4   Examples of Moldovan
            Neologisms, 1929   69

Table 5   MSSR Population, 1941–89   97

Table 6   National Composition of the
            Communist Party of Moldova   99

Table 7   First Secretaries of the Communist
            Party of Moldova, 1941–91   100

Table 8   Language and Ethnicity in the
            MSSR, 1989   113

Table 9   Moldovan Elections, 1991–98   158

Table 10   Population of Transnistria,
                1897–1989   185

Table 11   Transnistria in the Moldovan
                Economy, 1991   186

Table 12   Chronology of the Transnistrian
                Conflict, 1989–98   190

Abbreviations

CIS	Commonwealth of Independent States
CMU	Committee for Moldovanization and Ukrainization
CPM	Communist Party of Moldova
CPSU	Communist Party of the Soviet Union
DC	Democratic Convention of Moldova
DMR	Dnestr Moldovan Republic
MASSR	Moldovan Autonomous Soviet Socialist Republic
MDPM	Movement for a Democratic and Prosperous Moldova
MSC	Moldovan Scientific Committee
MSSR	Moldovan Soviet Socialist Republic
OGRF	Operational Group of Russian Forces
OSCE	Organization for Security and Cooperation in Europe

OSTK	United Council of Work Collectives
SSR	Soviet Socialist Republic
TIKA	Turkish Cooperation and Development Agency

The following abbreviations are used in the notes:

ANR-DAIC	Arhivele Naţionale ale României, Direcţia Arhiva Istorică Centrală (Romanian National Archives, Central Historical Archive Division, Bucharest)
ANRM	Arhiva Naţională a Republicii Moldova (National Archive of the Republic of Moldova, Chisinau)
AOSPRM	Arhiva Organizaţiilor Social-Politice a Republicii Moldova (Archive of Social-Political Organizations of the Republic of Moldova, Chisinau)
d.	*delo, dosar* (file)
f.	*fond* (archive group)
f.d.	no date (in Romanian archival references only)
FBIS-EEU	*Foreign Broadcast Information Service (Eastern Europe)*
FBIS-SOV	*Foreign Broadcast Information Service (Soviet Union)*
l., ll.	*list, listy* (page[s]) (f. and ff. in Romanian documents)
n/c	Moldovan archival sources not yet cataloged at time of research
op.	*opis'* (inventory)
SWB-EE	BBC *Summary of World Broadcasts (Eastern Europe)*
SWB-SU	BBC *Summary of World Broadcasts (Soviet Union)*

Foreword

The Moldovans are probably the least known of the former Soviet Union's republican nationalities. This book is the only comprehensive study of the subject. A great deal of attention was focused on Moldova in the brief period of its struggle for independence and the ensuing war with Transnistrian separatists in 1991 and 1992, but after that it generally faded from the headlines. Like other small states on the Russian periphery, once the fighting stopped Western interest seemed to fade as well, even though the conflicts that spawned the violence in the early 1990s have not been resolved.

The author places the fate of Moldova in its historical context, tracing the history of the lands of the present Moldovan state—mainly the Bessarabia region that was controlled for much of modern history by Russia or Romania—from the mid–fourteenth century to the end of the twentieth. This volume covers the origins of the medieval Moldovan principality, Bessarabia's place in the Russian empire from 1812 to 1918, the period of Romanian control from 1918 to 1940, and the making of the Moldovan Soviet republic after the Second World War. Further chapters focus on Moldova since independence, particularly the prickly questions of minorities such as the Turkic Gagauz and the mainly

Slavic Transnistrians. No other Western reseacher has been able to carry on research of such depth into the region's history. Sections covering more recent events are the product of a decade's close observation of Romanian and Moldovan affairs. The author has also conducted numerous interviews and conversations with leading political and cultural figures in the region.

The theme at the center of the book is the politics of culture and the vagaries of national identity in a European borderland. For much of this century, the idea of the Moldovans as a distinct historical nation served clear Soviet foreign policy ends. Although related to the Romanians by language and culture, the Moldovans were nevertheless held to be a separate nation that was flourishing within the boundaries of the Soviet Union. The languages spoken in Chisinau and Bucharest were indistinguishable, but it became a dogma of Soviet historiography and ethnography that the two peoples were distinct. Since the Moldovans inhabited a territory that had been forcibly annexed from Romania in 1940, the Soviet line on culture buttressed the territorial acquisitions of the Second World War. However, even though many observers predicted that the Moldovans would rush into the arms of the Romanians once the fiction of cultural separateness died with the Soviet Union, nothing of the sort has taken place. The calls for union by Moldovan and Romanian intellectuals have gone largely unheeded, with most Moldovans preferring to recognize their Romanian heritage while jealously guarding their new-found existence as an independent state.

This book also raises far broader questions about national identity and the ability of political elites to manipulate culture. To what extent can nations be forged, the author asks, without their appearing a forgery? Why do some attempts at nation-building succeed where others fail? What are the limits to which historians, ethnographers, writers, and others can shape culture and use it for political ends? The author suggests that the answers to these questions are likely to lie less in the content of culture-building—how authentic or objectively accurate the cultural forms are—than among the culture-builders themselves. The ability of political and cultural elites to take their task seriously, to adopt new alphabets, literary languages, national symbols, and other accoutrements of nationhood, is a critical component of culture-building. When the elites themselves have qualms about the cultures they are making—as in the Moldovan case—the success of planned cultural change is highly dubious.

The work before us is most welcome. The author is an outstanding scholar, broadly educated and interdisciplinary in his research work. He has mastered a number of major and minor languages, some spoken by few Europeans. A volume of this substance and quality merits the attention of the best scholars in the field. It would serve well as the centerpiece for a seminar on the problems of nationalism and national identity.

Wayne S. Vucinich

Preface

It is a myth that Moldova changed its name from Moldavia. What happened in the 1990s was simply that we in the West became better informed about what locals themselves had always called it. The region has always been known to most inhabitants as Moldova or Bessarabia, although it was often referred to as Moldavia by speakers of English or Russian. I use the labels *Moldova* and *Moldovan* consistently throughout the text, since even during the Soviet period the republic was known to its majority population as the Moldovan (not Moldavian) Soviet Socialist Republic—*Republica Sovietică Socialistă Moldovenească*.

Given the frequent spelling changes in Soviet Moldova, no attempt has been made to standardize spellings in original documents or publications. Romanian items originally written in the Cyrillic alphabet (Moldovan) have been transliterated using modern Romanian conventions, a system that is easier on the eye than the cumbersome, Slavic-based variant. With a few exceptions, current Romanian place names are preferred to their Russian or Ukrainian equivalents for Moldovan locales. The region east of the Dnestr River is referred to by its Romanian name, *Transnistria*. Latin-Slavic hybrids such as *Trans-Dniester* and *Trans-dniestria* have become common in English, but *Transnistria* is both more accurate and more easily pronounceable. I refer to the unrecognized separatist state in eastern Moldova as the Dnestr Moldovan Republic, since this is the most accurate translation of the name in both Romanian and Russian (*Republica Moldovenească Nistreană* and *Pridnestrovskaia Moldavskaia Respublika*).

The term *Moldovan language* is used often in the text, even though since 1989 there has been nothing to separate Moldovan in its standard form from what most people know as Romanian. In portions of the book that refer to events after 1989, the term *Romanian* is generally used. How this seemingly minor issue became a problem of high politics is one of the subjects of this study.

The pronunciation of Romanian is regular and straightforward. The English equivalents of Romanian sounds are given below:

a   a in *father*
e   e in *bet*
i   ee in *beet*
o   o in *stole*
u   u in *rule*
ă   a in *about*
â   approximately, i in *cousin*. (This sound does not exist in English, but is made by pronouncing an "ee" sound far back in the throat. It is the sound heard in the word *România* and its variants.)
î   same as â

In combination, vowels retain their regular values. For example, ea is simply e and a pronounced separately but quickly, becoming something like "ya." Likewise for ai ("eye"), oa ("wa"), oi ("oy"), eau ("yow"), and other combinations. Consonants generally have the same values as in English, with the following exceptions:

c   before e or i, pronounced as ch in *cheese*; otherwise, c in *cat*
ch   always c in *cat*
g   before e or i, pronounced as g in *gentle*; otherwise, g in *goat*
gh   always g in *goat*
ş   sh in *ship*
ţ   ts in *cats*

The proper spelling of Gagauz in the Latin alphabet is still a matter of some scholarly dispute, but the reader will not be far wrong in using the following:

a   a in *father*
ä   approximately, ya in *yak*
e   e in *bet*
ê   approximately, e in *bet*
ı   approximately, i in *cousin*
i   ee in *beet*
o   o in *stole*
ö   ö in German *Köln*
u   u in *rule*
ü   u in French *tu*
c   j in *jam*
ç   ch in *cheese*
ş   sh in *ship*
ţ   ts in *cats*

Russian, Ukrainian, and Bulgarian words have been transliterated using the Library of Congress conventions.

Acknowledgments

It is difficult enough to conduct research on contentious questions of identity and community, issues over which politicians and publics sometimes come to blows. It is even more difficult when the basic facts of the case—who did what to whom and when—are unknown outside a tiny band of foreign scholars and archivists. I am therefore profoundly grateful to the many specialists in Romania and Moldova who have helped me piece together the history of the borderland between Romania and Russia and who have aided me in the quest to place the study of this fascinating European region in a broader political, cultural, and conceptual context. There is always a certain tension between getting the story straight and formulating conclusions of interest to nonspecialists, but if I have managed to use this tension creatively it is because of the assistance of many gifted east European scholars who continue to toil for rewards that are never more than intellectual. No doubt some of those who have been indispensable in this project will not agree with the conclusions reached here, but their help is much appreciated nevertheless.

I owe a debt of gratitude to a number of people who have unfailingly provided support and guidance in Romania, Moldova, and elsewhere since I began work on this project: Igor Boțan, Ioan Chiper, Viorel

Cibotaru, Ion Ciobanu, Dimitrie Ciubaşenco, Elena Bivol, Hülya Demirdirek, Valerii Dimidetskii, Emilian Drăgulescu and family, Bogdan Dumitrică and family, Anatol Golea, Mihai and Argentina Gribincea, Iurie Leancă, Mihai and Angela Michicina, Sonia and Albert Misak, Vladimir and Svetlana Mischevca, Anton Moraru, the late Nicolae Movileanu, Igor Munteanu and family, Oazu Nantoi, Vasile Nedelciuc and family, Valeriu Opincă, Igor Pădure and family, Cătălin and Ioana Partenie, Costel and Constanţa Partenie, Adrian Pop, Branimir Radev, the Honorable Ion Raţiu, Iurie Reniţa, Nicolae Sali, Aurel and Voichiţa Sasu, Konstantin Sîrf, Alla Skvortsova, Vladimir Socor, Ion Şişcanu, Radu Tocan and family, Jan Arveds Trapans, Dorin Tudoran, Nicolae Turtureanu, the late Ion Vatamanu, Trevor Waters, the staff at Romanian and Moldovan embassies in London, Washington, Brussels, Sofia, Bucharest, and Chisinau, the staff of the OSCE mission in Moldova, and many other people whose assistance is no less appreciated for their not being named here.

The following persons have read portions of the manuscript in various forms and have thankfully saved me from some embarrassing oversights and errors, although I am wholly responsible for any that remain: William Crowther, Dennis Deletant, Donald L. Dyer, Jonathan Eyal, Kyril Haramiev, Irina Livezeanu, Mary McAuley, Iver Neumann, Susan Gross Solomon, Ambassador John Todd Stewart, and Wim van Meurs. Archie Brown served brilliantly as supervisor for the Oxford doctoral thesis in which this book had its distant origins. Jeff Chinn and Steve Roper offered sage advice and the loan of several photographs. Felicia Roşu provided research assistance in the final stretch.

I would also like to express sincere gratitude to the staff at the following libraries and archives. Those in eastern Europe allowed me to cut the pages of books that had never been opened and to read dusty documents that, but for the vigilance of their predecessors, would surely have been destroyed by those whom Boris Pil'niak called "leather men in leather jackets": National Library, Bucharest; Library of the Romanian Academy, Bucharest; National Library, Chisinau; Library of the Academy of Sciences of the Republic of Moldova, Chisinau; the Archive of Social-Political Organizations of the Republic of Moldova, Chisinau; the National Archive of the Republic of Moldova, Chisinau; the National Archives of Romania, Central Historical Archive Division, Bucharest; Radio Free Europe/Radio Liberty "Krasnyi Arkhiv," Munich; Bodleian Library, Oxford; British Library, London; Library of the School of

Slavonic and East European Studies, London; Seton-Watson Collection, New College Library, Oxford; Library of Congress, Washington; Bavarian State Library, Munich.

Funding for this project was provided at various stages by the British Marshall Commemoration Commission, in the form of a British Marshall Scholarship; St. Antony's College and New College, Oxford; the Social Science Research Council, via a Graduate Training Fellowship; and Georgetown University, through the Ion Raţiu Chair of Romanian Studies, to which I was elected in 1996.

Some of the research for this book appeared in very different form in articles and book chapters, and I thank the editors of *Slavic Review, Nationalities Papers, Ethnic and Racial Studies*, and *Romanian Civilization* for the chance to air ideas and conclusions in the pages of their publications.

Professor Wayne Vucinich, the editor of the Studies of Nationalities series, and Pat Baker and the editors at Hoover Institution Press made the journey from manuscript to book truly enjoyable.

This book is dedicated to my parents who, although often puzzled by my fascination with eastern Europe, have never failed in their moral support, and to the late Miss Pearlie Acheson, in whose ramshackle clapboard house in the Ozark Mountains I first discovered a window on another world.

Introduction:
The Physical Setting

Moldova is the second-smallest republic among the Soviet successor states, after Armenia, and has sometimes been known by its Russian and Latin name, *Moldavia*. The majority population, though, have always used the name *Moldova*, even under the Soviets. Perhaps the least known of the states to emerge from the Soviet federation in 1991, the Moldovan republic today comprises some 33,700 square kilometers, making it about a third the size of Indiana or Portugal. It is landlocked between Romania and Ukraine; however, in 1999 a border treaty with Ukraine recognized Moldova's access to the Danube (but only a few hundred meters of river frontage). The country consists of two broad regions: to the west, Bessarabia, the area between the Prut and Dnestr Rivers, to the east, Transnistria, the thin strip of land beyond the Dnestr that has effectively functioned as an autonomous state since a separatist conflict in 1991 and 1992. The arid southern steppeland of Bessarabia is known as the Bugeac, or Budjak.

In 1989, the republic's population was reported on the Soviet census as 4,335,360, but because of out-migration and a falling growth rate, the population was an estimated 4.32 million in 1997—about that of Norway.[1] Moldova is the least urbanized of all the Soviet successor states outside Central Asia and has the highest population density of all the republics. According to the 1989 census, still the most reliable figures available, the majority Romanian-speaking population accounted for 64.5 percent of the total, followed by Ukrainians (13.8 percent), Russians (13.0 percent), Gagauz Turks (3.5 percent), Bulgarians (2.0 percent), and other smaller minorities. About 83 percent of the population lives in Bessarabia and 17 percent in Transnistria. Moldovans form the largest single ethnic group in both regions, about 67 percent in Bessarabia and 40 percent in Transnistria. Over 70 percent of all Russians and Ukrainians in Moldova live west of the Dnestr River, in Bessarabia.

Throughout the 1990s, the country experienced a fall in the birth rate, a uniformly high level of infant and maternal mortality, a further increase in the general mortality rate, and a decline in the natural population growth rate. The mortality rate rose from 9.7 per 1,000 in 1990 to 11.9 in 1997. Infant mortality likewise rose from 19.0 to 20.0, while the birth rate fell from 17.7 to 11.9 over the same period. Life expectancy at birth declined, sliding to 62.9 years for men and 70.4 years for women in 1996.

The economy suffered from many of the problems common to most post-Soviet states. Agriculture, which employs about 40 percent of the population, suffered from periodic droughts, continuing problems with transportation, and the disruption of export markets to the other post-Soviet countries. Overall output fell steadily, standing at less than 40 percent of the 1990 value by the end of the decade, a decline far more dramatic than in some other republics. The average monthly salary for employees in the state sector was only 437 Moldovan lei (about $90) in mid-1998, a sum that covered less than 60 percent of the estimated monthly consumer budget. Huge wage arrears meant that employees often went without salaries for months at a time.

In macroeconomic terms, though, Moldova proved initially far more successful than its neighbors. Annual inflation in 1997 was only 12 percent, compared to 20 percent in Ukraine, 55 percent in Belarus, and 100 percent in Romania. The Moldovan leu—which is not connected to the Romanian currency of the same name—was introduced in 1993 at 3.85 lei/dollar and fell to only around 4.7 lei/dollar by late 1998, making it one of the most stable currencies in the region. The tight monetary policy of the National Bank, however, came at the cost of continual draw-downs on hard currency reserves. With the economy hard hit by the Russian financial crisis, in late 1998 the bank decided to halt the policy of propping up the leu, and the currency slid precipitously, reaching over 11 lei/dollar by mid-1999.

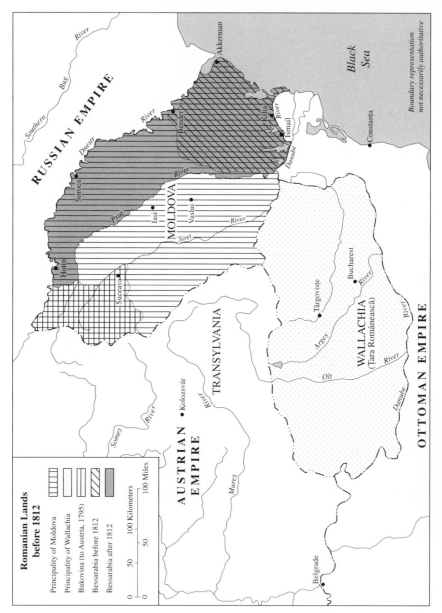

Romanian Lands before 1812

Principality of Moldova

Principality of Wallachia

Bukovina (to Austria, 1795)

Bessarabia before 1812

Bessarabia after 1812

0   50   100 Kilometers

0   50   100 Miles

RUSSIAN EMPIRE

Southern

Bug

River

Dnestr

River

Soroca

Hotin

Prut

River

Suceava

MOLDOVA

Iași

Vaslui

Siret

River

Bender

Akkerman

Kilia

River

Ismail

Danube

River

Constanța

Black
Sea

Boundary representation
not necessarily authoritative

AUSTRIAN
EMPIRE

Kolozsvár

TRANSYLVANIA

Someș

River

Mureș

River

Belgrade

Târgoviște

Argeș

Olt

River

Bucharest

WALLACHIA
(Țara Românească)

River

River

Danube

OTTOMAN EMPIRE

Map 1. Romanian Lands before 1812

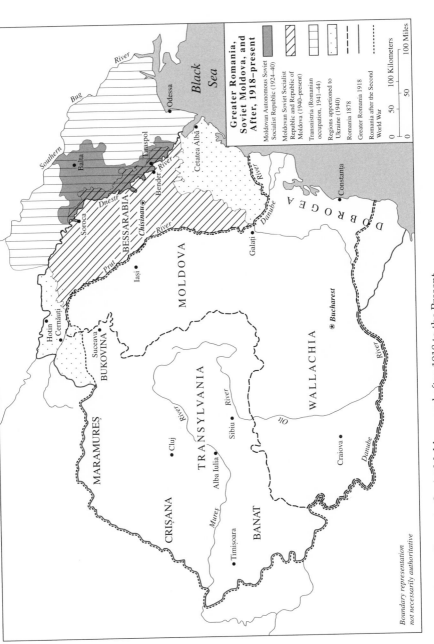

Map 2. Greater Romania, Soviet Moldova, and after, 1918 to the Present

Map 3. Republic of Moldova

1 Contested Territories, Contentious Identities

This book is about the malleability of national identity—the degree to which individuals' conceptions of self and community can be changed through education, cultural policy, and other forms of state intervention. This book asks why some attempts by political elites to mold identity succeed while others become quaint footnotes in the national history of a given people. It is about the perils of building nations from scratch, and about the incorrigibility of the nation itself. It is about what happens to nation-builders when the nations they build turn out to be rather different from what they expected.

Despite a venerable tradition of writing on nations and nationalism by historians, anthropologists, and political scientists, we know little about what might be called "nationalisms that failed." We often say that ethnic groups and nations are "constructed" by political and cultural elites, but we seem to know very little about why, in the universe of possible identities that politicians and cultural leaders might construct, only some seem to endure. In other words, to borrow from Marx, if nationalists do in fact make their own history, do they make it just as they please?

That ethnic identities are mutable, multiple, overlapping, and often inconsistent is one of the few things we say we understand about ethnicity and nationalism. The volume of publications on the invention or construction of everything from national symbols to national histories to national costumes is today truly unfathomable. A glance through any library catalog will uncover a host of titles in this genre, ranging from *The Invention of George Washington* to *The Invention of Sodomy*. Indeed, it has become a cliché to assert that ethnonational identities are "imagined" and that their particular content is as much the product of conscious nation-building by state, quasi-state, and elite institutions as of more natural processes operating at the grass roots within preexisting, bounded cultural communities. Linguists create national, standardized languages out of the messy and heterogeneous speech patterns of particular groups. Ethnographers formalize the bounds of membership in an ethnic population. Historians craft national histories and chronicle the deeds of a pantheon of national heroes. State-sponsored educational systems, the media, and elite-driven political ideologies communicate all these formal accoutrements of nationhood back to the people themselves. Thus are traditions invented and communities imagined by an array of political and cultural entrepreneurs—nation-builders whose task is to homogenize cultural practice and create a unified and standard national culture from a congeries of perennial or primordial attachments to clan, caste, or commune.[1] In Ernest Gellner's memorable formulation, it is nationalism that creates nations and not the other way around.[2]

If in fact nations really are invented things, then can members of any human group be made to embrace any ethnic or national identity and, if so, what precisely are those conditions that would allow political, economic, cultural, or other elites to compel them to do so? Or to put it slightly differently, what are the limits to which ethnic groups, nations, and languages can be forged—in both senses of the term—out of heterogeneous cultural practices? In the marketplace of identities, why do only a few visions of the nation attract buyers? Why do some nationalisms fail?

This book focuses on a Soviet nation-building project that failed, but one that failed in a rather peculiar and ambiguous way. Before the 1920s, few specialists thought of the Moldovans as anything more than an eastern offshoot of the Romanians, whose dialect had over the centuries been heavily influenced by the languages of neighboring Slavs. Spoken in parts of Ukraine and the provinces of eastern Romania, the dialect shared the same origins as Romanian in the vulgar Latin of the eastern Roman Empire, its structure was largely the same, and except for a larger number of words borrowed from Slavic languages, there was little to distinguish it from the numerous varieties of standard Romanian spoken in any other region within the historical Romanian lands. For this reason, the Romanians and Moldovans were generally considered part of a single, pan-Romanian nation.

In the 1920s, though, a new people and language suddenly seemed to spring onto the world stage. In the small Moldovan Autonomous Soviet Socialist Republic (MASSR), established on the western border of Soviet Ukraine in 1924, Moldovan histories, textbooks, grammars, newspapers, and other publications were hailed by the Soviet authorities as the first fruits of a Moldovan nation in the making. Persons whose language and ethnicity had previously been termed "Romanian" seemed overnight to become "Moldovans," and Soviet propagandists began to agitate for the unification of all Moldovans, who lived mainly in portions of Ukraine and the Romanian province of Bessarabia, into a single Soviet Moldovan state. Especially after 1940, when parts of the Romanian provinces of Bukovina and Bessarabia were annexed by the Soviet Union and mostly absorbed into an enlarged Moldovan Soviet Socialist Republic (MSSR), two independent "eastern Romance" peoples seemed to arise where before there had been only one.

Just as suddenly, however, it all came to an end. In the style of a mass confession, in August 1989 the Moldovans rejected the key feature that had long distinguished them from Romanians: the use of the Russian alphabet. Many publicly affirmed that the peoples of Romania and Soviet Moldova shared a single, pan-Romanian national identity. Moldovan, now written like Romanian in the Latin alphabet, was declared the sole official language of the republic. Its identity with Romanian was recognized by law. While gatherings in Tallinn, Vilnius, Riga, and other Soviet capitals celebrated the revival of indigenous cultures and identities in the late 1980s, crowds in the Moldovan capital of Chisinau (Kishinev) seemed to do exactly the opposite, rejecting the existence of a separate Moldovan nation and adopting the tricolor, national anthem, and official language of another country, Romania. Moldovan nationalism ultimately proved to be a rather strange beast: a nationalism that succeeded in gaining an independent state but seemed to fail in making an independent nation.

In the Republic of Moldova, which exited the Soviet Union in August 1991, exposing the falsehoods of Soviet cultural policy quickly became a cottage industry. Innumerable books, pamphlets, essays, and academic articles were published denouncing the cultivation of an independent Moldovan identity in the Soviet period as a vast exercise in Stalinist denationalization. For Moldova's younger generation of writers, artists, and academics—the intellectuals who led the national movement of the late perestroika period and hastened the republic's flight from the union—the Soviet era produced an unprecedented case of cultural fraud. Works in Moldovan linguistics, ethnography, and historiography published in the Soviet Union, they argued, were designed simply to justify the illegal annexation of Romanian territory in 1940 and to force Moldovans into a state of collective amnesia about their authentic culture and true national identity. For these pan-Romanian intellectuals, the adoption of the Latin alphabet and the recognition of Moldovan-Romanian cultural unity in 1989 were acts of historical justice, the first steps toward reappropriating a Romanian identity obscured by some seven decades of Soviet propaganda.

However, since the declaration of independence in 1991, Moldova's government and population at large have been far less sanguine about their Romanian identity than either the pan-Romanians or most Western analysts (who predicted a quick political unification of Moldova with Romania) had imagined. In the 1990s relations between Chisinau and Bucharest cooled considerably, with mutual recriminations sometimes replacing the warm avowals of pan-Romanian brotherhood that followed Romania's anticommunist revolution in December 1989 and the Moldovan declaration of independence a year and a half later. A full-scale war in 1992 between the central Moldovan government and groups intent on separation and reintegration with Russia polarized the population and intensified debates over cultural identity and relations with both Bucharest and Moscow. In reaction to the pan-Romanians, a small Moldovan nationalist movement reemerged, arguing that the Moldovans were in fact a distinct nation with a timeless past, related to but separate from Romanians. By early 1994 the Moldovan president, Mircea Snegur, had begun to direct historians and linguists to concentrate on the scientific origins of Moldova's independent identity, rather than on the cultural commonalities between Moldova and Romania. The parliament adopted a new constitution that made no mention of the putative Romanian identity of the Moldovan people and language. Most citizens in the republic, chastened by an enduring economic crisis, seemed content to split the difference between the two camps, holding that Moldovans and Romanians, like Britons and Americans, were two peoples divided by a common language.

Thus, in post-Soviet Moldova as in the Soviet period, the question Who are the Moldovans? continues to concern politicians as much as scholars. It does not have an easy answer. The politics of identity in this European borderland has in fact been far more complicated than any of the sides in these debates has admitted. The curious history of the Moldovans is not about Stalinist denationalization followed by national rebirth, nor is it about the struggle of an ancient Moldovan nation for self-determination. Rather, it is a history of fretful and sometimes violent projects to define the boundaries of the Romanian nation, the desiderata of authentic national culture, and the meaning of nationhood itself. Throughout this century, nationality among the Moldovans has been a decidedly negotiable proposition, a protean yet powerful conception of community in a region where the mutability of cultural boundaries has been matched by the fluidity of political ones. The territory of present-day Moldova has been a classic borderland, fought over and divided by outside powers eager to remake the Moldovans in their own image. Where the Moldovans have come from, why many have dismissed them as Romanians in denial and, most importantly, how far ethnic identities can be forged without their appearing a forgery form the focus of this study.

The twists and turns of cultural politics recounted in this volume, as well as the traumas of reconstructing a post-Soviet identity after the demise of communist rule, will be familiar to students of Soviet, post-Soviet, and east European affairs. What stands out about the Moldovan case, though, is the unsettled nature of the essentials of nationality. Belarusians, Kazakhs, and Latvians may still debate the interpretations of their national histories, the more and less authentic folk traditions from which these histories flow, and the appropriate cultural and political relationships with neighboring peoples and states; but in no post-Soviet republic except Moldova have inhabitants continued to argue about the existence of the nation itself. Why there has never been general agreement on who the Moldovans are and where the manifestly multiethnic Republic of Moldova is likely to go in the future are central questions in the chapters that follow.

This book devotes the most attention to the twentieth century, for it is only in this period that the questionable proposition of a distinct Moldovan nation—much less the possibility of a modern Moldovan state—became an issue in the international politics of southeast Europe. From the fourteenth century, there have been states, quasi states, and administrative regions that have laid claim, with varying justification, to the name *Moldova*. But it was not until the twentieth century, with the cataclysmic changes of the two world wars, the nation-building projects of the Bolsheviks, and the emergence of new peoples and states from the rubble of Soviet communism, that difficult questions about the Moldovans' ethnic identity and their right to self-determination came to the fore.

The idea of the Moldovans as a distinct nation, in the normal sense of the term, is today problematic. The language they speak is Romanian, even though it has long been called *Moldovan* by men and women in the countryside and is still referred to by that name in the constitution of the post-Soviet republic. The history of modern Moldova is an inextricable part of the broader history of the lands of eastern Latinity, the region stretching from the forests of Transylvania and the hills of Bukovina in the north, south to the Danube plain and the Black Sea, and east to the gentle hills and steppeland along the Dnestr River. All of these areas, including most of the present-day Republic of Moldova, were included in the Greater Romania produced by the First World War and destroyed by the Second. Today's Moldovans spent only a few decades in the same state as the Romanians, but their culture, language, and folk traditions spring from incontestably common roots. The national heroes and cultural luminaries of one are also those of the other. There are today, in this sense, two culturally "Romanian" states in eastern Europe, even though both are also home to a wide variety of ethnic minorities— Hungarians, Ukrainians, Russians, Roma, Turks.

There is, nevertheless, a separate sense of identity among the Moldovans. Apart from the three decades of Greater Romania, from 1918 to 1940, the inhabitants of postcommunist Romania and post-Soviet Moldova have spent most of the last two centuries apart. The Romanians and their cousins east of the Prut River have lived under separate legal, administrative, political, and religious systems, all of which in various ways were intent on creating as wide a gulf as possible between them. Both history and history-makers have produced an uncertain sense of distinctiveness among today's Moldovans. Most freely admit that they speak something akin to Romanian (indeed, there is now nothing to distinguish the two languages in their literary forms), but most also refuse to describe their nationality as "just" Romanian.

The Moldovan story is thus an unconventional tale. Unlike the other constituents of the Soviet Union, Moldova was the only union republic whose majority population was culturally bound to a nation-state across the border and therefore the potential object of irredentism, a situation that simply replayed within the socialist camp an older confrontation between the Romanian kingdom and the Russian empire. For this reason, the Moldovans have long been the object of intense nation-building projects, designed either to convince them of their separateness from the Romanians or, when under Romanian rule, to convince them that their purported separateness was a fiction of Russian propaganda. As in much of eastern Europe, shifting borders meant shifting cultural policies, and the peculiar sense of identity among modern Moldovans is the legacy of both. It is thus impossible to give a linear account of Moldovan nationhood, for whether they even constitute a nation in a cultural sense is highly dubious. There is no distinct literature, no separate language, no history apart from that of the states and empires of which they have been a part. Yet most Moldovans feel themselves to be something other than simply Romanians, and since 1991, they have had their own state to show for it. This book tells how, in a frontier zone full of situational and often puzzling identities, this particularly fascinating case came about.

BESSARABIA BETWEEN ROMANIA AND RUSSIA

PART ONE

2 From Principality to Province

In 1919 Emmanuel de Martonne, a professor at the Sorbonne, set out on a journey through the kingdom of Romania. Unlike any of its neighbors, the kingdom had emerged from the First World War with more territory, more people, and more nationalities than when it had entered, and Martonne was eager to explore the newly created Greater Romania. The province of Bessarabia, recently acquired by Bucharest after the collapse of the Russian empire, was his ultimate destination.

As he traveled by motorcar from the Danube port city of Galaţi northeastward across the Prut River into the Bessarabian steppe, Martonne noted that, all claims to being a Romanian province aside, Bessarabia seemed "inhabited by a motley population where mixed marriages must be very common and the notion of race rather hazy." With throngs of curious onlookers gathering around his car near Cahul, a market town on the edge of the Prut River valley, Martonne took the opportunity to examine his company more closely:

> [S]everal own up to a nationality different from what might be expected. This man with a broad and beardless face, typical of the Little Russian, calls himself a Gagaoutze. The other styles himself a Bulgarian, but his kindly face with grizzled mustaches, his fur cap as well as his racy Roumanian speech, remind me of the Oltean type of the Valachian Carpathians. That Jew might be a genuine Aryan, that Russian

looks like a Bulgarian. . . . One of them, who claims to be Russian, calmly admits that his father is Moldovan and his mother Bulgarian.[1]

In all of southeastern Europe, ethnicity has long been a rather hazy notion, mutating and adapting in a region where a change in political fortunes can still mean a change in political frontiers. But Martonne's observations are particularly pertinent to the peoples of Bessarabia. From the early nineteenth century, debates over the political status of the region—the "Bessarabian question"—were a fixture of European diplomacy, as Turks, Russians, and later Romanians argued over rights to the region between the Prut and Dnestr Rivers.

At the base of these conflicting territorial claims often lay the issue of the ethnonational identity of Bessarabia's majority population. As Martonne observed in 1919, the question of identity was even more perplexing than the territorial problem. Not only were over forty separate languages represented in Bessarabia by the end of the nineteenth century, but the identity of the region's largest ethnic group—normally called *Moldovans* or *Bessarabian Romanians*—also remained in some doubt. Were they merely Romanians long estranged from the Romanian motherland? Or had their tenure inside Russia caused them to become more Slav than Latin? Or, as Martonne wondered, did they represent a distinct population that had developed as the product of centuries of migration and intermarriage and might therefore "own up to a nationality different from what might be expected?"

This history of shifting borders and political allegiances has long been reflected in the overlapping and situational identities of Bessarabia's inhabitants, including their descendants in present-day Moldova. Although neighboring powers, from Russia to Romania to the Soviet Union, usually attempted to treat the Bessarabians as pure exemplars of a single cultural heritage, the picture that visitors encountered on the ground normally turned out to be rather different. It is thus difficult for modern Moldovans to trace their lineage to a distinct political entity or to carve out of history a homogeneous cultural identity. There is little in history to which the Moldovans can stake a unique proprietary claim. Moldova's most prominent historical figures are also those of the Romanians, and the territory of the present-day republic has not existed within a truly independent Moldovan state since 1538. Even the term *Moldova* itself has, since the fourteenth century, been applied to a variety of political entities, none of which has had exactly the same territorial boundaries.

THE EMERGENCE OF THE PRINCIPALITY OF MOLDOVA, 1359–1538

According to Dimitrie Cantemir,[2] whose *Descriptio Moldaviae* (ca. 1714) provides one of the richest descriptions of the early Moldovan lands, the foundation of a medieval Moldovan state came about as a result of an ill-fated hunting trip. In the early 1300s, Dragoş, a Romanian prince (*voievod*) from west of the Carpathian Mountains, set out across the wooded slopes on a hunt. At one point in the journey, having ventured far to the east, the party came upon a wild European bison, an aurochs, in a mountain stream. Dragoş unleashed his hounds on the unfortunate creature, and in the ensuing melee his favorite dog, Molda, was gored by the ox and drowned. Distraught at the loss, Dragoş decided to name the stream in honor of the hound, take the aurochs's head as his personal crest, and build a principality in the newly christened Moldovan land.[3] The aurochs-head emblem can be seen today on the seals of both Romania and the Republic of Moldova.

The Dragoş story is surely the stuff of legend, but it was used by early Moldovan chroniclers to establish the rights of Romanian-speakers to the lands east of the Carpathians. According to the story, Dragoş and his company met only a single man on their journey into the new land, so that when the prince stepped down from his horse, he stepped onto uninhabited, virgin soil. This process itself is reflected in the name that chroniclers and later Romanian historians would give to the act of founding the first Moldovan state: *Descălecarea*, literally, "the dismounting." At the time, though, the region was hardly a desert, since by the fourteenth century it was already home to a mixture of peoples: Magyars, Tatars, Cumans, and also Romanian-speaking Wallachs, the general term for Latin populations north and south of the Danube who had remained after the withering of Roman imperial control in the third century A.D.[4] Small Wallach principalities (*knezates*) gradually arose in the lands between the Carpathians and the Danube beginning in at least the tenth century, but it was not until the thirteenth century that foreign chroniclers came to refer to the region as the "land of the Wallachs." Before then, the dominance of Turkic tribes—Pechenegs and Cumans— led cartographers and chroniclers to use names such as *Patzinakia* or

Cumania, based on the names of groups who successively exercised control over the lower Danube.[5]

Regardless of the circumstances surrounding the Dragoş legend, a Moldovan state did emerge in the early fourteenth century and was probably founded by a Wallach prince from Maramureş in northern Transylvania, then under the suzerainty of the Hungarian king Ludovic I of Anjou. The original expedition to the east may have been an attempt to end a series of fratricidal wars among local Wallach princes along the Siret River or part of Ludovic's campaigns against the Tatars, who controlled much of the land beyond the Carpathians.[6] Hungarian, Polish, and Romanian chronicles all mention the assistance provided by local "Wallach" or "Olach" leaders in the battles against the Tatars.[7] In the early 1340s, though, the Wallachs in Maramureş had already begun to assert their independence from Ludovic's control, and at the end of the 1350s under the Wallach *voievod* Bogdan a distinct Moldovan state began to expand its power east of the Carpathians.[8] It is from this period that historical accounts begin to use both the terms *Wallach* and *Moldovan* to describe the inhabitants of this land.

Bogdan's consolidation of authority east of the mountains was paralleled by a similar process taking place in the south, between the mountains and the Danube. In the first half of the fourteenth century, Basarab I carved a unified principality out of the small Wallach fiefdoms along both banks of the Olt River. By the end of the 1350s, two broad entities existed in the territory beyond the Carpathian crescent: to the east, the principality of Moldova, and to the south, the Ţara Românească (Romanian Land), also known as *Wallachia*. Both Moldova and Wallachia quickly became important forces in southeastern Europe. They lay directly on the north-south trading route linking the Hanseatic states with the Genoese and Byzantine settlements along the Dnestr River and Black Sea at Hotin, Bender (Tighina), Akkerman (Maurocastro), and Kilia (Lycostomium).[9] The two principalities also stood at the center of conflicts between Poles, Hungarians, and Ottomans after the fifteenth century, as often collaborating with foreign invaders as standing together against them.

Any talk of a Moldovan—or even Romanian—nation during this period is, however, misplaced. Official court documents and chronicles from the Middle Ages often used the term *moldovean* to describe the inhabitants of the Moldovan principality, but one can also find instances of other terms such as *vlah* or *român*, the former generally used by western European chroniclers (based on the same Germanic root for Romans and other foreigners also seen in "Welsh" and "Walloon") and the latter used by indigenous writers.[10] In fact, who the Moldovans were at this stage usually depended on who the writer thought they were not. Against the Wallachians in the Ţara Românească, they were Moldovans. Against the Poles or Hungarians, they were Romanians. Against the Turks, they were Christians. It was not until the eighteenth and nineteenth centuries, with the rise of contemporary notions of the nation, that these changeable labels would take on political significance.

Moldova grew in strength under two important princes, Alexandru cel Bun (the Good) and Ştefan cel Mare (the Great). Alexandru (1400–1432) spent much of his reign developing the institutions of the principality and defending its borders against increasingly frequent attacks by the Ottoman Turks and Hungarians, and assisting the Poles, to whom he had sworn allegiance in 1402, against the Teutonic Knights. It was under Ştefan, though, that the principality reached its apogee and began its rapid decline. Through a series of alliances, Ştefan (1457–1504) was able to shore up Moldova's power against the encroachments of the Ottomans to the south, Hungarians to the west, Tatars to the east, and Poles to the north. At the 1475 battle of Vaslui, 40,000 Moldovan, Hungarian, and Polish troops commanded by Ştefan defeated a Turkish and Wallachian force numbering over 100,000. Campaigns by the Ottomans continued, however, and Ştefan's death in 1504 left the principality in the hands of less able successors. In 1538 the Ottoman host under Süleyman the Magnificent defeated the army of the Moldovan *voievod* Petru Rareş and occupied the principality's capital, Suceava.

Moldova, like Wallachia, eventually became a vassal state of the Ottoman Porte, but neither of the two principalities was ever incorporated fully into the empire. Already under Ştefan's son, Bogdan III, Moldova began paying an annual tribute of 4,000 pieces of gold, 40 horses, and 24 falcons to the sultan, figures that rose and fell according to the power of Moldovan nobles to resist the Turks.[11] Unlike the regions south of the Danube River, neither Moldova nor Wallachia experienced direct rule by Muslim landlords or the "child tax" (*devşirme*) levied against the Christian populations of the southern Balkans. For most of the period after the 1530s, the Romanian principalities continued to be ruled by native princes, recognized as rulers, or *domni,* by the sultan in exchange for annual tribute and other taxes. Periodic revolts by Moldovan leaders, often in concert with Hungarian or Russian forces, challenged the authority of the Porte and kept the relationship one of suzerainty rather than outright domination, with *domni* as frequently fighting the Turks as willingly surrendering their tribute.

MOLDOVA UNDER THE OTTOMANS, 1538–1812

Although Moldova had been an important Christian principality in the fifteenth and early sixteenth centuries, under the Ottomans it became an often ignored part of "Turkey in Europe," a frontier zone where none but the most intrepid foreign visitors ventured. Those who did often found the welcome less than satisfactory. William Lithgow, the famous Scottish adventurer, stumbled through the area on his way to Constantinople in the early seventeenth century, only to be stripped naked, tied to a tree, and relieved of sixty Hungarian gold ducats by a band of outlaws.[12] Other visitors found a principality more Turkish than Christian. Under Ştefan, the Moldovan principality had been at the center of the tumultuous politics of Europe's southeast, forging and breaking alliances with Hungarians and Poles in disputes with the advancing Ottomans. Within a century of Ştefan's death, though, Moldova's rulers had become nearly unrecognizable to visiting Europeans. The clothing and customs of the Moldovan divan mimicked those of the sultan's palace, with an elaborate series of ranks and courtly privileges—from grand vizier (*logofătul cel mare*) to chief cup holder (*ceaşnicul cel mare*)— extended to leading families of nobles, or *boiars*. The massive changes in Moldova from the sixteenth to the eighteenth century are evident in one striking detail: Portraits of Ştefan the Great show a typical medieval knight indistinguishable from his contemporaries in England or France, but portraits of his successors two centuries later depict rulers clad in the flowing robes and elaborate turbans of Turkish pashas.

The incorporation of Moldova into the Ottoman empire accelerated after the early eighteenth century. With Turkey in decline and conscious of the growing power of Austria and Russia, strengthening control over the border regions along the Danube and Dnestr became one of the Porte's major strategic goals.[13] After an anti-Ottoman war launched by the Moldovan prince Dimitrie Cantemir, the sultan rescinded Moldova's status as a vassal state in 1711 and appointed Greek nobles from the Fener district of Constantinople to administer the principality, a change that would be effected also in Wallachia in 1716. Known as "Phanariots," the Greek princes or *hospodars* destroyed the autonomy that the principality had enjoyed and treated the region as a source of personal wealth, a situation that earned the principalities the epithet of "the Peru of the Greeks."[14] Greek became the language of court, and the Orthodox Church fell under Hellenic influence. Political intrigue and poor governance became the hallmarks of the Phanariot system. A French observer, the Count d'Hauterive, was impressed by the absolute authority of the Phanariots. "Although the *hospodar* of Moldova pays a tribute to the Porte and does not reign forever in his province, the time that he does reign he reigns absolutely."[15] The French diplomat François de Tott, traveling through Moldova in the 1760s, was likewise astounded by the corruption of the Phanariot court and the misery of the population:

> I would compare Moldova with Burgundy, if this Greek Principality could enjoy the inestimable advantages that would result from a moderate Government. . . . An annual tax, grown immoderate by increases in the enormous loans taken out by the feudal ruler in order to purchase his investiture, at an interest of twenty-five percent; other sums used to insure against pretenders to the throne; the pomposity of these new parvenus; and the creative avarice of these ephemeral beings are together the causes that contribute to the devastation of the two most beautiful Provinces of the Ottoman Empire. . . . It seems that the Despot, concerned solely with destruction, thinks that he may gain advantage only in the measure that the people decrease in number and the land in fertility.[16]

As these and other travelers discovered, the Moldovan lands under the great Phanariot families—the Mavrocordats, the Ghicas, the Callimachis, and others—little resembled the independent principality of Ştefan, in which rulers succeeded to the throne either by dynastic right or after election by the nobles. Some Phanariot princes instituted progressive reforms, but in the main, ruling clans battled against each other for the tax-farming opportunities in the principalities, or for transfer from Moldova to the more prosperous Wallachia. Such was the instability among the Phanariots that the average duration of reign in the entire century of Phanariot rule was less than three years.[17] More often concerned with political intrigues in Constantinople than with developing the principalities, the Phanariots kept permanent representations in the Ottoman capital, paying huge sums to maintain elaborate palaces. Sadly, though, the once-grand Boğdan Saray, the Moldovan palace atop the Sixth Hill, is today an Istanbul tire repair shop.

Besides the Phanariot system, the eighteenth century also saw the growth in the importance of Russia and Austria in Moldova's fortunes, as the Romanian principalities became pawns in the struggles between the decaying Ottoman Empire and the Romanovs and Habsburgs to the north. Both powers had for the previous two centuries been on the sidelines of Moldovan politics, with the real power being exercised by Poles and Hungarians. Ştefan cel Mare had begun to strengthen ties between Moldovan and Russian princely houses when he gave his daughter, Ileana, in marriage to the son of Tsar Ivan III in the early sixteenth century, and later Ion Vodă cel Viteaz (the Brave, 1572–74) called on the assistance of the Zaporozhian Cossacks in his battles with the Turks. But it was in the eighteenth century that the Moldovan principality became a borderland in a series of wars among Europe's three great land empires. Under Peter the Great, the Russians intervened to support the uprising led by Dimitrie Cantemir. Although the Russian-Moldovan forces were soundly defeated at the battle of Stănileşti in 1711, Peter did manage to secure Russian control of the territory up to the Dnepr River.[18] For the rest of the century, Russian territory continued to expand at the expense of the Porte. Under Catherine the Great, Russian territory grew to include the lands between the Dnepr and the Bug, Crimea and the Kuban, and the territory between the Bug and the Dnestr. In 1774, under the Treaty of Küçük Kaynarca, Russia attained the right to represent the principalities before the Porte and began to assert a role as intercessor on behalf of Ottoman Christians, including those in Moldova and Wallachia. A year later, Austria annexed the northern portion of Moldova, Bukovina, which included Suceava and other important historical sites from the medieval principality. Throughout this period, both Romanian principalities were under foreign military occupation for more than two decades, as conflicts between Ottomans, Austrians, and Russians were played out along the Danube in a series of devastating wars: 1711, 1736–39, 1769–74, and 1787–92.[19] It was during the next major conflict, the Russo-Turkish War of 1806–12, that the Moldovan principality would itself come under direct Russian control.

THE FIRST BESSARABIAN ANNEXATION AND RUSSIAN RULE, 1812–1918

Convinced of the weakness of the Ottomans and frightened of Napoleon's designs on the Balkans, Russia occupied the eastern half

Remains of the Boğdan Saray, the former palace of the Moldovan princes in Constantinople, now an Istanbul tire repair shop.

of Moldova in 1806. After six years of warfare, Tsar Alexander I formally annexed the eastern reaches of the principality, the Bessarabia region between the Prut and Dnestr Rivers. At the time, the area included between 240,000 and 350,000 people, most of whom were Romanian-speaking Moldovans.[20] The total amount of land annexed by Russia was some 45,630 square kilometers—7,400 square kilometers more than remained under the control of the Phanariot princes in the rump principality.[21] Local *boiars* in the truncated principality originally opposed the annexation and argued that, since Moldova was only a vassal of Turkey rather than a Turkish province, the sultan had no right to accept the cession of territory without their consent. Nevertheless, the territorial changes were enshrined in the treaty of Bucharest concluded between Alexander and Sultan Mahmud II in May 1812.

The Romanian novelist Paul Goma amusingly recounted his grandfather's claim that the name *Bessarabia* had come from the Russian *bez arabov* (without Arabs), a reference to the flight of the Muslim Ottomans from the southern Bessarabian steppe before the army of Tsar Alexander.[22] Goma's grandfather was of course misguided, but the name does have a convoluted origin. The area between the Prut and Dnestr

DEMETRIVS CANTEMIR.
S.ROSSIACI IMPERII.
et MOLDAVIÆ. PRINCEPS.
PETRI.M.RVSSORU *Imperatoris*
SENATOR.et AB IN TIMIS CONSILIIS.

Dimitrie Cantemir, prince of Moldova, 1710–1711, and ally of
Peter the Great. Courtesy Cabinetul de Stampe, Library of the
Romanian Academy.

Rivers was never considered a distinct territory, but rather merely the eastern part of the Moldovan principality. Historical Moldova was defined by three north-south river valleys, the Siret, the Prut, and the Dnestr, and the real geographical division in the principality was between the northern mountainous area (*Moldova de sus*) and the hills and plains along the Black Sea (*Moldova de jos*). Before 1812, the eastern half of the principality thus had no particular name, least of all *Bessarabia*. The original region known by that name was in fact not in Moldova, but in the other Romanian principality, Wallachia, and applied to the swath of territory stretching between the Danube and the Dnestr and washed by the waters of the Black Sea. The Wallachian prince Mircea cel Bătrân (the Old, 1386–1418) had wrested the region from the Tatars and incorporated it into the Țara Românească.[23] The area thus came to be known as the land of the Basarab dynasty, of which Mircea was a part; the same practice of naming newly conquered lands after the houses that ruled them led the Turks to call Moldova *Boğdan* or *Kara Boğdan*, after the founding prince.

However, in the shifting boundaries of southeast Europe, Bessarabia moved north in 1812. In negotiations at the end of the 1806–12 war, Russian representatives had managed to secure Turkish agreement to the evacuation of Bessarabia and its cession to the tsar, although no documents identified precisely what that area was meant to be. Russian commanders interpreted *Bessarabia* to mean the entire region between the Prut and Dnestr, north as far as the fortress at Hotin, rather than simply the southern region along the Black Sea. From that point, a new Bessarabia was born.[24]

The Russian annexation of the Prut-Dnestr region initially promised to eradicate the legacy of Phanariot rule and bring European forms of administration and a cultural renaissance to the region, much as the Austrian annexation of Bukovina had helped achieve after 1775.[25] In the first years after the annexation, the Moldovan *boiars* managed to carve out a special autonomous district within the empire. Led by Gavril Bănulescu-Bodoni, the Orthodox metropolitan of Chisinau and Hotin, the Bessarabian nobles petitioned Alexander to establish a civil government for the region based on the traditional laws of the Moldovan principality. Under a special statute of 1818, the Bessarabians were given wide latitude in local government, with Moldovan serving alongside Russian as the official language of local administration.[26] Bodoni was also able to establish a seminary and printing works, which produced books and other liturgical works in Moldovan between 1815 and 1820, and to maintain the autonomy of the church within a distinct Bessarabian eparchy loyal to Moscow.[27]

This experiment in Bessarabian autonomy, however, proved to be short-lived. The death of Bănulescu-Bodoni in 1821 robbed the Bessarabians of a strong leader, while the growing national assertiveness of nobles across the border in the rump Moldovan principality and in Wallachia frightened tsarist authorities into retracting many of the freedoms allowed in the first years after the annexation. *Boiars* in Wallachia and Moldova led an insurrection against Phanariot administrators in 1821, and although Tsar Alexander held little enthusiasm for the Turks, he held the revolutionary actions of the Romanians in even lower regard.[28] Further still, by the early 1820s it had become clear to many administrators in Bessarabia that the autonomous status of the region served mainly to cover the rapaciousness of native nobles.[29] These factors worked together to bring a gradual end to Bessarabia's special place in the empire.

The coronation of Nicholas I in 1825 led to a further diminution of Bessarabian autonomy as the new tsar initiated a series of reforms aimed at extending central control over the newly acquired western borderlands. The constitution that had been awarded to Bessarabia in 1818 was repealed and, in 1829, replaced with a new code drafted by the governor of New Russia and Bessarabia, M. S. Vorontsov. Article 63 of the code halted the obligatory use of the Moldovan language in public pronouncements, and a further act of 1854 made Russian the region's official language.[30] The use of Moldovan was purged from the province's schools after midcentury, and Romanian books from west of the Prut were prohibited. One visitor in 1899 found no Romanian books at all in the Chisinau public library.[31]

From the end of the Crimean War to the Congress of Berlin (1856–78), three southern districts of Bessarabia were returned to the Romanian principalities, and Romanian authorities worked to reverse many of the cultural reforms of the tsarist era, including establishing Romanian schools and bringing the local church under the authority of the Bucharest patriarchate. But the return of the districts of Cahul, Bolgrad, and Ismail to Russia once again placed all of Bessarabia within the empire. With the exception of these two decades, all of Bessarabia's territory remained inside the Russian empire and outside the movement for pan-Romanian union that arose in Wallachia and western Moldova in the latter half of the nineteenth century. The return of southern Bessarabia to Russia in 1878 and the general conservative turn in Russian domestic policy after 1881 contributed to the loss of the relative political and cultural autonomy that the region had enjoyed in the first half of the century. Bessarabia's status was changed from an imperial region (*oblast'*) to a Russian province (*guberniia*) in 1871, an indication that it formed an inseparable part not only of the Russian empire but of the Russian heartland itself.

Bessarabia had never been a truly prosperous region even under the Moldovan principality, and under the Russians it remained the most backward region in the empire's western reaches. When Tsar Alexander I visited in 1818, he was astonished to find the Christian nobles dressed in elaborate Turkish gowns rather than jackets and breeches.[32] Chisinau was little more than a village on a swampy river at the time of the annexation, and rapid immigration after its selection as the provincial capital outran the ability of governors to improve city services.[33] Literacy among the Bessarabian population remained low, just over 15.6 percent by 1897; for ethnic Moldovans the figure was only 6 percent.[34] Located on the fringes of the empire, the province became a haven for smugglers and other criminals operating along the Danube and the Black Sea.[35] It was so out of the way, in fact, that Lenin's underground *Iskra* newspaper was printed in Chisinau in 1901 and 1902, a minor connection to the world socialist movement in which later communist historians would take great pride. Russian Bessarabia was frequently characterized as the Siberia of the west, a place about which Pushkin, exiled there from 1820 to 1823, was unequivocal: "Accursed town of Kishinev," he wrote, "to abuse you the tongue will grow tired."[36]

By the end of the century, Moldovans formed at least 47.6 percent of the population, but the province was home to a wide variety of ethnic groups.[37] Migrations of Bulgarians, Turks, Germans, and French-speaking Swiss colonists in the wake of the 1812 annexation added to an already multiethnic countryside. By the middle of the century, the province had seventeen synagogues, six Lutheran churches, and four Roman Catholic churches, as well as hundreds of Orthodox churches and monasteries attended by Russians, Moldovans, and Orthodox schismatic sects.[38] City life was dominated by Jews and Russians. Over 50,000 Jews were living in Chisinau in 1897, accounting for nearly half the population; almost all the city's factories were owned by Jews, and sixteen separate Jewish schools were functioning by the turn of the century.[39]

The Bessarabian capital was also one of the great centers of antisemitism. Many of the Russian empire's most infamous pamphleteers and organizers were of Bessarabian extraction, and local anti-Jewish organizations were instrumental in propagating the *Protocols of the Learned Elders of Zion*. The Chisinau pogroms of 1903 and 1905, in which 68 Jews were killed and hundreds of businesses looted, drew international attention to the plight of Jews in Russia.[40]

Some measure of liberty and local government came in the form of the emancipation of the serfs in 1861 and the introduction of the *zemstvo* system of local councils in 1869, but greater local control in Bessarabia usually meant greater power for the most reactionary elements among Russians and russified Moldovans.[41] A small stratum of nobles, especially the Kroupensky family, exercised firm control over a region far from the imperial capitals and far from the eyes of central officials. Prince Sergei Urussov, dispatched to Bessarabia as provincial governor

TABLE 1
BESSARABIAN POPULATION IN THE
NINETEENTH CENTURY

	1858		1871		1897	
Moldovans	600,000	66.4%	692,000	67.4%	920,919	47.6%
Ukrainians[a]	120,000	13.1	—	—	379,698	19.6
Jews	78,750	8.6	93,590	9.1	228,168	11.8
Bulgarians	48,216	5.2	25,684	2.5	103,225	5.3
Germans	24,160	2.6	33,501	3.5	60,206	3.1
Great Russians	20,000	2.1	162,252[b]	15.0	155,774	8.0
Roma (Gypsies)	11,490	1.0	18,983	1.5	8,636	0.4
Armenians	2,725	0.2	—	—	2,080	0.1
Turks[c]	—	—	—	—	55,790	2.9
Poles	—	—	—	—	11,696	0.6
Other	—	—	—	—	9,220	0.5
TOTAL	—	—	—	—	1,935,412	100.0

[a]"Ruthenian" in some statistics. Does not include 6,000 "Little Russians" reported in 1858 in fishing villages in southern Bessarabia.

[b]Includes all East Slavs.

[c]"Ottoman Turks," which probably included Muslim Turks along with Muslim Roma, Christian Gagauz, and Turkic-speaking Bulgarians.

NOTE: Dashes indicate no figure available.

SOURCE: A. Zashchuk, *Materialy dlia geografii i statistiki Rossii: Bessarabskaia oblast'* (St. Petersburg: n.p., 1862), p. 186; Zamfir C. Arbore, *Basarabia în secolul XIX* (Bucharest: Institutul de Arte Grafice, 1898), p. 118; 1897 Russian census.

in 1903, found a generally peaceful *guberniia*, except for the agitation of antisemitic circles, but one in which the local administration seemed something from Gogol:

> While I was passing through the prison wards several people asked me, imploringly, to interfere in their behalf, stating that they had been kept in confinement for several months after their sentence had expired. . . . When I asked the prison superintendent why more people were not allowed to go, he . . . pronounced the unintelligible verdict, "They are vicious foreigners, your Excellency." . . . [U]pon my return home, I discovered that on the recommendation of the provincial authorities the Minister of the Interior had the right to expel from Russia all foreigners found guilty of misdemeanors by the courts. It is customary, therefore, to detain all foreigners sent to prison, even after the expiration of their term, until the ministerial order is received. When I asked what objection there might be to the liberation of the prisoners at the proper time, I was told they might leave the country, and then it would be impossible to carry into effect the Minister's order for their expulsion.[42]

The period after 1812 also brought to the fore the question of the ethnonational identity of the Moldovans themselves. In the nineteenth century, tsarist views on Moldovan identity often shifted depending on the prevailing balance of power in southeastern Europe. Following an initial period of cultural liberalism after the 1812 annexation, tsarist officials became increasingly concerned about the growth of Greek-inspired nationalism along the lower Danube. From the late 1820s, cultural policy in Bessarabia therefore centered on the russification of the administrative system and the progressive integration of the region into broader imperial structures. The introduction of Russian as the province's official language, the subordination of the Bessarabian church to the Moscow patriarchate, and the elimination of Moldovan customary law were all designed to secure Bessarabia's place inside the empire and to strengthen its position as an Orthodox bastion along the Ottoman frontier. Official russification policies waxed and waned during the century of Russian rule, though, with most successes registered in the provincial administration and in the church, which after the death of Bodoni became the chief advocate of state-led russification. Archbishop Pavel Lebedev forced Moldovan churches and monasteries to conduct services in Russian, but even at the end of his tenure (1871–82), there were still 417 churches in the province that used Moldovan in the liturgy, with a further 608 in Russian only.[43]

Later Romanian propagandists would denounce the russification of the Bessarabian peasant under tsarism, but cultural politics often involved less russification than ruralization. Indigenous Moldovan culture was relegated to the countryside, with the urban centers dominated by Russians, Jews, and russified Moldovans. As in other parts of the empire's western frontier, Russian performed the dual functions of an official language and the language of polite society, while Moldovan was considered the crude language of the simple peasant. Provincial administrators, both natives and immigrants, lived in a world culturally detached from the customs of the village. "They spoke in about ten different languages, with only two of which I was familiar," the governor Urussov wrote of petitioners who visited his office in Chisinau. "The Moldavians were on their knees, holding their petitions on their heads, and muttering their requests while looking on the ground. . . . I usually allowed them to have their say, and then dismissed them, for which purpose I learned to speak a few Moldavian words. In cases where the matter appeared of unusual importance, I found at hand interpreters, who performed their duties admirably."[44]

At no time, though, did the Russians argue that Moldovans and their neighbors in the Romanian principalities somehow formed nations apart. Rather, the intent was to extinguish any manifestations of non-Russian nationalism, of whatever stripe, and erect in their place a sense of loyalty to tsar and empire. Imperial censuses used the term *Moldovan* to describe Bessarabia's majority population, but this term was the self-designation of the population, not an invention of the Russians. Imperial ethnographic studies of the Bessarabian region did not deny that important cultural commonalities existed between both banks of the Prut, and even committed local russophiles saw little need to conceal the Romanian identity of the Bessarabian Moldovans. "The inhabitants of upper Bessarabia," wrote one observer in the journal of the Russian foreign ministry in 1846, "are essentially Romanians [*rumuny*], that is, a mixture of Slavs and Romans, and sons of the Greek Orthodox Church."[45] Similarly, members of the Slavophile movement in Russia in the 1840s, although convinced that the Romanians were probably Slavs in Latin disguise, had nothing to say about possible differences between the Bessarabians and their neighbors to the west. After the mid-nineteenth century, Russian writers argued that Bessarabia belonged to Russia not because it was inhabited by a distinct nation, but because the area had been first settled by Slavs and only later conquered by Romanian Wallachs.[46] Even in the period after 1905, when local tsarist officials sought to stifle a growing Bessarabian national movement, ethnographic works identifying Moldovans and Romanians as two parts of a single nation were still published in St. Petersburg.[47] The one-hundredth anniversary of the Bessarabian annexation in 1912 was celebrated with special publications and demonstrations in Chisinau, but the justification for the union remained much as it had in 1812: the liberation of Bessarabian Christians from the Ottoman yoke and the reconquest of an ancient Slav land, not the liberation of a distinct Moldovan nation.[48]

Throughout the century, events in the western half of the old principality moved in a very different direction from those in Bessarabia. After the Bessarabian annexation, western Moldova remained formally within the Ottoman Empire and under the control of the Phanariots. A rising in 1821 was quashed by Ottoman troops, but in the long run, it proved to be a boon for local Moldovans and Wallachians. The Phanariot system was ended and the previous custom of the *boiars'* electing their own prince was reinstated. A period of Russian military occupation from 1828 to 1834 led to the rationalization of the local administration and, under the Russian administrator Pavel Kiselev, the eradication of Ottoman-era institutions. The germ of a common pan-Romanian identity took root in the two provinces as the century progressed. Historians explored the common cultural origins of Wallachians and Moldovans, and writers worked to Latinize the language of the principalities, which had evolved as a mixture of Latin and Slavic characteristics. Further political reforms brought some degree of uniformity to the institutions of the two principalities. In 1859, noble assemblies in the principalities' capitals of Iaşi (Jassy) and Bucharest elected the same man, Alexandru Ioan Cuza, as prince or *domnitor*, effectively creating a single Romanian state.

After the establishment of the United Principalities, later to become Romania, political figures began to call for the integration of all areas inhabited by Romanian-speakers—including Bessarabia—into a unified nation-state. Wallachia and western Moldova had long been the place of exile for Bessarabian writers dissatisfied with Russian rule in the province, and these intellectuals pressed strongly for the newly unified Romanian government to address the question of their brothers east of the Prut. With Romania's independence from the Porte in 1878 and its transformation into a dynastic kingdom in 1881, the debate over the

Romanian identity of Bessarabia and its population assumed greater significance.

POLITICAL CURRENTS IN RUSSIAN BESSARABIA

The early twentieth century saw the development of several conflicting political currents in the Bessarabian province. Young Bessarabian intellectuals, influenced by the radicalism of their counterparts in the imperial capitals, sought to spread the message of land reform, universal suffrage, and social justice to the backward *guberniia*. Other young Bessarabians, supported by artistic and philanthropic circles in Bucharest and Iaşi, looked to pan-Romanian nationalism as the chief tool for transforming cultural and political life in the region. Older Moldovan nobles hoped to use their positions of power to gain minor cultural concessions from the tsarist authorities, thus aiming to placate the young nationalists while using them as a lever against the radicals. Non-Moldovan property owners, russified intellectuals, and local reactionaries, facing the twin threats of socialist radicalism and pan-Romanian nationalism, urged the imperial authorities to remain vigilant against any manifestations of disloyalty to the tsar.

The 1905 revolution gave impetus to the radical discussion groups and literary circles that had begun to form among Bessarabian intellectuals in the latter half of the nineteenth century. Already at the turn of the century, Bessarabians studying at the University of Dorpat (Tartu) in Estonia, many of whom would later become central figures in the liberation movement, had established an underground students' association, the Bessarabian Countrymen (Pământenia Basarabeană). The group set up correspondence with intellectuals in Romania and organized festive literary evenings at which they spoke Romanian and ate *mămăligă cu brânză*, the polenta and cheese combination considered the Romanian national dish.[49]

Although the organization's leader, Ion Pelivan, was arrested by tsarist authorities in 1902, he returned to Chisinau after the 1905 revolution and in October, along with Pantelimon Halippa (another former Dorpat student), founded the Society for Moldovan National Culture. When few Moldovans managed to secure election to the first Russian State Duma in 1906, Pelivan and Halippa encouraged several sympathetic Bessarabian nobles to fund a newspaper in order to spread the message of national awakening to the region's peasant masses. In May 1906 the first Romanian-language newspaper (printed in the Cyrillic alphabet) was published in the province. Articles in the twice weekly "national-democratic gazette" *Basarabia* called for land reform, Bessarabian autonomy and self-government, and the introduction of the Moldovan language in schools and administrative organs, and included pieces signed by such local luminaries as Halippa, Pelivan, the lawyer and editor Emanuil Gavriliţă, and the eminent Iaşi University professor and populist Constantin Stere.

The *Basarabia* circle fell victim to the conservative reaction that swept the empire in 1907. Rumors that the newspaper was funded by a group of Romanian irredentists led by Stere eventually reached the ears of the Bessarabian governor, A. N. Kharuzin. After the newspaper printed the incendiary poem "Romanian, Awake!" in its March 1, 1907, issue, Kharuzin ordered the closure of the editorial offices.[50] The newly appointed archbishop in Chisinau, Serafim Chichagov, then cooperated with the Kroupensky family and other nobles to help purge the church and cultural institutions of Moldovan nationalists. Many of the newspaper's leading supporters were forced to flee to Iaşi, where with Stere's help they were able to enroll as students at the university. A more moderate publication, *Viaţa Basarabiei* (Bessarabian life), briefly continued the work of the *Basarabia* circle and appeared in two separate forms, one written in literary Romanian with Latin characters and the other written in the Moldovan dialect of the Bessarabian peasant and using the Cyrillic alphabet.[51] By mid-1907, after only six issues, *Viaţa Basarabiei* had likewise disappeared.

Besides the growth in nationalist sentiment among some young Bessarabian intellectuals, the years after 1905 also saw the emergence of other political groupings that rivaled the pan-Romanians. One, centered initially around the weekly "independent national gazette" *Moldovanul* (*The Moldovan*), represented the more moderate face of local nationalism in Bessarabia. Edited by Gheorghe Madan, the newspaper pressed for national reawakening and economic emancipation in the province, but since it largely represented the interests of Moldovan nobles loyal to St. Petersburg, its supporters were loath to challenge the legitimacy of tsarist rule. *Moldovanul* itself only lasted from January 1907 to October 1908, but the interests that it represented proved to be a significant challenge to the pan-Romanian nationalists. Indeed, it was in the course of a polemic between Gavriliță and Madan that the editorial board of *Basarabia* decided to print the nationalist poem "Romanian, Awake!" the ostensible reason for the newspaper's proscription.[52]

Another major political grouping opposed to the pan-Romanians were those forces in the republic with an unwavering loyalty to Russia and the tsar. Centered on local members of the Octobrist union, the rightist faction that split from the Russian Constitutional Democrats in 1906, this group also included the Bessarabian far right, represented by organizations such as the League of True Russians and the Union of Russian People, whose members had been largely responsible for instigating the Chisinau pogrom of 1903. Such far-right activists as the antisemitic publicist Pavalache Krushevan, the leader of the Rasputin assassination plot V. M. Purishkevich, as well as more moderate members of Bessarabia's Russian and Moldovan elite, were able to secure election to all four State Dumas, thus further radicalizing those groups pushing for the cultural and political autonomy of the Bessarabian province.

The forces of the Right eclipsed the political influence of the pan-Romanians after the closure of *Basarabia*. However, operating from Iaşi and financed by the Bessarabian philanthropist Vasile Stroescu, the nationalists launched a new publication in 1913. Again involving Pantelimon Halippa and other former members of the Society for Moldovan National Culture, *Cuvântul moldovenesc* (The Moldovan word)—a twice-monthly "journal of literature, village life, cooperation, and practical knowledge"—appeared in May 1913 in both Cyrillic and Latin script and, after January 1914, as a separate weekly newspaper under the same name. The initial editions included a range of literary and practical topics: poetry, fables, riddles, songs, public health information, war dispatches, news from Russia, and other items of public interest aimed at the enlightenment of the Moldovan people and the defense of their interests.

The disruption of war and revolution after 1914 opened up the possibility of treating more overtly political subjects. By April 1917 the Society for Moldovan National Culture had been transformed into an openly political organization, the Moldovan National Party. The party's program initially articulated demands not unlike those of the Provisional Government in Petrograd: suffrage by universal, equal, direct, and secret ballot; freedom of speech, press, assembly, and religion; a special Bessarabian legislative assembly; use of the Moldovan language in education; and an autocephalous Bessarabian church, all within a reconstituted

Russian federation.[53] However, with the Bolshevik seizure of power, the growth of new, more radical political movements across the empire, and the increasing militancy of soldiers along the Romanian front, full independence for the Bessarabian province became one of the party's central goals.

Developments in Chisinau after 1905 attracted the attention of many Romanians who sought to bring the same message of national awakening to the benighted Bessarabians that the rest of the historical Romanian lands had discovered already in the last century. Especially after late 1917, when Romania's misfortunes on the battlefield eventually forced an unfavorable peace treaty with the Central Powers, refugees from Transylvania, the Banat, and other Romanian irredenti saw in Bessarabia "a wonderful virgin soil" for continuing the national struggle that now seemed lost in their own regions.[54] Stroescu and Stere, both originally from Bessarabia, were instrumental in financing the nationalist movement and in protecting young Bessarabian writers when they fled across the Prut River to Iaşi before the February revolution. Other Romanians decamped to Bessarabia itself, working in Chisinau and the villages to build schools and libraries, train teachers, and resurrect a sense of Romanian identity in the province. It was not an easy task. "The Romanians in Bessarabia," recalled a visitor from the Banat in 1918, "have lost all sense of national sentiment as a result of the systematic idiocy of russification. Even today, the people call themselves 'Moldovans' and think of themselves more as brothers of the Russians . . . than of Romanians, whom the policy of denationalization has portrayed as a nation lower than the Gypsies."[55]

Onisifor Ghibu, a Transylvanian writer and educator, set up schools and language courses and collaborated with Halippa and other nationalists. Ghibu's journals, though, reveal the frustration that many pan-Romanians felt when they encountered the difficulties of sparking a Romanian renaissance. Not only were local Russians resistant to the efforts to turn the growing Bessarabian social revolution into a Romanian national one, but the central targets of Ghibu's efforts—the Moldovans—were themselves often less than enthusiastic. As Ghibu wrote on his first class session with Bessarabian teachers:

> The absolute majority of the teachers had no familiarity at all with Romanian culture—they did not even know the Latin alphabet—and no national consciousness. Their Russian training wiped away at least

95 percent of everything that was Romanian. . . . In the first week, every time I came into the classroom I found at the back of the room a little group of Russian teachers, mumbling and complaining that "We don't need Moldovan classes," "This isn't Romania; this is Russia," and "We've got better things to do." In general, the Moldovan teachers did not take part in these protests, but neither did they feel obliged to speak out against them.[56]

In 1912, the historian Nicolae Iorga had decried the "rape of Bessarabia" a century earlier and encouraged Romania to help reawaken the sense of nationality in the lost land.[57] But as Ghibu and others would later discover, it was less a matter of resurrecting a lost identity than building one from scratch.

THE SFATUL ȚĂRII AND UNION WITH ROMANIA

In the end the leaders of Bessarabia's awakening, the National Party and the intellectuals centered around *Cuvântul moldovenesc*, were overtaken by events. The turmoil of war, the fall of the tsar, and the rise of the Bolsheviks left the Bessarabian province in an uncertain state. Following calls for an elected national assembly from several social and military organizations throughout the summer of 1917, representatives of Moldovan military units in the former tsarist army convened an assembly in Chisinau in October 1917. At the congress the more than 900 delegates declared the autonomy of the Bessarabian province and called for the convocation of a National Council, or Sfatul Țării, to ratify the declaration and serve as the government of the new autonomous republic.

Elected indirectly through soldiers' councils, peasants' associations, and other social organizations, the 138-member Sfatul Țării convened on November 21, 1917, and included mainly Moldovans but also many members of the region's ethnic minorities. Ion Inculeț served as president, with Pantelimon Halippa as his deputy. Inculeț and Halippa represented two very different sets of interests within the assembly. Inculeț, although a former member of the original *Basarabia* circle, was a Socialist Revolutionary most concerned with political change and land reform; he had already served in Bessarabia as the official representative of Kerensky's Provisional Government. Halippa, who became one of the leaders of the so-called Moldovan Bloc in the assembly, was also a reformist, but his zeal for reform was tempered by his commitment to the ideal of pan-Romanian union.[58] Both groups were brought together by the fear of anarchy and an increasingly militant Ukraine, which seemed ready to occupy Bessarabia and declare it part of the new Ukrainian People's Republic. On December 2 the assembly declared the creation of an autonomous republic within Russia. As local leaders argued at the time, Bessarabia should remain firmly within the new Russia, but its status should be like that of Finland in the tsarist empire or one of the cantons of Switzerland.[59] The assembly quickly set about forming a council of ministers, organizing further self-defense units to protect the republic, and drafting legislation on agrarian reform.

It was Romania, though, that ultimately determined the fate of the Bessarabian government. The turmoil in Russia gave the Romanian kingdom a chance to acquire the territory taken from the Romanian principalities in 1812 and again in 1878. On the pretext of securing supply lines against raids by Bolsheviks and armed bandits, Romanian troops arrived in Chisinau in mid-January 1918 and, by the end of the month, had driven Bolshevik forces east of the Dnestr River. On January 24, 1918, with Bolshevik units on the run and Ukraine threatening to annex the region, the Sfatul Țării proclaimed an independent Moldovan Democratic Republic of Bessarabia.

The occupation of Bessarabia by the Romanians, although carried out after an appeal by members of the Sfatul Țării and other Moldovan organizations, was not universally welcomed.[60] Some Romanian officers seemed to think that their mission was to restore the property of the Bessarabian nobles that had been spontaneously seized by the peasants; the army's commanders were forced to issue specific orders threatening with court-martial any officers who attempted to intervene on behalf of the landowners.[61] Many members of the Sfatul Țării were themselves less than supportive of the Romanian presence. An appeal to the citizens of Chisinau signed by members of the Bessarabian government denied that the Romanian troops had ever been invited to occupy the republic and argued that their sole purpose should be to take control of the railways from the Bolsheviks.[62]

Regardless of the details surrounding their arrival, the presence of Romanian troops unquestionably augmented the power of those groups looking to Romania for deliverance from the triple peril of Bolshevism, Ukrainian expansionism, and political anarchy. A Sfatul Țării vote on

Members of the pro-Romanian "Moldovan Bloc" in the Sfatul Tării, after the passage of Bessarabia's land reform legislation, 1918. Courtesy National Archives of Romania.

March 27, 1918, declared Bessarabia's union with Romania. Support for the union was mixed. The vote did not break down along clear ethnic lines, but with Romanian troops already in Chisinau, Romanian planes circling above the meeting hall, and the Romanian prime minister waiting in the foyer, many minority deputies chose simply not to vote.[63] Eighty-six members voted for the union to only three against, but forty-nine representatives either abstained or failed to appear.[64] The vote would later be treated as a "quasi-unanimous" expression of the will of the Bessarabian people,[65] but the motion only managed to pass because of a compromise with those groups hesitant about the union. The Sfatul Țării's declaration listed fourteen special privileges that Bessarabia would retain inside an enlarged Romania, including the continued existence of a freely elected regional assembly, control over local budgets and administrative organs, respect for the rights of ethnic minorities, a general amnesty for crimes committed during the war and, most importantly, the completion of land redistribution.[66]

By the autumn, however, events had once again overtaken the Bessarabian leadership. With assemblies in Transylvania, Bukovina, and other Romanian irredenti voting for immediate union with Romania, Halippa's Moldovan Bloc urged the Bessarabians to follow suit. Although lacking a quorum and voting in the middle of the night,[67] on November 27, 1918, the deputies renounced the previous conditions, declared union with Romania, and voted to dissolve the assembly, thus placing a definitive end to Bessarabia's brief tenure as an independent republic. Winning international recognition of the border changes proved to be more difficult than simply declaring union and remained one of the major goals of Romanian diplomacy between the wars. As in the past, though, the mixed culture and problematic identity of Bessarabia's inhabitants—from ethnic minorities to the Moldovans themselves—would become a central object of dispute.

3 Greater Romania and the Bessarabian Question

Immediately after the First World War, Western observers were largely optimistic about the future of the new Romania. According to the prognosis of R. W. Seton-Watson, one of Romania's chief intercessors in London and Paris, "Two generations of peace and clean government might make of Roumania an earthly paradise."[1] As it turned out, however, Greater Romania had neither. Politics continued to be as corrupt as in the Regat, as the "old kingdom" of Wallachia and western Moldova was known. The 1920s remained relatively stable by Romanian standards, with political life dominated by the Liberal Party and the personality of its leader, Ionel Brătianu. But the deaths of both Brătianu and the Romanian king, Ferdinand, in 1927 heralded a period of rapid government change and palace intrigues. Twenty prime ministers and twenty-nine separate cabinets—only two of which served for a full legislative term—were appointed in the two decades of Greater Romania.[2] The political instability was so great that by February 1938, Ferdinand's successor, Carol II, had followed the examples of Albania, Yugoslavia, and Bulgaria and declared a royal dictatorship, the first step on Romania's road to the authoritarian politics that engulfed most of Europe by the end of the decade. The budding democracy that sympathetic Western commentators hoped for in the early interwar period, whether real or illusory, was soon crushed beneath the weight of corruption, court intrigues, and right-wing reaction.

Still, the initial optimism of Seton-Watson and others was understandable. Romania's role in the war had highlighted its strategic importance to the Western Allies. The country's rich petroleum deposits, its long Danube frontage and Black Sea coastline, as well as its position as an outpost of Latinity in an otherwise slavophile or germanophile portion of Europe, made Bucharest the logical ally of strategists in Paris and London. Especially after 1917, with the lesson of the October Revolution in Russia weighing heavily on political leaders in western Europe, France and Britain were eager to maintain strong ties with Romania as a buffer against the Bolshevik menace to the east.

In addition, the country had survived the war with its governmental structure and monarchy intact. The revolutions, putsches, and palace coups that confronted politicians in other parts of east central Europe after 1918 were alien to Greater Romania. Although the war had led to serious splits within the once-powerful Conservative Party, two of the great mainstays of Romanian politics before the war—the Liberals and the Brătianu family—emerged stronger than ever. The elections of November 1919 (the first with universal male suffrage) and the growth of new, reform-minded political groupings drawing their strength from the new provinces of Transylvania, Bukovina, and Bessarabia, also seemed to point toward the development of a political system more responsive to Romania's vast peasant population and less reliant on backroom pacts among Bucharest politicians.

Romania had also emerged as a clear winner in the postwar territorial settlement. Nearly all of the Habsburg lands secretly promised to Romania in August 1916 as an incentive to join the war on the side of the Allies were included in the state's new boundaries. All of Bukovina, Maramureş, Crişana, Transylvania, and a portion of the Banat, in addition to the former Russian Bessarabia and the Bulgarian Dobrogea, were added to the Regat, with most of the country's borders secured by the Treaty of Trianon in June 1920. By the end of the war, Romania had more than doubled its 1913 population and territory. Overcome with emotion, King Ferdinand remarked to a delegation of Transylvanian Romanians in 1918 that "you can just feel the pulse of the motherland beating in the same rhythm as your own. . . . After Bessarabia, after Bukovina, we lacked one of the most precious stones: Transylvania with the areas of Hungary inhabited by Romanians. Today you have brought us this final building block which crowns the great work of union. We can look with confidence to the future, for the foundations are strong."[3]

The territorial building blocks of Greater Romania, however, turned out to be its stumbling blocks. The increase in Romania's size also diluted its ethnic Romanian component. Whereas less than 10 percent of the Regat's prewar population consisted of non-Romanian minorities, by 1919 some 28 percent of Greater Romania's population was non-Romanian. Magyars, Germans, Jews, and other ethnic groups were sometimes seen by Romanian politicians as illegitimate foreign guests, at best a tolerable nuisance and at worst a dangerous fifth column supporting revisionist claims by neighboring states. Romania's treatment of its minority populations, particularly its refusal to incorporate the League of Nations' minority rights treaty into the 1923 constitution, contributed to the country's tarnished international image.[4] The demographic changes brought about by the territorial enlargement also gave impetus to the student radicalism and populist nationalism that would later find expression in the fascist Iron Guard movement.

One major source of instability arising from the territorial gains involved the status of Bessarabia—the only territorial acquisition whose place in Greater Romania was never secured by international treaty. Angered at the attempt by the "Bucharest oligarchs" to grab land from a weakened Russia, the Bolsheviks severed diplomatic relations with Romania in January 1918, confiscated the Romanian treasure that had been deposited in Moscow during the war, and from May to September 1919 supported an unrecognized "Bessarabian Soviet Socialist Republic" that had been proclaimed by Bessarabian communists.[5] Numerous formal complaints were lodged with the Paris Peace Conference contesting the annexation of the province, and at one stage in the early 1920s, the Soviets even drafted a secret plan for retaking Bessarabia by force, a project foiled by British agents in Istanbul.[6]

Resolving the dispute over the international status of Bessarabia remained one of the chief preoccupations of Romania's foreign ministry between the wars and also the personal crusade of the country's most talented diplomat, Nicolae Titulescu. Not only did the Soviet Union never recognize the union with Romania but, unlike the situation with the former Habsburg lands, it was never officially recognized by the Western powers either. The Bessarabian border was the last and most contentious issue to be addressed by Allied diplomats at the Paris Peace Conference. The Americans, especially Woodrow Wilson, felt uneasy that no plebiscite had been held in the province.[7] The British and French were similarly disinclined to make territorial changes that harmed the interests of the former tsarist forces still fighting the Bolsheviks in the Russian civil war.[8] However, after serious lobbying in Paris, in October 1920 the Romanian foreign minister, Take Ionescu, succeeded in concluding a treaty that would have recognized Romania's claim to Bessarabia and set out its obligations vis-à-vis the region's Russian population.[9] However, since the treaty was never ratified by Japan and failed to include the United States and Russia, it remained a legally worthless instrument.[10] The chief problem, complained the Romanian minister to the United States, was not that the Allied powers were opposed to the Bessarabian annexation, but that they could rarely be bothered to give much thought to it. "The same good people who used to believe that the Ukraine was a musical instrument imported from Hawaii . . . thought when they saw the name Bessarabia in print that it was part of Arabia."[11]

Successive rounds of negotiations were held throughout the 1920s and 1930s, but each failed to settle the Bessarabian question. In 1923 Romania attempted to normalize relations with the Soviet Union, but talks in Vienna failed once the question of Bessarabia was placed on the table. In 1929 both Romania and the Soviet Union signed the Kellogg-Briand pact outlawing war, but the problem of Bessarabia was raised at the protocol ceremony in Moscow. In 1932 talks were held in Riga on establishing a Romanian-Soviet nonaggression pact, but Moscow still balked at accepting recognition of the annexation. A year later, at talks in London on defining aggression, the Soviets indicated that they might accept Romania's de facto control over Bessarabia, but even after the complete normalization of relations between Bucharest and Moscow in 1934, no legally valid document existed guaranteeing the province's status.[12]

Two major political factors frustrated the effort to secure Romania's eastern border. First, Romania's relationship with Poland and France sometimes restricted the kingdom's freedom to maneuver in relations with the Soviets. Romania was linked to the former by a defensive military alliance signed in 1921 and to the latter by a treaty of cooperation and friendship concluded in 1926. The three countries promised to coordinate their foreign policies in important questions of European security, especially on the issue of their relationship to the Bolshevik state. What was meant to be a relationship of mutual security, however, sometimes placed the Romanians in a diplomatic straitjacket. Because of the commitment to coordinated foreign policies, Romania was obliged to forgo negotiations with the Soviets at times when resolving the Bessarabian issue might have been both profitable and possible (such as the early 1920s), and later was forced to normalize relations with Moscow at a less politically propitious juncture (in the mid-1930s).[13]

This was the argument repeatedly put forward by Alexandre Cretzianu, the Romanian foreign minister from 1939 to 1941. Cretzianu maintained that the French attempt to isolate the Bolsheviks in the early 1920s—France's so-called barbed wire policy toward the new Soviet state—was the chief impediment to resolving the status of Bessarabia. A decade later, although Romania's allies had all softened on relations with Moscow, Romania remained faithful to the earlier no-compromise policy and thus found itself the only neighbor of the Soviet Union with no official representative in Moscow.[14]

Second, the king's role in the Romanian political system frequently left Titulescu and other diplomats in an uncertain position. Since the installation of the Hohenzollern-Sigmaringen dynasty in 1866, the king had stood as the ultimate arbiter of Romanian politics. His support was the sine qua non of any party's viability, and having the king's ear ensured the leader of the party in power a say in the formation of any new government. Just as Carol I (1866–1914) had been the Conservatives' king, so Ferdinand (1914–27) became the patron of Ionel Brătianu and the Liberals. The death of both Ferdinand and the Brătianu family patriarch in 1927 seemed to mark an opening up of the political system to new parties, some of which drew their strength from the new provinces. These groups hoped to court Carol II (1930–40) and to find in him the patron that the Conservatives and Liberals had found in his great uncle and his father. However, the instability of the 1930s meant that politics in Romania was less about parties and more about personalities. No single political grouping could claim to occupy a special position in relation to Carol II, whose mercurial behavior was notorious. The king's personal affinity for a particular political figure often determined the leadership of new cabinets. This problem was especially evident in the case of Titulescu, with the king reneging on positions that Titulescu thought had been settled and then shifting support to his rivals within the foreign ministry.[15] The king's role injected an element of uncertainty in negotiations that frequently frightened the Soviets away from the bargaining table. Such institutionalized instability would have been difficult enough regardless of who held the throne, but it was particularly frustrating so long as the ultimate decision-making power remained in the hands of Carol, whose own father once described him as a man with a brain like a Gruyère cheese—with a few good bits but plenty of holes.[16] Even after the warming in Soviet-Romanian relations after 1934, the status of Bessarabia thus remained in dispute.

THE BESSARABIANS IN GREATER ROMANIA

In the 1920s and 1930s, Romanian scholars marshaled extensive data to illustrate the improved condition of Bessarabians under Romanian rule. It is certainly true that the Bessarabians' lot improved between the wars, as Romania sought to integrate the former tsarist province into the new kingdom. Agrarian reform, first voted by the Sfatul Țării in 1918 and accepted by the Romanian parliament in 1920, redistributed some 1.8 million hectares of agricultural land (over half the total) to 357,000 villagers.[17] A special state institution, Casa Noastră (Our House), was set up in Chisinau to give legal title to the newly propertied peasants and concluded the task of land reform by 1923. Public works projects accelerated. Chisinau's main streets were paved, and the swamps along the Bâc River in the lower city were drained to combat malaria.[18] New trains connected Chisinau with Bucharest and other Romanian towns, allowing Bessarabian produce to find its way west to markets in old Moldova and the rest of the Regat. New roads, bridges across the Prut, airports, telephone exchanges, and radio stations were all built in Bessarabia in the 1930s. Schools, adult education courses, and "cultural hearths" (*cămine culturale*) were established by the Romanian ministry of education, the army, and private philanthropic bodies, often with the dual goal of increasing literacy (in Romanian) and cultivating a sense of Romanian patriotism in the frontier province.[19] By 1930, literacy had risen to nearly 30 percent.[20]

Still, Bessarabia never managed to rise to the level of Transylvania or the Regat. Bessarabia had the largest relative rural population of all the provinces of Greater Romania. Some 87 percent of the entire population lived outside the cities (including nearly 93 percent of Romanian-speakers), and Russians and Jews alone formed over half the urban population.[21] In the late 1930s, one out of every four Romanian citizens had access to electrical power, but in Bessarabia the figure was one in seven. In the same period, Bessarabians suffered among the highest incidences of several major infectious diseases (typhoid, scarlet fever, diphtheria, encephalitis), as well as some of the highest mortality rates from these diseases.[22] The *zemstvo* system, which had allowed a degree of local autonomy in education, public health, and other spheres, was eliminated in 1918, with a corresponding decline in the access of Bessarabians to social services.[23] One American observer was so appalled by the living conditions that he could think of only poverty-stricken Arkansas as an American analogue.[24]

Infrastructural and economic difficulties also kept Bessarabia in a parlous state. Many of these problems had been inherited from the Russian empire. Only about 90 miles of paved roads existed in Bessarabia before its union with Romania, and the mud tracks that crisscrossed the province became impassable in the rain.[25] The Russians had built 657 miles of railroad in the *guberniia* before 1917, but since the railways were designed for strategic rather than economic purposes, they connected Bessarabian cities with Russia and Ukraine but not with each other; the primitive state of the rolling stock, as well as the Russian broad-gauge track, also proved to be major problems.[26] Revenues from wine production, previously one of the mainstays of the economy, were diminished by the loss of markets in Soviet Russia and the preferential access accorded to French wines on the Romanian market. A trade war with Poland after 1926 also disrupted one of the principal export routes for Bessarabian wine and continued to hurt production into the 1930s.[27] Serious droughts in 1921, 1924, and 1925 also dealt a harsh blow to an already ailing agricultural sector.

Corrupt and heavy-handed Romanian administrators, although not uncommon in the rest of the kingdom, seemed to be especially prevalent in Bessarabia. Transnistrian refugees, who had flooded into Bessarabia during the war, were seen by the Romanian secret police as potential Bolshevik agents, just as Bessarabians in other parts of Romania were accused of setting up communist "nests" in the universities.[28] The Siguranţa and local police agents worked to unmask these groups, often conducting surveillance of Russians and Jews, who were thought to be especially susceptible to Soviet propaganda.[29] The result, though, was a sense among locals that Bessarabia had been occupied by Romania rather than united with it.[30] Even the most ardent supporters of the 1918 union noted the harshness of the Romanian administration. Given the strength of the Bolshevik underground in the province, though, they argued that certain "human sacrifices" were justified when made "on the altar of order and peace."[31]

For locals, other aspects of the Romanian presence evidenced a simple lack of respect for Bessarabia as an equal part of the new Romania. Former members of the Sfatul Țării were awarded 50 hectares of land in Bessarabia in recognition of their service to the nation, but Romanian army officers who married Bessarabian women were eligible to receive 100 hectares.[32] The most widely recounted tale of Romanian behavior, still heard in Moldova in the 1990s, supposedly involved the Romanian commandant in the northern town of Edineț. In order to teach the Bessarabians to salute Romanian officers, the commandant apparently ordered his lieutenant to walk around town with his cap held aloft on a stick, requiring the townspeople to salute the cap for practice.[33] Such incidents, whether real or imagined, quickly became part of Bessarabian folk memory. "We joined the Romanians," complained a Bessarabian writer in 1930, "we weren't supposed to have been conquered by them."[34]

With the influx of new Romanian administrators and colonists from the Regat, as well as the region's status as a disputed territory, any examples of impropriety on the part of the civilian and military officials were necessarily magnified.[35] As the managing editor of *Foreign Affairs* noted in his travels through Bessarabia in the 1920s, the province's administration posed the most serious threat to Romanian security:

> [T]he Rumanian civil administration, nowhere noted for special efficiency, has fallen further short of proper standards in Bessarabia than anywhere else in the Rumanian realm. This is a pity because it is precisely in Bessarabia, exposed as it is to Bolshevist propaganda . . . , that the New Rumania should have put its best foot forward. . . . Until the Rumanian administration is able to give the economic life of the province a distinct turn for the better, agitators from over the border will always find favorable soil there for the sowing of communist tares.[36]

With communist agents active in the villages, Romanian carpetbaggers and provincial administrators provided Bolshevik propagandists with ready examples of the malicious nature of Romanian "landlord-capitalism."

Beyond all these problems, though, the Bessarabian people themselves proved to be the greatest obstacle to the region's complete integration into Greater Romania. Bessarabia was one of the most ethnically diverse regions in the kingdom, and the one in which the Romanian presence in the cities was least visible. By 1930 Bessarabia was home to 352,000 Russians, 314,000 Ukrainians, and 205,000 Jews; the Jews alone accounted for 26.6 percent of city dwellers.[37] Each of these groups had their own grievances against the Romanian center and in turn became the target of nationalist and antisemitic groups.[38]

Russians in particular were of some concern since, as the leader of the community complained, their being treated as "Bolsheviks in disguise" by the Romanians simply played into the hands of communist organizers.[39] Most Russian teachers and functionaries were purged from the local administration, and the few who remained were required to conduct business in Romanian or face expulsion themselves.[40] Private schools for ethnic minorities were allowed to function after 1925, but even in these instruction was in Romanian; by 1938 there were no state-sponsored Russian or Ukrainian schools and only one each in private hands.[41] Russian churches and libraries were also closed or romanized. Under Gurie, the Romanian Orthodox metropolitan (primate) of Chisinau, a campaign was launched to ensure that Russian congregations both adopted the Romanian religious calendar and conducted services in Romanian. When several Russians attempted to perform burial services without a priest rather than have a Romanian officiate, they were prohibited from processing down main streets during daylight hours.[42]

In 1939 the Romanian government began to address these complaints, largely in response to the German and Soviet attacks on Poland in September. Directives were issued to allow the importation of Russian books, introduce Russian- and Ukrainian-language classes in state schools, reopen Russian libraries, allow religious services in Russian, and other measures to coopt Slavic community leaders.[43] But by this time, resentment toward Bucharest's minorities policy already ran deep.

Apart from ethnic minorities, the Moldovans themselves proved to be another problem. After the Sfatul Țării vote on unification, King Ferdinand welcomed the Moldovans from Bessarabia as "brothers returning once again to the Motherland."[44] The task of integrating these brothers proved to be far more difficult than the pan-Romanian unionists had imagined. Charles Upson Clark, a prominent American interpreter of Romanian politics between the wars, noted the difficulty Romanian administrators encountered in introducing such seemingly trivial reforms as the Gregorian calendar and new shop hours. The former met with sharp opposition from Bessarabian clergy, who encouraged parishioners

"The Rape of Bessarabia," a parade float during a celebration in Chisinau, 1924. Two men dressed as Cossacks assault a woman in Romanian national costume, an allegory of the Russian annexation of Bessarabia in 1812. Courtesy Cabinetul de Stampe, Library of the Romanian Academy.

to continue using the Orthodox Julian calendar, and the latter, which attempted to institute a uniform opening time of 8:00 A.M. throughout the kingdom, came up against the Bessarabian tradition of opening later in the morning.[45] Even language was a problem. Older Bessarabians, accustomed to the Cyrillic alphabet, had difficulty reading modern Romanian.[46] Church leaders in Bessarabia also balked at the introduction of the Latin script, which was seen as a secular, non-Orthodox innovation; as late as the 1930s, Cyrillic letters could still be seen on street signs in Chisinau.[47]

Cultural propaganda in Bessarabia did yield some results, however. After their initial reticence, local teachers seemed to warm to the idea of learning Romanian, and scores applied for state-sponsored scholarships to improve their skills in continuing education courses in Chisinau.[48] Indigenous linguistic practice coupled with intense cultural propaganda by the Romanian government ensured that most Moldovans were Romanian-speakers; only some 12,000 (less than one percent of the total) did not consider Romanian their native language in 1930, even if not all Romanian-speakers could read the Latin alphabet.[49] Public education programs and adult literacy courses, built on the early cultural programs

TABLE 2

ETHNIC ROMANIANS IN GREATER ROMANIA, 1930

	Total (percent)	Urban (percent)
Oltenia	97.5	91.7
Muntenia	93.4	82.3
Dobrogea	44.2	52.4
Moldova (west of Prut River)	89.8	70.8
Bessarabia	56.2	31.5
Bukovina	44.5	33.0
Transylvania	57.6	35.9
Banat	54.4	35.0
Crişana-Maramureş	60.7	33.1
Romania total	71.9	58.6

SOURCE: Adapted from Sabin Mănuilă, *Studiu etnografic asupra populaţiei României* (Bucharest: Editura Institutului Central de Statistică, 1940), pp. 46, 48.

sponsored by the Romanian army during the war, continued throughout the interwar years. The coupling of national and strategic goals meant that cultural work remained a high priority, for culture-building served both to cement Bessarabia's place in Greater Romania and to counter the Bolshevik threat east of the Dnestr. "We need public libraries in Bessarabia," wrote a local teacher, "so that the fortress of Romanian bayonets along the Dnestr will be backed up by the fortress of the Romanian spirit."[50] Teachers and propagandists dispatched from the Regat worked to awaken a sense of Romanian patriotism in the Moldovan peasants. For some, the fact that the province was so backward provided a blank slate on which the ideals of Romanian nationalism could be inscribed. As one activist reported, "That Bessarabia has remained culturally backward is our greatest advantage. If there had been any culture at all in Bessarabia, it would have been Russian . . . [but] Russian books could not erase the clean and unaltered soul of the Moldovan. . . . We are working in an environment in which we have to create everything but destroy very little."[51]

After the initial successes of the early 1920s, problems became more apparent. Romanian-language periodicals and other publications were sparse by the 1930s. Although there had been an upsurge in Romanian publications during the First World War, by 1930 Chisinau could boast five separate Russian-language dailies but only two weeklies in Roma-

Women of Bulboca village, Bessarabia, 1924. Women were major targets of cultural programs in both Romanian Bessarabia and Soviet Transnistria. Courtesy Cabinetul de Stampe, Library of the Romanian Academy.

nian, a situation that the Association of Bessarabian Journalists attributed to the province's being treated like "an African colony" by Bucharest.[52] The lack of Romanian newspapers, however, was as much a result of linguistic preference as of the capital's neglect. The reading public continued to prefer Russian over Romanian, a situation denounced as "unnatural," "anti-national," and "immoral" by ardent pan-Romanians.[53] These practices seemed to confirm the Romanians' often repeated quip about the locals' paradoxical identity: *Tată rus, mamă rus, dar Ivan moldovean*—"Father is Russian, mother is Russian, but Ivan is Moldovan."[54]

Bessarabian politicians as well found life in Greater Romania far less welcoming than they had expected. Most lacked the political acumen necessary to compete with experienced politicians and other powerful *jokey-clubmenii*—members of the exclusive Jockey Club on the outskirts of Bucharest—who controlled Romanian politics.[55] The *zemstvo* system and the State Duma notwithstanding, leaders from the Bessarabian *gub-*

erniia had had little familiarity with electoral politics, especially the un-orthodox kind found in Greater Romania. Because of the rather peculiar institution of the king's naming a prime minister before elections were held, success in politics necessitated both a powerful political machine to determine the outcome of the elections and close ties to the court to ensure that the appropriate candidates were asked to form a govern-ment. The Bessarabians had neither the machine nor the preferential access to power necessary for electoral success and soon found them-selves overwhelmed by the corruption and palace gossip that character-ized Bucharest political life. Within a few years of union, they had been absorbed by older political parties, the Liberals and the National Peas-ants, and any sense of the Bessarabians as a distinct regional bloc had completely disappeared.[56] Ion Inculeţ and Pantelimon Halippa served in various Romanian governments in the 1920s and 1930s, but they never returned to the status that they held at the center of the Bessarabian national movement in 1918.

Inculeţ in particular had initially been skeptical about a merger be-tween the Bessarabian republic and Romania. As the representative of Kerensky's Provisional Government in Bessarabia and a member of the Socialist Revolutionary Party, he had little affinity for the Romanian kingdom, especially the Conservative government of Alexandru Marghi-loman in power at the time of union. For Inculeţ and other reform-minded members of the Sfatul Ţării, there would have been little point in rushing from Russian autocracy to Romanian oligarchy. Even when the chaos of revolution made entry into Greater Romania a necessity, Inculeţ and his colleagues still maintained that the agrarian and electoral reforms that had already been initiated by the Sfatul Ţării could serve as a model for the rest of the kingdom. "We thought that if we could hold on to the universal vote and resolve the agrarian question in this little corner of Romania," Inculeţ later reflected, "then this would be a guar-antee for the resolution of these questions in the future in Romania as well."[57]

Inculeţ would eventually make his peace with the union, serving as a minister in several Liberal governments and garnering the opprobrium of his Bessarabian colleagues for changing his political stripes. But de-spite the panegyrics to the ideal of pan-Romanian unity and the warm welcome extended to the brothers from across the Prut, most Bessarabi-ans and their political leaders remained on the social margins of Greater Romania. As Bessarabia's leading church historian, Nicolae Popovschi, complained in 1922, such a situation could only lead to the weakening of links between Bessarabia and the Regat, the failure of nation-building, and the regrettable triumph of Bucharest-style "politicking" (*politicianism*). "As far as politicking is concerned, . . . we have had excellent training. We know it not only theoretically, but practically as well. We know how to use skillfully all its methods and tools, including slander and intrigues aimed against our adversaries. . . . And when we observe that it has so easily and so deeply poisoned the soul of our intellectuals, we wonder: What will nation-building in Bessarabia come to along this path? Is this national awakening?"[58]

The union may indeed have been a "painful disappointment," wrote the National Peasant Party leader Iuliu Maniu, but this was because of problems with Romanian politics, not problems with the historic union.[59] By the 1930s, even the most impassioned advocates of integration had begun to have doubts about the ability of the Romanian state to reform itself—and the willingness of central authorities to respect the specific regional identity of Bessarabia. Provincial intellectuals urged writers, ethnographers, and linguists to explore the indigenous folk culture of the Bessarabian peasant, fearing that the "culturalizing" policies of Bucharest might eventually lead to the disappearance of the Moldovan dialect and its replacement by the "gallicized" language of the Bucharest aristocracy.[60]

The reticence of Bessarabians to embrace the pan-Romanian ideal and the disillusionment experienced by some provincial leaders should not have been surprising. After 1812 the Prut had become an ever-widening gulf between the Bessarabians and their western neighbors. The Bessarabians had missed out on the defining moments in the emergence of Romanian national consciousness among political elites in Wallachia and the rump Moldova. At each historical turning point, they had been absent: the rebellion against the Ottomans in 1821, the standardization and latinization of the Romanian language and alphabet in the 1840s and 1850s, the creation of a unified Romanian state in 1859, the creation of a Romanian dynastic house in 1866 and 1881, and the achievement of independence from the Porte in 1878. The Moldovan peasant's view of his own national identity was thus not solely the product of Russian assimilationist policies, but had remained virtually frozen since the Russian annexation of 1812, a time when the idea of a Romanian nation stretching from the Tisza to the Dnestr—even the idea of a "nation" in a modern sense—was still in its infancy. "The Bessarabians of

Ion Inculeț, Prince Mihai, and King Carol II of Romania (seated left to right), during an official visit to Hotin in northern Bessarabia, June 1935. Courtesy Cabinetul de Stampe, Library of the Romanian Academy.

today," noted a Romanian cavalry officer in 1918, "are the sons and grandsons of the Moldovans of 1812. This is as far as their idea of their origins goes."[61]

A similar point applied for Bessarabian elites. Dependent on Moscow and St. Petersburg for education, jobs, and promotions, after the 1820s few urban Bessarabians saw anything to be gained from links with Iași, Bucharest, or other Romanian centers. By the end of the century, imperial policies had not only created a loyal, Russian-speaking elite to govern the frontier province, but had also inadvertently ensured that even socialists and other radical circles in the region—the groups most opposed to tsarism—still looked to their Russian counterparts rather than to the Romanians for guidance and inspiration. Both reactionary and revolutionary leaders in Bessarabia, pushed to the fore by the cataclysmic events of 1914–17, shared a certain skepticism about Romanian avowals of brotherhood and goodwill. For the former, Bucharest posed as great a threat as the Bolsheviks, since both aimed at the destruction of the tsarist state and the erection of radically new political or social structures on its ruins. For the latter, there seemed little reason to trade Tsar Nicholas II for King Ferdinand, to mortgage the commitment to land reform and universal suffrage for a pan-Romanian nationalism whose most vocal proponents were supported by irredentists in the Regat. After 1918, Bucharest's policies seemed to underscore the reservations with which many Bessarabians, whatever their political hue, had entered the Romanian state.

SOVIET POLICIES ON THE ROMANIAN BORDER

The Soviets continually professed their willingness to work out a peaceful solution to the Bessarabian question, but their extensive agitation and propaganda efforts contradicted their avowals of good faith. Just as the Romanians were attempting to integrate the Bessarabians into Greater Romania, the Soviets worked to pull them in the opposite direction. Throughout the 1920s and early 1930s, Bolshevik agents were active in the Bessarabian countryside, Soviet planes dropped pamphlets in the province, and shots were exchanged between Soviet and Romanian soldiers from either bank of the Dnestr. Criminal bands, often associated with Bolshevik agitators, roamed the countryside preying on local peasants and finding shelter among those dissatisfied with the Romanian presence.[62] According to Romanian figures, as many as 118 separate Bolshevik incursions across the Dnestr were recorded between 1921 and 1925, and from 1918 to 1925 the Romanian foreign ministry cataloged over 3,000 separate "terrorist" incidents sponsored by the Bolsheviks, ranging from spying and agitation to demonstrations and outright rebellion.[63]

The effectiveness of these efforts on the ground was dubious. Although Bessarabian peasants were hardly enthusiastic about the presence of Romanian gendarmes and soldiers, they were even less receptive to Bolshevik calls for the collectivization of land and the expropriation of the peasants' property.[64] Refugees continued to flood across the Dnestr into Romania through the 1930s, a trend that communist authorities attributed to the prominence of "kulaks" and other anti-Soviet elements in Ukraine.[65] But the Soviets' pressing the territorial question at both the bargaining table and in the Bessarabian villages kept relations between Moscow and Bucharest necessarily tense. The Romanians held Soviet *agents provocateurs* responsible for risings in the Bessarabian towns of Hotin (January 1919), Bender (May 1919), and Tatar Bunar

(September 1924), brief jacqueries that were ruthlessly suppressed by the Romanian army. Tatar Bunar in particular loomed large in the Soviet propaganda effort, which centered on the lawlessness and oppressive policies of the "Bucharest capitalists" and their secret police, the Siguranța.

The Society of Bessarabians, based in Moscow, was the major organization responsible for Soviet agitation and propaganda. Supported by the Communist International and the International Organization for Aiding the Fighters of the Revolution,[66] the Society's full name made its demands unambiguous: "The All-Union 'Get the Hands of the Romanian Invaders Off Bessarabia!' Society of Bessarabians" (*Vsesoiuznoe obshchestvo bessarabtsev "Proch' ruki rumynskikh zakhvatnikov ot Bessarabii!"*). Its publications, including the bimonthly journal *Krasnaia Bessarabiia* (Red Bessarabia), decried the harshness of the Romanian regime and encouraged the Bessarabian peasants to rise up and join the workers of the Soviet Union in a single proletarian state.[67] Other groups, such as the Association of Bessarabian Emigrés in Paris, were funded indirectly by the Soviets and worked to convince Western governments of the injustice of Romanian territorial claims.[68]

By the mid-1920s, the repeated failure of territorial negotiations, the lukewarm reception to communist propaganda in the countryside, and the Bolsheviks' inability to foment large-scale rebellion (exemplified in the failure of Tatar Bunar) all provided the impetus for a new tactic in Soviet policy on Bessarabia: the creation of an autonomous Soviet republic across the Dnestr on Romania's eastern border. The new "Moldovan Autonomous Soviet Socialist Republic" (MASSR) was established inside Soviet Ukraine on October 12, 1924. Carved from portions of the Ukrainian regions of Odessa and Podolia, the MASSR comprised some 7,516 square kilometers and stretched from the Olshanka River region in the north, south nearly to the Dnestr estuary, and 95 miles eastward almost to the Southern Bug River.[69] During the civil war, the area had changed hands no fewer than twelve times, as the Red Army, Cossacks, independent Ukrainian forces, Whites, and roving bandits established temporary control. After the victory of the Bolsheviks in the autumn of 1920, the region, known in Romanian as Transnistria, fell within the boundaries of Ukraine and thus after 1922 within the Soviet Union. The MASSR accounted for less than 2 percent of Ukraine's total land area and population, and although nominally a "Moldovan" republic, it consisted mainly of Ukrainians. Ethnic Ukrainians formed nearly 49 percent

Nicolae Titulescu (1882–1941), who served as Romanian foreign
minister and president of the League of Nations, at the Ministry
of War in Paris, March 1933. Titulescu worked throughout the
interwar years to secure Soviet recognition of Romania's eastern
border. Courtesy Cabinetul de Stampe, Library of the Romanian
Academy.

of the republic's 1926 population of 572,114, while less than a third of the population was Moldovan. Russians (9 percent), Jews (8 percent), and Germans (2 percent) were also represented in significant numbers.[70] Even after the creation of this Moldovan "homeland," some 85,000 persons classed as Moldovans remained in other parts of Ukraine outside the MASSR.[71]

The MASSR, ostensibly set up on the request of the toiling masses of Transnistria, was primarily intended to increase the effectiveness of Soviet propaganda across the river, to put pressure on Bucharest in negotiations over Bessarabia's future, and to serve as a political magnet drawing Bessarabia even farther away from Bucharest. As a Soviet publication on the new republic noted in 1926, "the creation of the MASSR is the beginning of the liberation of Bessarabia. Once the economic and cultural growth of Moldova has begun, aristocrat-led Romania will not be able to maintain its hold on Bessarabia."[72] The republic was also to be a way of influencing politics in Romania as a whole, a first step toward sparking the revolution that would liberate all the peoples of Romania from the landlord-capitalist yoke.

The MASSR was part of the broader Soviet policy of using the logic

TABLE 3
MASSR POPULATION, 1926 AND 1936

	1926			1936	
	Population	Percent	Percent Rural (1926 only)	Population	Percent
Ukrainians	277,515	48.5	89.4	265,193	45.5
Moldovans	172,419	30.1	96.4	184,046	31.6
Russians	48,868	8.5	60.7	56,592	9.7
Jews	48,564	8.5	48.3	45,620	7.8
Germans	10,739	1.9	98.3	12,711	2.2
Bulgarians	6,026	1.0	98.2	—	—
Poles	4,853	0.8	73.3	4,450	0.8
Roma (Gypsies)	918	0.2	95.8	—	—
Romanians	137	—	77.4	—	—
Other	2,055	0.4	—	13,526	2.4
TOTAL	572,114	100.0	85.6	582,138	100.0

NOTE: Dashes indicate no figure available.
SOURCE: *Vsesoiuznaia perepis' naseleniia 1926 goda* (Moscow: Izdanie TsSU Soiuza SSR, 1929), 13: 39–41; and AOSPRM, f. 49, op. 1, d. 3997, l. 108.

of national liberation to draw border regions away from bourgeois states. In the 1920s, in addition to the MASSR, two other autonomous republics were set up in border regions that were especially contentious: the Karelian autonomous republic, established on the border with Finland in 1920 and upgraded, as the Karelo-Finnish republic, to the status of a union republic from 1940 to 1956; and the Buriat-Mongol autonomous republic, established on the border with Mongolia in 1923 but reduced considerably in size and renamed after 1937. Each of these territorial-administrative entities was the putative political instantiation of a nation separated by international frontiers. They were meant to place pressure on neighboring states—Finland, Romania, and Mongolia—for the relinquishment of all or part of their territory and were styled as bridgeheads of Soviet influence in northern Europe, central Europe, and the Far East as a whole. In each of the ASSRs, the content of cultural policy at various times stressed the divisions between local populations and related groups across the international border and at other times underscored the basic commonalities of language and culture between the two. The focus, however, was largely the same: the effort to use nationalities policy and nation-building as tools of foreign policy, thus countering the claims of "bourgeois nationalists" in neighboring states on their own terms.

To underscore these points, the MASSR's capital was declared to be Chisinau and all of Bessarabia included in the official borders of the republic, with the Transnistrian cities of Balta and later Tiraspol named as provisional capitals pending the liberation of Bessarabia.[73] Mykola Skrypnyk, then the people's commissar of justice in Ukraine, highlighted the border issue in a speech shortly after the MASSR's foundation:

> We consider the border to be not along the Dnestr, but along the Prut. Yes, for the time being the capitalists have Bessarabia in their hands. That is a question of fact, not of right. The right is on our side. On our map, Bessarabia is also included inside the red borderline, since Bessarabia should be an inseparable part of the MASSR.[74]

According to the Soviets, Bessarabia was as much a part of Soviet Moldova as the east-bank region. Such epithets as "the cradle of Red Moldova" and "Bessarabia in miniature" for the MASSR were used to stress Moscow's claim that Bessarabia remained an illegally occupied portion of Soviet Moldova. The banks of the Dnestr were heavily fortified, shots fired across the river were frequent, and sorties into Bessarabia from the

Soviet republic were commonplace. The MASSR authorities even ordered that bright lights be kept perpetually burning in Tiraspol, which looked across the river to the Romanian city of Bender, in order to impress upon the Bessarabian peasants the advantages of life in the technologically progressive Soviet republic.[75]

With the birth of the MASSR, the Soviet Union embarked on a radically new justification for its claim to Bessarabia, one based on nationality rather than on international law. In its early disputes with Bucharest, the Bolshevik government had marshaled largely legal and political arguments against the Romanian annexation. Christian Rakovsky, Titulescu's most vocal adversary on the Bessarabian issue in the 1920s, castigated the Romanians for using ethnic and historical arguments to justify their hold on the region. Rakovsky held that since the province's incorporation into the kingdom did not express the will of the Bessarabian people, Romanian diplomats were obliged "to deduce from the sciences of ethnology, anthropology and philology theories to substantiate such phrases as 'the sovereign right' of Roumania to Bessarabia." To Rakovsky, the fact that the main inhabitants of Romania and Bessarabia spoke the same language was completely irrelevant:

> [W]e do not deny the fact that a comparatively large part of the population of Bessarabia is Moldavian. . . . What is important is not the percentage of population of this or that ethnographic element, but the will of the population. . . . We know that a majority of the population of Switzerland speaks German, and that a part speaks French, but no one therefore suggests that the German-speaking cantons should be joined to Germany and the French-speaking to the French.[76]

Numerous protest notes issued to the Romanian government by the Soviets after January 1918 put forward similar arguments: that the workers and peasants of Bessarabia had never been given the chance to decide their own fate, and that the Romanian occupation of the Prut-Dnestr region merely represented an attempt by Romanian capitalists to undermine the Bolshevik revolution. As late as March 1924, seven months before the creation of the MASSR, the Soviets abjured the notion of historical or ethnic rights to Bessarabia in a position paper prepared for a new round of Romanian-Soviet negotiations in Vienna:

> The government of the Soviet Union believes that the population of Bessarabia should itself decide whether it wants to remain part of the Soviet Union, whether it wants to leave the Union and unite with Romania or, finally, whether it would rather exist as an independent, sovereign state. . . .

The government of the Soviet Union stresses that, on the Bessarabian question, it is not arguing from the point of view of the historical rights to Bessarabia which it inherited from the tsarist government.[77]

In short, argued the Soviets, the Sfatul Țării had not been a truly representative assembly, the vote on union had been far from unanimous, no plebiscite had ever been held among the Bessarabians, and the Romanian occupation troops had committed grave atrocities. For all these reasons, there existed a fundamental animosity between Moldovans and Romanians, which the latter were merely fueling by treating the Bessarabian land and people as their rightful chattels. Similar arguments had already been offered by former Bessarabian nobles at the Paris Peace Conference,[78] and Titulescu himself worried that they were in fact the strongest legal claim against Romania's hold on Bessarabia.[79]

However, the establishment of the MASSR signaled the crystallization of a new argument against the Romanian occupation of Bessarabia that had begun to develop shortly after the end of the Russian civil war: the notion that the majority population in Bessarabia constituted an ethnonational group separate from the Romanians and that, therefore, their incorporation into a unitary Romanian state had usurped their right to national self-determination. Although Rakovsky had earlier inveighed against the Romanians for appealing to ethnic arguments in defending their claim to Bessarabia, by the mid-1920s the Soviets had turned away from using purely juridical counterarguments and had begun to elaborate their own ethnic vision of "Moldovanness." For both sides in the dispute, ethnography thus became the handmaiden of diplomacy, as both Romanians and Soviets looked to history and the nascent disciplines of cultural anthropology, ethnolinguistics, and even ethnobiology for ammunition in increasingly heated diplomatic battles. With the appearance of a "Moldovan nation" and the creation of its provisional homeland in the MASSR, the ethnonational identity of the Moldovans themselves became the centerpiece of Soviet propaganda efforts.

DEFINING MOLDOVANS AMONG ROMANIANS AND SOVIETS

For Romanian historians, publicists, and politicians in the interwar period, the 1918 union of Bessarabia and Romania represented the culmination of a centuries-old struggle for the unification of the lands populated by the Romanian nation. From both a historical and an ethnic perspective, the right of the Romanians to Bessarabia was seen to be indisputable.[80] The situation was, of course, far more complex. Despite the best efforts of Bucharest intellectuals to awaken the Bessarabian peasant to his own "Romanianness," many Moldovans remained cool on their putative Romanian identity. The creation of the MASSR sharpened the debate on the identity question by providing an ostensible homeland for the Moldovan nation. But the view that the inhabitants of the Regat and the majority population of Bessarabia formed a single ethnic group was neither self-evident nor universally accepted before 1918 nor, indeed, even after the Act of Union.

It was a situation that infuriated pan-Romanian nationalists inside Greater Romania. The 1920 pamphlet *What Nation Are We?*, written by the Bessarabian essayist Porfirie Fala, complained of the use of the term *Moldovan* in Bessarabia, pointing out that the term was geographic rather than ethnic and that the inhabitants of the province should ignore any attempts by "foreigners" to convince them otherwise.[81] As late as 1938, two decades after the Great Union, the former Sfatul Ţării member Ion Pelivan argued that such a situation could never be remedied so long as Bessarabian intellectuals insisted on speaking Russian, thus divorcing themselves from Romanian culture and failing in their duty to bring the pan-Romanian message to the Bessarabian villages.[82]

Contemporary pan-Romanian nationalists looked on the Moldovans with the populist's characteristic double vision. On the one hand, the Moldovan peasant was praised as the repository of timeless Romanian traditions and cultural values. Despite the russification of the Bessarabian elite, the closure of Moldovan schools, and other tsarist efforts to dampen national sentiment in the province, the Moldovan villager had largely retained his characteristic dress, traditions, and language throughout the period of Russian rule. Bessarabia, argued Pantelimon Halippa, had thus become Romania's Piedmont, a region that looked beyond its own regional interests to press toward the goal of national union.[83] On the other hand, when the Moldovan peasant was slow to adopt wholeheartedly the pan-Romanian message—when he failed to recognize the simple equation between Romanian identity in the Regat and the language and culture that he had long known as "Moldovan"—

pan-Romanians denounced him as a Russian stooge, an uneducated victim of tsarist deceit who remained blind to his true national identity.

This ambivalent view, like the economic and social position of the Bessarabians inside Greater Romania, provided substantial grist for the Soviet mill. The Romanians' sense of their own *mission civilisatrice* in Bessarabia, argued one of the leaders of the MASSR in 1928, illustrated the bourgeois and essentially racist character of the idea of Romanian-Moldovan unity:

> [T]he bourgeois pen-pushers in Romania have proffered the slogan "Latinity means civilization, while Slavism means wistfulness and destruction." This is the most recent invention, the latest slogan, that [they] have put forward in order to win over bourgeois public opinion on Bessarabia and on the necessity of enlarging the territory of aristocratic Romania to the Bug River.

Such chauvinistic arguments, the author held, simply provided further evidence to support the adage that "The Romanians are not a nation but a profession."[84]

Propagandists in Moscow or Balta were not completely consistent in their views on Moldovan identity, however. Some Soviet negotiators and propagandists initially stressed the political rather than the ethnic aspects of the Bessarabian issue. Rakovsky and other Soviet writers were perfectly willing to admit that Romanians and Moldovans formed a single ethnonational group, but at the same time, they denied the relevance of this fact to the resolution of Bessarabia's international status. In two definitive works on Bessarabian history and ethnography published after the revolution,[85] the Russian ethnographer L. S. Berg saw the label *Moldovan* as purely geographic rather than ethnic:

> Moldovans are Romanians living in Moldova, Bessarabia and the neighboring parts of Podolia and Kherson *guberniias;* a small number also live in Ekaterinoslav *guberniia.* . . . Insignificant dialectal elements distinguish them from the Romanians of Wallachia, or Wallachs.[86]

The most prolific Soviet propagandist on the Bessarabian issue, Vladimir Dembo, was equally convinced of the unimportance of the ethnic factor. His 1924 tract, *Never Forget! The Bloody Chronicle of Bessarabia,* denounced Romanian attempts to read politics from ethnography.[87] Although Dembo speculated that there was in fact little affinity between

Romanians and Bessarabian Moldovans because of the latter's hundred-year tenure in the Russian empire, he was prepared to admit, for the sake of argument, that both groups might in fact form part of a single pan-Romanian nation. Nevertheless, the ethnic identity of the Moldovans was insignificant since they had never had the opportunity to vote freely on the Act of Union.

Although Bolshevik publications abjured the ethnic chauvinism of the Romanians, after 1924 Soviet writers gradually articulated their own ethnic arguments to support their claim to Bessarabia. In his *Soviet Moldova and the Bessarabian Question*, published only a year after *Never Forget!*, Dembo proffered two original arguments in favor of Bessarabia's cession to the Soviet Union. First, Dembo argued that the Moldovans represented not so much a nation apart as a class apart. The Moldovan population of Bessarabia had been formed, in the main, from peasants who had thrown off the yoke of Wallachian and western Moldovan nobles, refugees from the Regat who had settled east of the Prut River a century ago. The descendants of these free peasants thus had little in common with their former masters living west of the Prut.[88]

Second, Dembo held, the peasant refugees who had formed the substratum of modern Moldovan identity had not stopped at the Dnestr, but had in fact also settled the lands east of the river, the Transnistria region contained after 1924 within the MASSR. Hence, the population of the MASSR was "linked in the most intimate fashion and by the most kindred bonds to the population of Bessarabia."[89] The harsh regime imposed on the Bessarabians after 1918 only served to strengthen the class solidarity of the peoples of Bessarabia and Soviet Moldova. Dmitrii Milev, Dembo's contemporary and one of the MASSR's most prominent writers, lauded the proletarian roots of the Moldovans in his 1926 poem "Norod moldovenesc" (The Moldovan people):

> You have passed an entire century
> In heavy chains tormented;
> Made victims by your foes,
> You have never known the sun.
>
> For the nobleman and the landlord
> You have slaved for years on end;
> Born in toil and need,
> You were a wretch and a pauper.

Subjugated and nameless,
Without the right to be human,
For centuries forgotten by the world,
You were condemned to slavery.[90]

For Dembo, Milev and others, the emancipatory power of the Bolshevik Revolution had given a brighter future to the Moldovans, but the revolution would remain unfinished so long as their proletarian brothers in Bessarabia continued to toil "under the nobleman's heel."[91] It was to these class brothers beyond the Dnestr—rather than to their ostensible blood brothers beyond the Prut—that the Bessarabians should most properly turn.[92] Any attempt to obscure this bond of class with nationalist rhetoric would only remind the Bessarabians that their ancestors had once fled the "unbearable weight placed on them in the Danubian principalities by the forefathers of today's Romanian bankers, landlords, and industrialists, who now pretend to be the 'brothers' of the Moldovan peasant."[93]

Even if the Moldovans were separate from the Romanians, however, their underdeveloped culture still demanded active work by Soviet cultural planners. This view was clear in the pamphlet *Workers' Bessarabia and Soviet Power*, part of an early series of speeches and debates intended for use by Soviet agitprop workers. As the author maintained, the transformative power of the revolution should be harnessed to create an independent, Soviet, and genuinely Moldovan culture, and to raise the Moldovans to the level already attained by the other peoples of the former empire.[94] As another author noted in a survey of cultural policy in the MASSR, the Moldovan language and its literature were still in the stage of "primitive accumulation" of cultural forces; because of its low level of development in the tsarist period, Moldovan culture was, more than in any other part of the union, a genuine "child of the October Revolution."[95]

So long as Bessarabia remained under Romanian control, the revolutionary reshaping of Moldovan society was only a distant prospect. The creation of the MASSR, however, provided Soviet policymakers and cultural planners with a laboratory—"Bessarabia in miniature," as Vladimir Dembo often described it—in which to cultivate the seeds that would one day bear fruit across the Dnestr in occupied Bessarabia and beyond. "In this 'little Bessarabia,'" Dembo wrote in 1925, "they are organizing the forces that, maybe even without bayonets or rifles, will be the atom, the germ, from which will grow the government, administration, and culture of Bessarabia stretching to the Danube and the Prut."[96] The notion that Romanians and Moldovans in Bessarabia and the MASSR formed two wholly separate ethnonational groups, speaking different languages and possessing separate historical, cultural, and even biological traits, would eventually become a standard element of Soviet discourse on the Bessarabian question and the central justification for Moscow's territorial claims.

4   Forging a Soviet Moldovan Nation

The establishment of the MASSR in 1924 served two important ends in the emerging foreign policy of the Soviet Union. First, the new republic facilitated the penetration of Soviet propaganda into the kingdom of Romania, thus paving the way for a Romanian socialist revolution. Second, it ensured that the Bessarabian question remained a topical issue in international politics and a thorn in the side of Romanian diplomats at the League of Nations. But the origins of the effort to construct a distinctly Moldovan identity were not simply the result of Soviet foreign-policy needs. Moldovan nation-building in the MASSR emerged not as a mere by-product of Soviet expansionism, but rather as a result of the interplay of central foreign-policy goals, existing forms of indigenous identity, and the agendas of cultural and political elites inside the autonomous republic itself. Cultural planners were keenly aware of the political importance of the policy that came to be known as "moldovanization," but they were more than mere executors of a policy elaborated by the Soviet center. Professional disputes among linguists and historians and a genuine belief among many that they were helping to liberate the Moldovans from the oppression of Bucharest landlord-capitalism played a role in shaping the ideology of national distinctiveness in the 1920s.

The same cannot be said of the 1930s, a period when the official Soviet line on Moldovan identity underwent drastic changes. In two sharp reversals of policy, the Soviet center first denounced its own line on Moldovan separateness as a fiction created by "wreckers" of Soviet cultural policy, and then later changed tack again by returning to a version of the previous notion of the Moldovans as an independent nation. What had in the 1920s been an attempt by local nation-builders to forge a distinct national culture based on the indigenous cultural practices of Transnistrians and Bessarabians had become a decade later little more than the whim of Soviet central planners. The history of both these decades, including the debates over the boundaries of national identity, would leave an indelible mark on the Moldovan republic even after the territorial changes of the Second World War.

MAKING A MOLDOVAN LANGUAGE

The primary issue addressed by local elites in the MASSR was the creation of a distinct Moldovan literary language. Scholars from the West, in particular the German ethnographer Gustav Weigand, had noted earlier in the century that Romanian-speakers in Bessarabia and Bukovina spoke a dialect distinct from those in the Romanian kingdom, but that these differences were no more striking than regional variations inside Romania itself.[1] In the MASSR, however, these distinctions were imbued with political meaning and the dialectal differences in Transnistria hailed as the atom of a new national culture.

Pavel Chior, the people's commissar of enlightenment in the MASSR from 1928 to 1930, was clear on the political significance of language standardization. In an early work on Moldovan spelling, Chior argued that standard literary Romanian, controlled by Romania's ruling bourgeoisie, had become increasingly oriented toward France; the resulting melange—"not quite Romanian and not quite French"—had been rendered unintelligible to the large peasant population, both in the MASSR and in much of Romania. Bessarabians themselves did in fact complain about the "spoiled" language imported by Romanians after the 1918 union and its impact on local culture.[2] But for Chior, these linguistic differences had a political angle. "We can use this difference between the language of the ruling class and the language of the exploited class, if we do not lose sight of the political aspects of our spelling."[3] The chief significance of the MASSR was to provide a political buffer against future Romanian influence among the Moldovans, just as Romanian cultural policy among the Bessarabian masses served a similar political purpose for Bucharest.

The first tasks facing scholars in the MASSR were to select a dialect that would serve as the basis for a Moldovan literary standard and then to develop a grammar based on the linguistic peculiarities of that dialect. During his four expeditions to the MASSR from 1925 to 1930, the Moscow linguist M. V. Sergievskii mapped two general dialectal regions in the republic.[4] As with the relationship between "proletarian" Moldovan and "bourgeois" Romanian, however, the selection of a dialectal base was also a fundamentally political concern. As Chior argued, the dialect peculiar to central Bessarabia was not only the most widely spoken variety of Moldovan in both Bessarabia and the MASSR, but selecting this particular dialect as a literary base (as opposed to a form spoken exclusively in Transnistria) would also create a linguistic bridge across the Dnestr and thus pave the way for the national liberation of all Moldovans.[5]

Debates over dialect selection were largely preempted by the practical need for a grammar to use in the schools of the new autonomous republic. The first Moldovan grammar and dictionary, published in 1925 and 1926, were intended as interim texts by their author, Chior's predecessor as commissar of enlightenment, Gabriel Buciuşcanu. Buciuşcanu had been a Socialist Revolutionary deputy in the Sfatul Ţării—and therefore a colleague of Ion Inculeţ—but had been branded an outlaw by the Romanian authorities and fled to the Soviet Union after opposing Bessarabia's union with Romania. However, there was little to distinguish Buciuşcanu's grammar from Romanian ones published in the same period, except for the Cyrillic alphabet.[6] Its numerous typographical errors, as well as the sense among many local leaders that it was too "Romanian" in its orientation, caused it to be quickly pulled from circulation.

The choice of the Cyrillic alphabet had been a topic of debate among Soviet scholars even before the foundation of the MASSR. The alphabet, however, was never imposed on the Moldovans, as is often argued. Rather, Buciuşcanu's use of Cyrillic was very much in line with Bessarabian traditions. The adoption of the Latin alphabet and progressive gallicization of nineteenth-century literary Romanian had had little influence in Bessarabia and Transnistria. The best-known prerevolutionary Moldovan grammars and dictionaries, in fact, had normally used a version of the Cyrillic script.[7] Soviet Moldovan linguists owed a great deal to these prerevolutionary attempts at codifying Moldovan speech patterns, a debt that Buciuşcanu and his colleagues acknowledged. With the failure of the poorly received Buciuşcanu texts, responsibility passed to the newly created Moldovan Scientific Committee (MSC), chaired by Pavel Chior. Formed in December 1926, the MSC was the first state scientific research body in the MASSR and the precursor of the Moldovan Academy of Sciences.[8] Its original statute described the MSC's duties as the "comprehensive study of the region and culture of the Moldovan people, as well as the dissemination of scientific and applied knowledge about them."[9]

Chior's background was decidedly different from that of his predecessor, Buciuşcanu, and his revolutionary zeal as MSC chair would have an important impact on cultural policy in the MASSR. Born in Ismail *uezd* in southern Bessarabia in 1902, Chior was some thirteen years Buciuşcanu's junior. While Buciuşcanu had been sitting in an armchair in the Sfatul Ţării, Chior had been sitting on a horse. The birth of his political awareness had come at the same time as the birth of the Soviet state, and his civil war experience fighting on the southwestern front from 1918 to 1920 must have made an important mark on his political consciousness. His father, Ion Chior, had been active in the workers' movement in Ekaterinoslav, and Pavel was thus known to the Romanian secret police in Bessarabia by the nickname "the Bolshevik pup."[10] From June 1924 to January 1925, when Buciuşcanu assumed a leading political role in the new autonomous republic, Chior was once again with the Red Army, serving as a political commissar in a Cossack cavalry detachment. His background was typical of that of many young Bolsheviks whose political orientations were forged and tempered in the violence of the civil war and who brought the wartime imagery and transformative élan of their youth to Soviet cultural policy of the 1920s.[11]

Another figure within the MSC who would be crucial to cultural developments was Leonid Madan, the head of the committee's linguistics section. Born in 1894, Madan was firmly committed to the notion that Romanians and Moldovans formed two distinct peoples with their own independent languages. He had begun work on a Moldovan grammar while still a student in the early 1920s at the Institute of Public Education in Kyiv, long before the question of a distinct Moldovan language had become politically salient. After completing a preliminary draft of a standard grammar for Moldovan in 1924 in Kyiv, Madan tested his initial conclusions against the results of fieldwork in the

Pavel Chior (1902–43), commissar of enlightenment in the Moldovan autonomous republic and the chief architect of a new Soviet Moldovan culture in the interwar years.

MASSR at the end of 1925. In July and August 1926, a series of summer courses on "Differences between Romanian and Moldovan" was organized for schoolteachers in Balta and Zinovievsk. As a result of these courses, in November the MASSR Narkompros (people's commissariat of enlightenment) elaborated a project on "Changes in Moldovan Grammar" and encouraged debate on the project in the pages of the republic's newspaper *Plugarul roş* (The red ploughman). Over the following months, the Scientific Committee revised the project and issued a new version in June 1927, which in turn was debated the following month by over 100 participants in the Balta summer courses. Finally, in July 1927 the Scientific Committee produced a set of grammatical guidelines that would form the basis for a new grammar. Madan's *Moldovan Grammar* was then published later in 1929 by the State Publishing House in Tiraspol, with a second edition appearing the following year.[12] The grammar, which aimed to represent the spoken idiom of Bessarabians and Transnistrians, also used the Cyrillic alphabet and represented the most radical attempt to create a distinct Moldovan tongue, wholly separate from standard literary Romanian.

In his introduction to the text, Madan set out his general theory of linguistics and the main stages in the development of the Moldovan nation, both of which were consonant with theories being propounded by other Soviet scholars during this period.[13] According to Madan, over the centuries the Moldovan language had developed as an admixture of Latin and the language of the indigenous tribes of the Carpathian basin, the Dacii or Getae. After the disintegration of the Roman Empire, the Goths, Huns, Bulgars, Avars, Pechenegs, Polovtsy, Tatars, Poles, Turks, Greek Phanariots, Ukrainians, Russians, and others had also made their mark on the Moldovan language. These multiple influences eventually led to the emergence of a distinct Moldovan people speaking an independent (*samostoiatel'nyi*) Moldovan language.

This fact, moreover, was apparently confirmed by the most recent anthropometric investigations. As Madan argued elsewhere, research had apparently shown that Moldovans, in the main, had "an oblong cranial structure," whereas Romanians were "round-headed." The "dark type" (eyes, hair color) predominated among the Romanians, but Moldovans were "mainly brown with chestnut hair, something like the northern Russian type." The Moldovan character also differed substantially from the Romanian. "Wallachians" (Romanians) appeared "more mobile, more expansive," whereas Moldovans were "more leisurely in their movements."[14]

In addition, Madan held, the October Revolution and the establishment of the MASSR had ushered in a period of accelerated differentiation between the two east-Romance languages. Prior to the establishment of the MASSR, the natural development of a Moldovan literary language had been blocked by the refusal of the Romanian and Great Russian authorities to acknowledge the independent identity of the Moldovan people. In the Romanian case, as Chior had noted, a predilection for bourgeois gallicisms polluted the language and estranged the literary standard from the working masses along the banks of the Dnestr. Hence, Madan called for a revolution in the development of a Moldovan literary standard. No longer would foreign words and grammatical constructions be used to suppress the Moldovan toiling masses, but a new, Soviet literary language would be established on the basis of that dialect spoken by the majority of Moldovans in the MASSR and Bessarabia, a dialect that Chior had already employed in his collections of Moldovan proverbs and folk songs published before Madan's grammar.[15]

Besides the representation of peasant speech, efforts were made to introduce into the language new words based on rural speech. Chief responsibility for this effort lay with the MSC's linguistics section, particularly the subsection on terminology headed by the linguist and educator I. A. Malai. From the summer of 1929 to the summer of 1930, Malai's subsection compiled lists of new terms in the fields of history, politics, geography, chemistry, and zoology—a total of some 7,500 words—and submitted the proposed lists to the linguistics section for approval.[16] The popular roots used by the subsection were, in fact, mainly Russian loanwords or calques, designed primarily to increase the distance between Moldovan and standard Romanian. Many, though, would have been easily intelligible to Moldovan peasants, and some far more so than the French-inspired terms that had been introduced into literary Romanian since the 1860s.

Chior, Madan, Malai, and their associates were engaged in a standard

TABLE 4
EXAMPLES OF MOLDOVAN NEOLOGISMS, 1929

English	Standard Romanian	Russian	Moldovan
self-administration	autoadministrare	samoupravlenie	sîngurcîrmuiri
contemporary	contemporan	sovremennyi	amuvremnic
necktie	cravată	galstuk	galstuh
chronicle	cronică	letopis'	anoscriiri
dictionary	dicţionar	slovar'	slovari
English	englezesc	angliiskii	anglicesc
February	februarie	fevral'	făurari
January	ianuarie	ianvar'	jerariul
monotonous	monoton	odnoobraznyi	unofelnic
custom	obicei	obikhod	zîlnictreburi
like-mindedness	unitate de idei	edinomyslie	unogîndiri

NOTE: None of these terms was ever used consistently; indeed, it was the inconsistency of use as much as anything else that prevented the neologisms from ever gaining acceptance. In the context of Transnistria and Bessarabia in this period, some of the new words would not have seemed nearly as unusual as they appear today. Since Moldovan speech was already highly influenced by Slavic languages, and also contained many Romanian archaic forms, *galstuh*, *slovari*, and even *amuvremnic* would certainly have been more intelligible to a Moldovan peasant than the French-influenced *cravată*, *dicţionar*, and *contemporan*.

SOURCE: AOSPRM, f. 49, op. 2, d. 44, ll. 2–43; various issues of *Plugarul roş*.

nation-building project, played out in many parts of the Soviet Union, and indeed, earlier in Europe as a whole: taking peasant speech forms, formalizing them, building new words based on them, and elevating the result to the level of a new literary standard. Much the same processes were taking place from Belarus to Uzbekistan at the same time, but each within the context of the constraints of domestic politics and the exigencies of Soviet foreign policy.[17] There was, in this sense, nothing unique about the Moldovan experiment, nor anything more artificial in its designs than other projects of national construction in the Soviet Union and beyond. However, the practical problems of communicating this newly devised cultural standard to the Moldovan masses proved far more difficult than the MASSR's nation-builders had imagined and ultimately contributed to the retreat from "moldovanization" in the 1930s.

MOLDOVANIZING THE MASSES

The first step in making a Moldovan nation was to define who precisely the Moldovans were and to formalize the elements of their national culture, especially their language. But running parallel to the ongoing debates among MSC members was the attempt to bring this constructed vision of national identity to the Moldovans themselves— that is, to make the MASSR a genuinely Moldovan republic by educating the peasants and bringing them into the structures of the state and the party. Already in April 1923 the Twelfth Communist Party Congress had promulgated the policy of *korenizatsiia*, or indigenization, in the national republics, mandating that state and party organs institute preferential hiring and promotion policies for the benefit of non-Russian nationalities. Indigenizing the Soviet and party apparat would ensure, as Stalin argued, that local institutions "fully reflect not only the general needs and requirements of all the nationalities of the Union, but also the special needs and requirements of individual nationalities."[18]

Implementing the various components of cultural policy fell to the Committee for Moldovanization and Ukrainization (CMU), formed in September 1925. As in the rest of the Soviet Union, *korenizatsiia* in the MASSR covered a range of divergent, sometimes contradictory, policy goals. These included: (1) increasing the number of persons of Moldovan ethnicity in state and party institutions; (2) giving special attention

Plenary session of the Moldovan Scientific Committee (MSC), 1930. The MSC oversaw the development of a distinct Moldovan language and culture in early Soviet period. Photo from *Plugarul roş*.

to the role of women in the republic, especially illiterates; (3) building Moldovan schools and promoting the use of indigenous languages in education; (4) creating a Moldovan-language publishing industry; and (5) spreading the revolution and building socialism through native-language political education programs, mass literacy campaigns, and other areas of public education.[19] Implementing each of these policies demanded a particular strategy on the part of the MASSR authorities and, as well, revealed a unique series of unforeseen obstacles to identity construction—especially in a republic in which the chief targets of the policy, ethnic Moldovans, were in the minority.

The State and Party Apparat

Indigenizing the Soviet apparat was the most widely touted element of *korenizatsiia*. As Stalin had argued at the party's Twelfth Congress, Great Russian chauvinism and local nationalism would be eliminated only when "Soviet power in the republics becomes intelligible and native," a goal that itself could only be reached by enabling "titular nationalities on the periphery to have their own people on the boards [of the people's commissariats]."[20] In the MASSR such a policy was also intended to convince Bessarabian peasants in Romania that in the Soviet republic the Moldovan peasants controlled their own affairs.

In 1926, the MASSR's Central Executive Committee and Council of People's Commissars (Sovnarkom) passed a resolution "On the Moldovanization and Ukrainization of the Soviet Apparat," mandating that, by January 1, 1927, all central and district institutions (with the exception of areas with local Ukrainian majorities) were to conduct their work solely in the Moldovan language.[21] Moldovan language courses were to be held at all institutions and organizations, employing various versions of the new literary standard (including the Madan grammar after 1929). After the completion of the required period of study, students were to be issued with a special certificate confirming their linguistic status. The MASSR Narkompros also created a special "Inspectorate for the Moldovanization of the Soviet Apparat," eventually headed by Leonid Madan.[22] The inspectorate in turn organized "moldovanization brigades" (*moldbrigăzi*) to assist local authorities in carrying out language raids on institutions slow to implement the new cultural directives.

Despite this elaborate administrative structure, the indigenization of the apparat was never a genuine success. Although the achievements of moldovanization were lauded at party conferences, the Obkom (the central party institution in the MASSR) frequently castigated Moldovan officials for failing to "moldovanize themselves."[23] The intransigence of administrators and the indifference of the workers led to chronically low attendance figures at the language courses; administrators were also loath to promote less-qualified Moldovans to higher positions if there were better-qualified Russians or Ukrainians already available. As time went on, in fact, the numbers of Moldovans serving in central and *raion* (district-level) institutions actually dropped, a sign that local cadres had little interest in hiring and promoting individuals solely because of their nationality. As late as 1936, a decade after moldovanization had begun, local party secretaries in at least half the MASSR's *raions*, including the four *raions* in which Moldovans formed a plurality of the population, had no knowledge of the local language.[24]

The only areas where moldovanization actually succeeded were in those positions that turned out to be the most politically exposed. Since Moldovans largely controlled the institutions that were to serve as the vanguard of moldovanization—the commissariat of enlightenment and its subordinate organs, educational and cultural establishments, central and *raion* newspapers—blame for the policy's failure ultimately fell on Moldovan heads. This was, in fact, the central irony of indigenization in the MASSR. Moldovans such as Chior, Madan, and other members of the MSC and the CMU were attacked in the 1930s in part for their failure to follow the party's line on indigenization. Ironically, in criticizing the moldovanizers and eventually removing them from their positions within the state apparat, the MASSR authorities reversed any advances moldovanization might have made. Although their admonitions to managers to promote Moldovans up through the system and to allow workers to attend the language classes usually went unheeded, the failure of the indigenization policy was nevertheless laid at their feet.

Moldovanization within the MASSR party organization was initially far more successful than in the state apparat. Whereas in 1925 just over 6 percent of party members were Moldovans, by the end of the First Five-Year Plan Moldovans accounted for over 25 percent. They were the only major ethnic group whose party membership increased steadily from 1925 to 1932. After this peak, however, they were progressively purged from the party organization, as many were accused of "national chauvinism" in their exuberance for the moldovanization drive. By 1940 Moldovans were once again severely underrepresented in party structures, whereas Ukrainians, Russians, and especially Jews were significantly overrepresented relative to their share of the MASSR's total population. The post of first secretary, with the exception of 1931–32, always remained in the hands of a non-Moldovan, a situation that would remain unchanged until 1980.

Literacy and the Woman Question

The position of women in the MASSR was of special importance to the republic's cultural institutions. According to the 1926 census, women made up just over 51 percent of the MASSR's total population of 572,114; they accounted, however, for 61 percent of all illiterates.[25] Of all major ethnic groups in the MASSR, Moldovan women were the "least literate," with only one in ten being able to read.[26]

This situation, particularly in the countryside, presented Moldovan authorities with several difficulties. The inability to communicate effectively with women allowed religious mystics to hold sway over the rural population and to undermine atheistic education. During the 1920s the disciples of a local religious leader, Inochentie, were a particular problem for Moldovan propagandists. A monk at a monastery near Balta, Inochentie began preaching to the local peasant population in the local language well before the Bolshevik Revolution. By 1911 Balta had become a kind of Moldovan Lourdes and Inochentie a widely known miracle-worker. After being exiled from the region by the tsarist authorities, he returned to Balta in 1917 where, along with several hundred mainly female disciples, he constructed an elaborate commune in An-an'ev *raion*. The commune, which included an intricate system of underground cells and corridors, was known by the Inochentists as "Paradise" (*Rai*) since every evening Inochentie himself would supposedly ascend to heaven from a spot within the compound.[27]

Although Inochentie was killed before the establishment of the MASSR, "Paradise" continued to function throughout the 1920s, and its mainly female membership foiled several attempts by the MASSR authorities to transform it into the "From Darkness to Light" collective farm.[28] Although Inochentism never posed a serious threat to Soviet power, it did illustrate to Bolshevik authorities the strength of a movement that used the Moldovan language as its chief propaganda vehicle and that targeted the republic's female Moldovans. The "great religiosity, backwardness, and illiteracy" of Moldovan women, noted an official report in 1925, was the chief explanation for the continuing success of Inochentism and other mystic movements, which could only be eliminated by increasing cultural work among village women. [29]

Soviet authorities also worried that the high level of illiteracy among Moldovan women would impede collectivization. Periodic women's risings against collectivization were reported in the spring of 1930 in several *raions*. One of the most serious, in the village of Nezavertailovka, involved a group of about 400 women that released 40 to 50 "collectivized" horses and returned two "de-kulakized" peasants to their former home. Protests in other locales proceeded similarly, with women demanding "to dissolve the collective farms, return the grain supplies and seed-corn, abolish the grain requisitions, oust the local authorities, give a beating to the representatives of Soviet power, [and] stop the expulsion of kulaks."[30] Not only did the women's groups successfully encourage collectivized peasants to leave the collective farms (with as many as 400 per day exiting in some *raions*), but as a Communist Party report on the incidents argued, "we are 250 versts from the Romanian border, and this demands of us an even greater effort" to put an end to such instability.[31]

The party's official stance on the woman question continually stressed the need to involve Moldovan women more fully in the tasks of socialist and national construction, but the results were usually less impressive than the rhetoric. The work of the Bolshevik women's sections (*zhenotdely*) was hampered by the lack of educated women who could speak Moldovan. Moldovan women were to have enjoyed special treatment in promotion and training programs, but their movement up through the hierarchy of party, state, and trade union organizations proceeded slowly. Although the proportion of women in the party organization more than doubled by the end of the First Five-Year Plan (peaking at around 13 percent in 1931), few women were to be found in the top posts. Only 8 percent of delegates to the first MASSR party conference in 1925 were women, a figure that actually dropped by the time of the tenth conference in 1937.[32]

Women who did manage to achieve prominent positions in the MASSR—such as Ekaterina Voronovich, Niunia Bogopol'skaia, and Ecaterina Arbore—did so either by being the wives of leading Moldovan political figures or by working mainly in the field of cultural construction. Both paths, as it turned out, led to their eventual elimination. Voronovich (the wife of E. P. Voronovich, chair of the MASSR Central Executive Committee) was excluded from the party in 1937 along with her husband, while Bogopol'skaia (head of the Obkom cultural and propaganda section) and Arbore (an educator and member of the MSC) were arrested during the attacks on local nationalists in the late 1930s.

Schools and National Education

A special series of problems confronted the authorities in their attempts to introduce full-scale moldovanization in the republic's educational system. Over 80 percent of all schoolchildren in the MASSR were from peasant backgrounds, and the dearth of trained teachers in the republic exacerbated the difficulties of educating this largely peasant population.[33] Most non-Russian schools in the territory of the MASSR had been ukrainized during Ukraine's own indigenization campaign before the establishment of the MASSR, and local educators were thus forced to start from scratch in building a Moldovan school system. Indeed, given the republic's large Ukrainian population—48 percent of the total in 1926—indigenization necessitated a concentration on schools in Ukrainian areas over those in Moldovan locales. In the 1926–27 academic year, for example, Ukrainian schoolchildren outnumbered Moldovans by over four to one in the cities and by over two to one in the countryside.[34] A lack of teachers proficient in the Moldovan language, the scarcity of Moldovan-language textbooks, and the legacy of large-scale ukrainization in the region before the establishment of the MASSR meant that it was often difficult to use Moldovan as the medium of instruction.[35] Hence, although education policy in the republic did allow increasing numbers of Moldovan children to attend school, in the 1920s it was rarely the case that they were taught in the Moldovan language.

In the MASSR's schools, state inspectors identified two further sets of problems. First, the poor qualifications of the teaching staff made effective instruction difficult. By 1927 only 11 percent of the MASSR's teachers had started or finished higher education, while nearly 30 percent had not completed secondary school.[36] There was also little effort on the part of the teachers to impress on the students the importance of learning the Moldovan language; since many students would continue their professional or higher education in Ukrainian-language institutions, they saw no need to study Moldovan. Second, the preponderance of "non-working-class elements" in most schools meant that children of wealthier families were able to bring "hostile ideologies" from home and thus to exercise a certain influence over the children of peasants. This "petty-bourgeois influence" was reflected in "individualism, philistinism, and narrow-mindedness." On religious holidays, especially Easter, the children organized parties at which they charged one or two rubles admission and engaged in "fortune-telling, flirtation, serving wine and other drinks, kissing, music and a number of other philistine, hooligan forms of behavior." In some locales, the inspectors even found obscene picture-books, while antisemitism and religious practices (both encouraged by teachers) were observed in the professional schools.[37] This general disorder and lack of authority, the inspectors concluded, led to an incorrect interpretation of the party's moldovanization policy.

National Publishing

Moldovan publishing saw substantial gains in the late 1920s and early 1930s. In addition to *Plugarul roş*, which had been established in May 1924 and antedated the MASSR, a Ukrainian-language version, *Chervonyi orach*, appeared from September 1925. By the end of 1930, both papers had changed their names to *Moldova socialistă* and *Sotsialistychna Moldoviia* (Socialist Moldova) and were being distributed in 8,000 copies per issue.[38] A range of other periodicals appeared in the following years in Moldovan, Russian, German, and other languages, sponsored by *raion* executive committees, *raion* party committees, and machine tractor stations. A Moldovan-language children's journal, *Scînteiu leninist* (The Leninist spark), and an artistic magazine, *Moldova literarî* (Literary Moldova), were also published from 1930. The Moldovan State Publishing House began operating in 1925 and produced a wide range of books in Moldovan and Ukrainian.

The question of the intelligibility of these publications to the mass of the Moldovan population was of central concern to cultural elites. In the mid-1920s, *Plugarul roş* had been harshly criticized for being "too Romanian." Although the paper was printed in Cyrillic script, the grammar and vocabulary used by the editorial staff were denounced as alien to the peasants. However, by the late 1920s, with the adoption of the Madan grammar and the elaboration of new terms based on traditional speech, *Plugarul roş* had become completely moldovanized. Even this new version, however, would eventually come under attack in the 1930s as artificial and unintelligible, written in a strange, invented language by an editorial staff more concerned with differentiating the language from Romanian than communicating with the Moldovan peasants.

Mass Literacy and Political Education

As in other parts of the Soviet Union, mass literacy campaigns and political education programs were a common feature of the First and Second Five-Year Plans in the MASSR. Special series such as the Moldovan-language *Biblioteca colectivistului* (Library of the collective farm worker) and the *Biblioteca eftinî–literatura hudojnicî* (Easy fiction library), using various versions of the Madan grammar, were produced regularly in the late 1920s and 1930s by publishing houses in Balta, Tiraspol, and Kharkov.

Political education in the MASSR took several forms. Village clubs, reading huts (*khaty-chital'ni*), red corners (*krasnye ugly*), the central library in Balta, a museum in Anan'ev, and other cultural centers were functioning by the late 1920s, with a total of as many as 265 centers involving 200,000 Moldovan peasants by the 1926–27 academic year.[39] Lessons in improved agricultural techniques, natural history, sanitation and hygiene, cooperatives, and the internal situation of the Soviet Union were conducted in each of these centers under the auspices of political education circles subordinated to the CMU.

By the early 1930s, however, attempts at moldovanizing the countryside had become bogged down in the same problems that inhibited full-scale moldovanization in other arenas. The intransigence of local institutions, the peasants' low level of education and their suspicion of the political education programs, the lack of trained instructors and educational materials, and the incomprehensible neologisms used in *Plugarul roş* and other publications all impeded the work of the CMU and its associated organs. Even in the printed materials that did eventually reach the peasants, innocent grammatical and typographical errors in both Moldovan and Russian had the potential to create serious misinterpretations of the party's policies. The slogan "A cow to every collective farm worker," for example, had sometimes been rendered "Every collective farm worker is a cow."[40] The key problem, though, remained the peasant himself. "Religiously inclined, distrustful of any new undertakings," noted a CMU report, "he does not attach a great significance to any institution in which lessons are given which fundamentally contradict his way of life and spiritual constitution."[41] The practical difficulties of building a Moldovan culture, as well as changes in the political ends that the newly constructed culture was supposed to serve, would eventually bring an end to radical moldovanization.

ATTACKS ON THE MOLDOVANIZERS

During the late 1920s and 1930s, periods that witnessed wholesale attacks on the cultural elites that had engineered *korenizatsiia* after 1923, cultural policy in the MASSR was to a great degree derivative of attacks on writers, academics, and political figures in Ukraine and the rest of the Soviet Union. In Belarus, the effort to replace Russian or Polish loanwords with nativist constructs was denounced as an attempt to drive a wedge between Belarus and the rest of the Soviet Union. In Uzbekistan, the early successes of nativist literary circles in the field of language construction and "uzbekization" were likewise undone. Conversely, in Azerbaijan, long-standing debates between Ottomanizers and nativists were eventually decided in favor of the latter, as Soviet policy attempted to create a distinct Azeri national identity to counter the turkification policies of Kemalist Turkey. The origins of these moves against the cultural and political elites of the 1920s, both at the all-union level and in the national republics, lay in a range of personal and professional rivalries. The common result, however, was that by the late 1920s, in academic circles as well as in state and party institutions, scores of "little Stalins" exercised over their respective domains the ruthless dominance that Stalin would later exercise in the Kremlin.[42]

There had long been a fear among Moldovan culture-planners that local policies would overstep the boundaries imposed by the center, and the work of the MSC had frequently been the subject of significant discussion in the 1920s. Criticism increased from 1930. In February a report to the Ukrainian Central Committee noted that remnants of the "right deviation" existed in the MASSR and criticized the rise of local nationalism within the moldovanization campaign.[43] A special resolution of the Central Committee supported the report's findings and called on the Moldovan Obkom to carry out a more decisive struggle against Moldovan chauvinism.[44] Although the report mentioned no institutions or individuals by name, it represented the first high-level critique of the fundamental tenet of Moldovan cultural construction—that is, the belief that since Moldovans had never had their own national culture, other goals in the republic must be subordinated to the basic aims of building and promoting a distinctly Moldovan cultural and political identity. From this point, Chior and the MSC found themselves in an inescapable dilemma. Pressed to build a Moldovan culture in part to serve the interests of Soviet strategists, they were nevertheless criticized when the culture they built failed to give due weight to the guiding influence of the Russians.

The first open condemnation of the MSC came shortly thereafter, in September 1930. An unsigned, full-page article in *Plugarul roş* chided the committee for distancing itself from the masses, for working on esoteric issues of linguistics and ethnography without considering fully the political nature of its work, and for concentrating on moldovanization to the detriment of other equally important practical tasks. Although the article noted the committee's many achievements since 1926, an accompanying cartoon showed MSC members seated at a table perched high above the heads of the workers, building culture without deigning to consult the masses.[45]

The most important indication of this shift in policy was the appointment of Ivan Ocinschi as head of the MSC in 1931, with Chior leaving the MASSR to study in Moscow. Born to a Moldovan peasant family in 1888 near Czernowitz, Ocinschi had spent much of his professional life outside Transnistria. After joining the Communist Party in 1926, he was appointed head of departments of Leninism at various pedagogical institutes in Ukraine. Ocinschi's assignment to Tiraspol was a clear attempt to check the influence of Madan and other radical moldovanizers in the MASSR. Not only had he completed a doctoral dissertation on the "right deviation"—a label increasingly applied to those on the MSC considered soft on Moldovan chauvinism—but his previous career outside the republic also meant that he had not been influenced by the numerous debates on moldovanization in the 1920s.[46]

Once installed in Tiraspol, Ocinschi began a review of the MSC's work that led to a full-scale assault on Chior, Madan, and their associates. The only way to control the deviant tendencies of these cultural leaders, Ocinschi argued, was to disband the individual MSC sections and bring the committee under the direct control of the local government, a change soon effected by the Sovnarkom.[47] The attack on Madan and the policies associated with Ocinschi's tenure on the MSC hastened the demise of the committee that had once been at the center of Moldovan cultural construction. During the Second Five-Year Plan, in fact, the terms *Madanist* and *Madanism* would come to stand not only for crass artificiality in cultural policy, but also for the attempt to tear Moldovan culture away from the beneficial influence of the Russians and Ukrainians. It was the complete *volte-face* in cultural policy under Ocinschi, especially the introduction of the Latin alphabet in 1932, that brought to a definitive end the effort to build a wholly separate Moldovan nation.

NATION-BUILDING REVERSED: THE LATIN ALPHABET

The switch to the Latin script was sudden and unexpected. The Latin alphabet had always been seen as the embodiment of Romanian francophilia. Until 1932 political leaders in the MASSR and Ukraine frequently highlighted the vast divide between the cultures of Soviet Moldova and bourgeois Romania, as well as the need to widen this gulf by cultivating a distinct Moldovan identity. At a Moldovan Obkom plenum in May 1931, the Ukrainian commissar of enlightenment, V. P. Zatons'kyi, underscored the parallels between the MASSR and its political cousin to the north, Soviet Karelia:

> In the far north, there is a republic that is completely analogous to your own. There, 100,000 Karelians live inside the Soviet Union and around 400,000 in Finland. But it happens that a lot of "clever" leaders, because of the underdeveloped nature of Karelian culture, decided that it was necessary to take the Finnish language and to build the Karelian Republic on that basis. Obviously, the Finnish language is related to Karelian, although perhaps not as closely as Romanian to your Moldovan language, but it is unknown and unintelligible to the Karelians. Nevertheless, for a number of reasons, it turned out that they tried to build Karelian national culture on the basis of the Finnish language.

This, Zatons'kyi held, had been a mistake. Finnish and Karelian might differ in only a few respects, but given the appropriate political circumstances, such differences could assume an unusual significance:

> [I]n Russian, for example, we have *moloko* and in Polish *mlako*. The same thing in Russian and Ukrainian, and in general, all Slavic languages have a lot in common. But no one proposes that we unify them.

Moreover, [in the Karelian case] there is a clearly defined political situation: On the far side, Finnish bourgeois culture is developing, and on our side a culture is developing that is closer to us . . . and contradictory to the other one.[48]

Just as it had been a mistake to attempt to finnicize the Karelians, argued Zatons'kyi, it would be equally misguided to romanize the Moldovans.[49]

By early 1932, however, all this had changed. A local party resolution on February 2, 1932, announced the transition to the Latin alphabet by the end of the year.[50] The briefly worded resolution described the change as "timely and expedient" and called on Moldovan cultural cadres to base their work on the need to enrich the Moldovan language with words generally accepted by all Romanians, including the Moldovans of the MASSR. The basis for the Moldovan language was now to be not the peasants of central Bessarabia—as Chior and his colleagues had mandated—but the inhabitants of the region stretching from the Dnestr westward to the Carpathians. In other words, since the Latin alphabet was to be the same version used in Bucharest, there was now little to distinguish the Moldovan language from standard literary Romanian. Although the announcement gave no explanation for the transition, the implications were clear. The policy of differentiation between both banks of the Dnestr, the stress on representing the spoken language of the Moldovan peasant, the vigilant stance against the pollution of the Moldovan language by "bourgeois gallicisms," and the construction of neologisms based on popular roots were, from February 1932, immediately and radically reversed.

The source of the latinization decision is uncertain. Ivan Ocinschi later held that Stalin himself had ordered the change, but there is no specific evidence to support Ocinschi's claim.[51] However, the primary intent of the policy was clear: to facilitate Soviet influence in Romania and to hasten the day when Soviet power would include not only occupied Bessarabia, but the Romanian lands west of the Prut River as well. The failure in the early 1930s of Soviet-Romanian talks on normalizing relations stepped up the tension over Bessarabia and heightened Soviet rhetoric on the continued occupation of the province by the Romanians. The unsuccessful Riga round of Soviet-Romanian negotiations ended only weeks before the MASSR Obkom's final decision on introducing the Latin script, and radical cultural changes in the MASSR clearly paralleled the failure of Soviet negotiators to secure Bessarabia's status at the bargaining table.

Moreover, with the political turmoil of Romania in the early 1930s,

Soviet policymakers had a better chance than ever of pressing the Bessarabian question. In mid-1930 Prince Carol of Romania returned to Bucharest from Paris, violating the terms under which he had renounced his right to the throne three years earlier. The return of his mistress, Magda Lupescu, to Romania later that same year created a massive public scandal and eventually led to the resignation of Prime Minister Iuliu Maniu. The fall of the Maniu government, combined with the economic depression experienced by the country, created a crisis in Romanian political life. Viewed from Moscow, the situation was extremely propitious. With Romanian authorities occupied with palace scandals and other pressing concerns, the change of cultural policy in the MASSR may have been one way of building political bridges across the Dnestr and of increasing Soviet agitation in the province.

The political functionality of the alphabet change was the chief ex post facto justification offered by the Moldovans themselves. By using the Latin alphabet in Soviet Moldova, a 1934 pamphlet on the issue argued, "the common bond between the language of the Moldovans of the MASSR and of the Moldovans on the other side of the Dnestr is preserved, which increases the revolutionary influence of Soviet Socialist Moldova on the other side."[52] Whereas cultural policy had previously centered on exploring the differences between Moldovans in the MASSR and their neighbors in the rest of Romania, the new line on culture would seek to draw the regions closer together by highlighting "the common struggle of the toilers of Bessarabia and Romania against a common class enemy."[53] Moreover, as Ivan Ocinschi wrote in an editorial in *Octiabriu* (October), the organ of the MASSR writers' union, the new alphabet held certain advantages for the future development of the Moldovan people. It was the "weapon of the largest international powers"; it facilitated the study of other languages; it was the alphabet used by Esperanto, which "is now linking the workers of the USSR with the workers of the entire world"; and it had fewer letters than the Cyrillic alphabet and would, therefore, be easier to learn.[54]

THE LATINIZATION CAMPAIGN

As with full-scale moldovanization after 1926, the introduction of the Latin alphabet was accompanied by a broad mobilizational campaign designed to ensure the immediate acceptance of the new script. But plans to "latinize" the MASSR soon encountered many of the same difficulties as the moldovanization campaign. Funds were scarce, and new Latin-script typewriters were often in short supply. After raids carried out by newly created latinization committees, those institutions that had procured the appropriate typewriters were discovered to have made them useless by replacing the Latin type with Cyrillic. Special classes set up for *kul'tarmeitsy* and *latinizatory*—the "cultural soldiers" and "latinizers" who were to lead the alphabet campaign in the villages—reported low attendance figures and a lack of resources and trained teachers. Those who did bother to attend sometimes came drunk or showed up for the wrong class; few of the latinization schools held classes regularly, and those that were functioning did so without chalk, notebooks, or other teaching materials.[55] Already in mid-1933, the Moldovan leadership was harshly criticized by the Ukrainian center for their sluggishness in "carrying out the latinization of the alphabet and the romanization of the language."[56]

The latinization campaign may have had little real impact on the ground, but significant changes did take place at the level of official Moldovan culture. With the introduction of the Latin alphabet, the language used in schools, publishing, administration, and other spheres became Moldovan in name only. The 1932 edition of Madan's *Grammar of the Moldovan Language*, re-edited by a team that included Madan himself, was wholly Romanian.[57] Other works, intended both for scholarly consumption and for the public at large, were similarly purged of virtually any trace of nonstandard Romanian, including all the neologisms and grammatical innovations introduced by the MSC in the 1920s.[58] Most spectacularly, in addition to examples taken from Lenin, Stalin, and Gorky, school grammars and other textbooks also contained readings from important Romanian writers such as Mihai Eminescu and Vasile Alecsandri, figures who a short time before had been denounced as the mouthpieces of Romanian xenophobes and oligarchs.[59] The reform of 1932 was thus more than a simple alphabet change. It was also an abrupt and wholesale rejection of the indigenized Moldovan culture constructed after 1924.

THE RETURN TO THE CYRILLIC ALPHABET

The experiment with latinization came to an end as suddenly as it had begun. A resolution of the MASSR Central Executive Committee on May 19, 1938, returned the republic to the Cyrillic script and denounced the latinization drive as an ill-conceived detour along the road of cultural construction: "Enemies of the people operating in Moldova have carried out a hostile policy on the front of national-cultural construction, polluted the Moldovan language with Romanian salon-bourgeois words and terms, and introduced the Latin alphabet, which is unintelligible to the Moldovan toilers."[60] An editorial in *Moldova socialistă* was clear in its assessment of the political significance of the switch. "The transition to the Russian alphabet is a great strike against the Trotskyist-Bukharinist-bourgeois-nationalist-enemies-of-the-people-agents-of-fascism who wanted to tear flourishing Soviet Moldova from the Soviet Union."[61] Within weeks, lists of words had been prepared illustrating the "pollution of the Moldovan language by Romanian words" and were distributed to party and state institutions in the republic in order to root out any residual Romanian influences.[62] However, the new Cyrillic alphabet was decidedly different from that first used by Chior and Madan in the 1920s. None of the indigenized grammatical forms or neologisms were used even after the end of the Latin alphabet in 1938. The new standard represented little more than a Cyrillic version of literary Romanian—a compromise between the radical culture-building of the 1920s and the equally radical pro-Romanian policy of 1932.

The task of providing an academic justification for the compromise policy fell to I. D. Cioban, a young linguist who, like Ocinschi for the Latin campaign, would serve as the chief exponent of the return to the Cyrillic alphabet and the lead voice in condemning the policies of the 1920s. In an article entitled "A Little Something about Language," Cioban condemned the artificiality of the "Madanists" and criticized those who felt the language should develop on the basis of the spoken idiom of the Moldovan peasant:

> A few words about those who say we should write like the Moldovan villagers speak, without leaving out a single word. This is a mistaken view. The Moldovans speak in many different ways, with all kinds of words that cannot enter into the literary language. We must work to bring the literary language as close as possible to the language of the toiling masses, but we must not set about making it stupid.[63]

Cioban's words epitomized the massive transformation in Moldovan cultural policy since the late 1920s. Both Cioban and Pavel Chior, writing in the same newspaper over a decade apart, had used the same words to describe the task of local nation-builders. Their meanings, however, were completely opposite. In a 1926 article, Chior had spoken approvingly of the "simple" or "uncomplicated" (*prost*) nature of the peasant's speech; the language of the Transnistrian or Bessarabian village was simpler, more popular, more democratic than the bourgeois language of the Romanian city.[64] It was precisely this "simple" language, though, that Cioban condemned. Basing literary Moldovan on the language of the village would merely lead to its "stupidification" (*împrostiria limbii*). For Cioban, Moldovan was indeed a distinct language, but the artificial innovations of Chior and Madan only served to wreck the construction of a new socialist nation.

The reasons for the policy reversal in 1938 lie outside the MASSR itself. The recyrillicization campaign covered virtually the whole of the Soviet Union. Beginning in 1935–36, steps were taken to transfer the Latin-based alphabets of non-Russian peoples of the Russian Federation to Cyrillic. By 1939 all the languages of the Russian republic had been cyrillicized, and in September 1939, the first union republic to adopt the Latin script—Azerbaijan—also became the first non-Slavic republic to adopt the Cyrillic. Within a year, almost all the Soviet languages that had been latinized in the 1920s and 1930s had adopted the Cyrillic alphabet. In each instance, the recyrillicization campaign was only one component of the broader crackdown on "bourgeois nationalist" intellectuals in the Soviet republics. In the case of the MASSR, worries among Soviet authorities about the turn to the right in Romanian domestic politics also prompted the need for greater vigilance along the Romanian-Soviet border, a change in the international climate that seemed to work against the policy of cultural rapprochement introduced in 1932.

POLITICS AND THE END OF NATION-BUILDING

In the early years of the MASSR, the shape of Moldovan culture and language policy emerged as the product of prolonged, sometimes heated debates involving a range of policy actors. Local linguists and other cultural cadres, specialists dispatched from Moscow, the Moldovan party and state leadership, central Ukrainian authorities, and foreign policymakers in the Kremlin all influenced the formalization of a distinct Soviet Moldovan culture in the years following the establishment of the MASSR. Such plurality of opinion—which, if not respected, was at least tolerated before the early 1930s—ended with the introduction of the Latin alphabet. Local elites had little role in the decision to reverse the direction and fundamental assumptions on which cultural policy had been based before 1932. The change represented a major departure from the previous methods and goals of nation-building and opened the door to the criticism, and eventually the denunciation, of those who had engineered the policies of the 1920s.

The latinization drive also marked a significant change in the role of local professionals in the formulation of cultural policy. In the 1920s, Buciuşcanu, Chior, Madan, and other members of the MSC had been at the center of Moldovan cultural and political life. In the 1930s, the fate of these cultural engineers was little different from that of their counterparts at the all-Ukrainian level. A trip by the Ukrainian commissar of enlightenment, Mykola Skrypnyk, to Moldova in summer 1932 provided sufficient grounds for launching an assault on intellectuals in the MASSR.[65] Skrypnyk came under fire in June 1933 in a wave of denunciations of bourgeois nationalists in Ukraine, but took his own life before the campaign's climax. Within two weeks of Skrypnyk's suicide on July 6, the MSC condemned Ocinschi's lack of vigilance in rooting out local nationalists, whom he had supposedly allowed to link up with Ukrainian nationalists seeking to pull all of Ukraine out of the Soviet Union.[66] Ocinschi was branded a "party crook, false-scholar, and adventurer," removed from his post as MSC chair, and excluded from the party in August.[67] The MSC itself was then denounced as a nest of "Skrypnykist" bourgeois nationalists in an article in the Ukrainian journal *Komunist* in October 1933.[68] Similar condemnations at a Ukrainian Central Committee plenum in November 1933 and at the Ninth Moldovan Party Conference in January 1934 led to the committee's liquidation.

Most of the political and cultural elite of the MASSR followed a similar path. Madan, having first been attacked by Ocinschi and then grouped together with him as a "dyed-in-the-wool nationalist," was accused of wrecking the latinization drive and removed from his post as head of the MSC linguistics section in July 1933.[69] Those who had not fallen during the first wave of attacks in the early 1930s were swept away in the purges of the latter half of the decade. Pavel Chior fell under attack after his return to the MASSR from Moscow. Appointed first secretary of the Rîbniţa *raion* party committee in 1934, Chior was eventually denounced as having failed to carry out a thoroughgoing purge of bourgeois nationalists in the *raion* party organization and of having sheltered known Trotskyists. He was excluded from the party in April 1937, arrested in June, sentenced to ten years' imprisonment, and died in 1943 before his sentence expired.

Of the nine members of the Moldovan Obkom Politburo elected at the Tenth Party Conference in May 1937, only one survived politically in the MASSR until September of that year; seven had been declared "enemies of the people" and arrested; and one managed to escape from the republic.[70] Nearly all the former first secretaries of the local party organization and chairs of the Central Executive Committee were arrested and executed, along with virtually anyone who had played a role in the major organizations of cultural planning. Any trace of their having existed was erased. By the end of 1934, all works by Leonid Madan, along with all those of his colleagues on the MSC (some 3,231 volumes) had been removed from the MASSR's libraries.[71] After 1938, the "Moldovan language" and eventually most of Moldovan high culture would come to be little more than Romanian in disguise.

MOLDOVA AS A SOVIET REPUBLIC

PART TWO

5 A Stipulated Nation

The Little Entente with Yugoslavia and Czechoslovakia, the Balkan Entente with Turkey, Yugoslavia, and Greece, a strategic agreement with France, and a defensive alliance with Poland were all meant to secure Greater Romania's borders. The energetic diplomacy of the 1920s and 1930s, however, ultimately came to naught. Romania's post-1918 frontiers were part of the general postwar order in Europe, and once that began to fail, so too did the boundaries of Greater Romania.

In the secret protocols to the Molotov-Ribbentrop Pact signed between Germany and the Soviet Union in August 1939, Germany declared its lack of political interest with respect to the fate of Bessarabia and implicitly acknowledged the Soviet Union's claims on the region. Less than a year later, on June 26, 1940, the Soviet government acted on the terms of the secret treaty and issued an ultimatum to the Romanian minister in Moscow demanding the immediate cession of Bessarabia and the northern portion of the province of Bukovina. The justification for the demands had little to do with previous Soviet propaganda. In the written ultimatum, there was no mention of the Moldovan nation, nor of the class-based nature of Bessarabian identity, nor of the Moldovans' national oppression under the Romanians; the only oblique reference to national issues was the suggestion that Bukovina would be taken as recompense for the hardship experienced by the Bessarabians since 1918. Instead, the ultimatum argued that Bessarabia had a population that was "for the most part Ukrainian" and that the "overwhelming majority" of the population of northern Bukovina was "linked to Soviet Ukraine both by shared historical destiny and by shared language and national composition," both claims that were simply false.[1] On the map annexed to the ultimatum, the territories to be surrendered to Moscow were marked in a thick red pencil covering a seven-mile-wide swath of territory, so that the town of Herţa and other portions of Romania were haphazardly included in the area to be ceded, even though they were not mentioned in the text itself.[2] Italy and Germany, concerned primarily with stability and access to Romanian oil fields, urged King Carol II to accede to the Soviet demands. After several tense meetings in the Crown Council and the grim news that France and Britain were in no position to come to Romania's aid, Carol accepted Moscow's demand. On June 28 Soviet troops crossed the Dnestr River and occupied Bessarabia. Faced with the humiliating loss of Bessarabia to the Soviet Union, as well as the subsequent loss of northern Transylvania to Hungary, Carol transferred his principal powers to the authoritarian general, Ion Antonescu, and abdicated in September.

The Soviets' switch from supporting revolution in Bessarabia to the outright annexation of Romanian territory was occasioned by the changed international atmosphere of the late 1930s and, in particular, Bessarabia's position on the front line of antifascist defense. In 1934 high-level observers in the MASSR had noted that Romania's slide toward authoritarian government placed the kingdom in a situation "not far from Spain"; such a development, though, was seen primarily as a catalyst of revolution, not necessarily as a military threat to the Soviet Union.[3] By 1938, however, things had changed substantially. In the first half of the year, Carol II instituted a royal dictatorship, outlawed all political parties, and carried out a wholesale reorganization of the kingdom's territorial administration, eliminating the provincial system that had made Bessarabia a discrete administrative unit. In the MASSR such moves were seen as preparation for an attack on the Soviet heartland.[4] As early as February 1940, political leaders in the MASSR were already preparing population tables and other statistical data with a view to the eventual breakup of the autonomous republic and its union with a new, Soviet Bessarabia.[5] With Bessarabia's fortunes sealed in the Nazi-Soviet pact, Stalin had only to wait for an end to the war with Finland and the rolling victory of the Germans on the western front to launch the attack on Romania.[6]

The withdrawal of the Romanians from Bessarabia was chaotic. The Soviets had promised to allow the orderly removal of Romanian troops, but the cession of Bessarabia resembled more a retreat before an advancing conqueror than the quiet handover of territory. Romanian officials, former Sfatul Ţării members, and average Bessarabian citizens were rounded up or executed on the spot.[7] As many as 90,000 fell in the wave of repression and deportations that immediately followed the annexation.[8] Retreating Romanian troops, humiliated at the loss of the eastern province, also took their own revenge against those they held responsible for betraying Greater Romania. Jews attempting to leave Bessarabia were harassed or killed by Romanian officers, since as a confidential military report noted at the time "these antisemitic incidents spring from a sentiment of revenge for the horrors committed by the Jewish population in the abandoned territories against the Romanian army."[9] The total population of the regions annexed by the Soviet Union is uncertain, but the most reliable estimates are on the order of four million persons, of whom anywhere from half to three-quarters may have been Moldovan/Romanian.[10] As *Izvestiia* argued at the time, the "peaceful policy of the USSR" had "liquidated the Soviet-Romanian conflict" over Bessarabia forever.[11]

During the war, Romania—now allied with Nazi Germany—managed to recapture the annexed territory and press across the Dnestr into Ukrainian Transnistria as well. By late July 1941, Romanian and German troops had taken Bessarabia and Bukovina and officially reintegrated them into the Romanian state; at the end of the summer, Transnistria also came under Axis control.[12] Romania then created a special military district to govern the territory between the Dnestr and the Bug Rivers.[13] There was never any attempt to annex the occupied territory beyond the Dnestr, for it was generally considered by the Romanian government to be a temporary buffer zone between Greater Romania and the Soviet front line.[14] The region did, however, witness the worst atrocities of Antonescu and his German allies. It was to this special administrative unit that some 123,000 Jews from Bessarabia and Bukovina would be deported or killed during the war, along with scores of thousands of other Jews and Gypsies from Transnistria.[15] In 1930 there were 204,838 Jews and 13,518 Gypsies in Bessarabia; in 1959, the numbers had fallen to 95,107 and 7,265.[16]

At the time, Romanian politicians were fully supportive of the decision to wage war against the Soviets, even though this brought Romania into a conflict with its former allies, France and Britain. The decision to move across the Dnestr into Transnistria was more problematic. The two preeminent political figures of the day, Iuliu Maniu (chair of the National Peasant Party) and Constantin Brătianu (leader of the National Liberals), urged Antonescu not to take the war beyond the Dnestr. "Although the fight for the reconquest and liberation of Bessarabia and Bukovina was legitimated by the entire soul of the nation," they wrote in April 1943, "the Romanian people will never consent to the continuation of the struggle beyond our national borders."[17] Had Antonescu heeded their advice, Romania's fate after the war might well have been different. By reaching beyond Bessarabia, Romania became a de facto aggressor power, pursuing German war aims against the Soviet Union rather than simply retaking the territory stolen by the Soviets.

In April 1944, however, Transnistria again came under Soviet control as the Red Army advanced westward against the retreating Germans and Romanians. In late August, Carol's son and the new Romanian king, Mihai, initiated a royal coup against the Antonescu regime, switching sides in the war just as Soviet troops were preparing to enter Bucharest. It was too late for the turnaround to affect the fate of the ceded territories. Both Bessarabia and northern Bukovina were already under Soviet occupation, and the peace treaty of February 1947 established the Soviet-Romanian border along the Prut River.[18]

The new Soviet republic that emerged from the Soviet annexation and military reconquest was both more and less than historic Bessarabia. The redrawn Moldovan Soviet Socialist Republic (MSSR), formally established already on August 2, 1940, comprised six counties from Bessarabia plus the six westernmost *raions* of the MASSR. Northern Bukovina, the remainder of Transnistria, and part of the counties of Hotin, Akkerman, and Ismail in northern and southern Bessarabia fell to Ukraine when the MSSR's borders were settled in November 1940.[19] At the same time, a thin strip of territory east of the Dnestr that had never been considered part of Bessarabia was added to the new MSSR.

The territorial changes did have some demographic rationale. On ethnic grounds alone, there was some logic to apportioning northern and southern Bessarabia—the most ethnically heterogeneous and most Slavic of historic Bessarabia's zones—to Ukraine, although some 337,000 Moldovans were included in the bargain.[20] Likewise, the villages along the eastern bank of the Dnestr were the most Moldovan part of the old MASSR; in the areas apportioned from the autonomous republic, Moldovans formed almost 49 percent of the population, compared to only 32 percent in the MASSR as a whole.[21] More important, though, was the strategic usefulness of the administrative changes. The inclusion of Bessarabia's Danube and Black Sea frontage in the Ukrainian SSR placed these strategic assets in the hands of a reliable Soviet republic rather than leaving them under the control of a newly created entity and the potential object of Romanian irredentism. At the same time, by destroying the administrative unity of historic Bessarabia, Soviet policymakers created yet another hedge against potential claims by Bucharest. Just as Bessarabia moved north in 1812 when Russian negotiators redefined the meaning of the name *Bessarabia,* so too *Moldova* came to mean something very different in 1940: Although Romania still contained a region that locals called *Moldova* (the western half of the medieval principality), after the Soviet annexation *Moldova* or *Moldavia* would also come to be accepted as shorthand for the new MSSR.

The reshaped Moldovan republic emerged with a population of 2.4 million, of which 68.8 percent were Moldovan.[22] At 33,700 square kilometers, the new republic became the second smallest after Armenia.[23] Despite its size, though, the MSSR would continue to be a source of concern to Soviet policymakers. Not only did the problem of Moldovan identity remain on the agenda, but relations with Romania, despite its position as a socialist state after 1947, were also affected by the Bessarabian question.

THE FORGOTTEN SOVIET REPUBLIC

Leonid Brezhnev, who served as Communist Party first secretary in the MSSR from July 1950 to October 1952, later reflected that the new republic faced special challenges after the war. In Moldova, he noted, the processes of collectivization and sovietization had to take place within a much shorter period of time than in republics that had been part of the Soviet Union from the 1920s. "These remote *raions* lying along the Dnestr," he wrote, "had to break through to socialism by the shortest possible path."[24]

"Breaking through to socialism" exacted a harsh toll from the Moldovans. The Soviet invasion of 1940, the Romanian and German operation of 1941, and the Soviet reconquest in 1944 had already laid waste the Bessarabian countryside and uprooted hundreds of thousands of average Bessarabians. The war on the eastern front had eliminated nearly half of all horses and pigs and nearly a third of all sheep and goats; severe droughts in 1945 and 1946 further reduced agricultural production.[25] Immediately after the reoccupation, Soviet security forces organized the "repatriation" of Bessarabians who had fled before the advancing Red Army; refugees in Romania were handed over to the Soviet authorities, with many shot or deported as collaborators with Romanian and German fascists. The retribution fell on all ethnic groups, not just Romanian-speakers. For example, Bessarabia's German population, which numbered over 81,000 in 1930, had fallen to under 4,000 by 1959, the result both of wartime migration and forced removal as collaborators after the war.[26]

Famine and organized deportations inflicted further harm on Moldovans during the collectivization campaign (1946–50). Although famine and drought were not unusual in Bessarabia, there is ample evidence that the famine of 1946–47 was provoked by Communist grain requisitioning and was directed against the largest group in the countryside, Moldovans.[27] At a minimum, some 115,000 peasants died from hunger and related diseases from December 1946 to August 1947.[28] An official "de-kulakization" campaign aimed at supposed rich Moldovan peasants (*chiaburi*) eliminated still further families, most of them Moldovans, from 1947 to 1951.[29] On two days alone—July 6 and 7, 1949—11,342 Moldovan families were targeted for deportation to Kurgan, Tiumen, Irkutsk, and other destinations in Siberia and Kazakhstan in a plan labeled "Operation South" and directed by the notorious MSSR minister of state security, I. L. Mordovets.[30] In all, from 1941 to 1951, nearly 16,000 families were deported outside the MSSR.[31]

The turmoil in the countryside lessened with the completion of collectivization in 1950, but the removal of Moldovans continued, although under a different guise. In April 1951, "Operation North" targeted religious minorities in the MSSR, especially Jehovah's Witnesses, and more than 700 families were deported to Siberia.[32] In March 1955, the official newspaper *Sovetskaia Moldaviia* carried an article announcing a plan of "voluntary" migration to populate collective farms in Astrakhan and Rostov *oblasts* of Russia and the Pavlodar *oblast'* of Kazakhstan. The most heavily Moldovan districts of the MSSR were targeted for "volunteers," and as many as 40,000 Moldovans may have left the MSSR for the east.[33] Show trials and public terror campaigns

TABLE 5

MSSR POPULATION, 1941–89

	1941		1959		1970		1979		1989	
Moldovans	1,620,800	68.8%	1,886,566	65.4%	2,303,916	64.6%	2,525,687	63.9%	2,794,749	64.5%
Ukrainians	261,200	11.1	420,820	14.6	506,560	14.2	560,679	14.2	600,366	13.8
Russians	158,100	6.7	292,930	10.2	414,444	11.6	505,730	12.8	562,069	13.0
Gagauz	115,700	4.9	95,856	3.3	124,902	3.5	138,000	3.5	153,458	3.5
Bulgarians	177,700	7.5	61,652	2.1	73,776	2.1	80,665	2.0	88,419	2.0
Jews	—	—	95,107	3.2	98,072	2.7	80,127	2.0	65,672	1.5
Roma (Gypsies)	—	—	7,265	0.2	9,235	0.2	10,666	0.3	11,571	0.3
Romanians	—	—	1,663	0.06	—	—	—	—	2,477	0.06
Other	23,200	1.0	22,618	0.8	37,968	1.1	48,202	1.2	56,579	1.3
TOTAL	2,356,700	100.0	2,884,477	100.0	3,568,873	100.0	3,949,756	100.0	4,335,360	100.0

NOTE: Dashes indicate no figure available.

SOURCE: Compiled from V. V. Chembrovskii and E. M. Zagorodnaia, *Naselenie soiuznykh respublik* (Moscow: Statistika, 1977), p. 192; 1959, 1970, 1979, and 1989 Soviet censuses.

against supposed pro-Romanian secret societies in the early 1950s claimed even more lives.[34]

After the immediate postwar years, political life in the MSSR settled down considerably. After 1953, many of the deported "kulaks" and "collaborators" were rehabilitated, and those who remained alive were allowed to return to the MSSR. From this period, in terms of local politics, the history of Moldova as a Soviet republic is largely unremarkable. Its governmental and economic structures were copies of those in all the other Soviet republics. It became a generally quiet backwater on the periphery of the Soviet federation, and was a popular vacation spot for members of the Soviet party and state elite, with good weather, friendly locals, excellent wine and brandy, and decent Intourist hotels. The region's distance from Moscow and the difficulty of traveling to Chisinau from Romania meant that it was normally off the itineraries of all but the most adventurous foreign visitors. It was rarely featured in foreign analyses of the Soviet Union, with only one Western Sovietologist writing in depth about local political developments before the late 1980s.[35]

The Communist Party of Moldova (Partidul Comunist al Moldovei, CPM) was already established in August 1940 on the basis of the old MASSR Obkom and, after the return of Bessarabia to the Soviet Union, assumed the officially mandated "leading role" in Moldovan society. Within the local party, Russians and Ukrainians dominated; at the all-union level the Moldovans were the least represented nationality in the entire Soviet Union.[36] The few Moldovans who found prominent positions in the local and central organs were invariably from Transnistria—which had remained within the Soviet Union throughout the interwar years—rather than from Romanian Bessarabia. Moreover, the MSSR became a kind of training ground for future general secretaries of the Communist Party in Moscow. Brezhnev served as first secretary in the 1950s, and Konstantin Chernenko worked as head of the party's propaganda department from 1948 to 1956 and as a deputy in the MSSR Supreme Soviet from 1955 to 1959. Even Nikita Khrushchev had some familiarity with the thorny Bessarabian question in his capacity as a party functionary in Ukraine in the 1920s and as Ukrainian party first secretary after 1938. These trends continued throughout the Soviet period. Neither of the two longest-serving first secretaries, Ivan Bodiul (1961–80) and Semion Grossu (1980–89), was from Bessarabia, and both were more comfortable with Russian culture than with the language of the MSSR's ethnic majority. Like their forebears in tsarist Bessarabia, Moldovan political elites were among the most loyal in the union. Manifestations of local nationalism were sparse, and when they appeared in the form of arcane poems or Aesopian articles in literary journals, they were quickly eliminated in public campaigns organized by Bodiul and Grossu.

Soviet propaganda portrayed the MSSR as "a flourishing orchard," a region nestled in the rolling hills along the Dnestr, where happy peasants collected the bountiful harvest for delivery to the other fraternal peoples of the Soviet Union.[37] On one level, the image was not far off the mark. Only Kyrgyzstan had a larger proportional rural population, and after 1950 the MSSR became one of the great agricultural centers of the Soviet Union. Although it formed only 0.2 percent of the Soviet Union's total territory, by the 1970s the MSSR produced 10 percent of the union's canned foods, 4.2 percent of vegetables, 12.3 percent of fruits, and 8.2 percent of wines.[38] The "Moldovan model" of agriculture, which centered on the creation of regional councils to plan and coordinate production, was touted after the 1970s as the future of factory-farm production in the Soviet Union as a whole.[39] This "second collectivization," as it came to be called, did allow for increased agricultural production, but at the same time created a class of powerful agroindustrial managers virtually immune to the commands of central party and state organs.[40]

Industry also developed apace, although agriculture was the mainstay of the economy throughout the Soviet period, accounting for 42

TABLE 6
NATIONAL COMPOSITION OF THE COMMUNIST
PARTY OF MOLDOVA

	Moldovan	*Ukrainian*	*Russian*	*Jewish*
1925	6.3%	31.6%	41.6%	15.7%
1940	17.5	52.5	11.3	15.9
1989	47.8	20.7	22.2	2.5

NOTE: Figures for 1925 refer to the Moldovan *oblast'* party organization within the Moldovan Autonomous Soviet Socialist Republic (MASSR).
SOURCE: Adapted from E. S. Lazo, *Moldavskaia partiinaia organizatsiia v gody stroitel'-stva sotsializma (1924–1940)* (Chisinau: Ştiinţa, 1981), p. 38; William Crowther, "Ethnicity and Participation in the Communist Party of Moldavia," *Journal of Soviet Nationalities* 1, no. 1 (1990): 148–49.

TABLE 7

FIRST SECRETARIES OF THE COMMUNIST PARTY
OF MOLDOVA, 1941–91

	Period in Office	Place of Birth
P. G. Borodin	1941–1942	Ukraine
N. L. Salogor	1942–1946	Ukraine
N. G. Coval	1946–1950	Moldova (Transnistria)
Leonid I. Brezhnev	1950–1952	Russia
D. S. Gladkii	1952–1954	Ukraine
Z. T. Serdiuk	1954–1961	Ukraine
Ivan I. Bodiul	May 1961–Dec. 1980	Ukraine
Semion K. Grossu	Dec. 1980–Nov. 1989	Moldova (Transnistria)
Petru K. Lucinschi	Nov. 1989–Feb. 1991	Moldova (Bessarabia)
Grigore I. Eremei	Feb. 1991–Aug. 1991	Moldova (Bessarabia)

SOURCE: Compiled from *Moldavskaia Sovetskaia Entsiklopediia* (Chisinau: Glavnaia Redaktsiia MSE, 1979); and archival sources.

percent of the republic's net material product in 1991.[41] Industrial concerns, moreover, tended to be concentrated east of the Dnestr River. The steel mill in Rîbniţa, the Dubăsari and Moldavskaia power stations, and refrigerator, clothing, and alcohol facilities near Tiraspol were major industrial plants, but all were located outside Bessarabia. Just as Moldovan farm workers were sent to other parts of the Soviet Union on projects to build socialist agriculture, these new factories attracted industrial workers from Russia and Ukraine. In demographic and economic terms, the MSSR gradually developed as two republics in one: a largely rural, Moldovan, and indigenous population in Bessarabia employed primarily in agriculture and light agro-industry; and a more urban, Slavic, and generally immigrant population in Transnistria working in Soviet-style heavy industry.

The demographic hues of the MSSR changed considerably during the Soviet period. Jewish and German populations, once important constituents of the multiethnic Bessarabia of the nineteenth century, had decreased considerably by the 1980s, a result of the atrocities of the Second World War, postwar Soviet deportations, and emigration after the 1960s.[42] The MSSR also became less Moldovan as time passed. Deportations and out-migration reduced the Moldovan component and in-migration by industrial workers increased the Slavic component of the population. Some 68.8 percent of the population in 1941, Moldovans represented 63.9 percent by the 1979 census, rising slightly to 64.5 percent by 1989. Ukrainians rose from 11.1 percent in 1941 to 13.8 percent in 1989, but the most dramatic increase was among ethnic Russians, who almost doubled their share of the population in the same period, from 6.7 percent to 13 percent. Most other ethnic groups lost members throughout the Soviet years, further dissolving the multiethnic patchwork that travelers since 1812 had found the region's most remarkable trait.

Local intellectuals remarked on the increasing russification of the language and culture of the republic after the 1960s, but even more important was its rapid sovietization. The influx of migrants from other parts of the Soviet Union did not spark strong sentiments among locals; if anything the long history of multiethnicity and Russian dominance made accommodation rather simpler in Bessarabia than elsewhere. The creation of the MSSR was a relatively easier process than the integration of other territories annexed by the Soviets in 1940, such as the Baltic republics and western Ukraine. Unlike in these areas, there was no strong national sentiment in Bessarabia, and those in whom it might have flourished—such as the former members of the Sfatul Țării—remained in Romania after the war or were imprisoned in the Soviet Union. Even the Bessarabian church, tied to Bucharest during the years of Romanian rule, had long been oriented more toward Moscow than the West. The region had been a part of the Russian transport network and economic system less than four decades earlier, and for all the cultural activity of the Romanians between the wars, it remained the least integrated component of Greater Romania. During the final days of the war, Romanian officers had noted the serious desertion rates among Bessarabian soldiers fighting on the eastern front; whether leaving out of concern for their families or commitment to the Soviet cause, their loyalty to Greater Romania proved less than complete.[43] The germ of Soviet Moldova had been crafted in the MASSR in the 1920s and 1930s, and it was elites from the east-bank region who continued to dominate political and cultural life until the final years of the Soviet system. In relatively short order, the quiet MSSR thus became a well-integrated component of the Soviet state. By the time of the 1970 census, 16.5 percent of Moldovans were in ethnically mixed marriages, one of the highest rates among non-Slavic nationalities.[44]

Still, all was not well within the MSSR. The "Moldovan model" of agricultural production began to run into trouble already in the late 1970s. By the time of the Fifteenth Party Congress in January 1981, problems with the economy had been revealed.[45] In the past, First Secretary Bodiul attempted to play down difficulties by launching campaigns against "anti-Soviet feeling" and "local nationalism."[46] But with his replacement by Semion Grossu in December 1980, many of the deficiencies in the Moldovan economy came to light. Bodiul had been the last republican first secretary to be replaced under Brezhnev, and his long period in office came to be associated with the worst features of the period of stagnation. Even under Grossu, though, the party attracted still further criticism from the central authorities for padding economic results and other forms of local corruption. In December 1983, a special CPSU Central Committee resolution accused the Grossu leadership of inertia and a range of other shortcomings.[47] The next year, the Moldovan party newspaper was criticized as "banal, dull, timid, and superficial," and the entire party organization was once again censured for poor agricultural management at a Central Committee plenum in October.[48] Other reports in the all-union press throughout the early 1980s painted a picture of a Moldova rife with corruption and ruled by a party elite filled with holdovers from the era of "Bodiulism." In April 1984, the minister for light industry was sacked for drunkenness; in June the minister for meat production was dismissed for incompetence.[49] In October, the head of a major hospital was jailed for swindling more than 50,000 rubles by treating fictitious patients.[50] Although the evidence was mounting of serious corruption in the republic, local law enforcement organs did little to investigate the abuses.[51] Further, the factory-farm system and rapid industrialization in the 1960s and 1970s also began to pay dividends in the 1980s, although not in the form their designers had intended. The MSSR was the most densely populated of all the Soviet republics, and intensive farming and use of fertilizers caused massive health problems. Pollution along the Dnestr, both from agricultural runoff and because of temperature changes associated with hydroelectric production, created a nearly dead river.[52]

These trends were reflected in the MSSR's less than stellar demographic indicators. By the late 1980s, in demographic terms Moldova was closer to the Central Asian republics than to the more developed Soviet west. Moldovans had the highest infant mortality rate in the western Soviet Union; among the rural population, it was nearly twice as high as in neighboring Ukraine. Life expectancy, at 65.5 years for men and 72.3 for women, was lower only in Kazakhstan, Kyrgyzstan, and Turkmenistan.[53] The 1986 Chernobyl accident, although far more serious in Ukraine and Belarus, also left its mark on the MSSR, and the following years would see a remarkable rise in genetic disorders and birth defects.[54] These grim statistics, along with developments on the cultural front, would eventually undermine the authority of the Communist Party and serve as catalysts for the reform movement under perestroika.

SOVIET-ROMANIAN RELATIONS AND THE BESSARABIAN QUESTION

Even though the MSSR was largely ignored in the West, it was anything but a forgotten republic in Romania. The issue of the 1940 annexation was an officially forbidden subject in socialist Romania and off limits to historians; indeed, immediately after the war historians were encouraged to investigate the fraternal bonds between Romanians and Russians and to ignore the history of disputes between the two peoples earlier in the century. Raising the Bessarabian question was not only politically unpalatable, but Romanian Communists were also in a peculiar double bind. First, since the territory had been taken by a fraternal socialist state, the idea of irredentism was theoretically impossible. Second, in the 1920s the Romanian Communist Party had in fact encouraged the Soviet acquisition of Bessarabia as part of the Communist International's line against bourgeois imperialism, a policy that led to the party's proscription in 1924.[55] After the war, Romanian Communists were therefore in the difficult position of paying tribute to a foreign regime that had annexed significant portions of Romania's territory and that continued to laud the annexation as evidence of the Soviet Union's benevolent internationalism. For reasons of both propriety and past policies, the Romanians generally preferred therefore to keep silent and accept the loss of the eastern region.

From the 1960s, however, the Soviet annexation began to resurface. Under Gheorghe Gheorghiu-Dej, and later Nicolae Ceaușescu, Romania embarked on a hesitant policy of differentiation from the Soviet Union in a limited range of policy areas. Although often portrayed as a maverick in the Soviet camp, Romania in fact remained a steadfast member of the Warsaw Pact. But leaders in Bucharest tested the waters in certain policy areas in order to gain greater freedom to maneuver from Moscow. Military training, cultural policy, domestic economic policy, and relations with Israel and the West were areas in which Romania's leadership managed to differentiate itself from the policies of Khrushchev and Brezhnev.

When open political disputes did arise, they were often played out in the arcane language of historiography, linguistics, and other fields of scholarship, polemics that the staff at Radio Liberty in Munich labeled "the undeclared border war of historical materialism."[56] Romanian diplomats in Moscow monitored events in the MSSR and any discussions with Soviet historians that touched on Bessarabia were noted by the embassy and reported to Bucharest. Speeches by Soviet leaders were scrutinized for veiled references to Bessarabia and Bukovina, and Romanian visitors to the Soviet Union were encouraged to glean information on popular perceptions of relations between the two states; even Intourist maps and other tourist publications were scoured for information that might portray Romania in an unfavorable light. The Soviets in turn often criticized "hostile radio broadcasts," meaning those emanating from the powerful Romanian station just across the Prut River in Iaşi.[57] The polemics were usually capped by lengthy articles by the Moldovan first secretary in *Pravda* and other newspapers lauding the "age-old ties" between the Moldovan, Russian, and Ukrainian peoples.[58]

One of the most trenchant explicit examples of the impact of the Soviet Union's external relations on the cultural politics of the MSSR came in August 1967. At that time, relations between Bucharest and Moscow were near their nadir. Romania had been the only Warsaw Pact state not to condemn Israel in June for its actions in the Six Day War, Ceauşescu was well on his way to consolidating his rule by appearing to stand up to the Soviets, and Romania's political image in the West, especially in the United States, was quickly improving. Moreover, the Tenth International Congress of Linguists was due to open in Bucharest in late August, a forum at which the Soviets no doubt expected Romanian scholars to touch on the problem of an independent Moldovan language. At a meeting of the CPM Politburo on August 22, First Secretary Bodiul explicitly instructed the most prominent members of the republic's academic community to author articles that would "strengthen propaganda on questions of the history of Moldova, the Moldovan nation and statehood, the age-old relations of the Moldovan people with the peoples of the Soviet Union, and Soviet patriotism."[59] Bodiul directed several of the republic's best-known historians, ethnographers, and linguists to write articles on designated topics for publication both inside Moldova and abroad throughout 1967 and 1968. Nicolae Corlăteanu, director of the Institute of Language and Literature of the Moldovan Academy of Sciences, was assigned an article "On the Development and Flourishing of the Moldovan Language" for publication in the weekly *Kul'tura*; Artiom Lazarev, who had held the posts of minister of culture and of education and was, at the time, a distinguished researcher at the Institute of History, was to complete a major work on "The Struggle for Unification" of Bessarabia with the Soviet motherland. Each scholar was, in addition, instructed to use his international connections to help increase pro-Soviet propaganda outside Moldova's borders. The result was a massive increase in publications on the main nodal points in Bessarabian history, especially the 1812 union with Russia, the anti-Romanian risings in Bessarabia in the 1920s, and the "reunion" of Bessarabia with the Soviet Union in 1940.[60]

Similar incidents occurred throughout the Soviet period and were frequently pointed to by Western analysts as evidence of potential conflict between Romania and the Soviet Union.[61] In 1964 the Romanian Academy published a book containing Karl Marx's reading notes on the history of Wallachia and Moldova, which had supposedly been recently discovered at the International Institute for Social History in Amsterdam.[62] The notes, although no more than extracts that Marx had jotted down for future reference, mentioned the injustice of the 1812 annexation of Bessarabia and, implicitly, brought Marx himself into Bucharest's camp on the 1940 annexation as well. Likewise, during a speech to the Romanian Party Congress in July 1965, Ceaușescu quoted an 1888 letter from Friedrich Engels to a Romanian socialist journal in London in which Engels criticized the Russian takeover of Bessarabia; the focus of the quote was the "national unity" of the Romanians praised by Engels, but the subtext was anti-Russian.[63] During another speech in May 1966, this time marking the forty-fifth anniversary of the founding of the Romanian Communist Party, Ceaușescu made an overt reference to territories inhabited by Romanians but taken from Romania. He condemned as "erroneous" previous party resolutions adopted by the underground Communist Party in interwar Romania, supporting the occupation of Bessarabia and Bukovina by the Soviets.[64]

Even the Chinese and former Romanian nationalists became embroiled in the war of words. In an interview with a delegation of Japanese socialists in 1964, Mao Tse-tung cited the Bessarabian annexation as evidence of the expansionist aims of the Soviet Union, a comment that sparked harsh criticism from Moscow and quiet approbation from Bucharest.[65] In Romania, former Sfatul Ţării members such as Pantelimon Halippa joined the discussion as well. Halippa spent the early 1950s in prison in the Soviet Union, but once he was allowed to return to Romania he began a private campaign to keep the Bessarabian issue alive, writing letters to Ceauşescu and meeting on occasion with former colleagues to reminisce about the glories of Greater Romania.[66] As late as November 1989, with Romania's support in Moscow quickly dwindling, Ceauşescu attempted to raise the Bessarabian question again by denouncing, during the Fourteenth Congress of the Romanian Communist Party, the Soviet invasion. By then, of course, the writing was on the wall for socialism in Romania, but the president's return to a familiar theme illustrated the power of the Bessarabian issue in Romanian official discourse.

None of these disputes ever had a major impact on high-level policy. Indeed, the situation was rather the reverse: The Bessarabian issue was a barometer of overall relations between Romania and the Soviet Union rather than a cause of controversy in itself. After the conflicts of the late 1960s, relations between Bucharest and Moscow warmed considerably. Ceauşescu himself made a visit to the MSSR in August 1976, with his wife Elena and son Nicu in tow; he stressed the "friendly, brotherly" relations between Romania and the Soviet Union but indicated that there should be no special relationship with the MSSR.[67] Bodiul returned the visit shortly thereafter and inaugurated a series of cross-border collaborative projects in agriculture, industry, and energy production.[68] By and large, Romania remained a loyal member of the Soviet camp, so loyal in fact that it continued to follow the Soviet model even after the Soviets themselves had begun to realize the need for change. But the persistent disputes among historians and linguists in the two countries did have a much longer-term impact on cultural politics in the MSSR, an impact that would only become evident in the waning days of the Soviet order.

THE QUIET ROMANIZATION OF MOLDOVAN INTELLECTUALS

After the Bessarabian annexation, the Soviet line on Moldovan culture changed considerably. Soviet policy centered on the cultivation of a distinct Moldovan cultural identity, but avoided the radical indigenization and frequent changes that had characterized the MASSR. There were certainly open debates over the correct course to be followed in Moldovan cultural development, but these were never of the kind found in the earlier autonomous republic. After the war, the technical matters of the Moldovan language that had concerned elites in the MASSR gave way to more abstract arguments over the historical origins of the Moldovan nation and the ethnic links between the Moldovan and Romanian peoples. The settling of Moldovan cultural policy is evident in one telling detail: In the entire period from 1945 to 1989, only one major spelling reform was carried out in the MSSR—the introduction of a new letter in 1967—whereas no fewer than six separate alphabets had been in use from 1925 to 1941.

With the "liberation" of Bessarabia in 1940 and again in 1944 and the declaration of a Romanian People's Republic in 1947, the political context of cultural policy underwent a monumental shift. Since one of the original goals of Moldovan cultural construction had been attained—the absorption of the oppressed Bessarabian masses into the Soviet Union—continuing to tout the class-based distinctions between the peoples on both banks of the Prut was of little political utility. With the creation of a Romanian socialist state, the MASSR's other major goal—spreading the revolution west of the Prut—had also been achieved. The ideology of cultivated difference that had informed the work of Pavel Chior and Leonid Madan gave way to a policy of simply stating that Moldovans and Romanians were different, without really trying to make them so.

Moldovan cultural leaders would later decry the russification of the Moldovans under the Soviets, but the Soviet years if anything represented a rather different trend: the quiet acceptance of standard literary Romanian (albeit in the Cyrillic alphabet) as the linguistic norm for the MSSR and, by extension, the gradual romanization of Moldovan intellectual life. The increased Romanian influence on the Moldovan language was identified as early as 1960 by Romanian scholars[69] and by Western researchers in the 1970s.[70] By the 1980s, there was little except the Cyrillic alphabet and loanwords from Russian to distinguish the two languages. Most of the grammatical norms and peculiarities of pronunciation characteristic of the old MASSR had been definitively rejected in 1938, and the next five decades witnessed a gradual convergence of the grammar, pronunciation, and lexicon of standard Moldovan with those of standard Romanian.[71] A few peculiarities remained, such as the preponderance of Russian-based terminology for technological terms, but in the main, Moldovan in its standard form was more Romanian by the 1980s than at any point in its history. Linguistic practices that diverged from this standard were portrayed as non-Moldovan, the results of progressive linguistic russification that the prominent linguist Nicolae Corlăteanu denounced as a burlesque, "macaronic" form of the national language.[72] The putative separateness of the two languages was further undercut by the fact that catalog cards for Romanian-language publications at the republic's two major research libraries were often written in Cyrillic script—but with an additional note explaining that *Textul e dat cu caractere latine* (The text is in Latin characters). The fact that no Moldovan-Romanian dictionary was ever published in the Soviet Union is also illustrative of the difficulty of separating the two languages.[73] A dictionary of Madan's peasant-based speech would certainly have been possible, but that project had already fallen by the wayside before the creation of the MSSR.

There was a certain inevitability to this development. By the late 1930s, Moldovan nation-builders had rejected the pillar on which the idea of an independent Moldovan culture had been based: the commitment to representing the actual spoken language of the Moldovan peasant and fashioning it into a literary standard. After 1938, when linguists such as I. D. Cioban denounced the work of their predecessors as making "fetishes" of the peasant and soiling the Moldovan language with the simple tongue of the village, there was no place for linguists to turn except to standard literary Romanian. Indeed, since the Moldovan language was not to be based on the way Moldovans themselves actually spoke, and since at the same time linguists were still intent on promoting "correct" speech and spelling, the path chosen after 1938 could only lead to the continuous romanization of the Moldovan language. By the 1980s, a distinct Moldovan standard culture was more stipulated than cultivated.

There were other reasons, as well, for this gradual shift. In the first place, after the 1940s the view that Moldovans formed both a distinct class and a distinct nation—or rather, the idea that they represented the latter because of their position as the former—gave way to the search for the ethnic origins of the Moldovans in more strictly historical terms. For postwar Soviet scholars, the development of nations was a linear process, beginning with the existence of a social group or tribe (*plemia*) with unique linguistic, economic, cultural, and other characteristics; evolving toward an identifiable ethnic group (*narodnost'*) with a rudimentary class structure and increased social solidarity; and terminating with the emergence of a fully fledged nation (*natsiia*) with a distinct territory, system of economic relations, and developed language and culture. Each of these stages was associated with developments in the relations of production: The tribe was the typical form of ethnosocial organization in primitive economies, ethnic groups were to be found in periods characterized by slaveholding and feudal economic relations, bourgeois nations with their antagonistic classes were typical of the capitalist period, and socialist nations could develop only under an economic system that resolved the class contradictions inherent in capitalism.[74]

In Moldova, scholars were able to delineate these various stages with considerable precision. N. A. Mokhov, one of the republic's foremost historians and ethnographers, distinguished six stages in the development of the Moldovan socialist nation: First, Thracian and Illyrian tribes settled the region of the future MSSR. Second, in the first and second centuries A.D., Latin-speaking colonists arrived in the newly established Roman province of Dacia. Third, in the fourth through sixth centuries, Slavs entered the region from the north and the south, mixing with the local latinized population to form a new tribe, the Wallachs. Fourth, with the development of feudal societies in the lands north of the Danube and east of the Carpathians, as well as more extensive contacts with neighboring East Slavic peoples, a new ethnic group—the Moldovans—emerged from the Wallachs. Fifth, a Moldovan bourgeois nation evolved from the Moldovan ethnic group from the late eighteenth century to the early twentieth century. Sixth, the period of the formation of a Moldovan socialist nation was ushered in by the October Revolution and completed with the end of collectivization in 1950.[75] According to the official history of the republic, this final stage lasted longer in Moldova than in other regions because of the tortuous political history of Bessarabia, but the accelerated development of the republic in the late 1940s and 1950s ensured that a fully fledged Moldovan "socialist nation" (*sotsialisticheskaia natsiia*) now existed in harmony with the other peoples of the Soviet Union.[76]

For Soviet scholars, there was nothing unique in the developmental path of the Moldovan nation—as scholars in the MASSR had earlier contended—but only in its terminus, the rise of a second eastern Latin people and culture. The nation had emerged as the result of normal historical processes, and the task of the republic's historians was to investigate and elucidate them, especially those by virtue of which the paths of Moldovans and Romanians had diverged. In practice, such a project meant examining historical archives, uncovering literary and archaeological clues, and searching other sources in order to trace the evolution of the Moldovans from *narodnost'* to *sotsialisticheskaia natsiia* and to highlight the nodal points at which Moldovans and Romanians, despite their common origins in Roman Dacia, had begun to move apart: the establishment of a Moldovan principality in the fourteenth century, the Russian incorporation of Bessarabia in 1812, the "progressive influence" of the Russian revolutionary movement in the nineteenth century, the developmental hiatus during the Romanian occupation, socialist construction in the MASSR, the liberation of Bessarabia in 1940, and the path toward developed socialism after the war. The histories of the Moldovan people and of the Moldovan Communist Party were increasingly treated as separate issues,[77] a bifurcation that would have been unthinkable in the MASSR but that became institutionalized in the creation of separate research bodies for party and national history after the war.[78] Authorities worked hard to cover up the previous independent existence of most other territories annexed by the Soviet Union, but in the MSSR uncovering anything that might point to an independent sense of "Moldovanness" in history was an all-consuming task.

In addressing the issue of Moldovan identity by using the same tools as their colleagues in socialist Romania, Moldovan scholars put themselves in a difficult position. Since Moldovans and Romanians often used the same sources and methodologies but arrived at radically different conclusions about the origins and boundaries of the Romanian nation, conflicts between both scholarly communities were bound to arise. Moldovan scholars were increasingly dependent on carefully crafted turns of phrase or intentional oversights in order to escape the conclusion that Moldovans and Romanians in fact represented a single ethnonational group. In the MASSR, the task of proving the distinctiveness of the Moldovan cultural heritage was relatively easy, since local scholars could denounce the work of the Romanians as informed by bourgeois values wholly inappropriate to socialist scholarship. However, after the 1950s, when Romania and the Soviet Union were ostensibly on the same path, both developing apace as socialist nations, controversies between scholars in both countries were inevitable. The importance of these scholarly debates was magnified as political relations between Moscow and Bucharest cooled after the early 1960s. By the 1980s there was little to distinguish Moldovan research from that carried out in Romania, except that the conclusions reached in both countries using the same sources were often fundamentally opposed. Since both scholarly communities identified many of the same historical events and personages as fundamental to the development of Romanian and Moldovan culture, Soviet Moldovan scholarship—like the Moldovan language—became increasingly Romanian as the Soviet period progressed.

The rise of well-trained professional academics and popularizers of the Moldovan language in the late 1950s and 1960s also contributed to this trend. The establishment of the Institute of Language and Literature in December 1957 and the Moldovan Academy of Sciences in August 1961 created the institutional base for the growth of local scholarship. By the mid-1960s, a new generation of professionally trained scholars had begun to emerge. Whereas older researchers had received their education primarily at the Tiraspol Pedagogical Institute before the war, the second-generation scholars were younger, often ethnic Moldovans born in Bessarabia who had studied at the new Chisinau State University. In the 1980s, many of these scholars began to fill positions vacated by retiring scholars trained in the MASSR.[79] Furthermore, younger linguists were also involved in popularizing the Moldovan language and in promoting "correct" usage in schools and among the public at large.[80] Yet the particular form of the language that they promoted as correct speech was invariably urban Romanian rather than the distinctively Moldovan words and constructions found in the countryside. As Nicolae Corlăteanu, director of the Institute of Language and Linguistics from 1961 to 1969, would later reflect, many scholars "worked so that the idea of the linguistic unity of Moldovan and Romanian would always be presented," even if they could not argue directly against the separateness of the two languages.[81]

For all their increased professionalism, Moldovan academics rarely possessed the skills or resources of their colleagues in Romania. The opportunity for Romanian scholars to travel to the West, archival resources available in Bucharest and Iaşi (the capital of the Moldovan principality in the nineteenth century), and the greater openness in Romanian scholarship in the years following Ceauşescu's rise to power in 1965, all overshadowed the meager resources of researchers in the Moldovan Academy of Sciences and Institute of Party History. Younger Moldovan scholars eagerly read the works of their Romanian colleagues, even though they were often forced to denounce them as substandard. They made frequent trips to Moscow, where works by Romanian authors that were prohibited in Moldova could be easily purchased at the Druzhba bookstore.

The romanization of Moldovan academic life placed Moldovan linguists in a particular bind. Although they were compelled by the exigencies of Soviet politics to highlight the differences between Moldovan and Romanian (with more or less vehemence depending on the period), the objective differences between the two became more and more minute as the Soviet period progressed. The language that Moldovan intellectuals spoke in their own homes, taught to their children and students, promoted through popular books and newspaper articles, and hailed as the defining characteristic of the Moldovan nation was—to anyone outside the Soviet Union—known simply as "Romanian." In fact, there was a widening chasm between the linguistic peculiarities studied by Moldovan dialectologists and historical linguists (the rural speech forms that had been codified by Leonid Madan in 1929) and the actual linguistic practices of these scholars. Since the most educated and most literate Moldovan-speakers did not display the traits that they themselves identified as quintessentially Moldovan, the dissonance between scholarly word and linguistic deed became increasingly apparent.

"BOURGEOIS" SCHOLARS AND MOLDOVAN IDENTITY

Developments at the international level also had an important impact on culture in the MSSR. Beginning with the 1950s, historians and Romance linguists abroad began to turn their attention to the issue of the Moldovan language and its relationship to standard literary Romanian. One of the first to address the issue explicitly was the well-known Italian scholar Carlo Tagliavini in a paper presented to the Eighth Congress of Romance Studies in Florence in 1956.[82] Tagliavini surveyed a range of Soviet publications on the Moldovan language, but concluded that the only difference between Moldovan and Romanian was the Cyrillic alphabet and minor mutations in diphthongs (Rom. /ea/ > Mold. /ia/), the backing of some vowels after hard consonants (Rom. /i/ > Mold. /ɨ/ after /z/, /t/, and /g/), and a few other small variations in pronunciation.[83] Few of these, however, were represented in Moldovan spelling; such distinctions existed mainly at the level of popular speech. In his more extensive work on the origins of the Romance languages, Tagliavini was more direct in his dismissal of Moldovan, which he described as a mere "dogma of Soviet linguistics."[84] Other Western and émigré linguists and historians were equally condemnatory. Works by Eugene Lozovan,[85] Harald Haarman,[86] Klaus Heitmann,[87] Dennis Deletant,[88] Nicholas Dima,[89] and Michael Bruchis,[90] as well as regular reports by the staff at Radio Free Europe/Radio Liberty, were invariably critical of the Moldovans and highlighted the latest developments in Moldovan scholarship and Romanian-Moldovan polemics. Such Western attention kept the issue of Moldovan identity alive and forced Soviet scholars to proffer increasingly Byzantine explanations for Moldovan-Romanian separateness.

The rejection of the main arguments of Moldovan linguistics, historiography, and ethnography by Western specialists was reinforced by the propaganda work of Romanian and Bessarabian émigrés. Particularly in the late 1960s and 1970s, when battles between Romanian and Moldovan scholars were at their zenith, a range of publications appeared in the West denouncing the nationalities policies of the Soviet regime and warning of the ongoing denationalization of Romanians in the former Bessarabia.[91] Some of these publications were directed against specific scholars or trends within Moldovan academia. The most famous instance concerned the appearance in 1974 of the massive *Moldovan Soviet Statehood and the Bessarabian Question*, the magnum opus of the Moldovan historian and sometime government minister Artiom Lazarev, which still represents the premier synthesis of Soviet arguments on Moldovan national identity.[92] Lazarev's text was harshly criticized by Alexandru Şuga, a Romanian émigré in Germany who had earlier published a pro-Romanian history of the Bessarabian dispute.[93] The Soviet volume spawned a wave of veiled criticism in Romania as well, and the Ceauşescu regime even used a publishing house in Italy owned by an alleged sympathizer of the fascist Iron Guard to produce a pamphlet denouncing Lazarev as "a counterfeiter of history."[94]

The Moldovans, of course, were compelled to offer countercriticisms and refutations of the work of these "bourgeois falsifiers." Numerous books and articles emerged in the MSSR aimed expressly at denouncing the perfidious views of foreign scholars.[95] In some cases, the targets of these works were Romanian émigrés or scholars across the Prut River in socialist Romania, although Western "bourgeois" academics were most often named explicitly in order to deflect attention away from the divisions within the socialist world.

A by-product of refuting the "bourgeois falsifiers," especially for the younger generation of Moldovan researchers, was an intimate familiarity with Western literature on Bessarabia and Soviet Moldova. Spurred on by their political superiors, designated researchers in the Academy of Sciences and Institute of Party History had ready access to an extensive foreign literature on the history of Moldova and Bessarabia, some of it not even easily accessible in the West. The unintended consequence was the shaping of these scholars' views on Moldovan identity and their exposure to Western methodologies and writing styles. Ironically, in provincial Soviet cities such as Chisinau, the advent of glasnost under Gorbachev restricted rather than expanded the opportunities open to local cultural elites. Since there was no political need for Moscow to pass foreign works along to republican experts for refutation, the diffusion of Western literature to the periphery quickly came to an end.

Much of what Moldovan ethnographers, linguists, and historians had to say after the 1950s, if placed in a different historical or political context, would have seemed completely uncontroversial. That distinctions between languages and dialects are political rather than scientific, that historical circumstances and international relations play major roles in ethnic identity formation, and that there is no "natural" way for a national identity to evolve are all ideas that any modern academic would accept as truisms. However, the political functionality of Moldovan scholarship, as well as the increasing Romanian influence on Moldovan high culture, lent an air of insincerity to the work of Soviet scholars that their counterparts in the West were quick to condemn. The impact of consistent criticism of Moldovan cultural policies by a large international community cannot be overestimated. Trained linguists and historians, émigré scholars with personal axes to grind, and Western observers sympathetic to the Romanian national cause were all instrumental in the self-destruction of Soviet Moldovan scholarship in the 1980s. The eventual death of the Moldovan socialist nation was, in this sense, an assisted suicide.

SOCIAL TRENDS IN SOVIET MOLDOVA

These intellectual changes took place in an environment in which the demographics of Bessarabia and Transnistria were changing markedly as well. By the late 1980s, the demographic position of Moldovans relative to the local Russian population appeared secure. Although the proportion of Moldovans had fallen relative to the MSSR's total population, their growth rate remained the highest of any titular nationality in the western Soviet Union (including Russia) and higher than that of local ethnic Russians.[96] The local Russian and Ukrainian populations had clearly grown relative to the titular nationality, but not nearly so dramatically as in some other union republics.

The linguistic situation, however, was decidedly different. By 1989 Moldovans were the third most russified nationality in the Soviet Union; only in Ukraine and Belarus did a higher proportion of the titular nationality report Russian as their native language. The size of this russified population grew steadily after 1959, again with only Ukraine and Belarus showing sharper growth rates.[97] The generational differences were significant. Some 95.5 percent of Moldovans over fifty-five reported Moldovan as their native language in 1989, but 89.3 percent of persons under twenty-four still called Moldovan their native tongue.[98] The reverse side of these figures was equally striking. Of all the union republics, only in Central Asia did fewer Russians know the language of the titular nationality. Only 11.2 percent of ethnic Russians in the MSSR reported a fluent knowledge of Moldovan as a second language, and similar figures obtained for other minority groups: 15.2 percent for Jews, 12.8 percent for Ukrainians, 6.9 percent for Bulgarians, and a low of 4.4 percent for Gagauz.[99]

However, these aggregate figures hid an important component of Moldova's demographic landscape: the progressive moldovanization of the republic's urban centers, a development that would have an important impact on politics in the late 1980s. Moldova's urban population expanded rapidly throughout the postwar period and at a rate well above the all-union average.[100] In the interwar years, the urban populations of Bessarabia and the MASSR accounted for 13 and 14 percent of the respective totals.[101] By 1959 the MSSR's urban population amounted to 22 percent of the total, a figure that increased to 32 percent in 1970, 39 percent in 1979, and 47 percent in 1989.[102] The increase was partially the result of immigration from other Soviet republics, particularly Russia and Ukraine, as Moldova's newly established industries and pleasant climate attracted workers and retired members of the party and military elite. There was also substantial reclassification of villages to towns and of towns to cities as urban centers expanded to include outlying areas.

The primary source of urban growth, however, was the massive migration from villages to towns and "second stage" migration from towns to cities, with industrialization during the Soviet period pulling workers away from the agricultural sector and into industrial production or agro-industry.[103]

Not only were far more residents of Moldova living in the cities by 1989 than at any stage in the past, but the cities themselves had also become more "Moldovan" in the process. The cities of Bessarabia had traditionally been inhabited mainly by Jews and Russians, and the perception of urban centers filled with unwelcome foreigners was a major catalyst in the growth of local xenophobic and antisemitic organizations in the early twentieth century and between the wars. In 1897 Moldovans accounted for only 14 percent of Bessarabia's urban dwellers, even though they formed at least 48 percent of the province's total population.[104] By 1930, however, the figure for urban Moldovans had grown to 31 percent.[105] The share of Moldovans living in the towns and cities of the MSSR increased during the Soviet period from 28 percent in 1959 to 46 percent in 1989,[106] and between 1959 and 1970 Moldovans finally became the single largest ethnic group in the MSSR's cities, a position they would retain from the 1970s on.

The social effects of increasing urbanization and the concomitant moldovanization of urban areas were profound. The number and size of towns and cities undoubtedly experienced significant growth after 1940, but the link between rural and urban environments remained strong, and may even have been enhanced. Large numbers of workers commuted to jobs in the cities but maintained a primary residence in and cultural allegiance to the villages. Patterns of seasonal employment, with workers spending part of the year engaged in the agro-industrial sector in towns and the remainder in collective-farm agriculture in their villages, also perpetuated the link between urban and rural environments. Rather than creating a gulf between styles of life in both settings, the pattern of urbanization in the MSSR integrated the two "into a common network, using the raw material and labour resources from rural areas and the capital and organizational resources of [the] small towns."[107] The Moldovan writer Ion Druţă remarked on the social impact of these changes as early as 1971, in an article in *Komsomol'skaia pravda*:

> Chisinau has changed completely. It has become more earthy, more colorful, more picturesque. City-dwellers recently arrived from the

countryside retain in their walk, their speech, and their habits all the coloring of their native village. At times it seems that entire villages have emptied out and are walking down the streets of the city.[108]

An important part of this trend was the maintenance of traditional linguistic practices on the part of Moldovans in the cities. In the censuses of 1970, 1979, and 1989, respondents were asked to list their native language (*rodnoi iazyk*) and, if applicable, a second Soviet language in which they were fluent. Throughout the 1970–89 period, the number of urban Moldovans who spoke Russian increased considerably, while those speaking only Moldovan or only another non-Russian language dropped significantly between 1970 and 1979, but leveled off between 1979 and 1989. Learning Russian, though, was not normally associated with a loss of Moldovan-language skills; the vast majority of urban Moldovans remained either speakers of Moldovan only, or learned Russian as a second language, not as a mother tongue.

Other groups, such as Ukrainians, tended to assimilate to Russian in the cities. Between 1970 and 1989, the proportion of urban Ukrainian-speakers fell steadily, while those partially or completely assimilated to Russian rose apace. By 1989, nearly 40 percent of urban Ukrainians were fully assimilated to Russian. Urban Moldovans, however, tended to expand their linguistic repertoire rather than to adopt Russian at the expense of their ancestral language. Thus, although changes in all-union language policy after the war encouraged the acquisition of Russian at the expense of native languages, by 1989 Moldovans continued to claim competence in their national language even though more and more had begun to acquire Russian as a secondary language. Moreover, the lines between Moldovans and other ethnic groups remained relatively solid. Throughout the Soviet period there was never any net linguistic assimilation to Moldovan on the part of Ukrainians and Russians; there were always more Moldovans on Soviet censuses than there were speakers of the Moldovan language.

The continued salience of ethnolinguistic identity in the urban context contradicted standard Soviet notions of the results of urbanization. Soviet cities were normally seen as the locus of normalcy and everyday life, the great melting pot from which the new "Soviet people" would eventually emerge. However, as cultural solidarity became essential for success in the competitive urban job market, the importance of ethnicity and relationships among co-ethnics was often intensified rather than di-

TABLE 8

LANGUAGE AND ETHNICITY IN THE MSSR, 1989

(Percent of total ethnic group)

	Total population	Native Language			Fluent Knowledge of Another Soviet Language		
		Language of own ethnic group	Moldovan	Russian	Language of own ethnic group	Moldovan	Russian
Moldovans	2,794,749	95.4	—	4.3	1.7	—	25.7
Ukrainians	600,366	61.6	1.6	36.7	8.6	12.8	43.0
Russians	562,069	99.1	0.6	—	0.6	11.7	—
Gagauz	153,458	91.2	1.1	7.4	1.6	4.4	72.8
Bulgarians	88,419	78.7	2.4	18.1	—	6.9	68.3
Jews	65,672	25.9	0.8	72.9	6.9	15.2	23.1
Roma (Gypsies)	11,571	82.0	13.5	3.6	1.2	30.6	41.9
TOTAL	4,335,360	88.9	0.5	10.3	2.6	3.9	45.2

SOURCE: 1989 Soviet census.

minished. These demographic trends had another element as well, because of sharp distinctions between Bessarabians and Transnistrians. Having ties not only to a particular ethnic network, but also to a micronetwork of co-ethnics from a particular region of the republic, was essential to ensuring upward mobility in the party, administration, and other areas. Transnistrians had traditionally dominated party and state institutions, since they were seen as more politically reliable than their counterparts from the former Romanian Bessarabia. Within Bessarabia itself, persons with family ties to the north of the republic tended to win out over those from the center and the south in the party and state hierarchy. All these networks—ethnic, regional, and subregional—were later to become of critical importance.

By 1989 the MSSR was in demographic terms a Moldovan populist's dream: an economy based on agriculture; a largely rural society with the countryside inhabited mainly by members of the indigenous ethnic group; and urban centers populated by a mass of newly arrived immigrants from the countryside competing with "foreign" populations that had traditionally held the reins of political and economic power. Ethnic Moldovans who had moved to the cities were less than a generation removed from the villages, had not forsaken their national language, and lived in an environment in which they could be easily reached by newspapers, television, and other forms of mass communication. The conjuncture of these social features with trends in Moldovan scholarship and developments in elite politics provided the crucial point of departure for the national movement of the late 1980s.

6 Language and Ethnic Mobilization under Perestroika

Following massive demonstrations and extensive public debate, on August 31, 1989, the MSSR Supreme Soviet adopted three new language laws that declared Moldovan the "state language" (*limba de stat*) of the republic, mandated the transition to the Latin alphabet, implicitly recognized the unity of the Moldovan and Romanian languages, and set out a broad program for extending the use of Moldovan in government, education, and the national economy.

The new laws marked a radical break with the official line on Moldovan national identity and launched the republic on a course that would eventually lead toward both the declaration of independence and the outbreak of serious interethnic violence in Transnistria and among the Turkic-speaking Gagauz minority in the south. At a rally held outside the Supreme Soviet building on August 31, the Popular Front, Moldova's main opposition organization founded in mid-1989, called on the assembly to reinstate "the historic name of our people, which it has carried for centuries . . . the name *Romanian*, and the name of its language, the *Romanian language*."[1] The laws themselves described their chief goals as:

> eliminating the deformations that have occurred in language policy in the MSSR, taking the Moldovan language (one of the fundamental premises of the existence of the Moldovan nation in the framework of

its national-state formation) under the protection of the state, guaranteeing its functioning in all spheres on the territory of the MSSR, and regulating national-linguistic relations in the republic.[2]

A year earlier such pronouncements would have been unthinkable, but by 1989 the official line on national identity had undergone a transformation that seemed to represent a wholesale rejection of sixty-five years of Soviet history. It was the final chapter in the history of "Moldovan" as a wholly distinct cultural identity and the first step on Moldova's road to political independence.

The events of the late Soviet period, culminating in the new language laws in 1989 and the declaration of independence in 1991, have generally been portrayed as a crusade for rectifying and reappropriating the Moldovans' "genuine" national identity after a half-century of Soviet rule. The story, though, is rather more complicated than that. There was more to the national movement than simply a desire to seek historical truth. As became clear after 1991, the national movement included a variety of different political actors, all of whom were briefly united under the banner of national rebirth and political restructuring. They supported cultural—and eventually political—change for reasons that often had less to do with national sentiment than with securing their own positions in the tumultuous politics of the Gorbachev era. The success of the national movement of the late 1980s rested less on the mobilizing power of true and timeless identity, and more on the political uses of cultural questions to key social groups in the republic. It was these groups that would form the basis of new political parties once the collapse of the Soviet system produced a fully independent Moldovan state.

THE MOLDOVAN NATIONAL MOVEMENT AND THE CULT OF LANGUAGE

Major political changes had taken place in many Soviet republics by mid-1988, as Mikhail Gorbachev's policies of economic restructuring and political openness began to transform the Soviet system. The MSSR under First Secretary Semion Grossu, however, remained a relative backwater. There were repeated reprimands from Moscow throughout the 1980s concerning political and economic corruption,

Moldovan schoolchildren in Chisinau rally to support the declaration of Moldovan as the state language of the republic, August 1989. Photo by Tudor Iovu.

but the first secretary was able to keep the forces of change at bay, primarily by blaming any expressions of discontent on "local nationalism" and ineffective officials. At a CPM plenum in January 1988, Grossu engaged in the requisite self-criticism. He admitted that he had "not yet been able to take in fully all the ramifications of restructuring," and gave the standard castigations to the republican party organs for their sloth in strengthening reform.[3] There was little indication, though, that Grossu himself was interested in dismantling the personal fiefdom that he and his predecessor, Ivan Bodiul, had constructed since the period of stagnation under Brezhnev.

Culture issues began to come to light in the run-up to the 19th CPSU conference in June 1988. The conference was the first since 1941 and a milestone in the effort to reform the Soviet state, where Gorbachev would announce such fundamental reforms as multicandidate elections, a retreat from the party's dominance in the economy, and greater sensitivity to the nationalities question. In the weeks leading up to the conference, Grossu noted that cultural issues—especially the "language problem"—were of some concern to the party. Too little provision had been made during the Brezhnev period for native-language education, and one of the goals of perestroika would be to extend the use of all national languages (including Russian) in schools. However, Grossu stressed that any linguistic problems in the republic were to be solved by encouraging greater "national-Russian bilingualism," that is, promoting the use of both Moldovan and Russian rather than preferring one language over the other. In practice, though, this meant the continued dominance of Russian. He repeated the same assessment at the CPSU conference, reporting that the party had devoted "special attention to the development of national-Russian bilingualism."[4] Any calls for greater vigilance in resolving nationalities issues were always countered by assurances from Grossu and others in the republican press that they had already been solved.

Questions of Moldovan identity and interethnic relations began to receive special attention in early 1988. In January the materials of the 20th Moldovan Komsomol Congress were published. The congress, held some ten months before, had at the time been treated as a major example of the strength of restructuring efforts in the republic since several top Komsomol officials had been dismissed for failure to carry out their duties. But with the publication of the full materials from the congress, the seriousness of ethnic problems within Moldova became clear. *Komsomol'skaia pravda*, reviewing the materials, reported that "[w]e must frankly admit that Moldova, in addition to representatives of the indigenous nationality, is inhabited by tens of thousands of Bulgarians, Gagauz, Germans, and Gypsies, and that they are a long way from living in a cohesive and friendly family." Moreover, the most serious issue addressed at the congress was the parlous state of Moldovan language education, while addresses on other pressing topics "generated no particular enthusiasm in the auditorium."[5]

The recognition of ethnic questions by the all-union press as a legitimate subject for discussion gave impetus to the Moldovan "informal organizations" that emerged in the summer of 1988: the Moldovan Movement in Support of Restructuring and the Alexei Mateevici Literary-Musical Club, named for the author of the well-known poem "Limba noastră" (Our language) and a pillar of the Bessarabian cultural renaissance of the early twentieth century. The "informals" included prominent writers, journalists, and educators who called on the local party to increase Moldovan-language educational possibilities and address previously forbidden questions of Bessarabian history. The movements were not political parties, since the CPSU still exercised the offi- cially mandated leading role in Soviet society, but they were the first indication of organized political opposition to First Secretary Grossu. Similar voluntary organizations emerged in all the union republics and were encouraged by the Gorbachev leadership as pillars of reform. The informals, in turn, looked to Gorbachev's policies of glasnost and peres- troika as levers against local conservatives. By appealing directly to Moscow and portraying themselves as the local vanguard of reform, the leaders of these movements hoped to circumvent the republican party leadership and engender a rebirth of national culture within the frame- work of political and economic restructuring.

Initially, the two major informals issued a range of political and economic demands, including the transformation of the Soviet Union into a federal union of genuinely sovereign states, moves toward a mar- ket economy and plural forms of property-holding, legal guarantees on human rights, and greater environmental protection.[6] As the year pro- gressed, though, it was one particular plank of both informals' platforms that began to receive the greatest attention: the three-pronged demand that the republican government recognize the identity between the Ro- manian and Moldovan languages, that Moldovan be declared the state language of the MSSR, and that the republic switch to the Latin alpha- bet. The Cyrillic alphabet, the informals held, had led to the butchering of Moldovan proper names since it poorly reflected the structure of the Moldovan language. As one author complained, "It is simply revolting that, in a republic with a relatively high level of development, a large part of Moldovan family names are at present so disfigured."[7] *Literatura și arta*, the organ of the Moldovan Writers' Union and a consistent sup- porter of the informals, reported the case of one Andrei Mîță, none of whose six children seemed to be siblings: On the children's birth certifi- cates, the hospital secretaries had recorded six different Cyrillic spellings of his surname.[8] Conservatives within the local party organization de- nounced the informals and their increasingly frequent public rallies as threats to public order fomented by "nationalists" and "kulaks." But the informals' obvious public support, with the unsanctioned gatherings in public parks and Chisinau's outdoor Summer Theater growing too large to ignore, pressure grew on Grossu's party for an official response.[9]

As the language demands received greater attention, the republican government agreed in July 1988 to form a special commission of inquiry under the auspices of the Moldovan Academy of Sciences and the MSSR

Supreme Soviet.[10] The "Interdepartmental Commission for the Study of the History and Problems of the Development of Moldovan" was divided into four sections, each charged with examining a range of separate issues related to the history, alphabet, and status of the Moldovan language. However, before the commission had prepared its final report, the CPM issued a set of draft guidelines for implementing perestroika in the MSSR, titled "Let Us Affirm Restructuring through Concrete Actions."[11] The guidelines contained important admissions of mistakes made from the 1960s to the 1980s, many of which had resulted in a dire housing shortage, pollution, religious intolerance, the general demoralization of the republic, and "blank spots" in Moldovan history. On the language issue, however, the position of the party leadership remained the same: First, any talk of the need for greater development of Moldovan was to be seen in the context of Leninist nationalities policy and the development of the other languages of the republic—that is, no single language should have a privileged official status. Second, further steps were to be taken to develop full national-Russian bilingualism since Russian was the natural language of interethnic communication within Moldova and between Soviet republics. Third, the Cyrillic alphabet had served the Moldovan people for ages and corresponded exactly to the phonetic structure of Moldovan; not only would a transition to the Latin script negatively affect the cultural development of the nation and render the republic's population illiterate, but the cost of changing typographic equipment would be prohibitively expensive.

Finally, the guidelines addressed the issue of the relationship between Moldovans and Romanians:

> There is no doubt that Moldovan and Romanian are languages of the same Romance group. Between them, in fact, there does not exist a great deal of difference. But the recognition of their commonality, the identity [of Moldovan] with other languages from the same Romance group, cannot serve as a real reason for renouncing one in favor of the other.[12]

Romanian and Moldovan were, it seemed, somehow both identical and distinct. Such an admission, however convoluted, was crucial. For the first time, the party officially, though still only implicitly, recognized the unity of the two languages and, by extension, of the two peoples.

The party guidelines sparked a wave of protests in Chisinau organized by the informals, with participants denouncing the continued fiction of two separate languages. Demonstrators picketed party offices, numerous petitions were addressed to the interdepartmental group in support of its work, thousands of letters with tens of thousands of signatures arrived at the offices of local newspapers, and Chisinau students staged walkout strikes. First Secretary Grossu was forced to retreat a month after the guidelines were published. He stressed that they were merely a framework for discussion and not a policy statement.[13] By late December he had even conceded to the gradual transition to the Latin script.[14]

The first secretary seemed to have anticipated the outcome of the interdepartmental group's study. At the end of December 1988, the group published its report recommending acceptance of the three demands of the informals, arguing that at the very least the transition to the Latin alphabet would supposedly have the economic advantage of enabling printers to type 10 percent more characters per page.[15] Although he accepted the demand for the change of alphabet, Grossu remained firm on the uniqueness of the Moldovan people and their language and the need for balancing the use of both Moldovan and Russian. Even in his own home, he said, Russian and Moldovan were spoken with absolutely equal frequency.[16]

With time, the party's line on the language issue became increasingly untenable and contributed to the discrediting of the leadership. In accepting one of the three demands, Grossu put himself in an almost impossible position vis-à-vis the other two. Maintaining the claim of Moldovan-Romanian separateness had already become more difficult after the project of representing the actual linguistic practices of the peasants had been dropped in the late 1930s; once Moldovan was written in Latin characters, though, the two literary languages became impossible to distinguish. As Grossu attempted to defend his position against the growing opposition, his arguments became more and more bizarre, focusing on arcane points of pronunciation in a style reminiscent of the protracted debates over spelling and grammar in the 1920s and 1930s. Even if Moldova switched to the Latin script, he argued, it would have to be different from the one in Romania, since Moldovans and Romanians spoke differently.[17] Other party officials were equally Byzantine. In response to an interviewer's question about the Romanian flag, which had begun to appear at rallies sponsored by the informal organizations, one Communist official was adamant that the blue-yellow-red tricolor could never become the flag of the Moldovan republic since it was already used by another state—Chad.[18]

The party's position was further weakened by the performance of the Moldovan informals in the March 1989 elections for the Soviet Union's Congress of People's Deputies, the new super-parliament central to Gorbachev's effort to make the political system more democratic and responsive to voters. The informal groups could not openly support candidates and had to confine their nominally "independent" candidates to one-third of the electoral districts. Nevertheless, active members of the Moldovan Movement and the Mateevici Club defeated members of the CPM Politburo, the chair of the republican KGB, and several *raion* secretaries.[19] A total of ten seats went to members and supporters of the informals and thrust intellectuals and activists such as Nicolae Dabija (editor of *Literatura şi arta*), Ion Druţă (Moldova's most prominent writer), and Grigore Vieru (the republic's premier poet) into the political spotlight. In winning ten of the sixteen races in which they were allowed to stand, supporters of the informals proved that they had become a formidable threat to CPM hegemony. The victories also provided the groups with a union-wide platform from which to issue calls for fundamental change. It was these deputies, in fact, who along with their colleagues from the Baltic republics would lead the Congress toward officially condemning the Molotov-Ribbentrop Pact in December 1989, thus raising serious questions about the legality of the four republics' place inside the Soviet federation.

With the interdepartmental commission's pro-Romanian position on the language question and the progressive discrediting of the party leadership, the locus of power within Moldova shifted away from the party and toward the Supreme Soviet. In late January 1989, the Supreme Soviet instructed several of its permanent committees and a panel of experts to draft laws on the status of the Moldovan and Russian languages and the transition to the Latin alphabet.[20] The publication in the summer of the draft laws "On the Status of the State Language of the MSSR," "On the Transition of the Moldovan Language to the Latin Script," and "On the Functioning of the Languages Spoken on the Territory of the MSSR" marked a new stage in the debate over identity and culture. Thousands more letters flooded the editorial offices of several dailies and weeklies in response to an official government request for public views on the language issue. By the end of August, some 250,000 persons had written to the party daily *Moldova socialistă* expressing their support for the draft laws, which envisaged a transition to the Latin script and official-language status for Moldovan.[21]

These public debates were crucial. The language laws were the first piece of genuine legislation debated in the newly empowered Supreme Soviet. It was through the discussions about the most arcane aspects of language reform that the assembly began to assert its role as a deliberative legislative body, rather than as a rubber stamp for local Politburo decisions. Moreover, the language issue was the first instance of Moldovan politicians' acting politically—that is, taking firm and public positions on questions of republic-wide importance, attempting to communicate those positions to the public at large, and treating the republic's inhabitants as real constituents whose opinions on proposed legislation actually mattered in the political process. The open solicitation of public views on the language question in 1988 and 1989 by the Supreme Soviet's interdepartmental commission and the "war of letters" that it spawned in the republican press were Moldova's first experiments in democracy and marked the beginning of the transition to a more transparent and responsive form of politics.

The draft laws also had a deleterious effect on interethnic relations, however. Once the plans for major cultural changes in Moldova had been made public, tensions rose between the ethnic majority and minority populations, particularly Slavs and Gagauz who felt threatened by the prospect of the removal of Russian as the de facto official language. The language debate quickly took on an ethnic coloring as Moldovans, Slavs, and Gagauz created their own unified fronts in the mid- and late summer of 1989. Members of the Moldovan movement and the Mateevici Club, along with various smaller informals, formed the Popular Front of Moldova in May 1989. Some 200 delegates (including even some representatives from the republic's Russian, Bulgarian, and Gagauz populations) met at the Popular Front's founding meeting in Chisinau. The new organization issued a program and selected a nine-member executive committee, one of whose members was the writer and newly elected Soviet Congress deputy Ion Hadârcă. The Front's twenty-point program, which represented the most ardent call to date for political restructuring, sovereignty, and environmental cleanup in Moldova, still stressed the identity question and reiterated the demand that Moldovan be made the state language of the MSSR.[22]

Although some members of the Gagauz population had begun already in April to call for greater regional autonomy in the southern part of the republic, a representative from the Gagauz organization Gagauz Halkı (Gagauz People) was present at the founding congress of the Popular Front. At this stage, Gagauz Halkı was still in its infancy, having been formed in early May 1989, and the aims of the organization were still unclear. The movement had grown out of a Gagauz cultural club in the southern city of Comrat and had already convinced the major republican newspaper to carry a special Gagauz-language insert for the 153,000 Gagauz living in the MSSR.[23] Few overtly political goals, though, had yet been formally articulated.

A much more militant group in the summer of 1989 was the Slavic-dominated organization Edinstvo, a branch of the all-union Interfront movement that united minority populations and other opponents of cultural reforms initiated in the Baltic republics and elsewhere. Headed by Petr Shornikov and Vasilii Iakovlev, the group held its first local meeting in Chisinau in July 1989.[24] Edinstvo received strong support from well-known figures such as Marshal Sergei Akhromeev, a Soviet Congress deputy from the northern city of Bălți, and members pressed for equal linguistic status for both Russian and Moldovan.

As the summer progressed, leaders of the Gagauz and Russian-speaking minorities called for both Russian and Moldovan to be made equal state languages, rather than relegating Russian to the secondary position of "language of interethnic communication." To highlight these demands, workers initiated strikes at enterprises in cities with large Russian and Russian-speaking populations such as Tiraspol, Bender, and Rîbnița, and the Gagauz made plans to declare their own autonomous republic in the south. The strikes continued in the run-up to a Supreme Soviet session in late August. Scheduled for only two days, the session lasted for four, as delegates debated the language issue and the transition to the Latin alphabet. Outside the Supreme Soviet building in Chisinau, the Popular Front called a "Grand National Assembly" (*Marea Adunare Națională*), a mass rally meant to represent the mystical will of the Moldovan people and a label that harked back to similar gatherings by Romanians in the Habsburg empire. The assembly, attended by a reported 500,000 persons carrying Romanian flags and placards in the Latin script, featured speeches by leading intellectuals and public figures, as well as harsh denunciations of the Molotov-Ribbentrop Pact, the Soviet annexation of Bessarabia, and the decline of Moldovan culture over the past five decades. [25]

Opened with a blessing in Romanian by Father Petru Buburuz

(another Soviet Congress deputy), the assembly was addressed in turn by various prominent intellectuals, Congress deputies, Supreme Soviet chairman Mircea Snegur, and a representative of the Lithuanian independence movement.[26] The assembly was also the first major event at which linguistic reform was seen as just one of a number of equally important demands. The honorary president of the assembly, Ion Hadârcă, pressed for full sovereignty for the republic, and the president of the Mateevici Club called for the withdrawal of Soviet troops (the "army of occupation") from Moldovan territory.[27] As with similar rallies in the Baltic republics, speakers frequently referred to the illegal annexation of territory in 1940 and called on Soviet authorities to recognize the existence of the secret protocols to the 1939 Nazi-Soviet treaty.

All these views were expressed in the final document adopted by the assembly, "On State Sovereignty and Our Right to the Future."[28] The manifesto outlined the history of the Prut-Dnestr region, the carving up of historic Moldova by the Russian empire, the 1918 unification with Romania, and the Soviet seizure of Bessarabia from Romania. The document called for full national sovereignty, including local control of all resources and veto power over union laws that contravened the laws of the republic, as well as for republican control over relations with foreign powers, a law on citizenship, and the right of secession from the Soviet Union. The language issue—upon which the assembly had ostensibly been called to vote—had slipped to the middle of the list of demands.

Simultaneously, rallies were held by Edinstvo supporters in Chisinau and Tiraspol, and more than a hundred enterprises and work collectives, mainly in the Transnistria region, remained on strike to protest the draft laws then being debated by the Supreme Soviet.[29] Several members of the Supreme Soviet accused both the Popular Front and Edinstvo of pressure tactics during the session, but the parliament nevertheless adopted the final drafts of the language laws on August 31. Moldovan alone was granted the status of state language, "used in political, economic, social, and cultural life" and functioning "on the basis of the Latin script."[30] A special clause guaranteed the protection and development of the Gagauz language since the greatest proportion of Gagauz in the Soviet Union lived on the territory of the MSSR. Another clause guaranteed the conditions necessary for the development of Russian as the language of communication between Soviet republics and as the language of interethnic communication within the MSSR. Further provisions set out a plan for implementing the new legislation, including special classes for non-Moldovan speakers, and required language tests for state employees. Although no special legislation was adopted on the relationship between the Romanian and Moldovan languages, the preamble to one law mentioned in passing that it took into consideration the "really existing Moldo-Romanian linguistic identity" (*identitatea lingvistică moldo-română realmente existentă*).[31] The laws thus retained the designation "Moldovan" as the name of the republic's official language while implicitly recognizing that it was the same as Romanian.

SOCIAL GROUPS AND THE POLITICS OF LANGUAGE

Moldova's path out of the Soviet Union began with public discussion of the most esoteric questions of grammar and alphabet, subjects that major political figures as well as average Moldovans spent a great deal of time debating. More than in any other Soviet republic at the time, language was central to the national movement. But this issue came to the fore because of a unique convergence of political and social interests within the MSSR. Three major groups were able to find important political capital in the language question and to use it for their own ends. What might have looked to observers like a vast movement of national reawakening was in fact a political coalition of vested interests, one that for a time united distinct social groups but that proved to be remarkably fragile once their disparate goals were revealed after 1989.

The Generational Dimension: Moldovan Intellectuals

The leaders of the national movement on the ground were Moldovan cultural elites, the new generation of academics discussed in chapter 5. For these younger scholars, pressing for the transition to the Latin alphabet, official status for Moldovan, and recognition of Moldovan-Romanian unity represented the logical culmination of their efforts over the past decade or more. Beyond their own academic pursuits, the language question represented a useful weapon against older academics who still clung to power in the Academy of Sciences. Important changes in the leadership of the Writers' Union had been instituted in the mid-1980s, when younger writers assumed control of the union's main newspaper, *Literatura şi arta*, and other important cultural publications.[32]

Leadership changes were mirrored in other institutions, as older academics began to give way to their younger colleagues, usually because of retirement or failing health.[33] The result was the rise of cultural entrepreneurs who saw the language issue as a way of furthering their own careers while at the same time promoting a return to the "linguistic truth" that many had subtly encouraged since the 1960s.

Disputes between younger and older intellectuals were played out in the Moldovan press, with older conservatives publishing articles against the language reforms in the Russian-language daily *Sovetskaia Moldaviia* and various Transnistrian newspapers, and younger academics responding in the Moldovan-language *Moldova socialistă*, *Literatura şi arta*, and *Învăţămîntul public*.[34] Academics, schoolteachers, artists, and others staked out their positions on identity and language in letters to these publications. The Association of Historians, an informal organization founded in mid-July 1989 and allied with the Popular Front, made the conflict within the intellectual community explicit in an appeal launched at its first congress:

> Rooting out these evils [of historiographical distortion] demands the liquidation of a clan of functionaries in science and in the sphere of official ideology who have arrogated to themselves the right to formulate scientific tasks, to give opinions, to interpret historical events, and to pronounce verdicts that exclude the right of appeal. This highly influential group has long been a parasite [on the academic community].[35]

In the villages, the efforts of these Chisinau-based intellectuals were buttressed by the support of local Moldovan schoolteachers, whose numbers had expanded as a result of a special party resolution in May 1987 mandating increased provision for Moldovan-language education. Between academic years 1985–86 and 1989–90, the number of teachers of non-Russian language and literature, almost exclusively Moldovan, increased from roughly 3,400 to 4,200,[36] enhancing the potential grassroots support for cultural change in the countryside.

Cultural leaders such as these were intimately involved with the work of the interdepartmental commission established by the Moldovan parliament in mid-1988 to examine the history of the Moldovan language. One of the first public calls for the adoption of the Latin alphabet and the end of Moldovan linguistic uniqueness came in an open letter addressed to the commission by the republic's leading intellectuals.[37]

The commission was headed by two party stalwarts, Alexandru Mocanu, president of the presidium of the Supreme Soviet, and Nicolae Bondarciuc, the CPM Central Committee secretary in charge of ideology, but it also included prominent academics, writers, and journalists. Reform-minded members of the commission quickly found ways to work around their more conservative chairmen. For example, commission member Silviu Berejan, the newly appointed director of the Institute of Language and Literature, invited various "associate members" to join the commission, mainly reformist linguists who were encouraged to attend the meetings in order to put pressure on those reluctant to agree to the language reforms.[38] With younger leaders in the Writers' Union and academic institutes, as well as a growing population of sympathetic schoolteachers in the villages, the cards were stacked against the cultural conservatives.

Moldovan writers and academics, combining their forces in the work of the informals and the Popular Front, increasingly saw themselves as part of a movement for reform extending beyond the borders of Moldova and even outside the Soviet Union. A representative from Poland's Solidarity movement spoke at a Front meeting in August 1989 and proclaimed that "Solidarity and the Popular Front have the same goals."[39] Movements for cultural reform in other Soviet republics were also seen as models for similar efforts in Moldova. As a single issue, the language question received more attention in Moldova than in any other union republic, but similar linguistic demands voiced in the Baltics and elsewhere played a significant role in focusing republican attention on the status of Moldovan.

By mid-1989, as the debate on the upcoming Supreme Soviet session reached fever pitch, language laws had already been adopted in all the Baltic republics and Tajikistan, and a draft law had been published for discussion in Uzbekistan. These laws were usually reported in the Moldovan press without commentary, but the influence of the proponents of linguistic reform from these republics on their Moldovan counterparts was immense. The party ideology secretary, Bondarciuc, warned as early as June 1988 that certain elements within the Moldovan Writers' Union were under the influence of Estonian nationalists.[40] Less than a year later, *Glasul* (The voice), the first Moldovan publication to appear in the Latin script since the 1940s, was printed in Latvia under the aegis of the Moldovan and Latvian writers' unions.[41] Representatives from the Baltic popular fronts were often present at Popular Front rallies in

Chisinau, and a representative from Latvia gave perhaps the most memorable speech at the Grand National Assembly in 1989, beginning his
address with an apology for speaking in Russian, the "language of the
occupiers," and prompting a legal case against him for his incendiary
remarks.[42] The influence of the Baltic movements in Moldova was clear
by the time of the Supreme Soviet session in late August 1989. The Chisinau correspondent for *Krasnaia zvezda* even began one of his reports by
musing whether Moldova was following "the Baltic scenario."[43]

The Regional Dimension: Bessarabians and Transnistrians

Beyond the new generation of Moldovan intellectuals, another important group supporting culture reform included Moldovans with family and professional ties to the Bessarabia region. Traditionally, positions
in the party and state hierarchy had been filled by persons with links to
Transnistria—the Camenca, Rîbniţa, Dubăsari, Tiraspol, Grigoriopol,
and Slobozia *raions* that had formed part of the MASSR before 1940.
Persons from this region were seen as more politically trustworthy than
their counterparts from former "bourgeois" Bessarabia, and even members of the underground Bessarabian section of the Romanian Communist Party were viewed as politically suspect and denied membership in
the CPSU after the region was joined with the Soviet Union.[44] Moreover,
few Bessarabians had the practical experience or administrative skills of
their Transnistrian colleagues. Since the MASSR had been the "atom"
of socialist construction in Moldova, as propagandists in the interwar
period often stressed, it was reasonable to assume that Transnistrians
would take a leading role in socialist construction in postwar Moldova
as well. Until November 1989, the first secretary of the CPM had never
been from Bessarabia. Even within cultural institutions, persons from
the east-bank region controlled the top posts until well into the 1980s.
The relationship between Russians and non-Russians in the elite was at
least as significant as in any other Soviet republic, but there was also an
important axis of regional rivalry even among Moldovans themselves.

By the perestroika period, however, the traditional relationship between Bessarabians and Transnistrians had begun to change. A younger
generation of Bessarabians, trained at Chisinau State University or the
Chisinau Agricultural Institute and with further education in Moscow,
Kyiv, or other Soviet centers, had begun to rise up through the party and
state administration. Born in the 1940s, this new generation of Moldo-

van officials came of age in the 1980s, putting increased pressure on the older generation for a greater say in the affairs of the republic. They had come to power largely as a result of the preferential promotion of local Moldovans after the 1960s, when the CPM attempted to indigenize the party hierarchy. By 1989, Moldovans were in fact overrepresented in the party leadership relative to their proportion of the entire population.[45]

The careers of Mircea Snegur, Andrei Sangheli, and Nicolae Ţâu are representative of this new cohort. Snegur, born in Floreşti *raion* (northern Bessarabia) in 1940, graduated from the Chisinau Agricultural Institute in 1961 and began his career as an agronomist on a collective farm in his home *raion*. After taking an advanced degree in plant science, he moved on to a post in the MSSR ministry of agriculture, where he oversaw a number of departments and experimental horticulture projects. In 1981 Snegur moved into party work, serving first as chair of the *raion* party committee in Edineţ *raion* (northern Bessarabia) and then, from 1985, as Central Committee secretary with responsibility for agriculture. Andrei Sangheli was born in 1944 in Edineţ *raion*, graduated from the Chisinau Agricultural Institute, and worked as an agronomist on a collective farm in Donduşeni *raion* (northern Bessarabia). In 1986 Sangheli rose to the post of first deputy chair of the MSSR council of ministers and chair of the state agro-industrial committee. Nicolae Ţâu was born in 1948 in Cahul *raion* (southern Bessarabia) and, like Snegur, graduated from the Chisinau Agricultural Institute. Throughout the 1970s, he worked as an engineer, a collective farm president, and party secretary in Cahul and Ungheni *raions* (central Bessarabia). In 1986 he was elevated to the premier local party post, first secretary of the Chisinau city party committee. Snegur would later become the first president of independent Moldova, Sangheli would be appointed prime minister, and Ţâu would serve as foreign minister and as ambassador to the United States.

The social profile of this new elite was substantially different from that of the old. These new leaders had worked as *raion* officials or collective farm heads or in other positions that necessitated some interaction with the large Moldovan countryside. Many were themselves rural Moldovans who had come to Chisinau and other urban centers to take advantage of the expansion of educational opportunities in the late 1950s and 1960s. Most spoke Moldovan, since being at least conversant in the language was necessary for working with the Moldovan peasants. The older generation, by contrast, had been born in Transnistria or other areas outside Bessarabia and had been trained in the latter years of the MASSR or during the war. Few were as skilled in the Moldovan language as their Bessarabian colleagues. Their roots were not with the countryside, but rather with urban areas and with the Russian and Ukrainian settler communities that had grown up around the expanding industrial centers after the war.

For Snegur and his colleagues, the language issue proved to be a powerful weapon against older party and state elites. In the first place, increasing the use of national languages had been sanctioned at the all-union level as early as September 1987 in an editorial in the CPSU theoretical journal *Kommunist*, and endorsement of language reform at the republican level could be cast as support for Gorbachev's restructuring efforts.[46] In addition, the mounting criticism of First Secretary Grossu by central party organs underscored the need for change. Given Moldova's special position as a potential object of foreign irredentism, Soviet leaders had normally valued stability over efficiency in the Moldovan political system, fearing that any unrest would provide the occasion for the Romanians' raising uncomfortable questions about 1940. Semion Grossu, in office since December 1980, had been the last republican first secretary to be appointed under Brezhnev and would be the last to leave under Gorbachev. By the late 1980s, however, signs of Moscow's discontent with the local party leadership had become apparent. Grossu, accustomed to wide latitude in the running of his republic, did little in response. Throughout 1986 and 1987, he blamed any expressions of discontent on the machinations of local nationalists, slovenly bureaucrats, international conspirators, and Zionists.[47] In a February 1989 speech on republican television, Grossu attacked the informals and their unsanctioned rallies, but gave no indication that he recognized the legitimacy of their basic demands.[48]

On the language question, Grossu proved intransigent. As late as July 1989, one month before the Supreme Soviet session on the new language laws, he was still adamant about defending the separateness of Moldovan and Romanian, even after the proposed introduction of the Latin alphabet. Grossu's intervention in a Politburo meeting on July 27 was almost comical in its assertion of Romanian-Moldovan separateness:

> GROSSU: At the end of the day, the Ukrainians, Belarusians, and other nations could have pretensions of being identical with the Russians.

> That just doesn't wash. We are talking about the Romance origins, not the Romanian origins, of the Moldovan language. The Romanian language is also of Romance origin. What does the introduction of the Latin alphabet for Moldovan have to do with the Romanian language? Nothing at all! This is first of all from a scientific point of view. But it is also a political question. Why are we siding with the Romanians? We are talking about the Romance origins. But there are a lot of Romance countries and a lot of Romance alphabets.[49]

At the same Politburo meeting, various members then discussed the exact wording of the new language laws, particularly the issue of the legal basis for the transition to a new alphabet:

> GROSSU: Strike the phrase "on the proposal of the citizens." It doesn't sound very strong. Maybe "at the request of" or "on the demand of the workers" or "of the Moldovan people," or . . . That sounds good, it's strong.
>
> [UNIDENTIFIED]: That's not right either. We don't have the right to write "Moldovan people." Ukrainians, Russians, all inhabitants are also part of the Moldovan people.
>
> GROSSU: I understand. Well then, "Moldovan nation" or something . . .
>
> [UNIDENTIFIED]: Maybe "Moldovan nationality," but we don't want to single them out.
>
> GROSSU: "The workers of Moldovan nationality"—that's what we can say.
>
> [UNIDENTIFIED]: We really need to get away from that [about the workers].
>
> GROSSU: I agree. I also say that it is a question of how it sounds. If it were "citizen"—then that doesn't sound good at all.[50]

Compared to the bizarre verbal contortions of the first secretary, virtually any member of the younger party elite could easily portray himself as a rational defender of local interests and a champion of Moldovan cultural renaissance. Moreover, since many spoke Moldovan and had come up through the republic's large agricultural sector and local administration, their links with the Moldovan masses were inherently stronger than those of Grossu's cohort.

Snegur and others understood the necessity of co-opting the informal organizations rather than continuing to battle against them. In spring 1989, when the Moldovan informals united into the Popular Front, the new Moldovan political elite responded positively to their demands. Snegur spoke at a Popular Front rally a day after his election to the post of Supreme Soviet chair and was considered to be a major advocate of the informals' demands in top political circles.[51] Just as the language issue provided a useful conduit through which the new cultural elites could challenge the hegemony of their predecessors, Moldovan politicians likewise found it a lever against the older, predominantly Transnistrian leadership.

The Ethnic Dimension: Moldovans and Minorities

A final group of interests encompassed by the language issue concerned the Moldovan ethnic majority, particularly the large communities of first-generation urban-dwellers, and their relationship to the republic's minority populations. Leaders of the informal movements were at first careful to portray their goals as broad and inclusive rather than ethnically exclusivist; not only did they aim at supporting the reform program initiated by Moscow, but they also intended to mobilize all MSSR citizens, regardless of ethnicity, under the banner of openness, restructuring, and democratization. At the Popular Front's founding congress on May 20, 1989, representatives from many of the republic's ethnic groups were in attendance, including a representative from the Gagauz informal Gagauz Halkı which would later form the nucleus of a separatist movement in the southern *raions*.[52] The Front's name even reflected the attempt at interethnic coalition-building, since it was christened the Popular Front of Moldova (*Frontul Popular din Moldova*) rather than the ethnically suggestive Moldovan Popular Front (*Frontul Popular Moldovenesc*).

Even at the time of the Front's creation, however, the ethnic component of the language question was already evident. Ion Druță, the republic's best-known writer and a figure often at odds with Soviet officialdom, noted the importance of language reform for Moldovans in an article published in the party daily: "The request to declare Moldovan the state language and switch to the Latin alphabet is nothing other than the expression of the conditions necessary for existence. . . . Decreeing Moldovan the state language is not a goal in itself, but rather the search for . . . the reestablishment of our national ethnicity."[53] For Druță and other prominent commentators, the rebirth of the Moldovan people would necessarily come at the expense of those who had long oppressed them. As Druță noted in parable style in mid-1989:

The pure wheat is he who lives by his own labor. The chaff are those who devour the goods without paying for them with their own sweat. . . . The wheat is the sanctity of man before the land on which he lives, his care to leave it for his children in all its fullness and beauty. But the chaff is he who believes that the history of a region begins with the moment when he settles in it, and ends with his departure. . . .

The tragedy of the situation is that, unfortunately, we have too little wheat and too much chaff. . . . [U]p to now we have often found ourselves with the chaff at the head of the table, dictating when and how and where the wheat that remains will be cultivated, when it will be harvested, where it will be processed, what sort of bread will be made, and at what time it will be served.[54]

To any reader, it was clear who was the wheat and who the chaff. Nicolae Dabija, the editor of *Literatura şi arta*, was still more explicit: "Today the party and state leadership must decide: with the people or against the people. With the Moldovans or against them. . . . Many so-called 'internationalists' do not like the fact that our people has awakened. . . . For them, our people was good so long as it was hardworking and patient. If the Guinness Book of World Records had a category for 'The Most Somnolent People in the World,' ours would be in first place."[55]

Given the demographic changes in the republic since the Second World War, such views undoubtedly played well among Moldovans in the cities. While the number of Moldovans in the cities had grown since the 1970s, few members of the majority nationality had made it into the ranks of top-level managers in urban jobs. By January 1989, Moldova was in penultimate place (just ahead of Kazakhstan) in the percentage of management posts held by republican nationalities, with less than half of all posts in industry, transport, communications, and construction held by Moldovans.[56] In fact, the genuine strength of the national movement lay in urban centers, where Moldovans recently arrived from the villages were well aware of the advantages of official status for their ancestral language. In terms of their rhetoric, leaders of the Popular Front looked to the countryside as the locus of those qualities of hard work, respect for tradition, and self-sufficiency that would pull the republic out of the economic and social malaise into which it had sunk under first secretaries Bodiul and Grossu. However, it was in the cities—with first-generation, Moldovan urbanites competing with ethnic Russians and Ukrainians—where the message of language reform had its greatest impact. The eventual adoption of the new language laws in August 1989 was largely a result of the conjuncture of interests between younger Moldovan academics and their counterparts in the political elite, but the existence of a Moldovan constituency in the cities, persons for whom language reform represented a path toward increased social mobility, was important in galvanizing support for the new laws among the population at large. Responsibility for the final form and adoption of the laws lay within the interdepartmental commission and the Supreme Soviet, but the pressure exerted by mass demonstrations was of critical importance.

For all the efforts at portraying the national movement as a response by all Moldova's ethnic groups to the problems engendered by decades of Soviet rule, the purely ethnic implications of the movement for language reform were inescapable. By mid-1989 Russian-speaking elites in Transnistria had defected from the movement, focusing their attention on the language demands as a symbol of Moldovans' ethnic chauvinism and demanding a return to the respect for "internationalism" being urged by the CPSU leadership in Moscow. Although leaders of the Edinstvo organization agreed that Moldovan should be declared the state language, they urged that the position of Russian be secured by declaring it a second state language.[57] When the party newspaper of a Tiraspol factory prematurely published preliminary drafts of the new language laws in early August 1989—illustrating to the Russian-speaking population that the Supreme Soviet did not intend to declare Russian a second official language—local party cadres and factory bosses in Transnistria initiated a wave of strikes aimed against the language movement.[58] By early August, Moldova's ad hoc multiethnic opposition, which had allowed the Popular Front to emerge as a unified force from a plethora of informal organizations in May, was completely defunct. In the wake of the new language legislation, relations among Moldova's various ethnic communities deteriorated to the point that erstwhile allies were engaged in full-scale warfare by spring 1992.

RETHINKING THE NATIONAL MOVEMENT

Depending on whom one speaks with in post-Soviet Moldova, the national movement of the late 1980s is characterized as the rediscovery of the Moldovans' "true" Romanian identity after decades of official Soviet obfuscation, the assertion of Moldovan local sovereignty over imperial interests, or the defeat of Soviet "internationalism" by narrow ethnic chauvinism. As in all ethnic disputes, however, ethnicity is only part of the picture. The street demonstrations, Romanian flags, and nationalist slogans notwithstanding, the events of the late perestroika period involved three distinct social groups for whom questions of identity and language served a unique and, as it turned out, short-lived purpose.

Younger Moldovan elites from Bessarabia—exemplified by persons such as Mircea Snegur—found in the language issue a useful lever against the older, russified, and traditionally Transnistrian leadership. Long-term trends in Moldovan academic life and the republic's demographic landscape also heightened the effectiveness of the language issue as an instrument of elite politics. Without the progressive romanization of the language itself, the switch to the Latin alphabet would have been a much more radical and potentially unworkable proposal. The fact that the objective linguistic distance between standard Romanian and standard Moldovan had narrowed substantially since the late 1930s made these tasks considerably less difficult. Had it not been for the rise of pro-Romanian academics who had long argued in veiled terms for the revival of local Moldovan (read: Romanian) national culture, the movement for reform would likely have displayed something other than a national complexion. Further, the progressive moldovanization of the MSSR's urban centers, particularly Chisinau, provided a ready audience. Lauding the peasant as the embodiment of the Moldovan/Romanian national ideal, the informals and the Popular Front were able to cultivate relations with young urban Moldovans, themselves recently arrived from the villages, who saw in the national movement a chance to augment their positions in the Russian-dominated political, economic, and cultural elite. The prospect of raising the official status of Moldovan, thus privileging the linguistic skills that urban Moldovans had retained during their migration from the villages, held the promise of a competitive advantage over urban Russians and other ethnic groups. The power of the language question lay in its serving to obscure the boundaries between these various interest groups and to unite them behind the movement for cultural reform.

For all their achievements in 1988 and 1989, the early Moldovan informals and the Popular Front made one great strategic error. As the national movement gained momentum, with more and more radical demands being put forward after the adoption of the new language laws, the leaders of the Front increasingly misread the reasons for their success. They saw the great wave of public demonstrations in 1988 and 1989 as evidence of a national, pan-Romanian awakening, a view that was perpetuated and encouraged by the overthrow of the Ceauşescu regime in Bucharest in December 1989. Once the Front leaders began to stress only the exclusionary aspects of the movement for political reform—by seeing the language question as the first step in a mass movement for the integration of the Romanian nation and the rejection of the Russian yoke—the multiethnic coalition in support of restructuring was inevitably the first casualty.

Although culture served as an important mobilizational resource for a short time, it proved unable to unite the republic's various interest groups once other issues had been articulated. Already in mid-1989, the Transnistrians and Gagauz had defected from the once-unified movement for reform, the former incensed at the rise of Bessarabian elites as the patrons of the Popular Front and the latter convinced that the new language laws would lead to their forced assimilation to Romanian culture. Other fault lines began to appear among Moldovans themselves, as the most radical members of the Popular Front pushed for the destruction of the Soviet empire and pan-Romanian union, while more moderate groups seemed satisfied with local control over cultural and economic resources within a refashioned Soviet federation. The very issue that was able to bring together these disparate groups for a brief period in the twilight of Soviet socialism—Moldovan identity—became one of the primary areas of contestation among them in independent Moldova.

INDEPENDENCE AND CONFLICT

PART THREE

7 Politics, Identity, and Reform after the Soviet Union

In the late 1980s the language question initially represented an issue on which intellectuals and certain members of the political elite could agree. Eager to assert their power against the Soviet center, as well as against the local party leadership, Moldovan political figures from Bessarabia formed a united front with the younger generation of intellectuals. Their mutual interests were clear. Writers, artists, and historians hoped to engender a rebirth of Moldovan (that is, Romanian) national culture, a goal toward which many had been working covertly since the 1960s. Local politicians looked to the national movement as a way of extracting greater concessions from the center and of ousting the Brezhnev-era leadership of the Communist Party.

Through the 1990s, Moldova's political geography became considerably more complex. In the first post-Soviet parliamentary elections, held in February 1994, thirteen independent parties and electoral blocs competed for seats in the new assembly. The groups' political programs varied widely. On one end of the spectrum, radical pan-Romanians saw unification with Romania as the only salvation for a country plagued by economic crisis and territorial separatism. At the other end, an ultraconservative coalition based its campaign on a rejection of the national movement and called for the return of the Soviet Union. Other groups rejected the extremism of both camps and supported the maintenance of an independent Moldovan state participating in some, but not all, of the structures of the Commonwealth of Independent States (CIS). Still others urged voters to ignore the divisive rhetoric of nationalism—in either its pro-Romanian or pro-Russian forms—and to cast their ballots for candidates favoring quick privatization and agrarian reform.[1]

Presidential and parliamentary elections throughout the 1990s repeated this basic division among pro-Romanian, centrist, and pro-Russian or pro-Soviet camps. Party names changed rapidly, as politics became more a matter of allegiance to particular political figures than adherence to a clear ideology. The closest thing to an ideological dividing line, in fact, was the perennial identity question. The vehemence of cultural politics decreased considerably in the late 1990s, with the challenges of economic reform and the generally cool reception from Romania dampening the enthusiasm that many pan-Romanians had felt in the heady days of the national movement. More importantly, the vast constituency that the nationalists believed they had behind them seemed to disappear once Moldovans went to the ballot box. But the sharp divisions between pan-Romanians and their detractors remained the most important cleavage among independent Moldova's political elites.

FROM CULTURAL MOVEMENT TO INDEPENDENCE

The elections to the Congress of People's Deputies in March 1989 and to the MSSR Supreme Soviet in February–March 1990 sealed the fate of the Communist Party as an organized political force. Representatives of the Popular Front and the informals soundly defeated Communist candidates for seats in the new Congress and gave the organizations' most dedicated and articulate members an all-union platform. Likewise, although the Communist Party was the only party permitted in the 1990 Supreme Soviet elections, multiple independent candidates were allowed to stand in 373 of 380 electoral districts. Some 27 percent of all seats in the Supreme Soviet were taken by open supporters of the Front; along with moderate Communist Party deputies, mainly from rural districts, reformists commanded a majority of seats.[2] A pro-Soviet camp of mainly Russian-speaking deputies from urban centers, Transnistria, and the southern *raions* formed a small opposition, but when Gagauz and Transnistrian deputies walked out in protest over Romanian-oriented cultural reforms, Frontists and reform Communists gained complete control of the legislative body. For some, the road toward a repeat of the 1918 union seemed already prepared. The official newspaper of the Supreme Soviet was renamed *Sfatul Ţării* after the Bessarabian assembly of 1917–18, and deputies even toyed with the idea of renaming the parliament using the same name.[3]

From this period on, divisions within Moldovan society grew wider. Public opinion polls in 1990 indicated a clear ethnic division on the future of the republic. In one survey, 54.8 percent of Moldovans but only 8.8 percent of Russians and 8.4 percent of Ukrainians favored independence; on union with Romania, though, both Moldovans and minorities were in agreement: Only 3.9 percent of Moldovans and even fewer minorities voiced opinions in favor of unification.[4] The political fallout from the language laws and the emergence of a legislature controlled by the Front and the reformist-agrarian wing of the Communist Party marked the beginning of a new phase in Moldovan politics and the onset of violent conflict between Moldovans, the mainly Russian-speaking population in Transnistria, and the Gagauz in the south. In the eyes of the Transnistrian and Gagauz leadership, the republican government had taken up a position against the national minorities, counter to the "internationalist" message preached by Moscow and the Communist Party. The minorities thus found themselves at odds with the government itself, rather than just with individual nationalist political groups that had hitherto been the main supporters of cultural and political change.

The Transnistrians and Gagauz soon made moves to create their own governmental structures, eventually by declaring separate republics. The "Republic of Gagauzia," with its center in Comrat, was declared in five *raions* in southern Moldova in August 1990, while the "Dnestr Moldovan Republic" (DMR), with its capital in Tiraspol, was proclaimed in eastern Moldova in September 1990. Skirmishes between central government forces and armed irregulars supported by the separatists escalated over the coming months and culminated in full-scale fighting along the Dnestr River in the first half of 1992. Fault lines also began to develop between Mircea Snegur and the leadership of the Popular Front. An early supporter of the Front, Snegur soon found himself treading a tightrope between the republic's Transnistrian and Gagauz populations and the more radical, pan-Romanian elements of the Popular Front. What had in early 1989 appeared a rather unified organization, gathering members of the government, workers, peasants, and intellectuals under the broad banner of reform, rapidly disintegrated into various factions with competing goals and interests.

With the republican leadership more and more detached from central Communist Party control, Moldova was on the path toward a radically new relationship with the Soviet center. Despite repeated appeals by Mikhail Gorbachev for order and calm,[5] the Supreme Soviet renounced the leading role of the Communist Party in May 1990, enshrining multiparty democracy as the basis of political life, and declared state sovereignty on June 23, 1990, thus giving local legislation priority over all-union laws. In May 1991, the parliament voted to throw off the Soviet-era name, MSSR, and proclaim the "Republic of Moldova." In September 1990, the Supreme Soviet elected Snegur to the newly created post of republican president and adopted a version of the Romanian tricolor and ox-head seal of Ştefan cel Mare as the national flag, reforms that were immediately rejected by the Transnistrians and Gagauz.

Relations with Romania became one of the key issues on the Moldovan political agenda, a reorientation of politics that further frightened the republic's minorities and political leaders committed to the integrity of the Soviet state. Events in the disintegrating MSSR in 1989 and 1990 paralleled equally monumental changes across the border in Romania. Amid a popular uprising and machinations among party elites, the regime of Nicolae Ceauşescu fell in a violent revolution in December 1989, with Ceauşescu and his wife Elena executed on Christmas Day. The new National Salvation Front government, headed by the former party official Ion Iliescu, was eager to maintain strong ties to the Soviet Union but nevertheless sought to develop closer links with the newly assertive Moldovan republic. In talks in Bucharest less than a month after the revolution, Iliescu and Soviet foreign minister Eduard Shevardnadze reaffirmed the existing borders between Romania and the Soviet Union.[6] But shortly thereafter, the Moldovan party secretary Petru Lucinschi—who had succeeded Semion Grossu in late 1989—called for closer "mutually advantageous" ties between Romania and Moldova, a statement that would have been impossible just a few years earlier.[7] In late January 1990, seven transit points were opened up across the Prut River, and the 50-kilometer security zone that had previously flanked the river dissolved.[8] These renewed links were even more intriguing for their having been initiated by Iliescu, who as a local party secretary in Iaşi county in the 1970s was intimately involved in early contacts between Romanians and Moldovans.

This warming of relations allowed a kind of mutual rediscovery among Romanians and Moldovans, both among politicians and the public at large. Romanian newspapers began to publish poems and other works by Moldovan writers such as Grigore Vieru and Leonida Lari, individuals who had been central to the cultural movement of the late 1980s but whose work had long been prohibited in Romania.[9] In the early days of the Romanian Revolution, Moldova dispatched blood, food supplies, and other aid to Bucharest, while volunteers formed two military units to assist in the fight against the remnants of Ceauşescu's secret police.[10] On May 6, 1990, a massive demonstration—known as the "Bridge of Flowers" (*Podul de Flori*)—took place along the Prut, during which Moldovans and Romanians crossed what many described as a watery Berlin wall to see family members long separated by the international border.[11]

Not only did these renewed relations further radicalize the Transnistrians and the Gagauz, but they also widened rifts within the Moldovan political elite. After the euphoria of the Romanian Revolution and the national movement in Moldova, the Popular Front's leaders became increasingly militant about realizing political reunification. At a rally in March 1990, the Front adopted a resolution on the 1918 union, declaring it "natural and legitimate."[12] The young journalist Iurie Roşca, one of the Front's leaders, soon became the most outspoken proponent of union. "We want to unite with Romania," he told a Bucharest newspaper in March 1990, "but such a thing is not yet possible."[13] For Roşca and other pan-Romanians within the Front, national reawakening and pan-Romanian unification were the proper outcomes of the process of democratization. Once given the chance to express their will, the Moldovan people would inevitably opt for a return to the Romanian fold. Even those more moderate than Roşca placed relations with Romania at the top of the political agenda, for as the culture minister, Ion Ungureanu, argued at the time, Moldova was on the path to creating a "cultural confederation" with Bucharest that would prepare the way for closer political ties.[14]

Political figures in Bucharest encouraged the rhetoric of pan-Romanianism. During the Romanian national holiday celebrations in December 1990, Ion Iliescu—by this time Romania's president—denounced the "injustices committed against the Romanian people" in 1940 and expressed his conviction that "history will find a way to put things completely back on their normal track."[15] A few months later, the ruling

National Salvation Front held its national convention in Bucharest beneath a map that included the Moldovan republic as part of a resurrected Greater Romania.[16] The foreign minister, Adrian Năstase, began to speak publicly of an eventual "economic confederation" with Moldova and even unification "on the German model."[17] At the same time, though, Romania worked to shore up relations with the Soviet center, signing a treaty on good-neighborly relations and cooperation with Moscow in April 1991.

The militancy of the Popular Front and the apparent growth in irredentist sentiment in Romania caused other Moldovan political figures to become more public in their desire for the continued existence of a separate state. Snegur in particular became the chief spokesperson for the pro-Moldovan camp. Committed to local sovereignty, Snegur was reluctant to trade dependence on Moscow for a wholesale reorientation toward Romania. During a trip to Bucharest in February 1991, President Snegur addressed a joint session of the Romanian parliament and spoke favorably of "our sister country—Romania," but underscored the sovereignty of Moldova; in fact, his oblique reference to the historical borders of Moldova—including areas in Romania and Ukraine—pointed toward the birth of a "Greater Moldovan" nationalism to counter the calls for Greater Romania coming from Bucharest.[18] By the spring of 1991, Snegur and most of the Moldovan political elite had settled on a "two states" doctrine: obtaining complete sovereignty, and perhaps eventually independence, for the Moldovan republic while maintaining strong cultural ties with Bucharest.[19]

As in 1918, though, events outside Moldova ultimately determined the region's fate. The Moldovan leadership had already in spring 1991 signaled its desire to break with the Soviet Union. Snegur decreed that the republic would not participate in Gorbachev's March referendum on the future of the federation, and the removal of the labels "Soviet" and "Socialist" from the republic's name in May further placed Chisinau at odds with the center.[20] In early August, Moldova had already decided not to sign the new treaty on union; the August coup provided the final impetus for breaking with Moscow.[21] The reaction in Chisinau was swift. After some dithering among local party organs, the president and parliament issued statements condemning the putsch and calling on citizens to resist the return to authoritarianism.[22] On August 27, 1991, the Moldovan parliament declared the full independence of the Republic of Moldova, but the text of the declaration reflected the competing views of Moldovan independence within the assembly. The preamble spoke of the "dismemberment" of the Moldovan principality by Austria and Russia in 1775 and 1812, but it also called for the "liquidation of the political and legal consequences" of the Molotov-Ribbentrop Pact, a clause that seemed to point toward reunion with Romania.[23] Nothing in the declaration specifically mentioned Romania or the Romanian identity of Moldova's ethnic majority, but both issues would become the main fault lines within the new political system.

PAN-ROMANIANISM AND THE POLITICS OF DISCORD

The divide over relations with Romania had already in 1990 increased political dissension within the ranks of the Popular Front and, especially after independence, produced new political groupings with very different ideas about the future of the state. After the cultural triumphs of the perestroika period, the Front quickly became a victim of its own success. Once its goals had been reached—engineering a rebirth of Romanian culture, eradicating the notion of an independent Moldovan cultural identity, and pulling the republic out of the Soviet Union—serious questions about the organization's future naturally arose. For radical pan-Romanians, the logical culmination of the Front's activities was to be not only the destruction of a separate Moldovan identity, but the destruction of a separate Moldovan state as well. For more moderate figures, the organization's aim was to encourage increased cultural and economic links with Romania while proceeding more slowly on political union.

These internal disagreements between radicals and moderates were exacerbated by the Front's brief experience in government. Following its strong showing in the 1990 republican elections, one of the group's leaders, Mircea Druc, was named prime minister and presided over a government with significant Frontist representation, especially in the high-profile ministries of culture and education. The policies pursued by the Druc government, including a virtual purge of non-Moldovans from cultural institutions and the reorientation of educational policy away from Russian-speakers, sparked fears among ethnic minorities that the future would see their incorporation into a new Greater Romania.[24] Druc himself was usually pragmatic about union with Romania. "Let's

Crowds converge on central Chisinau to support the declaration of independence, August 1991. Photo by Tudor Iovu.

first set up a few hundred joint ventures and tens of thousands of mixed marriages," he told a reporter in 1990, "and then let's talk about union."[25] But from the perspective of non-Moldovans—who witnessed the rapid change of street names and other public symbols to reflect the Romanian heritage of the republic—the government seemed clearly committed to moving closer toward Bucharest.

The disputes with the Gagauz and Transnistrians, which had been brewing since mid-1989, escalated during Druc's tenure and culminated in the declaration of the Republic of Gagauzia and the DMR. These events had a major impact on the Front. For many Moldovan intellectuals, the adoption of the language laws represented a historical affirmation of the true identity of Moldova's ethnic majority, and the actions of separatists in Gagauzia and Transnistria were therefore undermining the cultural renaissance initiated in 1988. At its second congress in June 1990, the Front declared itself in opposition to the Snegur leadership, which it claimed was moving too slowly on pulling Moldova out of the Soviet Union and restoring order in the eastern and southern districts. At the congress, the Front's executive board under Iurie Roşca openly called for political union with Romania, and forced a change in the organization's statutes that made membership in the Front incompatible with membership in any other political organization. For Roşca, adopting such a position was an acid test: Once anti-Communism and pan-Romanianism were declared the organization's core values, it would be easy to separate the committed members from the fellow-travelers.[26] At its third congress in February 1992, the Front transformed itself from a mass movement into a political party, the Christian Democratic Popular Front, and included an overt commitment to Moldovan-Romanian union in its statutes: "The Christian Democratic Popular Front maintains its status as a national, unionist movement, whose major objective is the reintegration of the Unitary Romanian State."[27] So as not to add legitimacy to the existence of a separate Moldovan state, the refashioned Front rejected the name "Republic of Moldova" in favor of "Bessarabia," a usage that seemed a de facto recognition of the loss of Transnistria to the separatists.

The radicalization of the Popular Front certainly accomplished the goal of forcing Moldovan politicians and other Front members to come clean on union with Romania, but it also seriously weakened the numerical strength of the organization. The vast network of local groups that allowed it to organize so effectively in 1989 quickly diminished once union with Romania was revealed as the Front's ultimate aim.[28] The Front was able to attract hundreds of thousands of Moldovans to the Grand National Assembly in 1989, but only a few hundred supporters turned out for similar rallies in the summer of 1993. Several important members of the Front defected to newly created political parties or left Moldova altogether. Ion Hadârcă resigned as the Front's chair, leaving the position open to hard pan-Romanians such as Roşca. The national movement's spiritual leader, Ion Druţă, settled in Moscow, disillusioned at the hijacking of the movement by a pan-Romanian minority. Former Front supporters in the political establishment—such as Snegur, Sangheli, and Ţău—distanced themselves from the new party and moved toward establishing their own, the Agrarian Democrats, based around reform Communists within the republic's huge agricultural bureaucracy. Other Frontists left for different reasons, convinced that the cause of union had in fact been lost to Snegur and the old party elite. Mircea Druc moved to Romania, took Romanian citizenship, and stood in the 1992 Romanian presidential elections, running on the single-plank platform of Moldovan-Romanian union. He received only 2.75 percent of the vote, coming last in the field of six candidates. Other prominent members, such as the poets Leonida Lari and Grigore Vieru, also effected their own personal union with Romania by settling in Bucharest.

With the defection of Front members and a growing rift in parliament between Frontists and Agrarians, the pan-Romanian community split into two major wings: the rechristened Christian Democratic Popular Front and the Congress of the Intelligentsia, formed in April 1993. The Congress counted some of the Front's most highly respected members among its ranks, including the former chairman of parliament Alexandru Moşanu and parliamentary deputies Valeriu Matei and Vasile Nedelciuc. Although still dedicated to closer relations with Romania, its members aimed to temper unionism with calls for interethnic concord and, at least for the time being, continued independence. Its original statutes mentioned only "gradual economic and spiritual integration with Romania," rather than the immediate political union supported by the old Front.[29] The Congress would go through several name changes—finally becoming the Party of Democratic Forces by 1996—but the split between hard and soft pan-Romanians would remain in place for years after independence. Both camps, though, were opposed to the ratification of the Alma Ata accords on the CIS, which President Snegur had signed in 1991. These groups were able briefly to block the ratification in 1993 when the treaty was put to a vote, but the accords would later be approved and Moldova's place within the commonwealth secured.

Another result of the pan-Romanians' militancy on relations with Romania and the CIS was the corresponding radicalization of the emerging political groupings that strongly supported continued Moldovan independence. Chief among these groups was the Agrarian Democratic Party, formed in November 1991. The parliament with which Moldova exited the Soviet Union had been elected in 1990, when non-Communist parties were still banned. In the turmoil of post-independence politics, deputies exited and joined parties at will without losing their seats. In this environment, the Agrarians quickly became the most numerous bloc within the immediate post-independence assembly and the effective party of government until the parliamentary elections of 1998. The Agrarians, composed largely of the former Communist agricultural and agro-industrial elite, repeatedly stressed that Moldova should not become a mere "province" of either Romania or Russia—neither a *provincie* nor a *guberniia*, as it was often formulated.[30] The most radical of the Agrarians for a time even rejected the Front's practice of using the term *Romanian* to describe the Moldovans' ethnicity and language, and maintained a version of the former Soviet view that Moldovans were ethnically separate from Romanians west of the Prut River.[31] By the time of the 1994 parliamentary elections, this reborn "Moldovanism" had become one of the central tenets of the Agrarians' platform and an ideology promoted by the party's most prominent spokesperson at the time, Mircea Snegur.

In the campaign leading up to the 1994 elections, several newly formed parties attempted to play down the identity issue and to focus the electorate's attention on the bread-and-butter problems of privatization, land redistribution, and constitutional reform. However, the campaign's seminal political event, a special congress funded by the government, ensured that national identity would remain the centerpiece of the campaign. The congress, called "Our Home—The Republic of Moldova," was held in Chisinau on February 5 under the aegis of the Moldovan Civic Alliance, an umbrella organization consisting of those forces most opposed to the ideals of pan-Romanianism.[32] Speeches by Ion Druță and Agrarian party leader Dumitru Moțpan abjured the notion of union with Romania and underscored the need for consolidating independence and territorial integrity.[33]

A carefully worded address by President Snegur received the most attention and marked an important shift in the president's treatment of Moldovan national identity. In the past, Snegur had been careful to distance himself from the "Moldovanism" of the most radical Agrarians, a view of Moldovan-Romanian separateness that contained uncomfortable echoes of the Soviet policy discredited in 1989. While denying the possibility of political union, Snegur previously had spoken approvingly of the Romanian heritage of the Moldovan state and the need for closer cultural and economic integration with Bucharest. In his "Our Home" speech, however, his views were unequivocal. Snegur denounced the pan-Romanian message as "betrayal" and accused Moldova's writers and historians of doubting "the legitimacy and historical foundation of our right to be a state, to call ourselves the Moldovan people." In no uncertain terms, he stressed the existence of a distinct Moldovan nation as the foundation of the state and, in the style of former First Secretary Grossu, hedged his bets on the question of a separate Moldovan language:

> There has been a lot of commotion about the language spoken by Moldovans in the Republic of Moldova. Of course, we have the same

Mircea Snegur, first president of the independent Republic of Moldova. Photo by Tudor Iovu.

language as our brothers in Romania. But by the same token one cannot deny that there are certain nuances [to the Moldovan language]. . . . [I]n my opinion as an average speaker of this language, we cannot deny that our brother or our sister [in Romania] speaks a little bit differently from the way we do. The acceptance of this difference was characteristic throughout history, and I do not know why we are doing all we can to forget it now.[34]

The printed version of the speech included extensive footnotes referencing well-known Romanian historical and literary works in which the term *Moldovan* was used to describe the ethnic majority of Bessarabia. Snegur also pointed to the Bessarabian republic of 1917–18 as the logical precursor of the Republic of Moldova: "The decision of . . . parliament to proclaim Moldova an independent and sovereign state can and should be considered the satisfaction of the people's unaltered desires to continue the tradition of the Moldovans as a nation-state."[35] The "Our Home" speech was the beginning of an official ideology of Moldovan statehood, an idea that the pan-Romanians had rejected in 1989 and that had been only inchoate in the first years after independence. The early Front had seen the nodal points in Moldovan history—from the medieval principality to the brief Bessarabian republic—as leading inexorably toward union with Romania, but Snegur and his allies came to see the path leading in a rather different direction: toward the creation of an independent Moldova.

Not surprisingly, the speech was immediately condemned by the intellectuals. Representatives of the Writers' Union, the Institute of Linguistics, the Institute of History, Chisinau State University, and other institutions declared the speech an affront to the true identity of the republic's ethnic majority and an attempt to further "an invention of the Communist regime" by erecting a "barrier to authentic Romanian culture."[36] Historians, in particular, were outraged at Snegur's use of historical documents to perpetuate the division of the Romanian nation. In the style of the polemics of the late 1980s, an open letter to the president signed by forty-three leading scholars argued that the relationship of the label "Moldovan" to "Romanian" was analogous to that of "Milanese" or "Venetian" to "Italian." "In other words," the letter continued, "being Moldovans by virtue of the region where we were born, as an integral part of the Romanian people we are at the same time Romanians, whether we like it or not."[37]

Snegur's embracing the "Moldovanist" line on national identity surely aided the Agrarians in the February 1994 elections. The weakening of the Front after 1990 had already indicated that radical pan-Romanian ideals enjoyed little support on the ground, and Snegur's adopting a more anti-unionist rhetoric during the campaign helped seal the Front's political fate. The Agrarians emerged with over 43 percent of the popular vote and an absolute majority of seats in the new post-Soviet parliament; the Front and the Congress of the Intelligentsia together won only 20 seats.

An even more significant outcome was the strong showing by a local ultraconservative alliance that rejected the main ideals of both the pan-Romanian and the Moldovanist camps and called for, among other things, the use of Russian as the republic's official language. Composed of the Socialist Party (then the most direct heir of the former Communist Party) and the Edinstvo movement (the successor to the perestroika-era Interfront), the Socialist Unity Bloc garnered 22 percent of the vote, making it the second largest group after the Agrarians. None of the other nine parties and electoral alliances was able to pass the 4 percent threshold for parliamentary membership. In subsequent local elections, the leftists continued to garner strong support, mainly from Russian-speaking

TABLE 9

MOLDOVAN ELECTIONS, 1991–98

1991 Presidential Elections

Mircea Snegur (sole candidate)	98.17%

1994 Parliamentary Elections

Agrarian Democratic Party	43.2%	54 seats
Socialist Unity Bloc	22.0	27
Bloc of Peasants and Intellectuals[a]	9.2	11
Christian Democratic Popular Front[b]	7.5	9

1995 Local Elections

Agrarian Democratic Party	47.0%
Alliance of Democratic Forces[a]	19.7
Party of Communists[c]	15.7
Socialist Unity Bloc	7.2

1996 Presidential Elections

	1st round	2d round
Petru Lucinschi	27.7%	54.0%
Mircea Snegur	38.8	46.0
Vladimir Voronin[d]	10.2	
Andrei Sangheli[e]	9.5	
Valeriu Matei[f]	8.9	

1998 Parliamentary Elections

Party of Communists	30.1%	40 seats
Democratic Convention[g]	19.4	26
Movement for a Democratic and Prosperous Moldova[h]	18.1	24
Party of Democratic Forces[a]	8.8	11

NOTES:

[a]Includes former Congress of the Intelligentsia and other smaller, moderately pan-Romanian parties.

[b]Includes Popular Front and other smaller, more radical pan-Romanian parties.

[c]Established in 1994, but did not stand in the 1994 parliamentary elections.

[d]Candidate of the Party of Communists.

[e]Candidate of Agrarian Democratic Party.

[f]Candidate of Party of Democratic Forces.

[g]Includes Popular Front and Party of Rebirth and Reconciliation (supporters of Mircea Snegur).

[h]Includes supporters of Petru Lucinschi.

populations in the cities and older Moldovans dissatisfied with the ill effects of the economic transition.

The reason for the government's change of tack on the identity question was clear. By embracing an indigenous Moldovan nationalism as the basis for the republic, resurrecting not only the memory of the briefly independent Bessarabian state but also the notion of an independent Moldovan language, Snegur attempted to portray himself and his government as the guarantors of independence and territorial integrity. It was a theme that played well in the countryside. Two-thirds of all ethnic Moldovans lived in the villages, where they accounted for over 80 percent of the total rural population. Surveys carried out by William Crowther in 1992 showed that less than 10 percent of the ethnic Moldovan population supported union with Romania in the short or long term, and when given a choice between the ethnic tags "Romanian" and "Moldovan," some 87 percent of Moldovan-language speakers chose the latter.[38] Similarly, a government-sponsored referendum shortly after the elections seemed to yield a clear pro-independence result, with over 90 percent of participants voting "yes" to an independent republic within its post-Soviet borders.[39]

The new Agrarian-dominated parliament set about reversing many of the Frontist reforms of the early 1990s. The assembly voted overwhelmingly to change the national anthem, "Romanian, Awake!"—the same state hymn as in Romania, which had been adopted in 1991—and to initiate a competition for a new song that would reflect "the independence of the state and the aspiration of the people to prosperity."[40] Ironically, the parliament eventually opted for "Limba noastră" (Our language), based on the famous poem by Alexei Mateevici—a song that never mentions whether "our language" is called "Romanian" or "Moldovan." A similar policy reversal affected the highly divisive subject of language politics. In July 1994 the parliament voted in favor of continuing to describe the official language of the republic as "Moldovan" in the new post-Soviet constitution. Article 13 contained no reference to the relationship between Moldovan and Romanian, as did the earlier language laws, but stated simply that "The state language of the Republic of Moldova is the Moldovan language [*limba moldovenească*] and functions on the basis of the Latin script."[41] The language tests for state employees mandated by the 1989 laws were suspended, and the State Department of Languages—the institution that had previously carried out language "raids" on institutions to ensure that their employees knew

Moldovan—virtually closed down. The Institute of Linguistics and various other strongholds of the pan-Romanians denounced the use of the term *Moldovan language* as a betrayal of the ideals of the national movement and an affront to scientific truth.[42] Periodic demonstrations were held in Chisinau in favor of revisiting the language question, but the changes of 1994 marked the end of language politics as a major political issue. From that point, Moldova became a de facto bilingual state, a situation that all but the most vocal pan-Romanians seemed willing to accept. Romanian-language use began to gain ground in the late 1990s, but especially in the cities and among some business elites, Russian was heard more often than Romanian.

THE CHANGING POLITICAL LANDSCAPE

Throughout the first years of independence, Moldova's political parties were slow to develop either clear political ideologies or definable constituencies, apart from the rhetoric of pan-Romanianism and Moldovanism. Snegur's own political peregrinations were exemplary. In the late 1980s, he was a strong supporter of the national movement and, after being elected president, set about developing warm relations with Bucharest. By 1994, however, he had become the arch-enemy of the pan-Romanians, committed to an independent state and even to a distinct Moldovan culture. By 1996, though, he had begun to change tack yet again, calling on the Agrarian-dominated parliament to declare Romanian—rather than "Moldovan," as written in the constitution—the official language. In 1998, after losing to Petru Lucinschi in presidential elections two years earlier, he mended fences with the old Popular Front and stood for parliament in an electoral alliance with his former bête noire, Iurie Roşca.

Although shifting political alliances are common in all post-Soviet countries, the structure of Moldova's electoral system discouraged the creation of strong and stable parties linked to clear constituencies. In the first place, Moldova's proportional representation system functioned on the basis of a closed party list ballot, with the entire country considered a single electoral district. There was thus little incentive for parties to reach out to distinct constituencies, or for politicians, once elected, to feel a sense of obligation toward the voters who put them in office.

Cronyism, patron-client relations, and on occasion the rhetoric of ethnic identity became the driving forces behind electoral politics. The system of Soviet-era collective farms and agro-industrial enterprises produced a set of reform Communists with common material interests, and for a time this agrarian elite proved remarkably stable as a governing counterweight to the pan-Romanians. Within a few years of independence, however, even this group gave way to competing factions associated primarily with the presidential ambitions of ex-Communists such as Snegur and Lucinschi.

Furthermore, the sequence of events that led to Moldova's exit from the Soviet Union bequeathed to the post-Soviet leadership a political system perpetually in campaign mode. The presidency, parliament, and local government were all reformed at different times from 1989 to 1991, and new elections for the various levels of national and local government were never coordinated. The country had a major election almost every year after independence: presidential elections in 1991, parliamentary elections in 1994, local elections in 1995, presidential elections in 1996, parliamentary elections in 1998, local elections in 1999, presidential elections in 2000, and so on. It is little wonder that important economic and political problems remained unaddressed, since few political figures were willing to make bold moves that could be used against them or their party in the next election. Muddling through, for most Moldovan politicians, remained preferable to messing up. Nearly a decade after the demise of Soviet socialism, political parties thus continued to situate themselves along a spectrum ranging from those supporting some form of political union with Romania (if only in the long term), to those in favor of independence, to those desiring some degree of reintegration with Russia and the former Soviet republics. Although the high tide of identity politics seemed to have passed, the weakness of definite party ideologies meant that the identity question remained an important determinant of political affiliation.

By the late 1990s, new political parties had appeared on the scene and many of the parties that stood in 1994 had changed their names. In the 1996 presidential elections, Petru Lucinschi defeated Mircea Snegur in the second round with 54 percent of the vote. Lucinschi had had an illustrious career in Moldovan politics, serving as the penultimate first secretary of the Communist Party, then ambassador to Moscow, and finally as speaker of the parliament. There was little ideologically to separate him from Snegur, except his conviction that Moldova would be best suited by repairing its links with Russia. His victory in 1996, though, did little to change Moldova's fundamental foreign policy orientation. Lucinschi's first trip abroad was to Bucharest but was quickly followed by trips to the former Soviet republics, including Russia. Lucinschi himself had been at the center of Moldovan political life since the late 1980s, and his election to the presidential post represented little more than a continuation of the balanced foreign policy and moderate reform course that the country had pursued since independence.

The parliamentary elections in 1998, however, did signal an important change. The resurrected Party of Communists secured 30 percent of the vote and the largest number of seats in the parliament. Headed by Vladimir Voronin, one of the former leaders of the Interfront movement in the 1980s, the party was one of several successors to the old Communist Party of Moldova, which was banned with the collapse of the Soviet Union.[43] In previous elections, another leftist group, the Socialist Unity Bloc, usually represented the pro-Russian and antireform end of the political spectrum, but the Socialists were never able to move beyond their largely urban and Russian-speaking constituency and had begun to fade from the scene already in the 1995 local elections. By contrast, the Communists reached out across ethnic lines to garner support among even Moldovans disaffected by the dire economic situation.[44] Previously, language and ethnicity had been the primary dividing lines within the political system; Russian-speakers tended to support Socialist Unity since it was seen as the only group speaking on behalf of the republic's minorities. But once significant minority members gained seats in the assembly in 1994, nonethnic questions of economic reform tended to dominate the agenda. The economic malaise in the country allowed the new Communists to reach out to disgruntled Moldovans who had previously been alienated from the Russian-dominated Socialists.

The leftist resurgence also spelled the end of the Agrarian Democrats, the collective farm managers who had dominated politics since independence. Disputes among Agrarian sympathizers Snegur, Lucinschi, and Prime Minister Andrei Sangheli—all of whom stood in the 1996 presidential race—caused division within the party's ranks. The Agrarians eventually failed to win any seats at all in the 1998 elections. The Agrarians' demise also produced a plethora of short-lived and ill-defined political alliances intended mainly to support a candidate's presidential bid rather than to promote a particular party program. One of these groups, the Movement for a Democratic and Prosperous Moldova

Petru Lucinschi, elected Moldovan president in 1996.
Courtesy Associated Press.

(MDPM), mainly supporters of Lucinschi, managed to secure representation in the 1998 parliament by riding on the wave of Lucinschi's success in the presidential contest two years earlier. Snegur's Party of Rebirth and Reconciliation, however, eventually merged with the
president's former arch-nemesis, the Popular Front, to stand as the pro-
Romanian Democratic Convention (DC). The minority blocs within the
1998 parliament—the MDPM, the DC, and the Party of Democratic
Forces—were able to support a technocrat government under Prime
Minister Ion Ciubuc, mainly as a way of blocking the Communists. Divisions within the coalition, though, continually threatened to destroy the
uneasy center-right alliance, a problem that continued even under Ciubuc's successor, the young businessman Ion Sturza.

Despite the frequent party name changes and shifting allegiances
among politicians, the cleavages within the Moldovan polity remained

largely as they had been at independence: a pan-Romanian bloc supported by the small creative intelligentsia and Moldovans who benefited from the reforms of the early 1990s; a vast centrist bloc committed to maintaining their positions of power within the privatized agricultural and agro-industrial sector and motivated more by patronage than party ideology; and a resurgent left, composed both of disaffected ethnic minorities hard hit by the post-1989 cultural changes as well as a growing cadre of Moldovans dissatisfied with the political infighting and decline in the standard of living caused by the economic transition. Even the revived Communists, though, staked out positions on the identity question, pressing for the creation of an official holiday to celebrate the founding of the Moldovan principality in 1359—an attempt to undercut the pan-Romanians' annual celebrations of the 1918 union with Romania.

THE ROMANIAN DIMENSIONS OF DOMESTIC POLITICS

In a speech before a joint session of the U.S. Congress in July 1998, Emil Constantinescu averred that the "sensitive issues" that remained between Romania and Moldova had been "resolved without tension."[45] Despite the Romanian president's enthusiastic assessment, relations between Chisinau and Bucharest ran hot and cold throughout the 1990s. After the anticommunist revolution in Romania and Moldovan independence, there was a great deal of support in both capitals for closer ties. Many Romanians, in fact, saw in the August coup a parallel to the Bolshevik seizure of power in 1917: the political impetus that would finally drive the wavering Bessarabians back into the Romanian fold. Appeals to Moldovans toward unity and solidarity at the time of the putsch were a fixture of the Romanian media and conjured up similar images from earlier in the century. The National Christian Democratic Peasant Party and the Civic Alliance, two of Romania's major political formations, issued a declaration urging the government to take action to assist "Romanians in the occupied territories" on the model of 1918.[46] The governing National Salvation Front likewise called Moldovan independence the first step toward rectifying the "territorial amputation" of 1940.[47]

Moldova also became a source of inspiration for Romanian parties opposed to the generally antireform National Salvation Front. As democratic parties increasingly came to see the 1989 revolution more as a palace coup than a genuine revolution, Bessarabia was imbued with the same hopes that Onisifor Ghibu and others had seen there earlier in the century.[48] The Moldovans had risked their lives for the national cause, some Romanian observers argued, and might therefore teach Romanian democrats something about how to overthrow the legacy of communist dictatorship. "It is not only the Bessarabians who need reunification with the Motherland," wrote the political analyst Alina Mungiu, "the Motherland needs it, too."[49]

Relations developed apace. Romania was the first state to recognize Moldova's independence—only a few hours, in fact, after the declaration by the Moldovan parliament. Within only a few days, accords were signed on the establishment of embassies and consulates. Within a few months, a visa-free and passport-free regime was established along the Prut River, with Romanian and Moldovan citizens traveling back and forth with only an identity card.[50] Several Orthodox congregations in Moldova shifted their allegiance from Moscow to the Bucharest patriarchate, although this newly established "Bessarabian Metropolitan Church" was not recognized by the Moldovan government. Early in 1992 both states formed special interministerial committees on bilateral relations, the Romanian committee headed by the foreign minister and the Moldovan counterpart headed by a deputy prime minister.[51] Already in 1991, Romania began offering scholarships for Moldovan students as well as textbooks for Moldovan schools.[52] In 1993, the Romanian parliament passed a special law on the mandatory inclusion in each year's state budget of a fund for developing ties with Moldova; the amount of this fund, though, was largely symbolic—about 5 billion Romanian lei (less than $600,000) in 1997.[53] Romania became Moldova's largest trading partner outside the former Soviet countries and began supplying electrical power to Moldova in 1998. But because Chisinau's economy was overwhelmingly oriented toward the east, the level of cross-border economic activity remained low. By 1998, Romania accounted for only 11.5 percent of the value of Moldova's imports and 6.8 percent of exports; the former was a significant increase but the latter a marked decrease since 1995.[54]

Despite the special relationship that developed in the spheres of education and culture, relations between political elites oscillated between avowals of pan-Romanian brotherhood and harsh mutual denunciations. Immediately after independence, Moldovan public life was dominated by members and sympathizers of the Popular Front, who were intent on solidifying ties between the two states. Relations took a turn for the worse in the run-up to the 1994 Moldovan elections, reaching their nadir at the time of the "Our Home" congress. Snegur's resurrection of Soviet-era "Moldovanism" elicited a sharp reaction from political parties in Bucharest and an official condemnation by the Romanian parliament. In response, the Moldovan government and parliament, as well as several political parties, issued declarations denouncing Romania's meddling in another country's internal affairs.

There were clear reasons for the change from public speculation about political union in 1991 to mutual recriminations by 1994. In the first place, the national movement of the late 1980s was far more complicated than many observers recognized. At the heart were several groups who, though finding common ground in the calls for cultural revival and local self-government, had political interests that were fundamentally at odds. Once Moldova became independent and genuinely free political competition became a possibility, these conflicting interests quickly became evident.

More importantly, though, the "Bessarabian question" simply never became a major factor in Romanian domestic politics, and politicians thus had little incentive to push the issue onto Romania's foreign policy agenda. All parties and political figures in Bucharest agreed that the 1940 annexation was illegal, that there was no question about the true Romanian identity of the Moldovans (even if some Moldovans refused to recognize the fact), and that in an ideal world the two states would certainly be joined into a reconstituted Greater Romania. But since all parties and most Romanian voters accepted these basic tenets, no political grouping could use Moldova as a wedge issue. Among Romania's ultranationalist parties, only one—the Greater Romania Party—ever made Moldovan-Romanian union an explicit part of its campaign rhetoric, and that party barely crossed the threshold for parliamentary representation in the 1992 and 1996 elections. Some center-right parties, such as the National Peasants, attempted to use the Moldovan issue as ammunition against the largely unreformed administration of Ion Iliescu in 1992.[55] But soon thereafter, most parties came to accept the existence of two separate states. Even the influential weekly 22, generally a supporter of the National Peasant Party and its allies, published a lengthy report advocating a more mature relationship between Bucharest and Chisinau that would recognize the existence of two independent states with a common culture.[56] In 1992 the only Romanian presidential candidate to make Moldovan-Romanian union a key part of his platform, the former Moldovan prime minister Mircea Druc, finished last in the race. In the 1996 presidential elections, no candidate voiced the Moldovan question at all.

When Lucinschi succeeded Snegur as Moldovan president, there was some speculation that the new president would seek to move Moldova farther away from Romania. As a former party secretary in Tajikistan and member of the CPSU Politburo, Lucinschi's background certainly pointed in a more pro-Russian than pro-Romanian direction. But as a classic political survivor and pragmatist, he worked after the election both to restore cordial relations with Romania and to maintain the already strong ties with Russia. His first trip abroad, in fact, was to Romania, and in the first two years after assuming office, he met with the Romanian president, Emil Constantinescu, on more than five occasions. Ironically, both heads of state were born in Bessarabia, Lucinschi in the north-central region and Constantinescu in Bender along the Dnestr River.

There were, of course, outstanding issues between the two countries in the late 1990s. Moldova remained the only neighbor of Romania with which Bucharest had not signed an interstate treaty; finding a mutually acceptable wording to address the Soviet annexation and to describe the special links between the two countries was the primary obstacle to settlement. But the coming to power of moderates in both capitals allowed the relationship to mature beyond the national euphoria of 1991 and the sniping of 1994. Beyond Romania, however, Moldovan identity politics was also affected by other domestic and international developments. The long history of ties with Russia, the crises of territorial separatism in the south and east in the 1990s and, most importantly, the manifestly multiethnic nature of Moldova itself created particular challenges for the newly independent state.

8 The Multiethnic Republic

The changes of the late 1980s altered the balance of power between the majority and ethnic minorities, nearly a third of all Moldova's citizens. No longer were Moldovans a peripheral nationality, a culturally threatened population on the edge of a larger empire. Rather, as the majority ethnic group in a fully independent state, they suddenly had the power to reverse the political and cultural trends of the Soviet period.

Immediately after the adoption of the 1989 language laws, Popular Front supporters attempted to impose a radical restructuring of ethnic relations. The newly created State Department of Languages carried out surprise inspections of state institutions—more than 300 by the end of 1992—to make sure that the Moldovan language in the Latin script was being used on official forms and that employees were attending required Moldovan-language classes.[1] Intellectuals in the Academy of Sciences and other state institutions sought to reverse what many saw as the denationalization policies of the Soviets. The irony, of course, was that many of the historians, linguists, and writers who had been public defenders of "Moldovanness" in the 1970s became equally ardent defenders of "Romanianness" in the 1990s.

With the exception of that short period, however, the Moldovan government generally sought to craft a state built on the principles of citizenship and civic culture rather than the policies favored by the Popular Front and its descendants. The language laws mandated that state employees pass proficiency tests in the Moldovan language, but as the date for the initiation of language examinations drew near, in spring 1994 the Moldovan parliament voted to suspend the tests indefinitely. Several months later, a parliamentary commission elaborated a series of new regulations that significantly changed the 1989 legislation. Moldovan remained the official language of the country, but the provisions mandating national language examinations and sanctioning raids on enterprises that failed to "moldovanize" were dropped. By 1995, the State Department of Languages had faded into obscurity, focusing mainly on organizing cultural festivals rather than on implementing the defunct laws. Just as the 1930s had witnessed a retreat on the radical moldovanization of the 1920s, the mid-1990s saw a similar reversal of the pan-Romanian euphoria of the first years of independence.

Legislation in other spheres followed a similar line, with most politicians seeking to underscore the multiethnic heritage of Bessarabia and Transnistria rather than effect a pan-Romanian national awakening.[2] The 1994 constitution made no reference to Moldova as a "national" state, referring to the "people of the Republic of Moldova" rather than to any specific ethnic group as the locus of state sovereignty. Article 111 promised a special autonomous status for the most ethnically heterogeneous areas in the south and east of the republic. The citizenship law, adopted in 1991, was one of the most liberal in eastern Europe, allowing all persons living in the republic on the date of the declaration of sovereignty (June 23, 1990) to become citizens regardless of ethnicity, language, length of residence, or other criteria. Even during the ascendance of the Popular Front, Russian continued to serve as a de facto second language in the republican administration, and by the late 1990s, public advertisements and other displays in Chisinau were as likely to be in Russian as in Romanian. The publicly funded State Department for National Relations and the Institute for National Minorities within the Academy of Sciences functioned as the main conduits for government support of minority cultural activities, historical research, and native language education. International observers generally commended the government for creating a civic, inclusive state rather than the ethnically defined nation-states favored by the country's neighbors.[3] As a result, Moldova became the first post-Soviet republic to be admitted to the Council of Europe, in June 1995.

It is this history of inclusiveness, in fact, that many Moldovans came to see as the central point of difference between themselves and the

Romanians. Romania's constitution, for example, defined the country as a "national state" based on "the unity of the Romanian people."[4] The fear of ethnic and regional difference was one of the perennial themes in Romanian politics of the twentieth century, but the heritage of Bessarabian heterogeneity came, in the late 1990s, to be a source of pride for Moldovans. Surveys indicated that average Moldovans had a high degree of interethnic tolerance, far higher in fact than in Romania.[5] Few public figures denied the Romanian heritage of the Moldovans, as the brief resurgence in "Moldovanism" seemed to do in 1994, but even the most respected intellectuals began to explore the distinct cultural dimensions of Bessarabia.[6] Even the country's "foreign policy concept," adopted in 1995, set out multiethnicity as one of the sources of the country's friendly relations with the states of southeast Europe and the former Soviet Union.[7]

This shift in the mid-1990s resulted from the waning in enthusiasm for the pan-Romanian project, the tragedy of violence in the south and east, and most importantly the realities of the country's demographics. Moldova's population structure was similar to that of nineteenth-century Bessarabia, notwithstanding some important changes in the later Soviet period. In the 1990s, the villages remained largely Moldovan, while the major cities—Chisinau, Bălți, Tiraspol, Bender—contained large Slavic communities. Moldovans formed 80.2 percent of the rural population, but only 46.3 percent of the urban; they accounted for absolute majorities in most counties, but not in any of the major cities.[8] These demographic conditions and the generally inclusive nature of Moldovan political culture created a republic that, by the end of the decade, was truly multinational. The sections that follow briefly consider developments among Moldova's major ethnic groups as of 1999; later chapters address the more problematic questions of the Transnistrians and the Gagauz.

UKRAINIANS

Ukrainians were Moldova's largest minority and the largest relative Ukrainian minority in all the former Soviet Union, but they were the least politically mobilized of the republic's minorities. Their influence was far outweighed by that of numerically smaller groups such as the Gagauz. Most of the over 600,000 Ukrainians lived on the west bank of the Dnestr River, mainly in the cities and villages of the extreme northern and southern counties along the Ukrainian border; however, the 170,000 living in Transnistria formed a much more compact population.

Moldova included a clause in the 1992 basic treaty with Ukraine regarding the cultural development of ethnic Ukrainians, as it did with all states that have co-ethnic minorities inside Moldova. Besides this clause, however, there was little evidence that Kyiv was particularly concerned about respect for Ukrainian collective rights.[9] Some Ukrainian irregulars sponsored by the nationalist Ukrainian Self-Defense Forces were known to have participated in the Transnistrian war of 1992, but successive Kyiv governments praised Moldova's record on interethnic relations. The Ukrainian ambassador to Moldova spoke of "a real sea change" in Ukrainian cultural opportunities after independence and underscored the need for Ukrainians to be good Moldovan citizens in addition to being guardians of Ukrainian national culture.[10] There was no evidence that Ukraine sought either to mobilize ethnic Ukrainians in Moldova or to raise the ethnic issue as part of the Transnistrian problem.[11]

From 1990 on, a department of Ukrainian language functioned at the pedagogical university in Bălți, the city with the largest Ukrainian population outside Transnistria. As early as February 1991, President Snegur issued a decree introducing Ukrainian-language education in areas with compact Ukrainian settlements.[12] Movement on this issue was slow, but classes were eventually initiated in village schools in counties with sizable Ukrainian communities, mainly in the extreme north.[13] By early 1994, Ukrainian was being taught as a subject in sixty-nine schools throughout the republic, including one high school in Chisinau, but only a few classes used the language for instructional purposes.[14] For the first time in the 1992–93 school year, a small number of students at state universities were enrolled in sections with Ukrainian as the language of instruction, although they accounted for only about one-tenth of 1 percent of the total student population.[15]

Ukrainians fell in the middle of the spectrum of linguistic assimilation. In 1989, just over 60 percent reported Ukrainian as their native language, a figure significantly lower than that for Moldovans, Russians, Gagauz, and Roma, but higher than Jews and smaller ethnic groups; about 43 percent named Russian as a fluent second language, and nearly 13 percent claimed second-language competence in Moldovan. Ukrainians were second only to Jews in their level of complete linguistic assimilation to Russian, with nearly 30 percent counting Russian as their native language with no knowledge of Ukrainian. There were thus no large-scale movements for Ukrainian-language educational or cultural reform, with most Ukrainians seeing themselves as part of a general "russophone" minority rather than specifically Ukrainian. There were several Ukrainian social and cultural organizations registered in Moldova, but none made a prominent impact on the political scene.

RUSSIANS

Russians were not Moldova's largest ethnic minority, yet they were certainly the most visible in the first years after independence. Because of the status of the Russian language in the Soviet period, as well as Moscow's insistence on championing the rights of Russian-speakers in the post-Soviet states, the position of ethnic Russians and the broader russophone population was of major concern in Chisinau.

Demographically, the ethnic Russian community in Moldova represented an amalgam of those traits found elsewhere in the fourteen former Soviet republics outside the Russian Federation. With ethnic Russian minorities ranging from a high of over 6 million in Kazakhstan (38 percent of the republican total) to a low of 52,000 in Armenia (under 2 percent), Moldova ranked near the middle, with just over 562,000 Russians accounting for around 13 percent.[16] The growth rate of the Russian population after 1959 was unremarkable compared to neighboring republics and largely paralleled the increase in Russian-to-native proportions in Lithuania and Ukraine.[17] As in other republics, ethnic Russians tended to settle in urban areas, particularly around industrial centers, and therefore formed a much higher proportion of the population in the cities than in the countryside; ethnic Russians accounted for some 27 percent of the republic's urban population but only 4 percent of the rural.[18]

Urban Russians have long been a fixture of Bessarabian society; in fact, of all the western republican capitals, Chisinau had the most stable proportional ethnic Russian population over the period 1897 to 1989, ranging from a low of 22 percent in 1930 to a high of 32 percent in 1959.[19] Outside the major cities, the most significant concentration was in Transnistria, where Russians formed a quarter of the region's population (although they nevertheless ranked third behind Moldovans and Ukrainians).

After 1991, Russian continued to have a high profile, particularly in the cities. Street signs were written in both Romanian and Russian, and it was often easier to find Russian-language editions of major newspapers than Romanian ones. Significantly, the main government daily, *Moldova suverană*, carried some advertisements in Russian, but its Russian-language counterpart, *Nezavisimaia Moldova*, did not do the same in Romanian. A special governmental decree in February 1993 authorized the use of Russian along with Romanian in official correspondence,[20] a move necessitated by the inability of government employees to communicate effectively in the state language. Romanian certainly began to displace Russian as the primary language of instruction in schools, but this was largely due to the opening of new Moldovan schools rather than the forcible conversion of Russian ones. The amount of Russian-language broadcast time on state television fell after 1989; however, because of the infinitely superior television broadcasts from Moscow, there were few complaints about lack of Russian air-time.

As in other post-Soviet states, Russian community leaders struggled to articulate a clear vision of a specifically Russian cultural identity in Moldova. A host of overlapping identities and political concerns existed within the community usually given the facile label "Russian."[21] Indigenous Russians and Soviet settler communities were initially represented by the Interfront movement in the late 1980s and, later, by the Socialist Unity Bloc within the Moldovan parliament. The reborn Party of Communists garnered similar support after 1995 but managed to extend its base of support beyond the minorities into the Moldovan community as well. On Transnistria, the non-Moldovans remained divided, with some sympathetic to the demands of the east-bank region but others generally supportive of the multiethnic message preached by Chisinau. There was, moreover, no significant movement of Russians or Ukrainians from Bessarabia to the Dnestr Moldovan Republic; in fact, given the dire economic conditions in the separatist republic, the net flow was in the opposite direction.

Post-Soviet Moldovan legislation did not permit dual citizenship. Despite this provision there was not a major outflow of Russians to the Russian Federation. The largest numbers left during the violence of 1992, mainly from Transnistria. During the height of nationalist rhetoric and violence, from 1989 to 1993, a total of 22,351 Russians left Moldova for the Russian Federation, the lowest figure for any non-Slavic republic except Armenia.[22] This outflow declined considerably in succeeding years. In 1995 the total number of refugees from Moldova registered in Russia was only 18,559, with some former refugees having returned to Moldova and others engaging in second stage migration outside the former Soviet states.[23] In the late 1990s, net migration flows were negative for Russians and Ukrainians—with more exiting Moldova than arriving—but the same was the case for Moldovans themselves, with many joining ethnic Slavs in seeking opportunities in other former Soviet republics or in western Europe.

JEWS

From 1959 to 1989, Jews were the only major MSSR nationality whose number decreased—from 95,107 in 1959 to 65,672 three decades later—mainly because of out-migration to Israel. Many more Jews left after independence, with Israel being the third most important destination for migrants after Russia and Ukraine.[24]

Most of Bessarabia's Jews were linguistically assimilated to Russian from the end of the nineteenth century, but after perestroika and independence, there was a considerable cultural renaissance. Encouraged mainly by the Israeli Cultural Society and the Lubavitcher Hassidim, many Moldovan Jews began to return to traditional religious practices that had been lost during the Soviet era. Two Jewish schools were opened in the early 1990s in Chisinau, a kindergarten and a summer youth camp were organized by the local Society for Jewish Culture, and a small Yiddish-language section was instituted at Chisinau State University.[25]

The Israelis and international human rights monitoring groups were generally laudatory of the improved atmosphere in Moldova, and there even seems to have been a net increase in the Moldovan Jewish population since 1992, with many "closet Jews" feeling safe enough to rediscover their ethnic heritage.[26] Some antisemitic incidents were reported, but according to the Institute of Jewish Affairs in London, these were confined mainly to Transnistria.[27] Unlike in Ukraine and Romania, there were no political parties or organized groups that put forward a recognizably antisemitic agenda or attempted to make use of antisemitic propaganda. Most Moldovan citizens seemed to recognize the important role of Jewish culture in the history of Bessarabia. Revealingly, Chisinau's two most popular restaurants throughout the 1990s were those that promised "Jewish" food and music.

BULGARIANS

Most of Moldova's 88,400 ethnic Bulgarians lived among the Gagauz in the southern districts and actually formed a plurality in Taraclia *raion* before administrative changes redrew the boundary lines for local government. There was some fear that they might side with the Gagauz in pushing for separation, but there were no signs of a pact between the Bulgarians and the Comrat leadership. If anything, the Bulgarians by 1999 had begun to call for their own form of self-government in Taraclia, just as the Gagauz had won in their region earlier. These demands, though, reflected more a desire for *raion*-level control over local resources than a desire for increased cultural rights.

In linguistic terms, Moldova's Bulgarian population was significantly assimilated to Russian over the past several decades. The proportion reporting Bulgarian as a native language decreased from 91.5 percent in 1959 to 78.7 percent in 1989. Nearly 70 percent reported Russian as a second language but less than 7 percent claimed fluent second-language competence in Moldovan.

Calls for Bulgarian-language education in the republic were therefore limited. The main Bulgarian cultural organization, Văzrazhdane (Rebirth), largely limited its activities to organizing Bulgarian cultural festivals and promoting relations with Sofia. By mid-1993, sizable numbers of Bulgarian students were studying at the Gagauz university in Comrat (in Russian-language classes), while a small Bulgarian pedagogical college and school were set up in 1992 in Taraclia, the only town in which Bulgarians formed a majority. Small Bulgarian sections were also functioning in the Chisinau Pedagogical Institute, and Bulgarian-speaking students from Moldova regularly took up scholarships funded by the Bulgarian government.[28] Apart from these initiatives, however, there were few indications of a distinctly Bulgarian cultural revival.

In any case, the mobilization of ethnic Bulgarians proved to be a useful resource for elites within Taraclia *raion*. In 1998 the Moldovan government redrew the boundaries of administrative districts, abandoning the forty small Soviet-era *raions* in favor of larger counties (*judeţe*) and thereby reducing the drain on the state budget for local administration. The *raion* executives in Taraclia, though, denounced the changes as a threat to Bulgarian autonomy, and organized a referendum to block their absorption into neighboring Cahul *raion*. There was little evidence that the referendum actually represented the wishes of ethnic Bulgarians—the twelve or so villages in Taraclia *raion*, in fact, were not all Bulgarian, nor did all Bulgarians in Moldova live in Taraclia *raion*—but it did illustrate the degree to which local elites could mobilize the ethnic question as a way of maintaining their hold over political institutions.

ROMA (GYPSIES)

The 1989 census counted 11,571 Roma in Moldova. The difficulties of achieving accurate figures for Romany populations are well known, and some leaders argued that the real number may be as high as 100,000 or more.[29] The large number in Romania—perhaps as many as two million and by far the largest Romany population in Europe—made achieving an accurate estimate all the more difficult. Roma are for the most part highly mobile; the few who established permanent residences did so either in the countryside or among other ethnic communities in large cites. There were no exclusively Romany settlements; Roma formed a plurality of the population in only two villages and made up a significant part of the local population in only four towns, with the most visible being the impressive homes constructed by wealthy Roma in the northern city of Soroca.[30] The largest communities were concentrated in the extreme northern counties in an arc following the border with Ukraine and Romania.[31] A huge majority still considered Romany their native language, but roughly a third or more counted Moldovan or Russian as a second language in 1989. More Roma claimed second-language competence in Moldovan than any of the republic's other minorities.

Because of the small size of the Romany population, its mobility, and the lack of effective organized groups speaking for the entire community, few attempts were made to cultivate Romany language and culture. In 1993, President Snegur issued special instructions to the Ministry of Science and Education to make greater efforts to aid Romany social organizations.[32] However, no schools used the Romany language either as a language of instruction or as a subject of study. A Romany cultural organization, Romii Moldovei (Roma of Moldova), was active after 1990, but traditional animosities toward Roma remained a major impediment. Debates over the proper standardization of Romany speech forms also blocked attempts to use the language in education.[33]

By the late 1990s, Moldova's interethnic politics had brightened considerably from the dark days of the immediate postindependence period. The republic settled into a situation in which clashes between majority and minority populations were virtually nonexistent. Russians and others who had lost their positions in major cultural institutions after 1989 still complained that too little attention was paid to the history and culture of minorities. The economic problems faced by the state, though, meant that little attention was paid to history and culture in general. Equality in misery may be no justice, but there was little to distinguish an impecunious professor of Romanian history with a job from a former Russian researcher without one.

However, the two disputes at the center of the crisis of the late 1980s and early 1990s—the Gagauz question in the south and Transnistrian separatism in the east—continued to be on the political agenda. The evolution of both conflicts after 1991 illustrated the degree to which "ethnic conflict" was more a convenient label applied by outsiders than a reflection of realities on the ground and the extent to which each dispute demanded tailor-made solutions.

9 The Transnistrian Conundrum

In 1992 Moldova experienced a brief but bloody conflict over the territory lying east of the Dnestr River, the region known to Romanian-speakers as *Transnistria* and to Russian-speakers as *Pridnestrov'ia*. The thin strip of land, less than 30 kilometers wide and only 4,118 square kilometers in area, had once been part of the Moldovan autonomous republic in the interwar period but was joined with Bessarabia to form the MSSR after the Soviet annexation in 1940. The separatist conflict that erupted there in the late 1980s, and sizzled until the outbreak of large-scale violence in the first half of 1992, left over 1,000 dead or wounded and produced 130,000 internally displaced persons and refugees who flooded into Ukraine, Russia, and the rest of Moldova.[1] For the government in Chisinau, it remained the state's foremost security problem, since the area along the Dnestr functioned as a de facto separate state, the Dnestr Moldovan Republic (DMR).[2] It was also the first post-Soviet conflict in which the Russian military actively intervened with the ostensible goal of stopping the violence, and a conflict that launched the career of Alexander Lebed', who as commander of the Russian Fourteenth Army stationed in Transnistria repeatedly affirmed the need to protect local Russians against the "genocidal" policies of the Moldovan government.

Despite the active involvement of the international community, primarily via the presence of the long-term mission of the Organization for

Security and Cooperation in Europe (OSCE) in Chisinau, the dispute remained unresolved throughout the 1990s. There was no serious outbreak of violence after 1992, but the standoff between the two sides settled into what seemed an uneasy acceptance of the permanent division of the Moldovan state. Transnistria became another of the many "black holes" throughout the former Soviet Union, regions such as Chechnya, Nagorno-Karabakh, and Abkhazia where no long-term settlement had been reached but where the writ of central governments no longer ran. By the late 1990s, the Transnistrians still maintained a large force of men under arms, a force far better equipped than Moldova's own tiny army. A multinational peacekeeping contingent remained deployed to keep the two sides apart.

The sources of the violence and the reasons for the long stalemate are not simple. Transnistria was often portrayed in both Russia and the West as an ethnic war between nationalists in Chisinau bent on union with Romania and ethnic Russians in Transnistria fearful of being swept up in an enlarged Romanian state. Things on the ground, however, were never that straightforward. It is the multifaceted origins of the Transnistrian conundrum, as well as the political and economic interests spawned by the war itself, that have made the dispute so difficult to resolve.

TERRITORY AND HISTORY

The Transnistrian war was in no sense about ancient hatreds between eastern Latinity and Slavdom, but history did play an important role. Unlike the rest of the Republic of Moldova, Transnistria was never considered part of the traditional lands of Romanian settlement. The territory east of the Dnestr River belonged to Kievan Rus' and the kingdom of Galicia-Volhynia from the ninth to the fourteenth centuries.[3] The expansion of the Moldovan principality from the fourteenth to the sixteenth centuries stopped at the Dnestr, and the expansion of Russia from the east in the eighteenth century moved the empire up to the Dnestr's eastern bank. The Turks controlled the great fortresses along the river—the former Genoese settlements at Kilia, Akkerman, Hotin, and Bender—and all became prizes in the contest between sultan and tsar. Even the Swedish king Charles XII made his mark on Transnistrian history when he took refuge in Bender (actually located on the western side of the Dnestr) after his stunning defeat by Peter the Great in 1709. At the end of the eighteenth century, the victories of Russian forces under Count Alexander Suvorov added the area up to the Dnestr to the tsarist empire, a conquest commemorated by a statue of the Russian field marshal in modern-day Tiraspol.

It was only in 1812 that the historical Dnestr dividing line was breached. After the acquisition of Bessarabia by the Russian empire, the region between the Prut and the Dnestr was considered to be an administrative region separate from the lands to the east. Bessarabia became an imperial *oblast'* and later a Russian *guberniia* during its century-long tenure within the empire, but Transnistria was part of the districts of Podolia and Kherson. Ecclesiastical authority in Bessarabia for a time extended to congregations east of the river; after the 1830s, however, the archbishop of Chisinau exercised authority only in the Bessarabian diocese.[4] Even with the rise of Romanian nationalism in the nineteenth century, the far reaches of Transylvania were considered the western boundary of the Romanian lands while the Dnestr River formed the eastern. The romantic ideal of Greater Romania usually fell within these boundaries. Even the national poet Mihai Eminescu, in his famous poem "Doina," spoke of a Romania stretching only "from the Dnestr to the Tisza" and not farther east.

During the First World War, there was considerable speculation about the fate of Romanian-speaking populations beyond the Dnestr. The population was significant—173,982 in Podolia and Kherson *guberniias* in 1897[5]—and representatives of these eastern Romanians had participated in the Bessarabian national movement in 1917 and early 1918, agitating for the incorporation of territory across the river into the new Romanian kingdom. But the Romanian government never took a serious interest in these demands, which would have entailed a massive military operation to meet, and in the end it settled for leaving behind those villages in what would become, after the Russian civil war, Soviet Ukraine.

Calls by Transnistrian Romanian émigrés continued in the 1920s. The Romanian government was involved in funding schools and cultural organizations for Vlachs and speakers of cognate Latin languages in the Balkans, and Transnistrian representatives argued that this should be extended to Moldovan villages across the Dnestr as well. Refugees flooded across the Dnestr into Romanian Bessarabia, and the government set aside special funds for housing and educating them.[6] In 1935,

Nichita Smochină, an educator and pamphleteer based in Paris, launched the journal *Moldova nouă* (*New Moldova*) to publicize the plight of these eastern Romanians, and founded the Association of Transnistrian Romanians to assist the roughly 20,000 refugees from the east.[7] Smochină and others at first welcomed the establishment of the Soviet Moldovan autonomous republic in Transnistria in 1924 as a recognition of the "Moldovan" (that is, Romanian) character of the region.[8] But apart from publications and émigré groups, there was little interest in Romanian governmental circles in the interwar years. The problem of Bessarabia—which remained Romania's only border not secured by international treaty—trumped any residual concern for Romanian-speakers left behind in the territorial alterations of 1918.[9]

The region beyond the Dnestr was at least as ethnically diverse as Bessarabia, but Romanian-speakers formed a much smaller proportion of the population. Moldovan villages were interspersed with far more numerous Ukrainian and Russian ones; Germans and Poles were also to be found in significant numbers, while as in Bessarabia Jews dominated the region's few towns. As the authorities in the MASSR were later to discover, even these Romanian-speakers thought of themselves as "Moldovans," and their language bore little resemblance to standard Romanian. In the 1990s, propagandists in Transnistria attempted to carve out a timeless and homogeneous historical identity for the region in order to cultivate among schoolchildren a sense of loyalty to the Transnistrian fatherland. But the region was, at an even deeper level than in Bessarabia, a classic borderland where ethnic identities were fluid and situational, and where Russian, Ukrainian, Romanian, Jewish, and German influences combined to create a mixed culture.

TRANSNISTRIA IN THE SOVIET PERIOD

The region today known as Transnistria is the remnant of the Moldovan Autonomous Soviet Socialist Republic established in 1924. The old MASSR included far more territory than present-day Transnistria, stretching eastward almost to the Southern Bug River. The capital of the autonomous republic was originally far to the east, in the city of Balta, but was moved to Tiraspol on the Dnestr in 1929. When Stalin annexed Bessarabia in 1940, six *raions* of the former MASSR were

Standoff between Moldovan and Transnistrian forces on the road to Dubăsari, March 1992. Photo by Tudor Iovu.

united with portions of Bessarabia to form the new Moldovan union republic. The decision to carve up the MASSR was determined mainly by ethnic concerns. The autonomous republic had, from its inception, been far more Ukrainian than Moldovan, and the *raions* joined with Bessarabia (those nearest the Dnestr) were the ones with the greatest concentration of Moldovans. *Raions* with larger Ukrainian and Russian populations were returned to the authority of Kyiv.

Although the Transnistrian strip accounted for only twelve percent of new Moldova's territory, it played a disproportionately important role in the MSSR. Since the region had been under Soviet control since the revolution and had, moreover, already been through collectivization in the 1920s and 1930s, it was already far more sovietized than the newly acquired Bessarabia. Party cadres from Transnistria were therefore considered to be more politically loyal than those from Bessarabia. There was, in Moldova, the same tension that existed in most east European countries after the war, between "home communists" who had spent the war years working in the communist underground and "Moscow communists" who had spent the war in the Soviet Union. Communist leaders from Bessarabia were deemed politically suspect—even if their communist credentials were in fact unimpeachable—whereas those who had spent their careers in the MASSR or other parts of the Soviet Union were the cadres appointed to top posts in the new MSSR. Until 1989, no first secretary of the Communist Party of Moldova ever came from Bessarabia, and indeed, immediately after the war, a series of purges ensured that the underground communists from Romania would play no role in the new Moldovan republic.[10]

Transnistria's privileged position continued throughout the Soviet period. The MASSR had been an industrial backwater in the interwar period, but after 1945 Transnistria became a central component of the Soviet defense sector and its heavy industry. Some four-fifths of the region's population was employed in industry, construction, and the service sector.[11] The hydroelectric center in Dubăsari, begun in 1955, supplied most of the power for the entire MSSR, while the newer Moldavskaia thermal power station, constructed in 1961, was one of the largest electricity plants in the southwestern Soviet Union. The steel works in Rîbniţa, opened in 1984, produced high-quality rolled metal. Electrical engineering plants and other facilities in Tiraspol were major suppliers of technical equipment and weapons for the Soviet military.

The industrial policies of the Soviet state also produced significant demographic changes. Internal immigrants arrived to work in the new factories, increasing the Russian and Ukrainian portions of the population. In 1936 the *raions* along the Dnestr had a Russian population representing about 14 percent of the total, but by 1989 Russians made up over a quarter of the Transnistrian population. Moldovans, although still forming a plurality of the region's population by 1989, were concentrated in the villages just east of the river. Moldovans formed some 60 percent of the rural population, but only about a quarter of the city dwellers.[12] The key issue, though, was not how Russian the region became after the war, but how quintessentially Soviet. The professional careers, livelihoods, and even identities of its inhabitants depended on their connections with the Soviet center—the Communist Party, strategic industrial enterprises, and the military—not with the local farmers and agricultural firms found west of the Dnestr.

The presence of the Soviet military in the region played the crucial role in this respect. The Soviet Forty-Sixth Army, the division that pressed through Romania to Vienna during the Second World War, retreated after the war to form part of the Odessa military district, with most of the units concentrated in Transnistria and a few in southwest Ukraine. Transformed into the Fourteenth Army, the military became central to the economic and social life of Transnistria. Numbering around 3,000 officers and tens of thousands of men and local reservists by the early 1990s, the Fourteenth Army was one of the showcase units within the Soviet military. It included the elite Fifty-Ninth Guards Motorized Rifle Division and was intended to be the spearhead through southeastern Europe to Greece and Italy in the event of a military conflagration with NATO. Many of the unit's recruits were taken from Transnistria itself and, given Moldova's mild climate, the area became a haven for retired military personnel and their families. Like Belarus, with its own high concentration of military personnel, Transnistria became one of the most highly sovietized territories within the union. The primary loyalty of individuals in the region was not to Russia—even though most spoke Russian and had ties to the Russian republic—but to the Soviet Union. Of course, these trends were also evident across the Dnestr in the Bessarabian part of the MSSR, but it was in Transnistria that the Soviet system became most entrenched. Most local Transnistrians were employed directly in the defense of the Soviet system and spent most of their lives reaping the particular benefits that this status afforded. Tiraspol and Chisinau were only a short distance apart—about 50 kilometers on the highway linking the two cities—but in terms of social development, economic structure, and status within the republic, by the late 1980s their citizens were living in two increasingly distinct worlds.

POLITICAL MOBILIZATION AND THE OUTBREAK OF VIOLENCE

It should not be surprising that the strongest opposition to the national movement that began in 1988 came from Transnistria.

TABLE 10
POPULATION OF TRANSNISTRIA, 1897–1989

	1897		*1936*		*1989*	
Moldovans	173,982	3.0%	122,683	41.8%	239,936	39.9%
Ukrainians	3,904,858	67.9	84,293	28.7	170,079	28.3
Russians	674,359	11.7	41,794	14.2	153,393	25.5
Jews	691,843	12.0	23,158	7.9	—	—
Other	306,869	5.3	21,873	7.4	38,252	6.4
Total	5,445,042	94.6	271,928	100.0	601,660	100.0

NOTE: Figures for 1897 are for all of Podolia and Kherson *guberniias*, a region much larger than the area that would later form the MASSR and the eastern MSSR. Figures for 1936 include only *raions* later incorporated into the MSSR (Grigoriopol, Dubăsari, Camenca, Rîbniţa, Slobozia, Tiraspol). Hence, the 1936 and 1989 figures are directly comparable; the 1897 figures are given only for information, not for comparison. Dashes indicate no figures available.
SOURCE: Compiled from N. A. Troinitskii, ed. *Obshchii svod po imperii rezul'tatov razrabotki dannykh pervoi vseobshchei perepisi naseleniia, proizvedennoi 28 ianvaria 1897 goda* (St. Petersburg: n.p., 1905), 2: 20, 22, 23, 27; AOSPRM, f. 49, op. 1, d. 3997, l. 108; and 1989 Soviet census.

From the outset, managers at Transnistrian factories and local party and council heads were the most vocal in their condemnation of the reforms being initiated in Chisinau. Already in the late 1980s there developed a dynamic that would culminate in full-scale war by 1992: Every move in Chisinau that pulled the republic farther away from Moscow was met by a countermove in Transnistria that drew the region itself farther away from Chisinau. It was a dynamic replicated in several Soviet republics at the time. While central elites in the capitals were arguing for greater control over local resources and the revival of indigenous languages, they were also initiating a policy of centralization within their own republics, attempting to gain control over local party and state institutions that might see Moscow—rather than the republican capitals—as the legitimate locus of authority. These centralization policies prompted their own movements for autonomy and independence within the republics. Although national symbols were the mobilizational tools wielded by political elites, the key issues were not symbols and national myths but rather real problems of political and economic control. In an environment in which everything quickly came up for grabs—local resources, local institutions, economic centers, factories—regional elites within the republics began to replicate the conflict between Moscow and the republican capitals.

TABLE 11

TRANSNISTRIA IN THE MOLDOVAN ECONOMY, 1991
(Regional production as percentage of national total)

Large electrical machines	100.0%
Power transformers	100.0
Gas containers	100.0
Cotton textiles	96.6
Electric energy	87.5
Cement	58.1
Low-horsepower electric engines	55.8
Sheet metal	23.5
Agricultural products	13.1

SOURCE: Adapted from *IMF Economic Reviews: Moldova, 1993* (Washington: International Monetary Fund, 1993), p. 46.

Throughout much of 1988, there seemed to be little conflict between the aims of the informal organizations in Chisinau and the interests of party and state officials elsewhere in the republic. Although the Alexei Mateevici Club was more open in its calls for redressing the balance between Russian and Moldovan language use, the more powerful organization from the outset was the Moldovan Democratic Movement, whose chief purpose was simply to support the party in its effort to implement perestroika. But as the informal groups took shape, finally coalescing into the Popular Front in the summer of 1989, rifts began to show between reformers in the center and groups in the east.

The issue that received the most attention was the proposal to adopt Moldovan as the republic's official language and to transfer to the Latin script. For the Popular Front, the language question became a battle standard, a highly charged symbol of the rights of the ethnic majority within the republic. For non-Moldovans, particularly many Transnistrians, the proposed language laws were clear evidence not only of the anti-Soviet and anti-Party views of the Moldovan informals, but also of the shifting balance of power to the Moldovan majority and away from those groups that had traditionally exercised authority. Opposition to the language movement was not, of course, limited to Transnistria. Indeed, the Front's shift from a broad reform movement to a more narrowly ethnic movement cost the support of several minority groups, particularly the Gagauz. Demonstrations against the draft laws were also held throughout Bessarabia, especially in cities with large industrial bases and the attendant Russian-speaking populations, such as Bălți in northern Bessarabia. But it was in Transnistria where loyalty to the Soviet system was strongest and where the language reforms, particularly the required language tests mandated by the new laws, promised to have the greatest impact.

The key question during this period, though, was never purely one of minority rights. Clearly, had the Popular Front avoided the appearance of chauvinism, it might also have avoided the sharp reaction against its policies after 1989 and, moreover, have remained a major and unified force in Moldovan politics after independence. But had the main issue been protecting minority rights, one would have expected the greatest opposition to have come not from Transnistria but from Bessarabia. There were far more Ukrainians and Russians west of the Dnestr River than in Transnistria, and in some northern *raions* and in the cities, the Slavic populations were just as concentrated as in the *raions* east of the Dnestr. In Transnistria as a whole, Moldovans formed nearly 40 percent of the total population of just over 600,000. Rather, although the Transnistrian dispute was generally portrayed as a revolt by Slavs against the nationalizing policies of Chisinau, the real source of the violence after 1990 lay in fact at the level of elite politics. The language laws and the attendant rise of a new generation of largely Bessarabian politicians threatened the position of Transnistrians within the political and social hierarchy. The reaction to the national movement was not a revolt by minorities, but a revolt by a displaced elite against those who threatened to unseat them.

The center of opposition was the network of local party and state institutions in Transnistria, particularly the *raion* executive committees and the coordinating committees of industrial concerns. Just as the system of collective farms and their chairmen would become the nucleus of the new Agrarian Democratic Party in Chisinau, so too the existing political and economic structures in Transnistria provided a mobilizational resource for those opposed to the center's reforms.

Organization began in the summer of 1989, shortly after the formation of the Popular Front in Chisinau. Beginning in August, workers at factories in Transnistria held demonstrations against the proposed language laws. Women workers, grouped in a newly formed Women's Strike Committee headed by Nina Andreeva, blocked railway lines lead-

Results of fighting between Moldovan and Transnistrian troops. The slogan on the tank reads "For the Motherland! Dnestr Moldovan Republic." Photo by Tudor Iovu.

ing across the Dnestr River and made special appeals to Moscow to assist in their efforts against "nationalists and chauvinists" in Chisinau. The parliamentary vote in favor of Moldovan as the official language brought events to a head. In response to the vote, local councils in Tiraspol and other cities voted against the ruling and held that the language laws were not to be considered valid east of the river. Tensions rose in the weeks following the vote. Clashes between Moldovan police and the growing band of armed Transnistrian "self-defense units" increased. The leader of the opposition movement, Igor Smirnov, was branded a separatist by Chisinau and expelled from the Communist Party in April 1990.[13] Smirnov had only been in Moldova since 1987, having moved from Ukraine to manage the Elektromash machine-building concern in Tiraspol. He managed to ride the wave of discontent with the Popular Front's cultural reforms, and in August 1989 was elected chair of the United Council of Work Collectives (OSTK), the organization that coordinated the industrial strikes and demonstrations. Further support came from some members of the Edinstvo movement in Chisinau, some of whom moved to Tiraspol to aid the Transnistrians rather than continue to work within the Moldovan political system.[14]

The MSSR Supreme Soviet, emboldened by the vote on language, continued to push through further cultural and political reforms. The Transnistrians, seeing each of these moves as evidence of Moldova's intention to leave the Soviet Union and join Romania, continued their own preparations for secession. In January 1990, the OSTK organized a referendum on Transnistrian autonomy, in which a reported 96 percent of voters favored a self-governing status for Transnistria within the MSSR and, if necessary in the future, the creation of a wholly separate Transnistrian republic.[15] In the summer, the Moldovans declared local sovereignty, and the change in the MSSR's status within the Soviet Union set off a chain reaction within Moldova itself. A congress of local authorities on the east bank declared a separate Dnestr Moldovan Republic on September 2, 1990, a move immediately condemned by Chisinau. Two months later, the Transnistrians set up their own local legislature, which included mainly Russians and Ukrainians, but also many local Moldovan, Bulgarian, and Gagauz deputies.[16] Both governments were still at this time formally part of the Soviet federation, but the Transnistrians held that they were no longer part of Moldova.

From 1990 things quickly spiraled out of the central government's control. Transnistrian workers armed themselves with weapons taken from Soviet army stores located in Transnistria and began to take over police stations and government institutions along the east bank. At the same time, police units still loyal to the central government took up positions along the river, barricading bridges and at times exchanging shots with their counterparts to the east. By 1991 most of the region east of the Dnestr was no long under the effective control of Chisinau and, in the chaos that was quickly descending on the republic, for all practical purposes formed a separate administrative region.

THE END OF THE SOVIET UNION AND THE TRANSNISTRIAN WAR

Throughout the fall and spring of 1990 and 1991, the Transnistrian side consolidated its hold over the region on the east bank of the Dnestr and, in a series of moves in the spring, also gained firm control over portions of the west bank, especially the important city of Bender. By the summer of 1991, Moldova was virtually cut off from the rest of the Soviet Union: The major rail and road links to Ukraine and beyond ran through the east-bank cities of Rîbniţa, Dubăsari, and

TABLE 12

CHRONOLOGY OF THE TRANSNISTRIAN
CONFLICT, 1989–98

August 1989	New Moldovan language laws
September–October 1989	Strikes in Transnistrian cities protesting language laws
November 1989–August 1990	*Raion* and city councils in Transnistria reject Moldovan reform legislation; organize local congresses calling for autonomy
September 2, 1990	Dnestr Moldovan Republic (DMR) declared
November 1990–August 1991	Clashes along Dnestr River between Moldovan police and Transnistrian irregulars
August 27, 1991	Declaration of independent Republic of Moldova
December 1991	Presidential elections in DMR and referendum on independence; increase in clashes along Dnestr
February–May 1992	Fighting between Moldovan and DMR forces; arrival of volunteer and Cossack forces from Russia and Ukraine; first involvement of Russian Fourteenth Army units
June 1992	Major fighting around Bender; intervention of Fourteenth Army; Moldovan forces driven from Bender; Alexander Lebed' appointed Fourteenth Army commander
July 1992	Snegur-Yeltsin agreement on ceasefire and "special status" for Transnistria; deployment of Russian-DMR-Moldovan peacekeepers
February 1993	OSCE mission established in Chisinau
July 1994	New Moldovan constitution promises special autonomous status for Transnistria
August 1994	"DMR ruble" introduced as currency in DMR
October 1994	Moldovan-Russian accord on withdrawal of Fourteenth Army
April 1995	Fourteenth Army renamed "operational group of Russian forces" (OGRF)
May 1995	Alexander Lebed' replaced as OGRF commander by Valerii Evnevich
January 1996	Joint Russian-Ukrainian-Moldovan statement recognizing Transnistria as constituent part of Moldova
May 1997	Moscow memorandum between Moldova and DMR committing sides to existence within a "common state"
March 1998	Odessa agreement between Moldova and DMR, guaranteed by Ukraine, Russia, and OSCE, outlines variety of measures to build confidence and security
November 1998	Unit of ten Ukrainian military observers deployed in the security zone

SOURCE: Adapted from John O'Loughlin, Vladimir Kolossov, and Andrei Tchepalyga, "National Construction, Territorial Separatism, and Post-Soviet Geopolitics in the Transdniester Moldovan Republic," *Post-Soviet Geography and Economics* 39, no. 6 (1998): 347–48; Vasile Nedelciuc, *The Republic of Moldova* (Chisinau: Parliament of the Republic of Moldova, 1992), pp. 90–116; and news reports.

Tiraspol, all of whose local councils had declared their allegiance to the Transnistrian republic.

The Moscow coup in August 1991 was a major turning point. Communist Party authorities in Chisinau from the outset sided against the plotters in the Kremlin; led by Lucinschi's successor, the reformist First Secretary Grigore Eremei, the local Politburo severed ties with the CPSU. The party, though, had already become largely irrelevant, with all important decisions being taken by the parliament and President Mircea Snegur. Within days of the putsch, on August 27, 1991, the parliament declared Moldova an independent republic and officially took control of Soviet and party assets on Moldovan territory.

The reaction of the Transnistrians to the coup was the complete opposite. Igor Smirnov publicly praised the putschists as saviors of the Soviet state and promised military assistance to support the state of emergency. Once it became clear that the coup had failed, ending the Soviet Union rather than saving it, the Transnistrians rushed to shore up their own state. In cooperation with the Gagauz, the Transnistrians suggested the establishment of a tripartite federation with Moldova.[17] The Moldovan parliament rejected the proposal and instead used the opportunity of the coup attempt to target the leaders of the separatist movements. Smirnov and several local Transnistrian officials, along with Stepan Topal and other leaders of the Gagauz movement in the south, were arrested and charged with supporting the illegal putsch.[18] In response, the DMR threatened to cut off gas and electricity supplies to the rest of Moldova, and Transnistrian women once again blocked rail lines leading west of the river. The central authorities eventually capitulated and released the leaders, but the incident served only to convince both the Gagauz and the Transnistrians that compromise with Chisinau was impossible. As local journalists quipped at the time, the Snegur leadership thus made two disastrous mistakes: The first was arresting Smirnov and the DMR leadership, the second was letting them go.

The role of the Soviet Fourteenth Army during this period proved critical. In March 1991, the Moldovan authorities issued protest notes to Gorbachev and the Soviet defense ministry complaining of the army's assistance to the Transnistrians.[19] Complaints in the summer pointed to the introduction of Soviet OMON special forces into the region, and further protest declarations throughout early 1992 urged Fourteenth Army officers to maintain military discipline.[20] The arms wielded by the DMR's newly formed army, the Dnestr Guards, originally came from poorly guarded Fourteenth Army stores. The central command of the Transnistrian forces also came from the Fourteenth Army officer corps. The army's commander, Lieutenant-General Gennadii Iakovlev, defected in early 1992 to head up the DMR's armed forces, and Colonel Ştefan Chiţac, the army's former chief of staff, became the DMR's defense minister.[21] Other junior officers soon followed suit. The move from Soviet to Transnistrian allegiance was a breach of military discipline, but it was also to some extent understandable in the chaos of 1991. In a situation in which soldiers lost the state to which they had pledged their lives, it was not unreasonable for officers to see their first loyalty as to their homes and families, and most saw Transnistria—not Moldova—as the closest thing to a homeland. By the time the Russian Federation asserted formal control over the Fourteenth Army, declaring it to be a Russian rather than a Soviet force in April 1992, the flow of men and materiel to the Transnistrians had already been substantial.

The arms race continued throughout the fall and spring of 1991 and 1992. Further defections from the Fourteenth Army swelled the ranks of the DMR forces, and Cossacks from Russia and Ukraine arrived to assist the Transnistrians. The Moldovans instituted a military draft and announced plans to build a 15,000-man professional army with a further 10,000-man force of *Carabinieri*, or interior ministry troops.[22] Moldovans admitted that they had received some military hardware from Romania, and both Alexander Lebed' and Russian defense minister Pavel Grachev would later allege that Romanian military advisors and pilots were active in Moldova.[23] It is likely, though, that most of the resources came simply from Soviet military and interior ministry stores over which the Moldovans had asserted control. At the same time, in what one observer called a "creeping putsch," armed Transnistrian forces increased their control over police stations in villages and towns east of the Dnestr and in some locales along the west bank as well.[24] An effort by Moldovan police officers to disarm the Transnistrian irregulars around Dubăsari led to an open clash on December 13, 1991, the first serious hostilities between the two sides.[25] The Dubăsari incident sparked a series of exchanges along the river, as local police organs transformed themselves into defenders of the new Moldovan republic. The firefights also illustrated the lack of control within the Moldovan armed forces, as police, armed civilians, interior ministry troops, and

Cossack forces in their barracks in Dubăsari, March 1992. Fighters from Russia and Ukraine assisted the Transnistrians in their battles with the central Moldovan government. Photo by Tudor Iovu.

former Soviet soldiers now loyal to independent Moldova acted virtually independently of Chisinau.

Tensions escalated over the spring and summer. Over a hundred people were killed in battles along the river in the spring, despite a shaky cease-fire negotiated between the two sides.[26] Bridges across the Dnestr were mined or destroyed by the Transnistrians, who also mounted extensive military operations west of the Dnestr, especially into the west-bank cities of Criuleni and Bender. The incursions prompted Snegur to announce a state of emergency effective over the entire republic at the end of March. A dozen or more cease-fires were agreed to and then broken, usually in response to attempts by the Transnistrians to seize police stations and local government offices, or attempts by the Moldovans to reclaim buildings taken by the separatists. By May, Fourteenth Army units had also become involved in the fighting, with the ostensible goal of pacifying the conflict but more often than not openly assisting the Transnistrians.

Over the summer, violence once again broke out on a large scale.

On June 19, Transnistrian forces, using armored vehicles from Russian army depots, stormed the last remaining police station in Bender still loyal to the Chisinau government. Moldovan forces from the surrounding area attempted to fight their way into Bender and succeeded in retaking most of the city. The city's population was largely Russian, but ethnicity had little to do with the aims of either side. Bender was also a major arms repository, and after the destruction of the bridge at Dubăsari earlier in the conflict, the city stood astride the only major road and rail artery still linking Chisinau to the rest of the former Soviet republics. Bender was thus not only militarily but also economically vital to the future of the Moldovan state, and the government's military action was an attempt to gain back a strategically important piece of territory.

Moldovan troops launched a mortar attack on the city and planes reportedly dropped bombs in an attempt to force the DMR troops to retreat to the east. Moldovan armored personnel carriers moved into Bender, and street-to-street fighting ensued. After a day of fighting, though, the Fourteenth Army intervened in the conflict and on the night of June 20–21 fought alongside the DMR troops to drive the government forces from the city. As Russian Federation vice president Alexander Rutskoi would later declare, the intervention had been occasioned by the Moldovans' committing "a bloody slaughter" against local Russians when they entered the city.[27]

Skirmishes continued until early July, but the Moldovan defeat in Bender marked the climax of the conflict. From the outset, the Moldovans were both outmanned and outgunned. The hastily organized national army consisted mainly of former police officers or interior ministry forces equipped with mortars, armored personnel carriers, and antitank weaponry. The DMR forces, by contrast, had at their disposal T-64 and T-72 tanks, Grad and Alazan rocket systems, trained specialists from the Fourteenth Army, and Cossack volunteers.[28] Casualty figures were widely disputed, ranging from a few dozen reported by the Moldovans to nearly 700 reported by the Transnistrians.[29] However, the longer-term effects of the battle were profound.

First, the violence in Bender secured official Russian involvement in the dispute. Until June, the Russian Federation had remained officially aloof from the conflict and, with the exception of minor periodic involvement by individual Fourteenth Army detachments, had continued to call for an equitable and peaceful settlement. So long as the Transnistrians were in the winning position, the Russians were content to let things go on as before. The escalation of the conflict, however, not only threatened Russian security interests in the region, but also posed a threat to the position of the Transnistrians, whom the Russian press and Duma had long portrayed as an embattled Russian minority fighting against chauvinistic Moldovan nationalism. The Bender attack came at a time when the rhetoric surrounding Russia's obligations toward the stranded russophone minorities in the post-Soviet states was at its height, and the Transnistrians were in many ways the archetypal version of "Russian-speakers": Although certainly not all ethnic Russians, the Transnistrian population and its leadership epitomized the loyalty to the Soviet state and Great Russian culture that characterized the disparate minorities grouped under that umbrella label.[30]

The actual decision to intervene was probably taken by the Fourteenth Army commander, Lieutenant-General Iurii Netkachev, rather than by the Yeltsin leadership. Only days before the battle, Yeltsin had warned that Russia would "react to defend people and stop the bloodshed,"[31] but by summer 1992, the lines of communication between the Fourteenth Army headquarters and Moscow had largely broken down. The Russian defense ministry never publicly claimed responsibility for ordering the intervention, although it would later be touted as a successful effort by the Russian military to halt the growing violence on the former Soviet periphery.[32] Netkachev's intervention, though, illustrated the degree to which Russian commanders on the ground were acting without the full control of Moscow, and within days of the Bender battle, the commander lost his post to Major-General Alexander Lebed', the respected young airborne officer and personal ally of the recently appointed defense minister, Pavel Grachev.

Lebed' had already had experience in Moldova, not all of it pleasant. He had been part of the Russian defense ministry's expert team sent to negotiate the status of Russian forces after the collapse of the Soviet Union, and he would later describe his conversations with General Ion Costaş, the Moldovan defense chief and architect of the Bender campaign, as "a real pig . . . and I apologize to pigs for making this comparison."[33] He thus came to Moldova convinced of the barbarity of the Moldovan government and the need to protect locals against the zeal of the nationalists in Chisinau. The Russians would later portray their role as that of a stabilizing force preventing a return to the tragic violence of Bender. But under both Netkachev and Lebed' the Fourteenth Army's methods were closer to those of a protection racket than a neutral peace-

Igor Smirnov, president of the Dnestr Moldovan Republic, in his office in Tiraspol, 1993. Photo by Tudor Iovu.

keeping operation: encouraging the Transnistrians under the guise of protecting embattled Russian-speakers and then intervening militarily when the war threatened to get out of hand.[34]

The escalation in violence and the active involvement of the Russian Federation, however, did lead to a formal cease-fire and the deployment of a multiparty peacekeeping force along the Dnestr. Shortly after the Bender battle, Yeltsin and Snegur met in Moscow and hammered out an agreement to halt the violence and lay the groundwork for peace talks. The Yeltsin-Snegur agreement, signed on July 21, 1992, provided for the cessation of hostilities, the creation of a security zone along the river, the deployment of a tripartite peacekeeping force composed of six Russian paratroop battalions (under separate operational command from the Fourteenth Army) and three each from Moldova and the DMR, and the initiation of talks on finding a political solution to the conflict. Overseeing the peacekeeping operation was a tripartite Joint Control Commission, to which complaints about violations of the security zone and the cease-fire could be addressed. Snegur lifted the state of emergency, and Transnistrian enterprises began to restore gas and electricity supplies to the west bank. Russian peacekeepers remained in the region throughout the 1990s, although after 1994 the Russians began to draw down their own forces, largely because of the huge cost of the deployment, and turn over more control to Moldovan and DMR troops, as well as to a small group of Ukrainian military observers that arrived in 1998.

A second effect of the Bender battle was to increase the legitimacy of the local DMR leadership and to harden their bargaining position. Those who had prosecuted the war—Smirnov, his chief advisor Valerii Litskai, the Supreme Soviet speaker Grigore Maracuţa, deputy speaker Vladimir Atamaniuk—retained their offices long after the end of hostilities. The violence of summer 1992 also quickly became mythologized as a war for the independence of the Transnistrian fatherland. A heroes' memorial was erected outside the DMR Supreme Soviet in downtown Tiraspol, including a small tank used by Transnistrian forces during the war, and awards were made to those who had fought as part of the Dnestr Guards for their part in "liberating" the region from Moldovan fascists. Schoolbooks and history texts used in Transnistria's schools also came to treat the 1992 violence as a war for national liberation. These textbooks, written by former Communist Party historians who moved to Tiraspol from Chisinau, used the language and symbolism of the Soviet Great Patriotic War and applied both to the conflict along the Dnestr. As one textbook maintained:

> The traitorous, barbaric, and unprovoked invasion of Bender had a single goal: to frighten and bring to their knees the inhabitants of the Dnestr Republic, to make them shudder with terror. However, the people's bravery, steadfastness, and love of liberty saved the Dnestr Republic. The defense of Bender against the overwhelming forces of the enemy closed a heroic page in the history of our young republic. The best sons and daughters of the people sacrificed their lives for peace and liberty in our land.[35]

Not only did the DMR leadership come to see compromise with the Moldovans as impossible, but Transnistrian schoolchildren were also taught that independence had been sanctified with the blood of their compatriots. Both outcomes made finding a solution that would allow Transnistria to remain within Moldova profoundly difficult.

The violence also had a third effect. Just as it helped consolidate the position of the Transnistrians, so it in many ways set the worldview of the Moldovans as well. Chisinau had long been less than enthusiastic about cooperation with Russia and the CIS, but the intervention of

Russian troops and the continual pro-DMR rhetoric from the Russian Duma convinced many leaders that the Russian Federation was intent on using the Transnistrian crisis as a way of exercising control over Moldovan domestic affairs. So long as Moldova remained divided, the argument went, Russia's security and political aims in the region could be realized. The violence also had a legitimizing role for the newly independent Moldovan leadership, who took on the mantle of defender of the territorial integrity of the young state. Since it was a war that the Moldovans clearly lost, however, monuments to the heroes of the conflict in Chisinau were more modest than those in Tiraspol.

INTERNATIONAL INVOLVEMENT AND STALLED NEGOTIATIONS

With the upsurge in violence in 1992, the Transnistrian dispute quickly attracted the attention of international organizations, particularly the OSCE. As in other post-Soviet conflict zones, the organization established a long-term mission in Moldova in 1993, with the goal of supporting the negotiating process and providing expert information and analysis for the international community. Consisting mainly of seconded diplomats and military personnel from OSCE member states, the small mission began to issue reports on the state of negotiations, human rights, and other issues of political and security concern. Although the heads of the mission changed frequently, the office played an important role in internationalizing the negotiations and providing an objective voice in the peace talks. Numerous OSCE resolutions, supported by the U.S. Congress and other bodies, reconfirmed international support for Moldova's sovereignty and territorial integrity, a peaceful solution in Transnistria, and the quick and complete withdrawal of Russian forces.

From the outset, though, the OSCE's role was controversial. Several reports leaked to the Moldovan press were criticized for being too "pro-Russian," especially an early report that recommended that the Moldovan language law be changed to make both Moldovan and Russian equal official languages. In other instances, the OSCE was criticized by the Transnistrians for meddling and, at the worst, for being too "pro-Moldovan." OSCE observers were not allowed by the DMR peacekeepers into the security zone for nearly a year after the cease-fire.[36] In 1997,

Alexander Lebed', commander of the Russian Fourteenth Army in Moldova, being welcomed by the residents of Bender in 1993. Lebed' would later use his prominence in the Moldovan-Transnistrian dispute to launch a political career in Russia. Photo by Tudor Iovu.

under the tenure of Donald Johnson, a former U.S. ambassador to Mongolia, OSCE representatives were declared personae non grata in the DMR and were frequently blocked from crossing the cease-fire line.[37]

In such conditions, the role of external actors was necessarily limited. However, with the OSCE's assistance, several agreements were reached that seemed to pave the way toward a final settlement. The basis for negotiations was the 1992 Yeltsin-Snegur accord, but since that document was little more than a cease-fire agreement, there was need for comprehensive talks on the political structure of the Moldovan-DMR relationship. Regular meetings were held between Snegur and Smirnov at restaurants along the Chisinau-Tiraspol highway, and specially appointed expert groups followed up the meetings with technical discussions. Petru Lucinschi continued the talks after succeeding Snegur as Moldovan president, and both presidents also worked to settle the status of Russian troops in frequent talks with Moscow.

One important result of these multilevel contacts was the agreement between Moldova and the Russian Federation regarding the withdrawal of the Fourteenth Army from the republic. Russian troops, including the Three-Hundredth Guards Airborne Regiment in Chisinau commanded by Aleksei Lebed'—the younger brother of Alexander Lebed'—had been pulled out in the first two years following independence, but little had been done about the Fourteenth Army in Tiraspol. Some troops had been reassigned to Russia and a considerable number had resigned their posts and joined the DMR army. The Moldovans continued to insist, though, that the Russian army was an illegal foreign military presence, specifically forbidden in the neutrality clause (Article 11) of the 1994 Moldovan constitution.

Moreover, as commander, Alexander Lebed' became a frequent and bellicose commentator on the Transnistrian problem, repeatedly accusing the Moldovan side of instituting a form of ethnic cleansing during and after the Bender operation. "The Transnistrian people are being systematically, hypocritically, and brutally annihilated," he told the newspaper *Sovetskaia Rossiia* shortly after taking command, "in a way that makes the SS of fifty years ago look like amateurs."[38] He portrayed himself as the pacifier of the Transnistrian conflict, but it was in fact under his predecessor, Netkachev, that the decisive intervention on behalf of the Transnistrians took place; although Lebed' was more vocal than Netkachev, by the time he arrived on the scene the Moldovans had already lost Transnistria. The public statements of Lebed' soon became so outrageous that he was ordered by the Russian defense ministry to have no further contact with the press. Until he left his post in 1995, though, Lebed' proved to be an egalitarian critic. His condemnation of Smirnov and his associates as corrupt war-profiteers, of the Moldovans as fascists, and of his superiors in the Russian military as incompetents earned him enemies on all sides.[39]

Eventually, Russian and Moldovan negotiators managed to agree on the status of the army, with Yeltsin and Snegur signing a final agreement on withdrawal in Moscow in October 1994. According to the accord, all Russian troops would be withdrawn from Transnistria within three years, and the withdrawal process was to be "synchronized"—a term left undefined—with the granting of a special territorial status to the separatist region. The agreement was welcomed by both the Moldovans and international observers, but several problems were evident from the outset. The Duma insisted that, since the document was an international agreement on Russian military forces, it needed first to be ratified by the

Russian parliament. However, because there was no support for abandoning the DMR within the Russian legislature, there was also little chance that the document would be approved. As a result, it was unclear when the "three-year" time clock was supposed to start ticking. The Moldovans insisted that the withdrawal period began when the document was signed by the two heads of state, the Russian president and foreign ministry indicated that it began with the granting of autonomy to the Transnistrians, and the Duma stressed that it began only after the document was ratified by the lower house. In addition, the Fourteenth Army was later officially downgraded to an "operational group of Russian forces" (OGRF) making it uncertain whether the 1994 agreement still legally applied to the renamed military units located in Moldova. Unlike Georgia, the Moldovan government had repeatedly rejected Russian insistence on military basing rights in the region, and many in Chisinau felt that Moscow's stalling on the withdrawal process was simply a way of putting pressure on Moldova over the base issue.[40]

Beyond the legal problems of ratification and the withdrawal period, though, the document also illustrated the extreme complexity of the Transnistrian dispute. While the Moldovan side insisted that Russian troops must leave the territory, for most members of the Russian army "withdrawal" meant little more than a tram ticket across Tiraspol. Most of the army's large officer corps saw Transnistria as their homeland. Many had been born there or had arrived long before the breakup of the Soviet Union; their wives and children also grew up in the region, and most were loath to be relocated to a place that few saw as their legitimate homeland. The army's rank-and-file soldiers were in a similar position, and in contravention of international law, the Russian army had actually taken Transnistrian conscripts into its ranks after 1991. The real challenge was therefore not getting Russian troops off Moldovan territory, but rather finding creative ways of demobilizing or integrating these soldiers with the Moldovan armed forces, a politically sensitive issue rarely broached by anyone in Chisinau or Tiraspol.

Furthermore, the 1995 agreement said nothing about the tough issue of Russian weapons and other military equipment. Transnistrian, Moldovan, and Russian negotiators worked on this problem throughout the 1990s, but the sides were deeply divided. The Moldovans and Russians agreed that the equipment should either be destroyed or removed to Russia; the small Moldovan army had no need for the massive Fourteenth Army arsenal, nor did they have the money to pay for destroying or guarding the older ordnance, some of which dated back to the 1930s. The Transnistrians, on the other hand, insisted that the weapons should be turned over to the DMR. On more than one occasion, DMR detachments attempted to take control of ammunition depots, leading the commander of the Tiraspol garrison, Colonel Mikhail Bergman, to place mines around several storage centers.[41]

By the end of the 1990s, the size of the OGRF had decreased considerably, to fewer than 2,500 officers and men.[42] Some military equipment had been destroyed or withdrawn to Russia, but huge stockpiles remained in the arms depot in Cobasna in northern Transnistria. Under the successor to Lebed'—Lieutenant-General Evgenii Evnevich—the army played a much more conciliatory role; there was no more rhetoric about Moldovan fascists or orchestrated genocide. Just as no love had been lost between Lebed' and the DMR, so too did the DMR leadership sometimes butt heads with Evnevich. In one embarrassing incident, in 1998 Evnevich invited the OSCE mission and all the diplomatic representations in Chisinau to a special ceremony at the Russian barracks in Tiraspol to consecrate a newly constructed Orthodox church. The move was meant to be a sign of conciliation and an example of the army's commitment to remaining on good terms with the international diplomatic community. But when the delegation from Chisinau reached the security zone, DMR troops refused to let them enter. The entire convoy returned to Chisinau after having been harassed and searched by the DMR soldiers, whose presence in the security zone, in any case, contravened the cease-fire agreement.

Another important development in Moldovan–DMR negotiations was the signing of a memorandum of common negotiating principles in May 1997 in Moscow. Much of the previous eighteen months had been taken up with negotiating the wording of the two-page document, which was pushed by the OSCE as a way of breaking the impasse that had set in by 1995. The document set out the areas of agreement that both sides shared and, most importantly, committed both teams to negotiating from the position that Moldova should remain a "common state" within its internationally recognized borders. The Moldovans were concerned about how the Transnistrians might interpret particular portions of the text, as had happened with the 1992 cease-fire, and therefore insisted on a separate annex, guaranteed by Russia, Ukraine, and the OSCE, that elaborated each of the points and committed all signatories to working toward a peaceful and equitable solution to the dispute.

With the signing of the memorandum document, newspapers and wire services immediately reported that the Transnistrian conflict had been resolved. As it turned out, though, nothing could have been farther from the truth. In many ways, in fact, the memorandum represented a serious defeat for the Moldovan negotiating side. Much of the problem rested on the minutiae of interpretation. In the first place, the document was signed at the bottom by President Petru Lucinschi and by Igor Smirnov, identified in the text as representatives of Moldova and Transnistria. The DMR leadership viewed this formulation as an implicit recognition by the Moldovans that the DMR formed a separate entity from Moldova proper. Moreover, the term *common state* was also seen by the DMR as a victory for their cause, since Smirnov interpreted the phrase to mean a confederal state formed by two sovereign political entities, a solution repeatedly rejected by Moldovan negotiators. Within a week of the memorandum's signing, these disputes came into the open. The Moldovans had anticipated these problems, and had therefore insisted on the separate interpretive annex guaranteed by the OSCE and regional powers. But since the DMR never recognized the annex as valid, the negotiators were stuck with a document whose basic meaning was in dispute. If anything, the document merely reinforced the DMR's sense of separateness and, in the end, created even more ill will between the two sides. Further agreements signed in Odessa in March 1998 outlined a series of measures to build confidence and security, including the opening of bridges across the Dnestr and the gradual demilitarization of the security zone. These agreements too, however, faltered on the widely disparate bargaining positions of both sides.

The final solution to the Transnistrian problem was also wrapped up with Moldova's complex relations with Russia. In 1997 Russia accounted for over 80 percent of the value of Moldova's exports and nearly half of all imports.[43] The republic's energy debt to Russia amounted to some $215 million, or roughly 11 percent of Moldova's GDP.[44] Russia's gas monopoly, Gazprom, periodically reduced deliveries and threatened on occasion to cut off supplies entirely. Although many Moldovan policymakers were concerned about the political influence that Russia could wield via Gazprom, both on domestic politics in general and on Transnistria in particular, this aspect of the Russian-Moldovan relationship had more to do with simple economics than with any Russian grand strategy. Still, with ultranationalists in Russia seeing the Transnistrians as an important foreign policy cause, any pressure from Russia in the economic sphere was interpreted in Chisinau as at least indirectly related to the problem of the separatist east.

MOLDOVAN POLITICAL CHANGES AND TRANSNISTRIAN STATE-BUILDING

Conditions for a resolution of the Transnistrian dispute were far more propitious by the late 1990s than at any time since the eruption of violence. The euphoria of Moldovan independence had passed, and not even the most committed pan-Romanians talked publicly of union with Romania. The new president, Lucinschi, had strong links with Russia and little incentive to stoke nationalism of any sort—whether pan-Romanian or Moldovanist, both of which Snegur had attempted to use at various stages. The post-Soviet constitution made specific provision for territorial autonomy for Transnistria, and the parliament had illustrated how far it was willing to go by granting territorial autonomy to the Gagauz in 1995. The Bessarabia region had become an effectively bilingual society, with street signs and public announcements in two languages; in the major urban areas, such as Chisinau and Bălți, Russian was more in evidence than Romanian, and in still other areas, such as the extreme north and south of the republic, there was little Romanian-language use at all. While still facing monumental economic difficulties, the Moldovan government had managed to widen the gap between Bessarabia and Transnistria, the former clearly on the way to building a market-based economy, the latter an even more corrupt version of Brezhnev-era clientelism.

Russia, as well, had changed its position on the Transnistrians. By the end of the decade, the plight of Russian-speakers in the former Soviet republics was no longer a major issue in Russian domestic politics.[45] Despite continued interest within the Duma, the Russian foreign and defense ministries, as well as the president's office, had far larger problems to worry about than the DMR. Transnistria's massive energy debt to Gazprom (about two-thirds of Moldova's total) and the perception of the DMR as a state existing merely to serve the economic interests of its leaders caused growing dissatisfaction in Moscow.

Moreover, at every turn, the Transnistrians had shown themselves more than willing to bite the hand that fed. They strongly supported the

1991 coup plotters against Gorbachev, sent fighters to aid the Russian parliament against Yeltsin in 1993, and remained a major source of support for opposition groups such as Vladimir Zhirinovsky's Liberal Democratic Party and Gennadii Zyuganov's Communist Party of the Russian Federation. The internal security forces of the DMR were controlled by Colonel Vadim Shevtsov, the former OMON commander in Latvia considered responsible for the deaths of protestors in Riga in January 1991. The Russian leadership thus had little reason to associate itself with the DMR, which increasingly came to represent the most unsavory forces in post-Soviet politics.

Ukraine—long a silent regional player in the Transnistrian game—began to take a greater interest. Relations with Moldova were strong from the outset, with Kyiv already in 1992 working to halt the transit of Cossack forces across Ukrainian territory to Transnistria. Seeing uncomfortable parallels between Crimea and the DMR, both presidents Leonid Kravchuk and Leonid Kuchma were strong supporters of Moldovan territorial integrity. By becoming an official guarantor of the negotiation process, Ukraine took its first tentative steps as a foreign policy counterweight to Russia. The deployment of ten Ukrainian military observers in 1998, although a largely symbolic contribution to Moldovan peacekeeping, was also an important step toward making resolution of the dispute a genuinely multinational concern. A Ukrainian-Moldovan treaty in 1999 recognized Ukraine's commitment to respect Moldova's borders and settled the delineation of the interstate boundary, even providing for a small exchange of territory and ensuring Moldovan access to the Danube. A few Moldovan and Romanian politicians remained wary of putative concealed interests behind Ukraine's policies. However, by offering another perspective at the bargaining table, Ukraine was able to move the conflict from a purely Moldovan-Russian standoff to a broader discussion about security issues in the wider Black Sea–Dnestr zone.

Despite these developments, a final political solution remained elusive. Since the cessation of violence, the DMR continued to function as an independent state in all but name. It had its own constitution, flag, anthem, and currency, the DMR ruble introduced in 1994. It held regular elections, however undemocratic, for a president, parliament, and local authorities. Its army was estimated at around 5,000 to 6,000 men, smaller than Moldova's 11,000 troops but probably better equipped.[46] Its schools taught Transnistrian young people a version of history meant to inculcate loyalty to the DMR, which was seen as the legitimate successor to the Moldovan autonomous republic of the interwar years.[47] The region's economic situation was dire, but no more so than in many parts of the former Soviet Union. The large industrial concerns on the east bank continued to function, mainly through barter trade with firms in Russia and Ukraine. In every major economic area except consumer goods, in fact, Transnistria remained a net "exporter" to the rest of Moldova, delivering more energy, ferrous metals, chemicals, and construction materials than it received from areas under central government control.[48] In the case of some of the more productive industrial concerns, such as the steel mill in Rîbniţa, which provided roughly half the revenues for DMR's state budget, contracts were negotiated directly with foreign companies.[49] It is indicative of the DMR's international links, in fact, that the DMR ruble was printed in Germany, not in Russia. Most disturbingly, by the end of the 1990s the DMR had once again become a significant supplier of the small arms and ammunition that it had produced during the Soviet period. Igor Smirnov frequently trumpeted the region's arms exports as an example of its importance on the world stage, and it is likely that Transnistrian arms found their way to Kosovo, the north Caucasus, and other conflict zones.[50]

The longer such a situation obtained, the more difficult it was to change. The dispute with Transnistria remained throughout the 1990s formally unresolved, but the Transnistrian case illustrated that, as in many other parts of the world, individuals can learn to live with political ambiguity. So long as average Transnistrians and Moldovans could travel across the Dnestr River relatively freely and find some way to feed their families, there was little concern about who controlled which piece of territory. For those who did care about the region's political future, far more preferred either union with Russia or adherence to the Russian-Belarusian union than reintegration with Moldova.[51] What little political opposition existed in the DMR was usually even more hardline on relations with Chisinau than the Smirnov leadership. Former Popular Front supporters or others vocally sympathetic to Moldova were arrested and charged with a host of crimes against the Transnistrian state; several activists, including Ilie Ilaşcu (a deputy in the Moldovan parliament), remained in prison throughout the decade and became a major concern to international human rights organizations. The only vocal protests against Tiraspol came from Moldovan schoolteachers and parents' associations in the region, who were forced by the DMR to continue giving and receiving instruction in the Cyrillic script or face school closures.

Ilie Ilaşcu, representative of the Popular Front, and his associates on trial in Tiraspol, 1993. Ilaşcu was sentenced to death by a Transnistrian court and became a symbol of the resistance of local Moldovans to the Dnestr Moldovan Republic. Photo by Tudor Iovu.

The crux of the problem was that no one really had a major incentive to resolve the Transnistrian issue. So long as fighting was not going on, the problem slipped off the agendas of regional powers and the international community. The Moldovans were carrying on with their own economic and political reforms, hoping that the promise of prosperity in Bessarabia would eventually draw the Transnistrians closer. Moreover, since the Moldovans' economic reform program did not have to deal with the mammoth Soviet-era factories in Transnistria, the first stages of privatization and marketization were somewhat simpler for Chisinau. There was also some suggestion in the press that Moldovan political figures were benefiting from the untaxed production and trade in the DMR, and therefore had little reason to seek a negotiated solution that would halt it.

For the Transnistrians, nothing could induce them to change a status that they had worked to achieve since the late 1980s. The reason was simple: Transnistria was not a case of stalled conflict, but a straightforward instance of military victory. With Russian assistance, the Transnistrians won the war against the Moldovans in 1992. There was thus little reason for the victors to negotiate with the vanquished, even if their newly won state lacked a seat at the United Nations and the other trappings of international recognition. The DMR thus settled into a semblance of statehood, but the effects on the local population were severe. Inflation was rampant, with local newspapers printing notices instructing citizens on how many zeroes to add to the printed bills to keep up with the ruble's depreciation: two zeroes to the blue 1,000 ruble note for a value of 100,000, one zero to the brown 50,000 ruble note for a value of 500,000, and so on. In mid-1999 the value of the DMR was 3 million to the dollar. The size of the population fell steadily—decreasing by over 10 percent between 1991 and 1997—as both Moldovans and Slavs moved to Bessarabia or left to seek better fortunes in Ukraine and Russia.[52] Economic reform was virtually nonexistent, and the democratic reforms instituted in the rest of Moldova were alien to Bender and the areas east of the Dnestr. Visitors frequently characterized the DMR as a living museum, where public murals and placards still praised the achievements of the Soviet Union and urged the workers of the world to unite.

The real tragedy of the Transnistrian conundrum, though, was not that it remained unresolved for so long, but that even a final agreement on the region's political status would do little to improve the lot of ordinary Transnistrians. With an entrenched and powerful elite in office in Tiraspol, the minimum price of settlement seemed to be the recognition in law of the power that the DMR elite already exercised in fact—an elite whose commitment to democracy, human rights, and the market was highly dubious.

10 The Gagauz

Among the various ethnic groups in Moldova, the position of the Gagauz—Orthodox Christian Turks—is unique. Although they are only the fourth largest ethnic group in the republic, they are the only minority population that cannot claim a clear "protector" state abroad, unlike Russians, Ukrainians, and Bulgarians. The vast majority of the world's Gagauz inhabit southern Moldova, an area known as the Bugeac or Budjak, with other communities located in southwestern Ukraine and Bulgaria, Romania, Turkey, and perhaps Greece.[1] In 1989, a total of 197,768 Gagauz were reported in the Soviet Union as a whole, of which 153,468 (77.6 percent) were living in Moldova, mainly in the southern *raions* of Basarabeasca, Comrat, Ciadîr-Lunga, Taraclia, and Vulcăneşti. The remainder were found primarily in the southwest corner of Ukraine's Odessa *oblast'*, part of historical Bessarabia.[2] The Republic of Moldova is thus, as some Gagauz leaders argue, as much their homeland as the Romanian-speakers'.[3]

The conflict with the Gagauz that erupted in the late 1980s and remained largely unresolved until 1995 was the only dispute in Moldova that evolved along clearly ethnic lines. Although the scale of the armed conflict with the Transnistrians dwarfed the minor skirmishes that took place among armed Gagauz and Moldovans, the demands put forward by Gagauz leaders were substantially different from those voiced by the Transnistrians. In Transnistria, the dispute with the Moldovan authorities involved the desire of a historically privileged region to maintain that status and, more broadly, to resist the drift away from the Soviet—and later Russian—center that began under perestroika. But in the south, a history of official neglect of the southern districts and serious concerns about the future of Gagauz culture contributed to the intensity of discontent between Chisinau and Gagauz separatists, centered in the cities of Comrat and Ciadîr-Lunga. The Gagauz and Transnistrian leaderships frequently worked together against Chisinau, especially during the early 1990s, but the Gagauz question evolved differently from the problem of Transnistria. Indeed, it was precisely because it involved mainly demands for greater rights from a small and compact ethnic population that the devolution of power to local authorities proved sufficient to quell the conflict.

GAGAUZ ORIGINS

The ethnic origin of the Gagauz is in dispute. One scholar has counted as many as nineteen separate theories of Gagauz ethnogenesis.[4] Over the past century, some have argued that the Gagauz are descended from the Pecheneg or Cuman tribes that inhabited the lands along the Black Sea until the thirteenth century; others have held that they are simply part of the Oğuz division of Turkic peoples, who migrated to southeastern Europe from the steppe region north of the Black Sea; still others have described them simply as christianized Turks, turkicized Slavic Bulgarians, turkicized Greeks, descendants of the Turkic Bulgars, or some combination of all the above.[5]

One of the most prominent theories, supported by the great Ottomanist Paul Wittek, among others, is that the Gagauz are in fact descendants of Turkic Oğuz tribes that already inhabited the area of Dobrogea or Dobrudja (in modern Romania and Bulgaria along the western Black Sea coast) in the first half of the thirteenth century.[6] Fleeing before the advancing Mongols, the Seljuk sultan, Izz al-Din Kay-Kaus, was given control over a portion of Dobrogea by the Byzantine emperor, Michael VIII Palaeologus. Kay-Kaus, from which the name *Gagauz* perhaps derives, established a state in the region among the Oğuz, with its capital in Kavurna and Orthodoxy recognized as the dominant religion under the authority of the patriarch in Constantinople. By the end of the fourteenth century, these Oğuz had come under the control of the Ottomans, but they retained their distinctive Orthodox faith even within the expanding empire, using Church Slavonic and Greek as liturgical languages.

Regardless of their more distant heritage, Gagauz and Bulgarian migrants arrived in southern Bessarabia from Dobrogea in several waves in the wake of the Russo-Turkish wars, beginning in the 1780s and ending in the late 1870s.[7] They were often treated by contemporary observers as a single population, and one nineteenth-century Russian observer simply dismissed the Gagauz as no more than "illegitimate children of Turks and Bulgarians."[8] The 1897 Russian census had no listing for the Gagauz in Bessarabia, but reported 55,790 "Ottoman Turks" and 103,225 "Bulgarians," categories that probably included Gagauz and Bulgarians as well as local Moldovans, Vlachs, Ruthenians, and Roma, who lived together in the cultural melting pot of the Bugeac region.

THE GAGAUZ IN THE ROMANIAN AND SOVIET PERIODS

In the poor steppeland of southern Bessarabia, the Gagauz have long been one of the region's most disadvantaged ethnic groups. At the end of the nineteenth century, Gagauz illiteracy rates stood at 88 percent for men and nearly 98 percent for women, considerably higher than those for local Moldovans or Russians.[9] There was a limited Gagauz renaissance in the 1920s and 1930s, almost entirely the work of one dedicated Bessarabian priest, Mihail Ciachir (1861–1938). Ciachir compiled the first Gagauz dictionary and grammar, translated the Gospels and liturgical works into the language, and wrote a short history of the Gagauz that remained noncommittal on the subject of their ethnic provenance.[10] But apart from Ciachir's cultural work, little was done under the Romanians to improve the social status of this tiny minority.

The same can be said of the Soviet period. A Cyrillic Gagauz alphabet was not developed until 1957—making Gagauz the last Soviet Turkic language to be cyrillicized—and a few schools were opened in southern Moldova in the 1957–58 academic year with Gagauz as the language of instruction. These, however, were liquidated by the early 1960s and replaced with Russian-only programs. The Gagauz language was no longer used even as a subject of study.

The quality of secondary education, regardless of the language of instruction, was relatively poor in the MSSR's southern districts. In 1990 the percentage of teachers with higher degrees was below the republican average in all the Gagauz *raions*, and around a quarter of all teachers in some *raions* had only a post-secondary teaching certificate but no higher degree.[11] By 1990, only 647 Gagauz were studying at institutions of higher education; at Chisinau State University, just over 1 percent of the total student population was Gagauz, and in no university or institute did the figure exceed 4 percent.[12] Of a total of 2,875 teachers at institutes of higher education, only 15 were ethnic Gagauz.[13] As a result of these trends, few Gagauz were to be found in the republic's administrative structures. Ethnic groups with smaller relative populations—such as Jews (1.5 percent of the MSSR total) and Bulgarians (2 percent)—had far higher proportions of their populations employed in city and village administration than did the Gagauz.[14]

Social and infrastructural problems in southern Moldova also took their toll. The areas of compact Gagauz settlement accounted for a tenth of the republic's total land area but, throughout the Soviet period, never provided more than 4 percent of the total industrial output.[15] Even though the local economy depended on the transportation of agricultural goods to markets in central Moldova, all of the southern *raions* were well below the republican average in terms of hard-surfaced highways and local roads. Water reserves, always problematic in the Bugeac's arid climate, were normally three to seven times lower than the republican average, and even potable water had extremely high mineral content. By 1990, these problems had led to a serious health crisis: Over 50 percent of children in Comrat district had functional health disorders, while 45 percent of final-year pupils in the *raion's* schools had serious kidney, respiratory, and digestive ailments. The provision of doctors and other medical personnel, however, was far below the republican average.[16] All of these problems were magnified by the damage caused by an earthquake in May 1990, which hit the districts of the south especially hard.

GAGAUZ LANGUAGE AND CULTURE

Social problems were mirrored in the cultural sphere. During the Soviet period, the mainly rural Gagauz became a largely russified minority, although their language and culture had long been influenced by interactions with Bulgarians, Ukrainians, and even Romanians. In 1989 a higher percentage of Gagauz considered themselves fluent in Russian as a second language than any other ethnic group in Moldova. Nearly 73 percent of ethnic Gagauz reported Russian as their second language, a figure that had risen from 68 percent ten years earlier.[17] Moreover, they ranked last in the percentage of minority groups with Moldovan as a fluent second language. Only 4 percent of Gagauz reported a fluent knowledge of Moldovan, while more than 10 percent of Ukrainians, Russians, Jews, and Roma said they knew the language. At the same time, however, most Gagauz retained some knowledge of their own ancestral language, or at least saw the language as important to their own sense of identity. Just over 91 percent of Gagauz reported Gagauz as their native language, a figure exceeded only by corresponding percentages for ethnic Russians and Moldovans.

Gagauz is part of the southwest division of Turkic languages, along with Turkish, Azeri, and Turkmen. However, it has been heavily influenced by Romanian and Russian, and before the late 1980s, little was done to make it a serviceable literary idiom. In fact, there was little demand among Gagauz villagers for using the language outside the home, for they had long functioned within a largely Russian-speaking social environment, even during the period when Romania controlled Bessarabia. The Moldovan Politburo approved a Cyrillic alphabet for Gagauz in July 1957, and a provisional program was elaborated for teaching the Gagauz language in secondary schools in both Moldova and Ukraine. After 1961, however, the Gagauz language disappeared from the MSSR's school system and, to a large degree, from cultural life in general. The first collection of poetry in Gagauz appeared in 1964, but few other works were published in the Soviet period.[18] Several ethnographic studies were completed by Gagauz specialists in the Moldovan Academy of Sciences, including a Gagauz grammar in 1990, but these were invariably published in Russian and, on occasion, then translated into Gagauz.[19] In the postwar period as a whole, no more than thirty to forty books, including translations, were published in Gagauz.[20]

Beginning in the late 1980s, the Moldovan government attempted to address the problems within the Gagauz community. The Supreme Soviet set up a special commission on "the Gagauz question" in August 1989, and the republican government assembled an advisory council on Gagauz affairs a year later.[21] After 1991, the newly independent republic organized a State Department for National Relations to act as a liaison between Chisinau and grassroots cultural organizations, and the department quickly became instrumental in focusing attention on Gagauz issues. Specialists within the department worked to revive traditional Gagauz festivals and folk culture through the quasi-official cultural association Kardaşlık (Brotherhood). These efforts sometimes met with little interest on the part of Gagauz villagers, whose distinctive music, dress, and folk art in large part disappeared under the Soviets.

The results of this increased attention were impressive. A weekly Gagauz-language newspaper, *Ana sözü* (Mother tongue), began in 1988 as a regular supplement to the main Moldovan-language daily. A Gagauz university, funded jointly by the Moldovan government and private donations, was opened in southern Moldova's administrative center, Comrat, in 1991. Over a thousand students were studying in the university's three faculties of agronomy, economics, and "national culture" by the late 1990s. About two-thirds of the teaching staff spoke Gagauz, with more than three-quarters of the students coming from ethnic Gagauz backgrounds.[22] Numbers also grew in other institutions of higher education, with Gagauz accounting for 2.4 percent of the total student population in academic year 1992–93, compared with 1.4 percent in 1989–90.[23] Because of a lack of local demand, Gagauz was not introduced as a language of instruction in schools, but several public schools had begun to teach the language as a subject; there were, by the late 1990s, also several kindergartens and a private high school with some lessons conducted in Gagauz. A Gagauz writers' union, a women's association, two small libraries, monthly Gagauz-language broadcasts on Moldovan television and radio, a small Comrat-based television station, and a modest Gagauz film studio were all established in the 1990s.[24]

Despite these successes, conflicts within the Gagauz community itself were a serious impediment. Some cultural leaders sought to inspire a Turkic renaissance, reorienting the historically slavicized Gagauz back toward their Turkic roots. Others embraced the Russian components of Gagauz culture and sought to maintain strong ties between local Gagauz communities and the Russian Federation. For obvious reasons, the central Moldovan government tended to support the former group, encouraging student exchanges with Ankara and Istanbul, and approving in 1993 a Latin alphabet for Gagauz endorsed by the official Turkish Language Society in Ankara. These cultural divisions, though, were indicative of broader political disputes that came to the fore in the 1990s, especially after the creation of a separate Gagauz administrative district in 1995.

ETHNIC MOBILIZATION IN THE GORBACHEV ERA

Just as intellectuals in Chisinau were mobilizing around demands for cultural and political change in 1988 and 1989, so too Gagauz leaders in the south began to call for greater attention to cultural and social needs in the disadvantaged region. A Gagauz cultural club in Comrat formed at about the same time as the Alexei Mateevici Club in Chisinau, and by 1989 had transformed itself into an umbrella association known as Gagauz Halkı (Gagauz People). A representative of Gagauz Halkı traveled to Chisinau and was present at the founding of the Popular Front of Moldova later in May. Underdevelopment, poverty, and educational disadvantage in the region made Gagauz intellectuals and local political elites eager to support the reformist goals of the Front.

However, the multiethnic coalition on which the Front was founded proved fragile. After the March 1989 elections to the Soviet-level Congress of People's Deputies, the renaissance of a distinctively Romanian culture became the main focus of the Front's activities, a shift that culminated in the August 1989 language laws. These changes both frightened the Gagauz population and challenged the vested interests of the local Gagauz leadership, which emerged from the array of district-level party and state structures in the south. Although Gagauz Halkı had been formed as a cultural organization, many of the group's supporters were members of the district-level administrative elite. These administrators, like their colleagues in other parts of Moldova, had hoped to use the movement as a way of gaining political and economic concessions from the Moldovan center; most were content to remain part of the Soviet Union and were wholly opposed to the Front's new pan-Romanian orientation.

In September 1989, in response to both the radicalization of the Front and the growing assertiveness of Chisinau vis-à-vis Moscow, Gagauz leaders proclaimed the creation of an autonomous republic. Throughout late 1989 and early 1990, tensions rose between the central government and the self-proclaimed administration, based in Comrat and headed by Stepan Topal, a former construction engineer. The

Stepan Topal, leader of the
Gagauz, in his office in Comrat,
1993. Topal led the movement for
a distinct Gagauz political entity
in the early 1990s but eventually
retired from politics. Photo by
Tudor Iovu.

republican parliamentary elections in 1990 were a major catalyst in the
growing Moldovan–Gagauz dispute. The new Frontist prime minister,
Mircea Druc, repeatedly condemned the Gagauz leadership; after the
proclamation of a wholly separate "Gagauz Soviet Socialist Republic"
in August 1990, the government outlawed Gagauz Halkı. Troops of
Moldovan volunteers, emboldened with vodka, hijacked municipal
buses in Chisinau and rushed to the Gagauz areas. Only the intervention
of Soviet interior ministry troops prevented the outbreak of serious violence between Moldovan and Gagauz irregulars. Small arms flowed into
the area from Transnistria, and the Gagauz organized their own local
self-defense unit, christened the "Bugeac Battalion." The Gagauz, however, were not united in their opposition to Chisinau. The former party
and *raion*-level elite, of which Topal and the speaker of the local parliament, Mihail Kendigelian were representatives, were intent primarily on
maintaining control of local resources in the crumbling Soviet Union.
Others, such as the economist Konstantin Tavşancı and the former political prisoner Leonid Dobrov, looked to inspire a Gagauz national renaissance, much as their counterparts in Chisinau had done with Moldovan
national culture.[25]

Over the following months, little progress was made in resolving the dispute between Chisinau and Comrat. The Moldovan declaration of independence in 1991 deepened the rift, since Gagauz leaders welcomed the Moscow coup as an attempt to forestall the breakup of the Soviet federation and were arrested by the Moldovan authorities in response.[26] Like minority populations in other Soviet republics, the Gagauz argued that the rising tide of local nationalism—not Soviet "international-ism"—represented the greatest threat to their future. It was not until 1994, with the victory of the Agrarian Democratic Party in Moldova's parliamentary elections, that the Gagauz problem would move toward resolution.

THE POLITICS OF TERRITORIAL AUTONOMY

The essential issue at the heart of the Gagauz problem in the early 1990s was the demand by ethnic elites for control over local resources and a revival of indigenous culture. Unlike the Transnistrians, the Gagauz leadership did not desire a full separation from Moldova, the nominal declaration of an independent "Gagauz republic" notwithstanding. Throughout the standoff with Chisinau, local *raion* committees continued to receive funding from the central state budget, and most leaders were aware that their sustenance came from central coffers. It is indicative of the rhetorical nature of these declarations that, as late as 1994, the president of the "Gagauz republic," Stepan Topal, could not produce a map showing which areas were supposedly under Gagauz control.[27] Still, just as Mircea Snegur and other Moldovan leaders used the national movement of the late 1980s to supplant their rivals within state and party structures in Chisinau, so local leaders in Comrat saw the popular mobilization of the Gagauz as a useful vehicle for extracting political and economic concessions from the central government. The language and symbols employed by the Gagauz seemed to point toward separation from Moldova, but the essential demand was in fact a greater share of the local control that Chisinau had begun to wrest from Moscow.

After the low point in relations between Chisinau and Comrat in 1990, most Moldovan politicians quickly came around to the idea that some form of territorial autonomy in southern Moldova was a reasonable demand. The 1994 elections, in which pan-Romanians lost to centrist candidates more interested in political stability than in national ideals, were a turning point. As part of a more general trend toward empowering district councils and invigorating local government, the devolution of political power to a distinctly Gagauz entity in the south became a widely accepted idea. Some politicians saw in Gagauz autonomy a dangerous first step toward the breakup of Moldova, a time bomb waiting to explode should Moldova move closer to Romania.[28] Still, after the elections, the new parliament dominated by the Agrarian Democrats, the government of Andrei Sangheli, and President Snegur all voiced support for some form of autonomy for the Gagauz districts.

The demography of Gagauz settlements, however, made the devolution of political, economic, and cultural powers to Gagauz localities rather difficult. Gagauz formed absolute majorities in only two of the five *raions* supposedly included in the Gagauz republic—Ciadîr-Lunga *raion* (64.2 percent) and Comrat *raion* (63.8 percent).[29] Gagauz accounted for absolute majorities in only twenty-eight settlements in the entire southern region. Only in Comrat *raion* were these Gagauz-dominated settlements in the majority, and the *raion* centers of Comrat and Ciadîr-Lunga were the only sizable towns with majority Gagauz populations.[30] The remainder of the population was composed mainly of Moldovans and Bulgarians, who formed pluralities in the other three *raions*. Thus, in the five ostensibly "Gagauz" *raions* as a whole, ethnic Gagauz, at 47.2 percent of the total population, did not form an absolute majority, a fact that local Moldovan and Bulgarian leaders were keen to impress on anyone who spoke of "self-determination" for the Gagauz people.

In the end, the Moldovan government proposed a form of self-determination designed to allow local populations—whether Gagauz or otherwise—to determine themselves which administrative district they wished to join. Article 111 of the 1994 constitution had already promised a "special status" for southern Moldova, but left that status undefined. A law on Gagauz autonomy, adopted by parliament and the Gagauz leadership in December 1994 and promulgated by President Snegur in January 1995, granted wide-ranging powers to local officials while at the same time giving individual villages the right to opt in or out of the new arrangement. Under the law, a special "territorial autonomous unit" was created as "a form of self-determination for the Gagauz" and as a "component part of the Republic of Moldova."[31] Villages with absolute Gagauz majorities could enter the new unit via referendum, and mixed villages could also hold their own referenda on joining in the future. In the first referenda in March 1995, three cities and over two dozen villages opted into the autonomous district, known in Gagauz as Gagauz Yeri (literally, "the Gagauz land"). A governor (Başkan), executive committee (Bakannık Komiteti), and legislative assembly (Halk Topluşu) were elected in local ballots in May and June 1995. The holders of these offices were endowed with power over local resources, the economy, justice, and other areas. Only major functions such as the granting of citizenship, foreign policy, currency circulation and issue, and national security remained exclusively in the hands of the central Moldovan government. Moreover, the law could only be modified by a three-fifths vote of the Moldovan parliament, virtually assuring its permanence.

Three languages—Gagauz, Moldovan, and Russian—were all made official in Gagauz Yeri, an attempt to assuage the fears caused by the declaration of Moldovan as the state's sole official language in 1989. Moreover, in the event of a "change in the status of the Republic of Moldova"—presumably, union with Romania—the Gagauz would retain the right to determine their own fate. Such a provision in the 1995 law not only relieved Gagauz fears of Moldova's eventually joining Romania, but also indirectly shored up Moldovan territorial integrity: Since any attempt at forcing a union of the two states would likely prompt the Gagauz to take this clause in the 1995 law seriously, pro-union forces in Chisinau and Bucharest have had a great disincentive to make any moves toward unification.

The local autonomy law, to a large degree, worked as planned—not because it provided the basis for a Gagauz cultural renaissance, but because it essentially met the major demands of local elites. Allowing former *raion*-level administrators a greater say in local government while at the same time ensuring that they would still receive disbursements from the central budget proved enough to quell the Gagauz independence movement. Moreover, unlike in Transnistria, Chisinau sought to address the problem of the armed irregulars who had threatened the security of the southern region and, especially during harvest time, remained a menace to local law enforcement bodies. Rather than simply disbanding the "Bugeac Battalion," the Moldovan interior ministry created a special detachment—Military Unit 1045—that absorbed most of the groups' members. Their weapons were registered, they were provided with uniforms and, most importantly, they were given reason-able salaries, all in exchange for loyalty to the Moldovan central authorities.[32]

After 1995, the Gagauz region was no longer a major problem for Chisinau. The Gagauz participated in all central and local elections, and the institutions of the new autonomous region were elaborated and seemed to function as well as any local institutions in the republic. In elections for the first Başkan of Gagauz Yeri in 1995, Georgi Tabunşcik emerged as winner with 64.1 percent of the vote in the second round.[33] Tabunşcik, a former *raion* party secretary, was generally considered more accommodating than Stepan Topal, but he remained committed to carving out as much local control for Gagauz Yeri as possible.[34] His main base of support was not substantially different from that of Topal or indeed many other powerful politicians in Moldova: the network of local administrators, workers' groups, and collective farm heads, many of whom had remained in power since the breakup of the Soviet Union. The new Party of Communists became a major force in the south after 1995, as well, accounting for nearly all Gagauz Yeri's deputies in the Moldovan parliament. But again, these developments were little differ-ent from electoral outcomes in other parts of the republic and, given the continuing problems of poverty and underdevelopment in the south, hardly surprising.

All of this took place within an environment, though, in which Mol-dovan politicians were still not united in their view of the Gagauz people themselves. Pan-Romanian groups in particular continually denounced the idea of a Gagauz nation as a fiction used by Moscow and Tiraspol to encourage the breakup of the Moldovan republic.[35] Others argued more pragmatically that drawing administrative units along ethnic lines virtually ensured the future disintegration of the Moldovan state.[36] The Romanian government, seeing an uncomfortable parallel between Ga-gauz local autonomy and the status demanded by some ethnic Hungari-ans in Transylvania, took a similar line during debates on Gagauz auton-omy in 1994 and 1995.[37] But after the granting of autonomy, the outcome was a fait accompli. Minor problems remained about the delin-eation of district boundaries, especially after the Moldovan parliament decided to discard the republic's Soviet-style system of forty *raions* in favor of a new arrangement of nine counties headed by prefects.[38] But these problems paled in comparison to the violence of the past.

TURKEY AND THE GAGAUZ

Moldovan officials early recognized that one way of easing strained relations with the Gagauz community and of convincing the most radical factions of the central government's good faith was by increasing ties with Turkey. Turkey recognized Moldova's independence in December 1991, and by February 1992 the two states had established full diplomatic relations. Accords on economic cooperation, trade, and agricultural development projects were signed in February 1994, and in mid-1994 the existing Turkish consulate in Moldova was upgraded to full embassy status. Turkey was also one of the first countries in which the Moldovans opened an embassy and, in the 1990s, remained one of only a few with a full embassy in Chisinau.

A high point in Moldovan–Turkish relations was the state visit by Turkish president Süleyman Demirel in June 1994, the first high-ranking foreign delegation to visit Moldova after independence.[39] Arriving with a large delegation of Turkish policymakers and business leaders, Demirel spent three days meeting with President Snegur and other Moldovan officials and signed several protocols on increased cultural and economic ties, as well as a basic treaty of friendship and cooperation. Demirel also announced a $35 million aid package for Moldova, most of which would be used for improving water supplies and infrastructure in the Gagauz region.[40] During his visit, Demirel traveled with Snegur to the Gagauz cities of Comrat and Ciadîr-Lunga, and repeatedly referred to the Gagauz as "a solid bridge of friendship between Turkey and Moldova."[41] A short follow-up visit in 1998, in which Demirel once again spent a day in Comrat, brought further commitments of Turkish development aid.

Through its embassy in Chisinau, as well as via the Turkish Cooperation and Development Agency (TIKA), Ankara provided significant financial and educational support to the Gagauz after 1991. Nearly 200 Gagauz students received places at Turkish universities in the 1992–93 academic year, a number that remained relatively constant throughout the 1990s. Under a special exchange program, over two dozen Turkish students and several teachers also studied and worked each year at Comrat University.[42] Turkish money was largely responsible for Moldova's two Gagauz/Turkish libraries, numerous exchange schemes for Gagauz artists, musicians, and television presenters, and a range of other aid programs initiated after Moldovan independence.[43] In early 1994, Ankara announced that it would fund the transition of the Gagauz language to the Latin script by donating a fully equipped printing works to be located in Ciadîr-Lunga.[44] The high school that opened in Ciadîr-Lunga in September 1993, offering instruction in English and Gagauz, was funded from private sources, probably indirectly linked with the Turkish religious leader Fetullah Gülen. Moreover, two of the most prominent Soviet and Turkish sociologists—Mikhail Guboglu and Kemal Karpat—were of Gagauz extraction, and these preexisting links made the Gagauz of some interest to Turkish intellectuals. Several books on the Gagauz, a rarity outside the former Soviet Union, appeared in Ankara after 1991, some of them published by the Turkish Ministry of Culture and the Turkish Language Society.[45]

Turkey's involvement in Moldova, though, was not universally welcomed. The most ardent pan-Romanian factions in the Moldovan parliament were highly critical of Demirel's visits, insisting that strengthening ties with Turkey would merely encourage Gagauz separatists to press for the full confederation of the Moldovan republic. However, Turkey's role remained very low-key, and if anything probably served Moldovan interests by providing an alternative to Russia as the natural pole of allegiance for the Gagauz.

FROM TERRITORIAL SEPARATISM TO LOCAL GOVERNMENT

The Gagauz problem, at least in territorial terms, had been largely solved by 1995. There were no Gagauz leaders who threatened to resurrect the separatist demands of 1989 and 1990, nor were there any major Moldovan politicians seriously looking to backtrack on the autonomy legislation. In 1999 the election of Dumitru Croitor—a former deputy foreign minister and centrist politician—as Gagauz governor and Tabunşcik's successor illustrated how far the region had been reintegrated into central Moldovan politics. What had once been a conflict threatening the integrity of the state had become, in only a few years, a problem of local government. Some local Gagauz officials commented wryly that the resolution of the dispute was not without its costs. Officials from the OSCE, the Council of Europe, and other bodies were frequent visitors to Comrat in the early 1990s and helped keep the city's one major restaurant in business. But once the autonomy legislation came into force, foreign visitors to the Gagauz capital were few and far between. A day trip to the region was de rigueur for Turkish officials visiting Chisinau, but apart from these occasional delegations, the Gagauz became once again a largely forgotten minority within an overlooked republic.

Given the clashes of 1990, no news from Gagauz Yeri is probably good news. Gagauz Yeri was still a backward region, where crime and corruption were rife; local elites still clashed, sometimes violently, over the division of resources from the center and, especially during harvest time, rival gangs fought for control of the produce. But in this sense, Gagauz Yeri was no different from any other outlying region of any other post-Soviet republic. The Gagauz university in Comrat, as well as local radio and television broadcasts and the efforts of the Chisinau-based State Department for National Relations, had done a great deal to revive Gagauz folk traditions. Gagauz students and teachers were regular visitors to Turkey, and the Gagauz language was on its way to becoming a more frequently used, if still not dominant, feature of cultural life in southern Moldova. Moreover, exploratory drilling by an American oil company led to the discovery of natural gas deposits in the south, producing wild speculation about the region as the future Emirates of the Black Sea. Apart from these encouraging trends, though, it is difficult to see how the Gagauz land can in the near future become anything other than the poor and disadvantaged region it was before the conflicts of the 1990s—except now one with its own flag.

11 A Negotiable Nationalism

The Romanians in Bessarabia awoke in the late 1980s, quipped the writer Ion Druță, but they forgot to get out of bed.[1] The disappointment that many intellectuals felt with the outcome of the national movement was part of a long history of disillusionment experienced by generations of nation-builders. At every turn, Moldova has turned out to be something other than what most observers had either hoped or expected. It was one of the most sovietized of the Soviet republics, with high rates of linguistic assimilation to Russian and marriage across ethnic lines. But it also witnessed a divisive and violent conflict between forces supporting independence and those intent on maintaining the unity of the Soviet state. It was a republic that had no clear historical antecedent within the same borders. But it nevertheless produced a strong movement of national renaissance and eventually independence. It was a republic that Western writers frequently criticized as artificial, the result of Stalin's redrawing of east European borders during the Second World War, and a territory that if given the chance would surely seek to reunite with its former motherland, Romania. But since 1991 public sentiment has been cool on the idea of unification between the two states.

Most unusual of all was the fact that the Soviet project of building a distinct Moldovan nation yielded a rather ambiguous result. Local political leaders in other national republics came to power in the late 1980s by defending an independent historical and cultural identity, but those in Moldova succeeded by denying theirs. An independent Moldovan state emerged with the breakup of the Soviet federation, but the idea of an independent Moldovan nation seemed to fade with Soviet-style communism. Since then, the legacy of Soviet-era nation-building and the contentious question of the "true" national identity of the Moldovans have remained topics at the center of political life.

Making a Moldovan nation should have been a relatively easy enterprise. The eastern Moldovan lands, both before and after the annexation of Bessarabia, were populated largely by illiterate peasants with few ties to the cosmopolitan cities. They had been politically separate from the closest co-ethnic group—the Romanians—for the past two centuries or more, and had been absent from all the historical turning points in the formation of Romanian national consciousness. They had been the subjects of a variety of contradictory cultural policies: russification in the Russian empire, romanization in interwar Romania, fitful moldovanization in the Moldovan autonomous and union republics, and sovietization in the entire Soviet period. Nation-building also accompanied broader processes of urbanization and industrialization, so that the rhetoric of national identity was linked with other powerful themes of enlightenment and modernity. All this took place among a population that, even before the Soviet Union, still called itself "Moldovan" and within an authoritarian political system that put a premium on ethnonational affiliation and often spared no expense in the effort to engineer it. One can think of plenty of modern nations that have been built under far less propitious conditions.

For all this, though, by the 1990s the Moldovans were still a nation divided over their common identity. For some, they were simply Romanians who, because of the treachery of the Soviets, had not been allowed to say so. For others, they were an independent historical nation, related to but distinct from the Romanians to the west. For still others, they were something in between, part of a general Romanian cultural space but existing as a discrete and sovereign people with its own traditions, aspirations, and communal identity. How one imagines the Moldovans has never been a straightforward issue. In most periods, in fact, the various projects for cultivating a sense of nationhood among them have turned out rather differently from how their designers had planned.

The first modern Moldovan political entity, the autonomous republic established in Ukraine in the interwar period, was founded with the explicit goal of furthering Soviet efforts to acquire Romanian territory, the Bessarabia region that belonged to Russia before 1918. The cultivation of a distinct Moldovan national identity, based on an indigenous Moldovan language, was to be the primary means to this end. From the 1920s, the Soviets argued that the majority population of Bessarabia and peasants in the lands immediately to the east shared a common national identity, and that such an identity could only truly flourish within the Soviet Union. After 1940, when the Soviets annexed Bessarabia and ostensibly united the Moldovans into a single national and socialist republic, claiming the existence of a second "eastern Romance" people was Moscow's chief bulwark against irredentist claims from Romania.

In the 1920s specialists in the MASSR worked to build a distinct Moldovan identity based on the culture of the peasant. By embracing the cultural and linguistic traits of the countryside and codifying them in a new, national cultural standard, scholars and party activists hoped to draw the Moldovans in Bessarabia farther away from bourgeois Romania. Just as the Romanians were working to convince the peasants of their proper place inside Greater Romania, so Soviet propagandists in the MASSR worked to pull them out of Romania and into an enlarged Soviet Moldovan republic. Culture and politics thus often amounted to the same thing. Soon, though, radical moldovanization came to an end. The sudden introduction of the Latin alphabet in 1932, the growing criticism directed at the main architects of cultural policy, and Moscow's forcible annexation of Bessarabia in 1940 all led to the political demise of the cultural elite that had stood at the center of Moldovan political life in the early years of the autonomous republic.

These events also marked a break with the main tenets of cultural policy set out in the 1920s. Cultural elites initially lauded the "simple" nature of Moldovan peasant life. By raising this uncomplicated and democratic culture to the level of a national standard, the party aimed to build a distinct Moldovan nation as a way of wresting Bessarabia from the Romanians. By 1938, however, these same cultural forms were denounced as "simple" in a different sense, as uneducated, stupid, non-literary, and unworthy of the modernizing zeal of the Soviet state. With the exception of the Cyrillic alphabet, after the 1930s the differences between standard Moldovan and its Romanian cousin became minuscule. Notwithstanding the vitriol thrown between Soviet and Romanian writers in the 1960s and 1970s, scholars in both countries shared a common disdain for the cultural peculiarities of the Moldovan peasant that elites in the MASSR had hailed as the germ of a new Moldovan national culture.

What had begun in the 1920s and early 1930s as a genuine project at identity-construction was abandoned by 1938. However, the rhetoric that surrounded it—the discourse of national distinctiveness—remained in place. The situation was nothing short of bizarre. By the 1980s Moldovan scholars were touting the existence of a language that no longer existed in any standardized form and were praising a project long abandoned, the building of a new socialist culture founded on the customs of rural Moldovans. The language the MSSR's intellectuals actually spoke at home, taught their children and students, and praised as fundamental to "Moldovanness" was, to the rest of the world, simply Romanian. The national movement of the perestroika years was in this sense not a break with the past, but the direct outcome of decades of quiet cultural romanization in the ostensibly "Moldovan" republic.

It is often said that the failure of the Soviets to create a distinct and durable Moldovan nation resulted primarily from the artificiality of the entire project. This is simply wrong. Cultural policies from the 1920s were no more artificial than similar efforts in the other republics of the Soviet Union and, indeed, no more politicized than similar developments in nineteenth-century France, twentieth-century Yugoslavia, or any other region in which the ethnic or national distinctiveness of a population becomes an issue of high politics. All nations and their accoutrements—standard languages, national anthems, official histories, national costumes—are artificial insofar as they are the products of human artifice, homogenized codes pared from the heterogeneous reality of human behavior. Rather, building a distinct culture in Moldova failed for a far simpler reason: After the Second World War, no one really tried. Although the rhetoric of national distinctiveness remained and was repeated at Soviet party congresses and scholarly conferences, cultivating a truly separate culture effectively ended with Stalin's annexation of Bessarabia. All that was left by the 1980s was to admit publicly what most Moldovan intellectuals had accepted privately for decades.

The reverse side of failed nation-building in the Soviet Union was not, however, wholly successful nation-building in Romania. Despite a consistent state-led effort in the interwar years to convince the inhabitants of Bessarabia of their Romanian origins, many remained ambivalent about their relationship to the Romanian state. Not only did the ethnically heterogeneous nature of Bessarabia's population sit uneasily with the idea of the province as a uniquely Romanian land, but even the Moldovans themselves were far from unanimous in their support for being incorporated into Greater Romania. Given this legacy of ambivalence, the mystery in 1991 was not why Moldovans proved reluctant to rush toward union with Romania, but rather why so many Western observers expected that they would.

In post-Soviet Moldova the politics of identity has become even more complex. Not only is the perennial question of the relationship between Moldovans and Romanians still a topic of some debate, but a range of other issues, especially relations between the majority nationality and the republic's minorities, has come to the fore as well. The once unified Popular Front of Moldova came to be dominated by a pan-Romanian wing intent on closer ties with Romania and, for some members, political union of the two states on the model of 1918. Members of the republic's ethnic minorities defected to form their own fronts in defense of what many perceived as the nationalist fervor of the Popular Front. Internal disputes within the Front, as well as public dissatisfaction with the turmoil of the early years of independence, led to the group's eclipse by the old agricultural and party elite—now transformed into defenders of Moldova's sovereignty.

These issues were sometimes played out in the same cultural arcana that occupied nationalists in both Greater Romania and the early Soviet Union. In fact, by 1999 how one spelled "dog" in Moldova could reveal a world of information about one's political proclivities. For pan-Romanians, who tended to use the same reformed spelling system as in postcommunist Romania, it was *câine*. For supporters of an independent Moldovan identity, who used an older spelling convention, it was *cîine*. And for Transnistrians, who still used the Soviet-era Cyrillic alphabet, it was *kyine*. All post-Soviet states were caught up in debates over identity and culture, but in few places were they as strikingly evident as in Moldova.

An independent Moldovan state is now a fixture of European politics. The arguments for Moldovan–Romanian union have largely fallen on deaf ears on both sides of the Prut River. For Moldovans, the promise of union with an economically desperate Romania held few advantages. For the Romanians, welcoming the prodigal cousins back into the pan-Romanian fold, with significant numbers of Ukrainians and Russians in tow, was hardly an appealing proposition. Even if all Moldovans were convinced of their Romanian heritage, the strong economic disincentives for union with Romania would remain a brake on pan-Romanian unifi-cation. Moreover, as Moldova continues to develop the structures of independent statehood and to produce new generations of leaders with loyalty to the Moldovan state—and not to any cross-border nation—independence is likely to become even more attractive. Why be mayor of Chisinau, the logic goes, if you can be president of Moldova?

The same argument can be made, though, about Transnistria. Mol-dova by the late 1990s was, by any measure, a divided state. It had two legislatures, two tax systems, two flags and, most importantly, two armies. Repeated rounds of unsuccessful negotiations had allowed the Transnistrians to develop all the attributes of statehood, and it is difficult to see how this situation could change without a major restructuring of the Moldovan state. Chisinau promised from the earliest days of the conflict to grant a special territorial status to Transnistria; the creation of a Gagauz autonomous unit in 1995 provided a ready template. But so long as Tiraspol continues to be supported by the most unreconstructed figures in the Russian Duma, local Transnistrian leaders have little incen-tive to accept anything short of a loose confederation.

If the existence of two "eastern Latin" states—or even three, given the Dnestr Republic's Moldovan plurality—is now generally accepted, what then of Moldovan identity? By the end of the 1990s, the impor-tance of questions of language and culture among the Moldovans had declined considerably. Even for many intellectuals—the chief protago-nists in the republic's cultural struggles—there was a clear sense in which the late perestroika years represented a kind of cultural overkill, with the constant concentration on esoteric aspects of history and linguistics taxing the attention of even the most devoted enthusiast.[2] Moldova still has an official "language day"—the *Limba noastră* (Our Language) hol-iday held on August 31—but celebrations receive little support from either the state or the public at large. The cult of culture, including the vast array of books and articles that celebrated the mystical link be-tween language and the spiritual essence of the nation, has long since disappeared.

Still, Moldova remained, even a decade after independence, the only country in eastern Europe in which major disputes existed among politi-cal and cultural elites over the fundamentals of national identity. Only in Moldova did a clear distinction exist between powerful groups whose members held divergent views on the basic question of what it means to be a member of the ethnic group for whom the country is named. It is unlikely that this underlying dispute will completely disappear from the scene, for the backlash against the Popular Front did not destroy the pan-Romanian ideal. Many of its supporters, in fact, retreated to the same institutions that had originally spawned the national movement: the State University in Chisinau, various institutes in the Academy of Sciences, and the Writers' Union. These latter-day nation-builders travel frequently to Bucharest and Iaşi, have strong links with Romanian intellectuals and, like their forebears in 1918, consider it their task to awaken a somnolent nation. So long as Moldovan schoolchildren and university students continue to study literary Romanian, to take advantage of Romanian scholarships, and to learn of Soviet-inspired denationalization, the question of national identity will not go away. Of course, greater familiarity with Romania may breed contempt, since Moldovans sometimes encounter the same patronizing attitudes from Romanians that estranged the Bessarabians in Greater Romania. Still, just as the rise of a new intellectual elite after the 1960s helped bring about the disintegration of Soviet conceptions of Moldovan identity, the growth of a new generation of young Moldovans, educated in the spirit of pan-Romanianism, may portend equally monumental changes to come.

The Moldovan story is fundamentally about the troubled relationship between political elites and the people they claim to represent, between nation-builders and the nations they aim to build. In the past, a deep chasm separated these groups. Cultural engineers, whether Russian, Romanian, or Soviet, went about their task with little regard for the existing cultural practices or political will of their target populations. "The people" have been both the source and the object of the competing visions of the nation promoted over the past two centuries, but what the people themselves desired rarely figured into the various schemes devised for their enlightenment. In the late 1980s, though, this gap began to close. For the first time in the region's history, the peoples of Bessarabia and Transnistria have been allowed a say in their own political, economic, and cultural future. It should not be surprising that they speak with many voices.

Notes

INTRODUCTION

1. Demographic and economic data are taken from various issues of the *Oxford Analytica East Europe Daily Brief* and from *Moldovan Economic Trends*, published by the Moldovan Ministry of Economy and Reform in cooperation with the European Commission.

CHAPTER 1

1. For the most important and insightful works in this field, see Benedict Anderson, *Imagined Communities*, rev. ed. (London: Verso, 1991); Eric Hobsbawm and Terence Ranger, eds., *The Invention of Tradition* (Cambridge, Eng.: Cambridge University Press, 1983); Eugen Weber, *Peasants into Frenchmen: The Modernization of Rural France, 1870–1914* (London: Chatto and Windus, 1977); Linda Colley, *Britons: Forging the Nation, 1707–1837* (New Haven, Conn.: Yale University Press, 1992); Werner Sollors, ed., *The Invention of Ethnicity* (New York: Oxford University Press, 1989); Anthony W. Marx, *Making Race and Nation: A Comparison of the United States, South Africa and Brazil* (Cambridge, Eng.: Cambridge University Press, 1998); and on the role of exter-

nal forces in "imagining" the nation, Maria Todorova, *Imagining the Balkans* (New York: Oxford University Press, 1997), and Larry Wolff, *Inventing Eastern Europe* (Stanford: Stanford University Press, 1994).

2. Ernest Gellner, *Thought and Change* (London: Weidenfeld and Nicolson, 1964), p. 174.

CHAPTER 2

1. Em. de Martonne, *What I Have Seen in Bessarabia* (Paris: Imprimerie des Arts et des Sports, 1919), pp. 9–10.

2. Cantemir's more famous work is his monumental history of the Ottoman Empire, Demetrius Cantemir, *The History of the Growth and Decay of the Othman Empire*, trans. Nicholas Tindal (London: Printed for James, John, and Paul Knapton, 1734–35).

3. Dimitrie Cantemir, *Descrierea Moldovei* (Chisinau: Hyperion, 1992), p. 13.

4. Gheorghe I. Brătianu, "Tradiţia istorică a descălecatului Moldovei în lumina noualor cercetări," *Analele Academiei Române, Memoriile Secţiunii Istorice* 27, no. 1 (1944–45): 24.

5. Victor Spinei, *Moldavia in the 11th–14th Centuries* (Bucharest: Editura Academiei Republicii Socialiste România, 1986), pp. 25–28.

6. Ion Nistor, *Istoria Basarabiei* (Bucharest: Humanitas, 1991), pp. 25–26.

7. C. Kogălniceanu, *Dragoş şi Bogdan seu întemeierea Principatului Moldova: Cercetare istorică* (Bucharest: Stabilimentul grafic Socecu şi Teclu, 1886), p. 8.

8. Dennis Deletant, "Moldavia between Hungary and Poland, 1347–1412," *Slavonic and East European Review* 64, no. 2 (1986): 187–211.

9. Dennis Deletant, "Genoese, Tatars and Rumanians at the Mouth of the Danube in the Fourteenth Century," *Slavonic and East European Review* 62, no. 4 (1981): 511–530.

10. T. J. Winnifrith, *The Vlachs: The History of a Balkan People* (London: Duckworth, 1987), p. 1.

11. Cantemir, *Descrierea Moldovei*, p. 110.

12. William Lithgow, *The Totall Discourse of the Rare Adventures and Painefull Peregrinations of Long Nineteene Yeares Travayles from Scotland to the Most Famous Kingdomes in Europe, Asia and Affrica* (Glasgow: James MacLehose and Sons, 1906 [1632]), p. 365.

13. R. W. Seton-Watson, *A History of the Roumanians from Roman Times*

to the *Completion of Unity* (Cambridge, Eng.: Cambridge University Press, 1934), p. 126.

14. William Wilkinson, *An Account of the Principalities of Wallachia and Moldavia* (London: Longman, Hurst, Rees, Orme, and Brown, 1820), p. 71.

15. Le Comte d'Hauterive, *Mémoire sur l'état ancien et actuel de la Moldavie en 1787* (Bucharest: Institutul de Arte Grafice "Carol Göbl," 1902), p. 340.

16. François de Tott, *Mémoires du Baron de Tott sur les Turcs et les Tatares* (Amsterdam: n.p., 1784), 1: 39–41.

17. Seton-Watson, *History of the Roumanians*, p. 128.

18. Cantemir reigned briefly as *domn* of Moldova, but he is, next to Ştefan cel Mare, the preeminent cultural and political figure in Moldovan history. Descended from a noble Tatar family, he immigrated to Russia and became one of the empire's foremost Oriental linguists and scholars. His son, Antioch, served as Russian minister in London and Paris, but is perhaps better known as one of the earliest satirists in the Russian language. See his *Satyres de Monsieur le Prince Cantemir, avec l'histoire de sa vie* (London: Jean Nourse, 1749).

19. Seton-Watson, *History of the Roumanians*, p. 134, n. 1.

20. Historians dispute the actual number of inhabitants at the time of annexation, but these are probably the lower and upper figures. Nistor, *Istoria Basarabiei*, p. 197; Andrei Popovici, *The Political Status of Bessarabia* (Washington: Ransdell, 1931), p. 80; Zamfir C. Arbore, *Basarabia în secolul XIX* (Bucharest: Institutul de Arte Grafice, 1898), pp. 91–92.

21. Nistor, *Istoria Basarabiei*, p. 178.

22. Paul Goma, *Din calidor: O copilărie basarabeană* (Bucharest: Editura Albatros, 1990), p. 44.

23. Nistor, *Istoria Basarabiei*, p. 22.

24. Ion I. Nistor, "Localizarea numelui Basarabiei în Moldova transpruteană," *Analele Academiei Române, Memoriile Secţiunii Istorice* 24, no. 1 (1943–44): 1–27.

25. See Ion Nistor, *Istoria Bucovinei* (Bucharest: Humanitas, 1991).

26. Ştefan Ciobanu, *Cultura românească în Basarabia sub stăpînirea rusă* (Chisinau: Editura Enciclopedică "Gheorghe Asachi," 1992), pp. 18–20. For detailed descriptions of the early Bessarabian administrative systems, see Ion G. Pelivan, *La Bessarabie sous le régime russe (1812–1918)* (Paris: Imprimerie Générale Lahure, 1919).

27. Nistor, *Istoria Basarabiei*, pp. 228–31.

28. Seton-Watson, *History of the Roumanians*, pp. 202–3.

29. George F. Jewsbury, *The Russian Annexation of Bessarabia: 1774–1828* (Boulder, Colo.: East European Quarterly, 1976), pp. 142–54.

30. Nistor, *Istoria Basarabiei*, p. 189.

31. Ibid., p. 260.

32. A. S. Weinberg, *Chişinăul în trecut şi prezent: Schiţa istorică* (Chisinau: Tipografia Carmen Silva, 1936), p. 23.

33. Arbore, *Basarabia în secolul XIX*, pp. 250–51.

34. *Pervaia vseobshchaia perepis' naseleniia Rossiiskoi imperii, 1897 g.* (St. Petersburg: Izdanie Tsentral'nago Statisticheskago Komiteta Ministerstva Vnutrennikh Del, 1905), 3: 1. Even this figure was probably high, since the standard for literacy was little more than the ability to sign one's name.

35. A. Zashchuk, *Materialy dlia geografii i statistiki Rossii: Bessarabskaia guberniia* (St. Petersburg: n.p., 1862), pp. 357–58.

36. Quoted in D. S. Mirsky, *Pushkin* (London: George Routledge and Sons, Ltd., 1926), p. 49.

37. It is likely that the figure was even higher, since the 1897 census tended to count all persons with some knowledge of the Russian language as "Russians."

38. Zashchuk, *Materialy*, pp. 260, 287.

39. "Kishinev," *Encyclopaedia Judaica* (Jerusalem: Encyclopaedia Judaica, 1971), 10: col. 1064.

40. Ibid., col. 1065.

41. Seton-Watson, *History of the Roumanians*, p. 563. In addition, Bessarabian peasants, while working for noble landlords, were not tied to the commune as were their counterparts in other regions of Russia. Another class of "free peasants" (*răzeşi*) from the old Moldovan principality also managed to retain their special privileges even under tsarism.

42. Prince Serge Dmitriyevich Urussov, *Memoirs of a Russian Governor* (London: Harper and Brothers, 1908), pp. 36–37. On these themes, see also the travel account by Shirley Brooks, *The Russians of the South* (London: Longman, Brown, Green and Longmans, 1854).

43. Ciobanu, *Cultura românească*, p. 118.

44. Urussov, *Memoirs*, pp. 24–25.

45. A. A. Skal'kovskii, "Istoricheskoe vvedenie v statisticheskoe opisanie Bessarabskoi oblasti," *Zhurnal Ministerstva vnutrennikh del* 1846, no. 13, p. 171.

46. See Zashchuk, *Materialy*; Aleksei Nakko, *Istoriia Bessarabii s drevneishikh vremen*, 2 vols. (Odessa: Tipografiia Ul'rikha i Shul'tse, 1875); I. P. Donchev, *Russko-rumynskie spravochnye razgovory* (St. Petersburg: Tipografiia V. Kandaurova, 1877); R. N. Batiushkov, *Bessarabiia: Istoricheskoe opisanie* (St. Petersburg: Obshchestvennaia Pol'za, 1892); A. Krushevan, *Bessarabiia: Geograficheskii, istoricheskii, statisticheskii, ekonomicheskii, etnograficheskii, literaturnyi i spravochnyi sbornik* (Moscow: Bessarabtsa, 1903).

47. See Polikhronii Syrku, *Iz byta bessarabskikh rumyn* (Petrograd: Tipografiia V. D. Smirnova, 1914). For an overview of tsarist ethnography on Bessarabia, see O. S. Lukianets, *Russkie issledovateli i moldavskaia etnograficheskaia nauka v XIX-nachale XX v.* (Chisinau: Ştiinţa, 1986).

48. N. V. Lashkov, *Stoletie prisoedineniia Bessarabii k Rossii, 1812–1912* (Chisinau: Tipografiia Bessarabskago Gubernskago Pravleniia, 1912).

49. Ioan Pelivan, "Mişcarea naţională în Basarabia până la unire," manuscript, ANR-DAIC, f. Ioan Pelivan, d. 292/1940, f. 13.

50. Alexandru Bobeică, *Sfatul Ţării: Stîndard al renaşterii naţionale* (Chisinau: Universitas, 1993), pp. 8–11.

51. Ciobanu, *Cultura românească*, p. 228.

52. Bobeică, *Sfatul Ţării*, p. 9.

53. Ştefan Ciobanu, *Unirea Basarabiei* (Chisinau: Universitas, 1993), pp. 86–88

54. Cassian R. Munteanu, *Prin Basarabia românească: Însemnări de călătorie* (Lugoj: Tipografia Iosif Sidon, 1919), p. 43. The Treaty of Bucharest, signed with the Central Powers in April 1918, forced Romania to cede territory to Austria-Hungary and to accept German control of the economy and transport on the Danube. However, the victory of the Allies on the western front and the Salonika offensive through the Balkans in summer and fall 1918 led to the collapse of the Central Powers and the annulment of the treaty.

55. Ibid.

56. Onisifor Ghibu, *Pe baricadele vieţii: În Basarabia revoluţionară (1917–1918), Amintiri* (Chisinau: Universitas, 1992), pp. 244–45. See also his *În vîltoarea revoluţiei ruseşti* (Bucharest: Fundaţia Culturală Română, 1993); *Trei ani pe frontul basarabean* (Bucharest: Fundaţia Culturală Română, 1996); *De la Basarabia rusească la Basarabia românească* (Bucharest: Semne, 1997).

57. Nicolae Iorga, *Basarabia noastră: Scrisă după 100 ani de la răpirea ei de către Ruşi* (Valenii de Munte: Neamul Românesc, 1912).

58. Halippa was convinced, though, that some sort of union with Romania was also the will of Trotsky and Lenin, with whom he met in June 1917. Pantelimon Halippa, *Basarabia noastră* (Bucharest: Universul, 1941), p. 10.

59. Ioniţa Pelivanu, *Adunaria întemeetoare* (Chisinau: Tipografia Ocîrmuirei Guberniale, 1917), p. 11.

60. General Broşteanu, "Oştirea României şi Basarabia," *România nouă*, March 3, 1918, p. 1.

61. Ciobanu, *Unirea*, pp. 224–25, 233.

62. Ibid., pp. 228–31.

63. Ghibu, *Pe baricadele vieţii*, p. 568.

64. "Isvodul deputaţilor Sfatului Ţării care au glăsuit Unirea," f. Preşedinţia Consiliului de Miniştri, d. 40/1918, ff. 1–5.

65. The term *quasi-unanimous* was used by Prime Minister Alexandru Marghiloman at the time of the vote. See his *Reintrarea Basarabiei în sânul patriei-mume* (Bucharest: Institut de Arte Grafice, 1924).

66. "Declaraţia Sfatului Ţării Republicii Democratice Moldoveneşti din 27 Martie anul 1918," ANR-DAIC, f. Preşedinţia Consiliului de Miniştri, d. 35/1918, f. 1.

67. Hamilton Fish Armstrong, "The Bessarabian Dispute," *Foreign Affairs* 2, no. 4 (1924), p. 666.

CHAPTER 3

1. R. W. Seton-Watson, *A History of the Roumanians: From Roman Times to the Completion of Unity* (Cambridge, Eng.: Cambridge University Press, 1934), p. 554.

2. Marin Nedelea, *Prim-miniştrii României Mari* (Bucharest: Viata Româ-neasca, 1991), p. 3.

3. Quoted in Ioan Scurtu, *Monarhia în România, 1866–1947* (Bucharest: Danubius, 1991), p. 70.

4. Jonathan Eyal, "International Protection of Ethnic Minorities: The Case of Romania between the Wars" (D.Phil. thesis, Oxford University, 1987).

5. "Sobytie istoricheskoi vazhnosti," *Sovetskaia Moldaviia*, October 12, 1989, p. 2.

6. Louis Fischer, *Men and Politics: An Autobiography* (London: Jonathan Cape, 1941), p. 131.

7. Ion Pelivan, *Ion Inculeţ şi conferinţa de pace dela Paris (1919–1920)* (Bucharest: Tipografia ziarului "Universul," 1920), p. 9.

8. Sherman David Spector, *Romania at the Paris Peace Conference* (Iaşi: Center for Romanian Studies, 1995), p. 273.

9. Andrei Popovici, *The Political Status of Bessarabia* (Washington: Rans-dell, 1931), pp. 251–55.

10. The treaty was ratified first by Great Britain in January 1921, followed by Romania in April 1922, France in March 1924, and Italy in March 1927. See Philip E. Mosley, "Is Bessarabia Next?" *Foreign Affairs* 18, no. 3 (1940): 559.

11. Prince Antoine Bibesco, *Redeeming Bessarabia* (New York: Society of the Friends of Roumania, 1921), pp. 1–2. It is also likely, though, that the Soviets actively discouraged Japan from ratifying the 1920 treaty, thereby preventing its entering into force. See Bruce A. Elleman, "The 1925 Soviet-Japanese Secret Agreement on Bessarabia," *Diplomacy and Statecraft* 5, no. 2 (1994): 287–325.

12. For detailed treatments of the negotiations over Bessarabia between the wars, see Walter M. Bacon, Jr., *Behind Closed Doors: Secret Papers on the Failure of Romanian-Soviet Negotiations, 1931–1932* (Stanford: Hoover Institution Press, 1979); Dov B. Lungu, *Romania and the Great Powers, 1933–1940* (Durham, N.C.: Duke University Press, 1989); Valeriu Florin Dobrinescu, *The Diplomatic Struggle over Bessarabia* (Iaşi: Center for Romanian Studies, 1996).

13. Dov B. Lungu, "Soviet-Romanian Relations and the Bessarabian Question in the 1920s," *Southeastern Europe/L'Europe du sud-est* 6, no. 1 (1979): 29–45.

14. Alexandre Cretzianu, *The Lost Opportunity* (London: Jonathan Cape, 1957), p. 24.

15. Lungu, *Romania and the Great Powers*, pp. 83–96.

16. Quoted in Cretzianu, *Lost Opportunity*, p. 21.

17. Ioan Scurtu et al., *Istoria Basarabiei: De la începuturi până în 1998*, 2d ed. (Bucharest: Semne, 1998), p. 146; Ion Nistor, *Istoria Basarabiei* (Bucharest: Humanitas, 1991), pp. 317, 322. The situation in Bessarabia was different from that in the other provinces of Romania, though, since much of the land had already been seized by land-hungry peasants in 1917 and 1918.

18. A. S. Weinberg, *Chişinăul în trecut şi prezent: Schiţă istorică* (Chisinau: Tipografia Carmen Silva, 1936), p. 39.

19. Irina Livezeanu, *Cultural Politics in Greater Romania* (Ithaca, N.Y.: Cornell University Press, 1995), p. 103.

20. Nistor, *Istoria Basarabiei*, p. 309.

21. Sabin Mănuilă, *Studiu etnografic asupra populaţiei României* (Bucharest: Editura Institutului Central de Statistică, 1940), pp. 34–36.

22. *Anuarul statistic al României, 1937 şi 1938* (Bucharest: Editura Institutului Central de Statistică, 1939), pp. 486–87, 150–53.

23. Teofil Ioncu, "Ce sunt zemstvele în Basarabia?" *Basarabia economică* 1, no. 4 (1919): 35–44.

24. Charles Upson Clark, *United Romania* (New York: Dodd Mead, 1932), p. 341.

25. Charles Upson Clark, *Bessarabia: Russia and Roumania on the Black Sea* (New York: Dodd Mead, 1927), pp. 18–19; Em. de Martonne, *What I Have Seen in Bessarabia* (Paris: Imprimerie des Arts et des Sports, 1919), p. 11.

26. Clark, *Bessarabia*, p. 22.

27. Romania imposed tariffs on the import of Polish coal; Warsaw responded by taxing Romanian wine imports. Scurtu, *Istoria Basarabiei*, p. 146.

28. Report from Deputy Inspector General of the Sigurana in Bessarabia to Director General, n.d., ANR-DAIC, f. Ministerul Instrucţiunii, d. 273/1921, f. 12; Letter from Minister of Education to Rector of University of Cernui, April 26, 1921, ANR-DAIC, f. Ministerul Instrucţiunii, d. 273/1921, f. 5.

29. Letter from Director General of Police, Chisinau, to Minister of Interior, October 20, 1921, ANR-DAIC, f. Ministerul Instrucţiunii, d. 273/1921, f. 17; Report by Gh. Teodorescu, inspector in Suceava *judeţ*, March 11, 1920, ANR-DAIC, f. Ministerul Instrucţiunii, d. 305/1920, ff. 4–5. See also the police reports in ANR-DAIC, f. Pantelimon Halippa, d. 70/1931, d. 73/1933, d. 77/1934.

30. T. Vicol, "Constatări triste," *Basarabia: Ziar săptămânal independent*, December 18, 1924, p. 1; D. R., "Cum se compromite autoritatea de stat în Basarabia," *Viaţa Basarabiei* [newspaper], August 6, 1933, p. 1.

31. Paul Cazacu, *Zece ani dela unire: Moldova dintre Prut şi Nistru, 1918–1928* (Bucharest: Tipografia ziarului "Universul," 1928), p. 283.

32. Letter from Daniel Ciugureanu to Minister for Bessarabia, n.d., ANR-DAIC, f. Ioan Pelivan, d. 793/f.d., ff. 1–2.

33. M. A. Baluh, *Cu ce vine URSS: Către animia Octiabrului a 15-a, şî RASSM în veţuiria de 8 ani* (Tiraspol: Editura de Stat a Moldovei, 1932), p. 33.

34. A. Trei Schini, *Dela regimul teocratic spre regimul democratic: Amintirile unui basarabean, 1870–1930* (Chisinau: Cartea Românească, 1930), p. 60.

35. Letter from General Râşcanu, Chief Commissar of the Government in Bessarabia and Bukovina, to Prime Minister Averescu, May 7, 1927, ANR-DAIC, f. Preşedinţia Consiliului de Miniştri, d. 10/1927, ff. 88–89.

36. Hamilton Fish Armstrong, *The New Balkans* (London: Harper and Brothers, 1926), pp. 158, 160.

37. Mănuilă, *Studiu etnografic*, pp. 34–35, 38–39.

38. Livezeanu, *Cultural Politics*, pp. 120–27.

39. Gheorghe M. Tzamutali, "Memorandum on the Situation of Russian Minorities in Romania and Their Rights to Attain Their Goals," October 30, 1930, ANR-DAIC, f. Pantelimon Halippa, d. 577/1930, ff. 12–15.

40. A. Iu. Skvortsova, "Russkie v Bessarabii posle ee prisoedineniia k Rumynii (1918-nachalo 20-x gg.)," in *Vne Rossii: Sbornik nauchnykh statei o russkikh i russkoi kul'ture Moldovei* (Chisinau: Institute of National Minorities, Moldovan Academy of Sciences, 1997), pp. 40–48.

41. Scurtu, *Istoria Basarabiei*, p. 164; Nistor, *Istoria Basarabiei*, pp. 308–9.

42. Letter from Police Inspectorate, Chisinau, to Minister for Bessarabia Pantelimon Halippa, February 16, 1931, ANR-DAIC, f. Pantelimon Halippa, d. 70/1931, f. 3.

43. "Report on the Agreements Concluded with Representatives of the Russian Minority," ANR-DAIC, f. Preşedinţia Consiliului de Miniştri, d. 145/1939, ff. 7–11; "Report on the Resolution of Claims Put Forward on September 29, 1939, by Representatives of the Ukrainian Minority," ANR-DAIC, f. Preşedinţia Consiliului de Miniştri, d. 144/1939, ff. 1–6. See also ANR-DAIC, f. Preşedinţia Consiliului de Miniştri, d. 144/139, ff. 6–11, 34–35

44. Quoted in Ştefan Ciobanu, *Unirea Basarabiei* (Chisinau: Universitas, 1993), p. 274.

45. Clark, *Bessarabia*, pp. 287–90.

46. "Fraţi Moldoveni, învăţaţi slova latină!" *Viaţa Basarabiei* [newspaper], February 1, 1925, p. 1.

47. D. J. Hall, *Romanian Furrow* (London: George G. Harrap and Co., Ltd., 1939), p. 207.

48. See the letters and applications in ANR-DAIC, f. Ministerul Instrucţiunii, d. 168/1925.

49. Mănuilă, *Studiu etnografic*, pp. 34–35, 54–55.

50. Porfirie Fala, *Cugetările unui luptător moldovean în timpul revoluţiei ruseşti din 1917* (Bucharest: Editura Casei Şcoalelor, 1927), p. 48.

51. Letter from Propagandist C. Stan to Minister of Education, April 26, 1920, ANR-DAIC, f. Ministerul Instrucţiunii, d. 118/1920, f. 53.

52. Constantin Mâţu, *O necesitate deconsiderată: Presa românească în Basarabia* (Chisinau: Cartea Românească, 1930), pp. 5, 14.

53. Ion Pelivan, *Să vorbim româneşte* (Chisinau: Gazeta Basarabiei, 1938), pp. 4–6.

54. Cassian R. Munteanu, *Prin Basarabia românească: Însemnări de călătorie* (Lugoj: Tipografia Iosif Sidon, 1919), p. 16.

55. Dimitrii Bogoş, "Regionalism," *Viaţa Basarabiei* [newspaper], September 27, 1931, p. 2.

56. Constantin Stere, "Cele două căi," ibid., October 23, 1921, p. 1; Pantelimon Halippa, "Cuvinte de îndrumare despre administraţie," ibid., January 31–February 7, 1932, p. 1.

57. Quoted in Stelian Stoian, "Viaţa politică din Basarabia în perioadă de autonomie provizorie (27 martie–27 noiembrie 1918): Activitatea Sfatului Ţării," *Revistă de istorie a Moldovei* 1992, no. 2, p. 49.

58. Nicolae Popovschi, *Problema naţionalizării în Basarabia* (Chisinau: Tipografia Societăţii de Editură Naţională "Luceafărul," 1922), p. 24.

59. Iuliu Maniu, "Zece ani dela unirea Basarabiei," *Viaţa Basarabiei* [newspaper], April 15, 1928, p. 1.

60. See Al. David, "Culturalizarea masselor in Basarabia," ibid., November 30, 1932, p. 1; Ştefan Ciobanu, "Basarabia care nu se vede," ibid., December 25, 1932, p. 1; I. Zaborovschi, "Basarabia: Câte-va precizări istorice," *Viaţa Basarabiei* [journal] 1, no. 2 (1932): 25–28; T. Porunciuc, "Lexiconul terminilor entopici din limba română din Basarabiei," *Arhivele Basarabiei* 2, no. 1 (1930): 1–33.

61. M. C. Schina, *Pe marginea unirii: Basarabia, ianuarie 1918-iunie 1919* (Bucharest: Institut de Arte Grafice, 1938), pp. 12–13.

62. Letter from Minister of War to Minister of Education, August 22, 1921, f. Ministerul Instrucţiunii, d. 282/1921, f. 13.

63. Antony Babel, *La Bessarabie: Etude historique, ethnographique et économique* (Paris: Librairie Félix Alcan, 1926), p. 212, n. 1; Gh. Tătărescu, *Internaţională a III-a şi Basarabia* (Bucharest: Independenţa, 1925), pp. 30–34. See also the extensive treatment by the Romanian secret police inspector general for Bessarabia, Z. I. Husărescu, *Mişcarea subversivă în Basarabia* (Chisinau: Atelierele Imprimeriei Statului, 1925).

64. Hall, *Romanian Furrow*, pp. 206–7.

65. Protocol of Politburo meeting, Moldovan Committee of the CPbU, February 2, 1932, "On the Attempted Mass Crossing of the Border in Slobozia Raion," AOSPRM, f. 49, op. 1, d. 2068, l. 1.

66. The organization, known as MOPR (*Mezhdunarodnaia organizatsiia pomoshchi bortsam revoliutsii*), existed from 1922 to 1947 and was involved in a range of Soviet agitprop activities outside Bessarabia as well.

67. For a history of the Society and the work of MOPR and other agitprop organizations, see Ia. M. Kopanskii, *Obshchestvo Bessarabtsev v SSSR i soiuzy bessarabskikh emigrantov (1924–1940)* (Chisinau: Ştiinţa, 1978).

68. See J. Okhotnikov and N. Batchinsky, *La Bessarabie et la paix européene* (Paris: Association des Emigrés Bessarabiens, 1927).

69. M. N. Bochacher, *Moldaviia* (Moscow: Gosizdat, 1926), pp. 5–7.

70. *Vsesoiuznaia perepis' naseleniia 1926 goda* (Moscow: Izdanie TsSU Soiuza SSR, 1929), 13: 39.

71. *Moldova: Materialile statistice* (Balta: Moldavskoe Statisticheskoe Upravlenie, 1928), p. 304.

72. Bochacher, *Moldaviia*, p. 46.

73. A. Repida, *Obrazovanie Moldavskoi ASSR* (Chisinau: Ştiinţa, 1974), p. 112. See also the map in Bochacher, *Moldaviia*, p. 58. The provisional capital was moved to Tiraspol in 1929.

74. Quoted in Repida, *Obrazovanie*, pp. 106–7.

75. Hall, *Romanian Furrow*, p. 208.

76. C. G. Rakovsky, *Roumania and Bessarabia* (London: W. Coates, 1925), pp. 9, 12, 18.

77. Quoted in A. Antosiak, "Osvobozhdenie Bessarabii i severnoi Bukoviny," *Mezhdunarodnaia zhizn'* 1991, no. 8, p. 154.

78. See Paul Miliukov, *The Case for Bessarabia: A Collection of Documents*, 2d ed. (London: Russian Liberation Committee, 1920); A. N. Kroupensky and A. Ch. Schmidt, *What Is the "Bessarabian Question"* (Paris: Imprimerie Lahure, n.d.); idem, *The Bessarabian "Parliament" (1917–1918)* (Paris: Imprimerie Lahure, n.d.). Kroupensky was the former marshal of the nobility in Bessarabia and Schmidt the former mayor of Chisinau.

79. Nicolae Titulescu, *Basarabia pămînt românesc* (Bucharest: Rum-Irina, 1992), pp. 55–58.

80. See Ion G. Pelivan, *The Right of the Roumanians to Bessarabia* (Paris: Imprimerie des Arts et des Sports, 1920); idem, *Chronology of the Most Important Events in the Life of Bessarabia* (idem); idem, *The Union of Bessarabia with Her Mother-Country Roumania* (idem).

81. Porfirie Fala, *Ce neam suntem? O lămurire pentru Moldovenii din Basarabia* (Chisinau: Glasul Ţării, 1920).

82. Pelivan, *Să vorbim*, p. 6.

83. Pantelimon Halippa, undated manuscript, ANR-DAIC, f. Pantelimon Halippa, d. 122/f.d., f. 11v.

84. V. Kholostenko, *3 goda natsional'nogo stroitel'stva v AMSSR, 10 let natsional'nogo ugneteniia v Bessarabii* (Balta: Gosizdat Moldavii, 1928), pp. 36–37, 56.

85. L. S. Berg, *Bessarabiia: Strana, liudi, khoziaistvo* (Petrograd: Ogni, 1918), and idem, *Naselenie Bessarabii: Etnograficheskii sostav i chislennost'*

(Petrograd: Rossiiskaia Akademiia Nauk, 1923). Berg was in fact a prominent tsarist ethnographer who, like many former "bourgeois" academics, continued to work in the Bolshevik period.

86. Berg, *Naselenie Bessarabii*, p. 29.

87. V. Dembo, *Nikogda ne zabyt'! Krovavaia letopis' Bessarabii* (Moscow: Krasnaia Nov', 1924).

88. V. Dembo, *Sovetskaia Moldaviia i bessarabskii vopros* (Moscow: Izdatel'stvo Moskovskogo otdela Obshchestva bessarabtsev, 1925).

89. Ibid., p. 15.

90. D. Milev, "Norod moldovenesc," *Plugarul roş*, July 28, 1926, p. 3.

91. Pavel Chior, *Basarabia sub călcîiu boiresc* (Balta: Editura de Stat a Moldovei, 1928).

92. A. G., "Pervaia godovshchina Sovetskoi Moldavii," *Krasnaia Bessarabiia* 1926, no. 1, p. 26.

93. V. Dembo, *Bessarabskoe krest'ianstvo pod vlastiu kulakov i pomeshchikov* (Moscow: Izdatel'stvo TsK MOPR SSSR, 1931), p. 9.

94. Viktor Garskii, *Trudovaia Bessarabiia i sovetskaia vlast'* (Moscow: Gosizdat, 1921), p. 16.

95. K. N. Derzhavin, "Literaturnoe stroitel'stvo v sotsialisticheskoi Moldavii," *Trudy Instituta slavianovedeniia Akademii Nauk SSSR* 1932, no. 1, pp. 239–96.

96. Dembo, *Sovetskaia Moldaviia*, p. 38.

CHAPTER 4

1. Gustav Weigand, *Die Dialekte der Bukowina und Bessarabiens (mit einem Titelbilde und Musikbeilagen)* (Leipzig: Johann Ambrosius Barth, 1904).

2. See Al. David, "Scrisul românesc în Basarabia," *Viaţa Basarabiei* [newspaper], November 17, 1932, p. 1; V. Prisacaru, "Să ne cinstim limbă!" ibid., September 23, 1933, p. 1.

3. P. I. Chior, *Dispri orfografia lingii moldovineşti* (Bîrzula: Comitetu di Ştiinţî Moldovinesc, 1929), p. 11.

4. M. V. Sergievskii, *Moldavskie etiudy* (Moscow: Izdatel'stvo Akademii Nauk SSSR, 1936), p. 11.

5. "Protocol of the Fifth Plenum of the Obkom and *Oblast'* Control Commission of the Communist Party of Moldova," AOSPRM, f. 49, op. 1, d. 516, ll. 51, 95–97.

6. Gabriel Buciuşcanu, *Gramatica limbii moldoveneşti* (Balta: Editura de Stat a Moldovei, 1925); *Slovar ruso-moldovenesc* (Balta: Editura de Stat a Moldovei, 1926); *Slovar moldovo-rusesc* (Balta: Editura de Stat a Moldovei, 1926).

Cf. August Scriban, *Gramatica limbii românești (morfologia) pentru folosința tuturor* (Iași: Institutu de Arte Grafice "Viața Românească," 1925).

7. See Stepan Martsell, *Rossiisko-rumynskaia grammatika* (St. Petersburg: Tipografiia Departamenta Narodnago Prosveshcheniia, 1827); Ia. Ginkulov, *Nachertanie pravil Valakho-Moldavskoi grammatiki* (St. Petersburg: Tipografiia Imperatorskoi Akademii Nauk, 1840); Mihail Ciachir, *Russko-Moldavskii slovar'* (Chisinau: Eparkhial'naia Tipografiia, 1907).

8. The Moldovan Academy of Sciences was established in 1961. See *Ocherki istorii organizatsii nauki v Sovetskoi Moldavii (1924–1961)* (Chisinau: Știința, 1980).

9. "Statute of the Moldovan Scientific Committee of the MASSR Narkompros," AOSPRM, f. 49, op. 1, d. 951, l. 35.

10. Personal file of Pavel Chior, AOSPRM, f. 49, op. 4, d. 1351, ll. 3–4.

11. See Sheila Fitzpatrick, "The Civil War as a Formative Experience," in Abbott Gleason, Peter Kenez, and Richard Stites, eds., *Bolshevik Culture: Experiment and Order in the Russian Revolution* (Bloomington: Indiana University Press, 1985), pp. 57–76.

12. L. A. Madan, *Gramatica moldovniascî* (Tiraspol: Editura de Stat a Moldovei, 1929).

13. See Michael G. Smith, "Soviet Language Frontiers: The Structural Method in Early Language Reforms, 1917–1937" (Ph.D. diss., Georgetown University, 1991).

14. "Protocol of Meeting of the Moldovan Scientific Committee, February 14, 1930," AOSPRM, f. 49, op. 2, d. 42, ll. 2–3.

15. P. I. Chior, *Zîcătoarele moldovenești* (Balta: Editura de Stat a Moldovei, 1926); idem, *Cîntece moldovenești (norodnice)* (Balta: Editura de Stat a Moldovei, 1927–28).

16. See the lists of new terms in AOSPRM, f. 49, op. 1, d. 1817, l. 2; op. 2, d. 44, ll. 1–22; d. 43, ll. 2–43.

17. See Isabelle T. Kreindler, ed., *Sociolinguistic Perspectives on Soviet National Languages: Their Past, Present, and Future* (Berlin: Mouton, 1985); Paul Wexler, *Purism and Language: A Study of Modern Ukrainian and Belorussian Nationalism (1840–1967)* (Bloomington: Indiana University Press, 1974); Michael Kirkwood, ed., *Language Planning in the Soviet Union* (London: Macmillan, 1989); William Fierman, *Language Planning and National Development: The Uzbek Experience* (Berlin: Mouton, 1991).

18. I. V. Stalin, "Natsional'nye momenty v partiinom i gosudarstvennom stroitel'stve" in *Sochineniia* (Moscow: Gosudarstvennoe Izdatel'stvo Politicheskoi Literatury, 1947), 5: 191.

19. For a general introduction to Soviet policies on these fronts, see Peter Kenez, *The Birth of the Propaganda State: Soviet Methods of Mass Mobilization, 1917–29* (Cambridge, Eng.: Cambridge University Press, 1985).

20. I. V. Stalin, "Doklad o natsional'nykh momentakh v partiinoi i gosudarstvennom stroitel'stve," in *Sochineniia*, 5: 257–58.

21. "Postanovlenie Tsentral'nogo Isponitel'nogo Komiteta i Sovnarkom AMSSR 'O moldovanizatsii i ukrainizatsii sovetskogo apparata,'" *Plugarul roş*, June 30, 1926, p. 6.

22. See the instructions and administrative structure in AOSPRM, f. 49, op. 1, d. 775, ll. 2, 4, 5; f. 49, op. 1, d. 3364, l. 19v.

23. See the resolutions and reports in AOSPRM f. 49, op. 1, d. 734, ll. 1–4; d. 935, ll. 17–18; d. 939, ll. 53–54; d. 1162, ll. 4–6; d. 2017, ll. 32–37, 48; d. 2181, ll. 18–20; d. 2401, ll. 5–7, 8–10, 55–58, 64–66; d. 3988, ll. 27–28; f. 32, op. 1, d. 522, l. 165.

24. Politburo report "On the Study of the Moldovan Language among *Raion* Party Secretaries," AOSPRM, f. 49, op. 1, d. 3123, l. 3.

25. *Vsesoiuznaia perepis' naseleniia 1926 goda* (Moscow: Izdanie TsSU Soiuza SSR, 1929), 13: 39–41.

26. Ibid. This does not include Roma (Gypsies), who, of all ethnic groups, had the lowest number of literate men and women. Only about 900 Roma, though, were recorded in the 1926 census. The "most literate" women were Germans, with 67 percent of German females able to read.

27. On the origins of Inochentism, see Nicolae Popovschi, *Mişcarea dela Balta sau Inochentizmul în Basarabia* (Chisinau: Cartea Românească, 1926).

28. Report by I. I. Badeev, first secretary of MASSR Obkom, n.d., AOSPRM, f. 49, op. 1, d. 159, ll. 15–16.

29. Ibid., July 1925, AOSPRM, f. 49, op. 1, d. 84, l. 65.

30. Letter from Dumitriu, deputy secretary of MASSR Obkom, to Central Committee, March 7, 1930, AOSPRM, f. 49, op. 1, d. 1648, ll. 55–56.

31. Ibid., l. 55v. Women's protests were common during this period. See Lynne Viola, "*Bab'i Bunty* and Peasant Women's Protest during Collectivization," *Russian Review* 45, no. 1 (1986): 23–42; and Viola, *Peasant Rebels under Stalin* (Oxford: Oxford University Press, 1996).

32. E. S. Lazo, *Moldavskaia partiinaia organizatsiia v gody stroitel'stva sotsializma (1924–1940)* (Chisinau: Ştiinţa, 1981), p. 39; AOSPRM, f. 49, op. 1, d. 9, ll. 1–261; d. 3623, ll. 1–280.

33. Report on "Schoolchildren by Social Class, 1926–27 Academic Year," AOSPRM, f. 49, op. 1, d. 1022, l. 2; V. M. Mireniuk, "Podgotovka kadrov srednei i vysshei kvalifikatsii v Moldavskoi ASSR (1926–1940), " in S. K. Brysiakin, ed., *Kul'turnoe stroitel'stvo v Sovetskoi Moldavii* (Chisinau: Ştiinţa, 1974), p. 249.

34. "Data on the Work of the MASSR Narkompros in the 1926–27 Academic Year," n.d., AOSPRM, f. 49, op. 1, d. 1082, l. 1.

35. Report by Gabriel Buciuşcanu, MASSR Narkompros, 1925, AOSPRM, f. 49, op. 1, d. 84, l. 76.

36. Narkompros report on teaching staff, January 1, 1927, AOSPRM, f. 49, op. 1, d. 1082, l. 63.

37. Report by party commission for the inspection of MASSR schools, n.d., AOSPRM, f. 49, op. 1, d. 1082, ll. 57, 58, 62.

38. "Table on the Distribution of Moldovan Newspapers," n.d., AOSPRM, f. 49, op. 1, d. 1890, l. 51.

39. Report by political education inspector Nikolaev, n.d., AOSPRM, f. 49, op. 1, d. 1082, l. 34.

40. AOSPRM, f. 49, op. 1, d. 2475, l. 168.

41. Report on political education in 1926–27, AOSPRM, f. 49, op. 1, d. 1082, l. 11.

42. James E. Mace, *Communism and the Dilemmas of National Liberation: National Communism in Soviet Ukraine, 1918–1933* (Cambridge, Mass.: Harvard University Press, 1983), p. 200.

43. F. Golub, "Om dizredecina clintiria dreptaşî la practicî," *Plugarul roş*, March 21, 1930, pp. 2–3.

44. "Hotărâria CŢ PC(b)U după docladu dispri lucru Comobului moldovinesc," ibid., p. 3.

45. "Lucru Comitetului Ştiinţîinic—la slujba zîdirii soţializmului," ibid., September 6, 1930, p. 3.

46. See D. T. Ursul and V. M. Topilina, *I. V. Ochinskii (1888–1970)* (Chisinau: Ştiinţa, 1979).

47. I. V. Ocinschi, "Nauku—na sluzhbu piatiletki," *Krasnaia Bessarabiia* 1932, no. 11, pp. 26, 30.

48. "Transcript of Combined Obkom and *Oblast'* Control Commission Plenum, May 21, 1931," AOSPRM, f. 49, op. 1, d. 1899, l. 39.

49. On the Karelian case, see Paul T. Austin, "Soviet Karelian: The Language That Failed," *Slavic Review* 51, no. 1 (1992): 16–35.

50. "Resolution on the Transition to the Latin Alphabet," AOSPRM, f. 49, op. 1, d. 2401, l. 59.

51. Ocinschi's statement was given in a 1956 KGB interview as part of an investigation regarding the rehabilitation of the MASSR writer Dumitru Milev. It was published for the first time in "Alfabetul latin în Transnistria—cap de pod pentru România," *Sfatul Ţării* 1992 (December): 19.

52. *10 ani de construire socialistă a RASSM (în ajutorul raporturilor)* (Tiraspol: Editura de Stat a Moldovei, 1934), p. 18. See also AOSPRM, f. 49, op. 1, d. 2861, l. 42.

53. M. Bochacher, "Ocherki moldavskoi literatury," *Krasnaia Bessarabiia* 1935, no. 5, p. 24.

54. "Latinizaria alfabetului moldovenesc—arma luptii di clas a proletariatului şî zîdirii soţializmului," *Octiabriu* 1932, nos. 5–6, p. 183.

55. MASSR Obkom report "On the Situation of Courses to Teach the Latin Script to Cultural Soldiers," AOSPRM, f. 49, op. 1, d. 2284, l. 63.

56. Letter from V. P. Zatons'kyi to Bulat and Staryi, June 22, 1933, ibid., d. 2599, l. 21.

57. L. A. Madan, *Gramatica limbii moldoveneşti: Fonetica, morfologia şi sintaxa* (Tiraspol: Editura de Stat a Moldovei, 1932).

58. See G. C. Gordinschi, *Dicţionarul terminologiei matematice* (Tiraspol: Editura de Stat a Moldovei, 1932); P. I. Craciun and D. E. Grigorieva, *Abecedar* (Tiraspol: Editura de Stat a Moldovei, 1936); A. P. Dîmbul, *Manual de limba moldovenească: Gramatica şi ortografia (clasă a 3-a şi a 4-a)* (Ibid.); N. Ploeşteanu, *Limba moldovenească: Gramatica şi ortografia (manual pentru şcolile de adulţi cu puţină ştiinţă de carte)* (Ibid.).

59. A. P. Dîmbul, *Gramatica, morfologia: Manual pentru şcoala medie, anul al cincilea de învăţămînt* (Tiraspol: Editura de Stat a Moldovei, 1933).

60. "Despre treşeria scrisului moldovenesc dela alfavitu latin la alfavitu rus," *Moldova socialistă*, June 6, 1938, p. 1.

61. Ibid., "Şerinţa norodului moldovenesc este împlinită."

62. Tiraspol city committee report, "On the Pollution of the Moldovan Language by Romanian Words, 1938," AOSPRM, f. 32, op. 1, d. 640, ll. 48–49.

63. I. D. Cioban, "Câte şeva despre limbă," *Moldova socialistă*, June 6, 1938, p. 2.

64. P. Chior, "Pe drumul moldovenizării," *Plugarul roş*, December 8, 1926, p. 2.

65. C. Stratievschi, "Victime ale Stalinizmului," *Tribuna* 1989, no. 4, p. 33.

66. "Resolution on the Open Meeting of the Party Cell of the Moldovan Scientific Committee, July 16–17, 1933," AOSPRM, f. 49, op. 1, d. 2309, ll. 11–14.

67. Obkom Politburo report "On National Cultural Construction in the MASSR," n.d., ibid., d. 2225, l. 19; "Alfabetul latin în Transnistria," p. 19. Ocinschi was also arrested and detained for several weeks. He was subsequently released and, by exposing other local nationalists, managed to survive the purges of the late 1930s. He was officially rehabilitated in February 1957 and died in Chisinau in 1970.

68. Stratievschi, "Victime," p. 34.

69. AOSPRM, f. 49, op. 1, d. 2225, ll. 15, 19. Madan's life after this point remains a mystery. There is some speculation among Moldovan historians that he managed to survive the purges by quitting the MASSR before the mid-1930s.

70. N. F. Movileanu, "Sledovat' pravde istorii," in *Vosstanavlivaia pravdu istorii* (Chisinau: Cartea Moldovenească, 1989), p. 12.

71. See the lists in AOSPRM, f. 49, op. 1, d. 2507, l. 25; d. 3880, ll. 59–61; d. 3881, l. 22; d. 3883, l. 134.

CHAPTER 5

1. "Ul'timativnaia nota pravitel'stva SSSR pravitel'stvu Rumynii," *Basarabia* 1991, no. 6, p. 43.

2. Grigore Gafencu, *Prelude to the Russian Campaign*, trans. E. Fletcher-Allen (London: Frederick Muller, 1945), p. 290; Alexandre Cretzianu, *The Lost Opportunity* (London: Jonathan Cape, 1957), p. 47.

3. "Transcript of Fourth Plenum of the MASSR Obkom, October 24, 1934," AOSPRM, f. 49, op. 1, d. 2475, l. 168.

4. "Transcript of First Session of MASSR Supreme Soviet, July 18, 1938," ANRM, f. P-2947, op. 1, d. 9, l. 35.

5. "Data on the Territory of Each *Raion* of the MASSR in Square Kilometers," ibid., d. 33, l. 14; Letter from O. Mezhzherin, secretary of the Supreme Soviet of the Ukrainian SSR, to Konstantinov, chairman of the MASSR Supreme Soviet, February 9, 1940, ibid., l. 16.

6. Keith Hitchins, *Rumania, 1866–1947* (Oxford: Clarendon Press, 1994), p. 445.

7. Letter from Ion Inculeţ to Ion Antonescu, n.d., ANR-DAIC, f. Pantelimon Halippa, d. 1018/f.d., ff. 1–6.

8. M. I. Semiriaga, *Tainy stalinskoi diplomatii, 1939–1941* (Moscow: Vysshaia Shkola, 1992), p. 270. See also the memoirs of a refugee from Bukovina, Dumitru Nimigeanu, *Hell Moved Its Border* (London: Blandford Press, 1960).

9. Report from Eugen Sturdza, state inspector general, ANR-DAIC, f. Preşedinţia Consiliului de Miniştri, d. 482/1940, f. 19v.

10. Anton Galopenţia, "Populaţia teritoriilor româneşti desprinse în 1940," *Geopolitica şi geoistoria: Revistă română pentru sudestul european* 1941, no. 3, p. 4; "Basarabia şi Bucovina de nord, 1939–1940: Documente," *Basarabia* 1991, no. 6, p. 54.

11. *Sovetskaia Bessarabiia i Sovetskaia Bukovina* (Moscow: Gosudarstvennoe izdatel'stvo politicheskoi literatury, 1940), p. 31.

12. Alexander Dallin, *Odessa, 1941–1944: A Case Study of Soviet Territory under Foreign Rule*, rev. ed. (Iaşi: Center for Romanian Studies, 1998), p. 59.

13. See Olivian Verenca, *Administraţia civilă română în Transnistria* (Chisinau: Universitas, 1993), by the former chief of staff to the Transnistrian governor.

14. See the memoirs of Gherman Pântea, the mayor of Odessa during the Romanian occupation, in ANR-DAIC, f. Gherman Pântea, d. 6.

15. Radu Ioanid, *Evreii sub regimul Antonescu* (Bucharest: Hasefer, 1998), p. 265. See also Julius S. Fisher, *Transnistria: The Forgotten Cemetery* (New York: Thomas Yoseloff, 1969); Siegfried Jagendorf, *Jagendorf's Foundry* (New York: HarperCollins, 1991); and the monumental study by Jean Ancel published in Romanian translation, *Transnistria*, 3 vols. (Bucharest: Editura Atlas, 1998).

16. Sabin Mănuilă, *Studiu etnografic asupra populației României* (Bucharest: Editura Institutului Central de Statistică, 1940), pp. 60–61; *Itogi vsesoiuznoi perepisi naseleniia 1959 goda: Moldavskaia SSR* (Moscow: Gosizdat, 1962), pp. 62–53.

17. Letter from C. I. C. Brătianu and Iuliu Maniu to Ion Antonescu, April 20, 1943, ANR-DAIC, f. Pantelimon Halippa, d. 1008/1941, f. 3.

18. *Treaties of Peace with Italy, Romania, Bulgaria, Hungary and Finland* (London: HMSO, 1947).

19. A. V. Surilov, ed., *Gosudarstvenno-pravovye akty Moldavskoi SSR (1924–1941 gg.)* (Chisinau: Cartea Moldovenească, 1963), pp. 149–52. The border with Ukraine remained a problematic issue throughout much of the Soviet period and would resurface after 1991. See Anton Moraru, "Documentele mărturisesc," *Cugetul* 1993, nos. 5–6, pp. 61–73.

20. "Basarabia și Bucovina de Nord," p. 54.

21. Ibid.

22. V. V. Chembrovskii and E. M. Zagorodnaia, "Moldavskaia Sovetskaia Sotsialisticheskaia Respublika," in *Naselenie soiuznykh respublik* (Moscow: Statistika, 1977), p. 192.

23. The Karelo-Finnish republic was smaller, but only existed from 1940 to 1956.

24. Leonid Il'ich Brezhnev, *Vospominaniia*, 2d ed. (Moscow: Izdatel'stvo politicheskoi literatury, 1983), p. 141.

25. Mihai Gribincea, *Basarabia în primii ani de ocupație sovietică, 1944–1950* (Cluj: Dacia, 1995), p. 72.

26. *Economia națională a Republicii Moldova, 1991* (Chisinau: Departamental de Stat pentru Statistică, 1992), p. 78.

27. See Gribincea, *Basarabia în primii ani*, pp. 71–104.

28. A. M. Țăran et al., *Golod v Moldove, 1946–1947: Sbornik dokumentov* (Chisinau: Știința, 1993), p. 9.

29. Ion Șișcanu, *Deșțărănirea bolșevică în Basarabia* (Chisinau: Adrian, 1994).

30. Gribincea, *Basarabia în primii ani*, pp. 129–48.

31. Ibid., p. 145.

32. Ioan Scurtu et al., *Istoria Basarabiei de la începuturi până în 1998*, 2d ed. (Bucharest: Semne, 1998), pp. 258–59.

33. Dennis Deletant, "The Molotov-Ribbentrop Pact and Its Consequences

for Bessarabia: Some Considerations on the Human Rights Implications," unpublished paper, 1991, p. 17.

34. Elena Postică, "Grupuri de rezistenţă pe teritoriul Basarabiei," *Arhivele totalitarismului* 15, nos. 15–16 (1998): 66–77.

35. Ronald J. Hill, *Soviet Political Elites: The Case of Tiraspol* (New York: St. Martin's, 1977).

36. Zev Katz and Roderic T. Harned, "Appendix: Comparative Tables for the Major Soviet Nationalities," in Zev Katz, ed., *Handbook of Major Soviet Nationalities* (London: Collier Macmillan, 1975), p. 449. This figure does not include nonrepublican nationalities.

37. A. F. Diorditsa, *Moldavia: A Flourishing Orchard* (London: Soviet Booklets, 1960).

38. Scurtu, *Istoria Basarabiei*, p. 282.

39. Paige Bryan, "The Soviet Leadership Endorses the Moldavian Model for Agriculture," January 24, 1974, Radio Free Europe/Radio Liberty Krasnyi Arkhiv, File Moldavskaia SSR.

40. Gheorghe Malarciuc, "Kuda devat' izobilie," *Literaturnaia gazeta*, June 25, 1975, p. 10.

41. *IMF Economic Reviews, 1993: Moldova* (Washington: IMF, 1993), pp. 45–46.

42. Despite the declining Jewish population, antisemitic campaigns continued. In 1964, the composer David Gershfeld was accused of illegal trading and other economic misdeeds and was removed from his position as head of the Moldovan Composers' Union.

43. Scurtu, *Istoria Basarabiei*, p. 247.

44. Rasma Karklins, *Ethnic Relations in the USSR: The Perspective from Below* (Boston: Unwin Hyman, 1986), p. 156.

45. "XV s'ezd Kompartii Moldavii," *Partiinaia zhizn'* 1981, no. 4, pp. 61–65.

46. S. Gamburtzev, "The Exacerbation of the Nationality Problem in Moldavia: Some Specific Aspects," April 20, 1966, Radio Free Europe/Radio Liberty Krasnyi Arkhiv, File Moldavskaia SSR.

47. "O rabote TsK Kompartii Moldavii po sovershenstvovaniia stilia i metodov deiatel'nosti partiinykh organizatsii v svete reshenii noiabr'skogo (1982 goda) Plenuma TsK KPSS," *Partiinaia zhizn'* 1984, no. 1, pp. 21–24.

48. Alexander Rahr, "Moldavian Party Chief Reprimanded," November 3, 1986, Radio Free Europe/Radio Liberty Krasnyi Arkhiv, File Moldavskaia SSR.

49. "MSSR Minister Sacked for Drunkenness," May 8, 1984, ibid.; Reuters (Moscow), June 26, 1984.

50. Reuters (Moscow), October 1, 1984.

51. E. Kondratov, "Tak gde zhe byl prokuror?" *Izvestiia*, December 2, 1986, p. 3.

52. Elena Torina, "Nistru: Un fluviu transfrontalier," *Arena politicii* 1997 (November): 22–23.

53. Goskomstat SSSR, *Demograficheskii ezhegodnik SSSR, 1990* (Moscow: Finansy i statistika, 1990), pp. 149–66, 390.

54. For example, the incidence of Down syndrome rose from 0.57 percent of newborns in 1987 to 1.32 percent in 1997. *FBIS-SOV*, February 12, 1997 (electronic version).

55. See Robert R. King, *A History of the Romanian Communist Party* (Stanford: Hoover Institution Press, 1980), pp. 29–32.

56. "Moldavian Party Secretary Bodyul on Friendship of Soviet Peoples," December 3, 1965, Radio Free Europe/Radio Liberty Krasnyi Arkhiv, File Moldavskaia SSR. For detailed accounts of these disputes, see George Ciorănesco, *Bessarabia: Disputed Land between East and West* (Munich: Editura Ion Dumitru, 1985); George Cioranesco et al., *Aspects des relations russo-roumaines: Rétrospectives et orientations* (Paris: Minard, 1967); idem, *Aspects des relations soviéto-roumaines, 1967–1971: Sécurité européene* (idem, 1971).

57. In the 1960s, the Romanians increased the power of the station so that its programs could be easily received in the MSSR. "Bodyul Again Attacks Anti-Russian Feeling in Moldavia," March 17, 1967, Radio Free Europe/Radio Liberty Krasnyi Arkhiv, File Moldavskaia SSR.

58. I. Bodiul, "Oktiabr' i sotsial'nye preobrazovaniia," *Pravda*, October 5, 1967, pp. 2–3; idem, "Slavnaia stranitsa geroicheskoi letopisi," ibid., August 22, 1969, p. 2; idem, "Utverzhdenie sotsialisticheskoi kul'tury," ibid., April 16, 1970, p. 2; idem, "Preobrazhennaia Moldaviia," ibid., June 28, 1970, p. 2; idem, "Plody velikogo bratstva narodov," *Literaturnaia gazeta*, July 12, 1972, p. 2; idem, "Sotsialisticheskaia po soderzhaniiu, natsional'naia po forme," *Pravda*, August 22, 1972, p. 2.

59. "Protocol from Meeting of CPM Politburo, August 22, 1967," AOSPRM, f. 51, op. 28, d. 19, ll. 35–41.

60. See the charts in Wim van Meurs, *The Bessarabian Question in Communist Historiography: Nationalist and Communist Politics and History-Writing* (Boulder, Colo.: East European Monographs, 1994), Chapter 6.

61. See, for example, Nicholas Dima, "Moldavians or Romanians?" in Ralph Clem, ed., *The Soviet West: Interplay between Nationality and Social Organization* (New York: Praeger, 1975), pp. 31–45.

62. Karl Marx, *Însemnări despre români: Manuscrise inedite*, ed. A. Oțetea and S. Schwann (Bucharest: Academia RPR, 1964). On the background to this incident, see Van Meurs, *Bessarabian Question*, pp. 270–77.

63. King, *Minorities under Communism*, p. 267.

64. Ibid., pp. 233–35.

65. "Po povodu besedy Mao Tsze-Duna s gruppoi iaponskikh sotsialistov," *Pravda*, September 2, 1964, pp. 2–3.

66. See ANR-DAIC, f. Pantelimon Halippa, d. 552/1967–71, ff. 1–4, 22–26; d. 556/1968, f. 1. Halippa was arrested in Romania in 1950, turned over to the Soviets in 1952, and sentenced to 25 years' imprisonment in Irkutsk. He was freed and allowed to return to Romania in 1955.

67. "Tovarăşul Nicolae Ceauşescu a facut ieri o vizită de prietenie la Chişinău," *Scînteia*, August 3, 1976, pp. 1, 3.

68. "Another Romanian Delegation in Soviet Moldavia," September 20, 1979, Radio Free Europe/Radio Liberty Krasnyi Arkhiv, File Moldavskaia SSR.

69. Al. Graur, *Studii de lingvistică generală* (Bucharest: Editura Academiei Republicii Populare Romîne, 1960), p. 311. Graur recognized the status of Moldovan as a "new eastern Romance language," but maintained that Moldovan and Romanian were likely to merge into "a single and common language for the entire people, the Romanian national language."

70. Dima, "Moldavians or Romanians?" pp. 31–45.

71. For a comparison of changes in Moldovan usage, see A. Lunacharskii, "Cîteva probleme de terminologie," *Cultura* 1972, no. 48, pp. 6–7.

72. See Corlăteanu's retrospective in "Nicolae Corlăteanu la 75 de ani," *Revistă de lingvistică şi ştiinţă literară* 1990, no. 4, p. 68.

73. Explicit comparisons of the two languages were frequent, but no attempt was made to publish a full dictionary. See L. A. Novak, "Chastotnyi slovar' moldavskogo i rumynskogo iazykov" (*Kandidat* diss., Leningrad University, 1962); P. G. Piotrovskii, "Lingvisticheskie otsenki raskhozhdeniia blizkorodstvennykh iazykov (eshche raz o sootnoshenii moldavskogo i rumynskogo iazykov)," *Voprosy iazykoznaniia* 1973, no. 5, pp. 36–42; T. P. Il'iashenko, *Formirovanie romanskikh literaturnykh iazykov: Moldavskii iazyk* (Chisinau: Ştiinţa, 1983).

74. See Iu. V. Bromlei, *Etnosotsial'nye protsessy: Teoriia, istoriia, sovremennost'* (Moscow: Nauka, 1987).

75. N. A. Mokhov, *Ocherki formirovaniia moldavskogo naroda* (Chisinau: Cartea Moldovenească, 1978), pp. 6–7.

76. *Istoriia RSS Moldoveneşti* (Chisinau: Cartea Moldovenească, 1970), 2: 653.

77. Van Meurs, *Bessarabian Question*, p. 193.

78. The Institute of Party History, subordinated to the CPM Central Committee, was established in January 1948 as an affiliate of the Marx-Engels-Lenin Institute in Moscow. The Institute of History was set up in December 1957 and, after the opening of the Moldovan Academy of Sciences in 1961, became the locus of historical scholarship within the Academy. The former was the descendant of Istpart, the institution for the study of party and revolutionary history set up in the MASSR in 1925. The latter evolved from the Moldovan Scientific Committee.

79. Van Meurs, *Bessarabian Question*, p. 195.

80. For examples of popular writing on the Moldovan language, see N. G. Corlăteanu, *Egale între egale: Limba moldovenească literară în perioada sovietică* (Chisinau: Academia de Ştiinţe din RSSM, 1971); idem, *În constelaţie de limbi înfrăţite* (Chisinau: Lumina, 1982); Arcadie Evdoşenco, *Comoara din străbuni* (Chisinau: Hyperion, 1992).

81. "Nicolae Corlăteanu," pp. 70, 72.

82. Carlo Tagliavini, *Una nuova lingua letteraria romanza? Il moldavo* (Florence: Sansoni, 1956). See also the collection of maps and other materials prepared for the congress, *Alcuni documenti sulla unità della lingua romena* (Florence: VIII Congresso Internazionale di Studi Romanzi, 1956).

83. Tagliavini, *Una nuova lingua*, p. 448.

84. Carlo Tagliavini, *Le origini delle lingue neolatine*, 6th ed. (Bologna: Casa Editrice Prof. Riccardo Petron, 1969), p. 361, n. 4.

85. Eugene Lozovan, "La linguistique roumaine de 1952 à 1954," *Zeitschrift für romanische Philologie* 1995, no. 71, pp. 391–407.

86. Harald Haarman, *Soziologie der kleinen Sprachen Europas* (Hamburg: Helmut Buske Verlag, 1973), vol. 1.

87. Klaus Heitmann, "Rumänische Sprache und Literatur in Bessarabien und Transnistrien (die sogenannte moldauische Sprache und Literatur)," *Zeitschrift für romanische Philologie* 1965, no. 81, pp. 102–56; idem, "Das Moldauische—eine eigenständige ostromanische Sprache?" *SüdosteuropaMitteilungen* 1987, no. 27, pp. 56–62; idem, "Probleme der moldauischen Sprache in der Ära Gorbačev," *Südosteuropa* 38, no. 1 (1989): 28–53.

88. Dennis Deletant, "The Soviet View of Bessarabia," *Slavonic and East European Review* 56, no. 1 (1978): 115–18; idem, "Romania and the Moldavian SSR," *Soviet Analyst* 12, no. 1 (1983): 6–8; idem, "What Would Self-Determination Mean for the Moldavians?" in Alexander Shtromas and Morton A. Kaplan, eds., *The Soviet Union and the Challenge for the Future* (New York: Paragon House, 1989), 3: 479–508; idem, "Language Policy and Linguistic Trends in Soviet Moldavia," in Michael Kirkwood, ed., *Language Planning in the Soviet Union* (London: Macmillan, 1989), pp. 189–216.

89. Dima, "Moldavians or Romanians?" and idem, *Bessarabia and Bukovina: The Soviet-Romanian Territorial Dispute* (Boulder, Colo.: East European Monographs, 1982).

90. Michael Bruchis, *One Step Back, Two Steps Forward: On the Language Policy of the Communist Party of the Soviet Union in the National Republics (Moldavian: A Look Back, a Survey, and Perspectives, 1924–1980)* (Boulder, Colo.: East European Monographs, 1982); idem, "The Language Policy of the CPSU and the Linguistic Situation in Soviet Moldavia," *Soviet Studies* 36, no. 1 (1984): 108–26; idem, *Nations–Nationalities–People: A Study of the Nationalities Policy of the Communist Party in Soviet Moldavia* (Boulder, Colo.: East European Monographs, 1984).

91. See, for example, Cioranesco, *Aspects des relations russo-roumaines*; idem, *Aspects des relations soviéto-roumaines*; Grigore Nandriş, *Bessarabia and Bucovina: The Trojan Horse of Russian Colonial Expansion to the Mediterranean* (London: Editura Societăţii pentru Cultura, 1968); and on the forced deportations of the 1950s, Association "Pro Bessarabia" de France et de Grande-Bretagne et al., *Pro Bassarabia: Mémoire* (Paris: Imprimerie Blanchard, 1955).

92. A. M. Lazarev, *Moldavskaia sovetskaia gosudarstvennost' i bessarabskii vopros* (Chisinau: Cartea Moldovenească, 1974). For an extensive analysis, see Jack Gold, "Bessarabia: The Thorny 'Non-existent' Problem," *East European Quarterly* 13, no. 1 (1974): 47–74.

93. Alexandru Şuga, *Ştiinţa şi polemică: Istoricii ruşi, falsificatori ai istoriei* (Freiburg: Institutul Român de Cercetări, 1976); idem, *Die völkerrechtliche Lage Bessarabiens in der geschichtlichen Entwicklung des Landes* (Bonn: n.p., 1958).

94. Petre Moldovan, *A. M. Lazarev: A Counterfeiter of History* (Milan: Nagard, 1976). "Petre Moldovan" was the pseudonym of the Romanian historian Constantin Giurescu, and "Nagard" referred to Iosif Drăgan, an alleged Iron Guard sympathizer and publisher in exile in Italy. See Van Meurs, *Bessarabian Question*, pp. 242–57, on this incident.

95. Some of the most notable examples of this genre are N. A. Mokhov, B. M. Kolker, and V. I. Tsaranov, "Istoriia Moldavii v sovremennoi burzhuaznoi istoriografii," *Voprosy istorii* 1970, no. 8, pp. 3–19; A. M. Lazarev, "Bessarabskii vopros v rumynskoi burzhuaznoi i sovremennoi istoriografii," in M. K. Sytnik, ed., *Stranitsy istorii Sovetskoi Moldavii* (Chisinau: Ştiinţa, 1973), pp. 32–43; A. G. Moraru, *Obrazovanie i razvitie moldavskoi sotsialisticheskoi natsii v krivom zerkale burzhuaznoi istoriografii* (Chisinau: Znanie, 1973); *Împotriva falsificatorilor burgeji ai istoriei şi culturii poporului moldovenesc* (Chisinau: Cartea Moldovenească, 1974); V. I. Tsaranov and V. I. Cozma, "Kritika burzhuaznykh fal'sifikatorov istorii kul'tury Moldavskoi SSR," in S. K. Brysiakin, ed., *Kul'turnoe stroitel'stvo v Sovetskoi Moldavii* (Chisinau: Ştiinţa, 1974), pp. 218–36; V. Stati, *Limba moldovenească şi răuvoitorii ei: Împotriva falsificatorilor burgeji ai dezvoltării limbii moldoveneşti* (Chisinau: Lumina, 1988).

96. Barbara Anderson and Brian Silver, "Demographic Sources of the Changing Ethnic Composition of the Soviet Union," *Population and Development Review* 15, no. 4 (1989): 634, 636.

97. Ibid., pp. 645–46.

98. *Itogi vsesoiuznoi perepisi naseleniia 1989 goda* (Minneapolis, Minn.: East View Publications, 1993), 7: Part 3, p. 110.

99. Anderson and Silver, "Demographic," p. 647.

100. Irina Livezeanu, "Urbanization in a Low Key and Linguistic Change in Soviet Moldavia, Part 1," *Soviet Studies* 33, no. 3 (1981): 334.

101. Mănuilă, *Studiu etnografic*, pp. 34, 38; *Vsesoiuznaia perepis' naseleniia 1926 goda* (Moscow: Izdanie TsSU Soiuza SSR, 1929), 13: 39–41.

102. *Narodnoe khoziaistvo Moldavskoi SSR, 1924–1984* (Chisinau: Cartea Moldovenească, 1984), p. 9; *Anuarul statistic al Republicii Moldova, 1992* (Chisinau: Universitas, 1994), p. 22.

103. Livezeanu, "Urbanization, Part 1," p. 343.

104. *Pervaia vseobshchaia perepis' naseleniia Rossiiskoi imperii, 1897 g.* (St. Petersburg: Izdanie Tsentral'nago Statisticheskago Komiteta Ministerstva Vnutrennikh Del, 1905), 3: 70–73.

105. Mănuilă, *Studiu etnografic*, p. 42.

106. *Itogi vsesoiuznoi perepisi naseleniia 1959 goda: Moldavskaia SSR* (Moscow: Gostatizdat, 1962), p. 90; *Itogi vsesoiuznoi perepisi naseleniia 1989 goda,* 7: Part 2, p. 526.

107. Livezeanu, "Urbanization, Part 1," p. 347.

108. Ion Druţă, "Khlebopashtsy v Kishineve," *Komsomol'skaia pravda,* March 21, 1971, p. 2.

CHAPTER 6

1. "Documentul final al Marii Adunări Naţionale," *Literatura şi arta,* August 31, 1989, p. 2.

2. *Actele legislative ale RSS Moldoveneşti cu privire la decretarea limbii moldoveneşti limbă de stat şi revenirea ei la grafia latină* (Chisinau: Cartea Moldovenească, 1990), pp. 3, 5.

3. *FBIS-SOV,* April 21, 1988, pp. 1–9.

4. "Cuvîntarea delegatului Grossu S. K.," *Moldova socialistă,* July 3, 1988, p. 1.

5. *FBIS-SOV,* January 12, 1988, pp. 52–53.

6. Vladimir Socor, "The Moldavian Democratic Movement: Structure, Program and Initial Impact," *Radio Liberty Report on the USSR,* February 24, 1988, pp. 29–35; idem, "The Alexe Mateevici Cultural Club: An Informal Group Becomes a Mass Movement," ibid., August 25, 1989, pp. 23–25.

7. A. Rotaru, "Durerea şi speranţa noastră—graiul matern," *Moldova socialistă,* December 3, 1988, p. 3.

8. Grigore Singurel, "Moldavia on the Barricades of *Perestroika,*" *Radio Liberty Report on the USSR,* February 24, 1989, p. 46.

9. William Crowther, "The Politics of Ethno-National Mobilization: Nationalism and Reform in Soviet Moldavia," *Russian Review* 50 (April 1991): 190–91.

10. Boris Vieru, ed., *O luptă, o suferinţă şi . . .* (Chisinau: Literatura artistică, 1989), p. 165.

11. "Să afirmăm restructurarea prin fapte concrete," *Moldova socialistă*, November 11, 1988, pp. 1–3.

12. "Să afirmăm," p. 3.

13. Jonathan Eyal, "Soviet Moldavia: History Catches Up and a 'Separate Language' Disappears," *Radio Liberty Report on the USSR*, February 24, 1989, p. 28.

14. S. Grossu, "Timpul acţiunilor concrete," *Moldova socialistă*, December 29, 1988, p. 3.

15. The commission's full report was published as "Cu privire la statutul lingvistic şi social al limbii moldoveneşti," *Limba şi literatura moldovenească* 1989, no. 2, pp. 13–41.

16. S. K. Grossu, "Organele de conducere sînt datoare să nu admită abateri de la realitate," *Nistru* 1989 (September): 71.

17. Denis LeGras, "Nationalisme: La Moldavie aussi," *Le Figaro*, February 28, 1989, p. 4. Grossu argued that even if Moldova switched to the Latin alphabet, it could not be the same one as in Romania because of the need for special symbols for distinct Moldovan sounds.

18. Jonathan Eyal, "Moldavians," in Graham Smith, ed., *The Nationalities Question in the Soviet Union* (London: Longman, 1990), p. 137. Romania, Chad, and Andorra all have the same blue-yellow-red tricolor.

19. Vladimir Socor, "Unofficial Groups Score Unexpected Gains in Elections in Moldavia," *Radio Liberty Report on the USSR*, May 12, 1989, pp. 17–20.

20. Vieru, *O luptă, o suferinţă*, pp. 236–38.

21. V. Odoleanu, "Vieţe în poate," *Moldova socialistă*, August 11, 1989, p. 4.

22. Vladimir Socor, "Popular Front Founded in Moldavia," *Radio Liberty Report on the USSR*, June 9, 1989, pp. 23–26; L. Busuioc, "Pe baza Mişcării Democratice—Frontul Popular din Moldova," *Învăţămîntul public*, May 24, 1989, p. 2.

23. Vladimir Socor, "Gagauz in Moldavia Demand Separate Republic," *Radio Liberty Report on the USSR*, September 7, 1990, p. 9.

24. Dmitrii Kazutin, "A Hot Summer," *Moscow News*, August 27, 1989, p. 8.

25. "Sărbătoare a sufletului," *Moldova socialistă*, August 31, 1989, p. 4.

26. "Manifestare de amploare," ibid.

27. G. Lupuşor, I. Misail, and I. Sandu, "Înseninata zi a demnităţii," *Tinerimia Moldovei*, August 30, 1989, p. 2; "Manifestare de amploare," p. 4.

28. "Documentul final," p. 2.

29. A. Khantsevich, "Kishinev, 25 avgusta," *Komsomol'skaia pravda*, August 26, 1989, p. 2; idem, "Kishinev, 28 avgusta," ibid., August 29, 1989, p. 1.

30. *Actele legislative*, p. 3.

31. Ibid., p. 5.

32. Crowther, "Politics," 188.

33. For example, the changes in the Writers' Union leadership were occasioned by the apparent suicide of its chair, Pavel Boțu, in early 1987.

34. See for example, A. Moșanu, I. Osadcenco, N. Matcaș, and I. Dumeniuc, "O istorie cu istorici," *Învățămîntul public*, July 15, 1989, p. 4; A. Ciobanu, "Reavoință," *Moldova socialistă*, July 27, 1989, p. 4.

35. "O nouă asociație: Într-un ceas bun," *Literatura și arta*, July 13, 1989, p. 3.

36. "Non-Russian" teachers were primarily Moldovan-language instructors, since only a few mainly experimental classes were held in languages other than Russian and Moldovan before 1989. *Narodnoe khoziaistvo Moldavskoi SSR* for 1985, 1986, 1987; *Economia națională a RSS Moldovenești* for 1988; *Economia națională a RSS Moldova* for 1989.

37. Vieru, *O luptă, o suferință*, pp. 17–23. Klaus Heitmann gives special attention to this letter in his "Probleme der moldauischen Sprache in der Ära Gorbačev," *Südosteuropa* 38, no. 1 (1989): 28–53.

38. Silviu Berejan, director of the Institute of Language and Literature, Moldovan Academy of Sciences, interview with the author, Chisinau, October 6, 1992.

39. "Mitingul Frontului Popular din Moldova," *Moldova socialistă*, August 16, 1989, p. 3.

40. Singurel, "Moldavia on the Barricades," p. 36.

41. Vladimir Socor, "Moldavian Writers Publish Unauthorized Periodical in Latin Script," *Radio Liberty Report on the USSR*, April 7, 1989, p. 25.

42. "Po negodnym retseptam," *Pravda*, August 29, 1989, p. 6; N. Muliar, "Nuzhny razumnye kompromissy," *Krasnaia zvezda*, August 31, 1989, p. 1; N. Stiazhkin and V. Gordienko, "Sessiia zakonchilas', problemy ostaiutsia," ibid., September 6, 1989, p. 1.

43. Muliar, "Nuzhny," p. 1.

44. Crowther, "Politics," p. 186.

45. Moldovans were significantly underrepresented in the party as a whole (47.8 percent compared with 63.9 percent of the total republican population), but overrepresented in party leadership positions (75.5 percent). William Crowther, "Ethnicity and Participation in the Communist Party of Moldavia," *Journal of Soviet Nationalities* 1, no. 1 (1990): 148–49.

46. "Internatsionalisticheskaia sut' sotsializma," *Kommunist* 1987, no. 13, pp. 3–13.

47. In February 1987, several Moldovan Komsomol officials were sacked for their inability to "cope with their work," and Grossu later blamed demonstrations that had broken out in the MSSR in May on the intrigues of informal organizations, Jews, and the West.

48. S. K. Grossu, "Timpul primenirilor—timp al acțiunilor de răspundere," *Moldova socialistă*, February 25, 1989, p. 2.

49. "Transcript of Meeting of the CPM Politburo, July 27, 1989," AOS-PRM n/c, l. 47.

50. "Transcript, July 27, 1989," l. 51. The phrase "on the proposal of the citizens of the republic" (*pe propunerile cetățenilor republicii*) was adopted in the final text of the law.

51. Nicolae Dabija, editor of *Literatura și arta*, interview with the author, Chisinau, June 29, 1994.

52. Busuioc, "Pe baza Miscării," p. 2.

53. Ion Druță, "Anevoioasa trecere de la vorbe la fapte," *Moldova socialistă*, March 5, 1989, pp. 1–2.

54. Ion Druță, "Grîul și neghina," *Tinerimia Moldovei*, August 30, 1989, p. 4.

55. Nicolae Dabija, "Ora mărilor răspunderi," *Moldova socialistă*, August 29, 1989, p. 3.

56. "Iazykom tsifr," *Argumenty i fakty* 1990, no. 2, p. 5.

57. "În Comisiile permanente ale Sovietului Suprem al RSS Moldovenești," *Moldova socialistă*, August 6, 1989, p. 3.

58. "Grabă strică treabă," ibid., August 17, 1989, p. 3; "Cititorul se alarmează greva," ibid., August 18, 1989, p. 3.

CHAPTER 7

1. A more detailed analysis of these parties' histories and programs is given in Charles King, "Moldova," in Bogdan Szajkowski, ed., *New Political Parties of Eastern Europe, Russia and the Successor States* (London: Longman, 1995), pp. 293–311.

2. Gheorghe Lupușor, "Confruntări parlamentare," *Adevărul*, May 29, 1990, p. 4.

3. "Televiziunea în RSS Moldova," *România liberă*, June 21, 1990, p. 4.

4. Vladimir Solonari and Vladimir Brutner, "Russians in Moldova," in Vladimir Shlapentokh, Munir Senoich, and Emil Payin, eds., *The New Russian Diaspora: Russian Minorities in the Former Soviet Republics* (Armonk, N.Y.: M. E. Sharpe, 1994), p. 80.

5. See Vladimir Socor, "Gorbachev and Moldavia," *Radio Liberty Report on the USSR*, December 21, 1990, pp. 11–14.

6. "Revoluția română este un fenomen de proporție europeană și mondială," *Adevărul*, January 7, 1990, p. 5.

7. "Piedicile artificiale au fost înlăturate," ibid., January 9, 1990, p. 4.

8. "Măsuri de democratizare la frontieră dintre RSS Moldovenească şi România," ibid., January 13, 1990, p. 6.

9. "Oaspeţi dragi: Scriitori basarabeni," *Contemporanul*, January 19, 1990, p. 4.

10. Th. Marcarov, "Dovezi emoţionte alē solidarităţii," *România liberă*, February 22, 1990, p. 4. The units, named after Ştefan cel Mare and the nineteenth-century revolutionary Tudor Vladimirescu, never reached Romania. There is some evidence that these units were encouraged by the Soviet defense ministry on the grounds that, in the event of a Soviet intervention in Romania, sending in Romanian-speaking Moldovans would be preferable to an invasion by Russians. Lucian Avramescu, "În direct, la Chişinău, revoluţia română," *Tineretul liber*, January 21, 1990, p. 1.

11. Dumitru Nicodim, "Podul de flori de la Prut," *Dreptatea*, May 9, 1990, pp. 1, 4.

12. "Declaraţie a mitingului FPM din 25 martie 1990," *Flacăra*, April 18, 1990, p. 1.

13. "Obiective prioritare ale Frontului Popular din RSS Moldovenească," *Adevărul*, March 27, 1990, p. 6.

14. Petru Călăpodescu, "Mai presus de orice noi dorim o confederaţie spirituală cu România," *Libertatea*, March 13, 1990, p. 4.

15. Ion Iliescu, "Din inima ţării, gînduri pentru ţară," *Adevărul*, December 2, 1990, p. 1.

16. "Lider FNS—Petre Roman," *Izvestiia*, March 19, 1991, p. 5.

17. "Declaraţia ministerului Adrian Năstase," *Moldova suverană*, March 27, 1991, p. 1; "În viitor o unificare după modelul german," *România liberă*, August 9, 1991, p. 8.

18. "Alocuţiunea Domnului Mircea Snegur," *Moldova suverană*, February 15, 1991, pp. 1–2.

19. "Ne cinstim înaintaşii," ibid., March 29, 1991, p. 1; "Răspunsurile sincere ale lui Mircea Snegur," ibid., April 20, 1991, p. 1; Victor Losak, "Interviu acordat de dl. Mircea Snegur," ibid., May 22, 1991, p. 1.

20. "Poporul şi decizie," ibid., March 14, 1991, p. 1; "Raportul domnului Mircea Snegur în problema schimbării denumirii republicii," ibid., May 24, 1991, p. 1.

21. "Moldova nu va semna tratatul unional," *România liberă*, 10/11 August, 1991, p. 8.

22. See the declarations in *Sfatul Ţării*, August 20, 1991, p. 1.

23. "Declaraţia de independenţă a Republicii Moldova," *România liberă*, August 28, 1991, p. 8.

24. Jeff Chinn and Robert Kaiser, *Russians as the New Minority: Ethnicity and Nationalism in the Soviet Successor States* (Boulder, Colo.: Westview Press, 1996), pp. 167–70.

25. Ion Pavelescu et al., "Cred în viitorul neamului nostru aşa cum cred în lumina soarelui," *România liberă*, June 26, 1990, pp. 1, 2.

26. Iurie Roşca, chair of the executive committee of the Christian Democratic Popular Front, interview with the author, Chisinau, April 15, 1993.

27. *Programul Frontului Popular Creştin Democrat* (Chisinau: FPCD, 1992), p. 8.

28. Vladimir Socor, "Why Moldova Does Not Seek Reunification with Romania," *RFE/RL Research Report*, January 31, 1992, p. 30.

29. "Statutul Congresului Intelectualităţii," *Literatura şi arta*, April 8, 1993, p. 2.

30. Svetlana Gamova, "Parlament Moldovy na grani samorospuska," *Izvestiia*, January 29, 1993, p. 2.

31. See Petre P. Moldovan, *Moldovenii în istorie* (Chisinau: Poligraf-Servis, 1993).

32. The organization had no connections with the Romanian group of the same name and was even officially denounced by it. "Spor ni o chem," *Nezavisimaia Moldova*, October 30, 1993, p. 1.

33. "Sîntem poate la cea mai hotărîtoare răscruce din istoria neamului nostru," *Pămînt şi oameni*, February 12, 1994, pp. 1, 3; Elena Shatokhina, "Drutse i 'Gazprom'—za Snegura," *Moskovskie novosti*, February 13–20, 1994, p. A10.

34. Mircea Snegur, "Republica Moldova este ţara tuturor cetăţenilor săi," *Pămînt şi oameni*, February 12, 1994, p. 3.

35. Ibid.

36. "O invenţie a regimului comunist," *Moldova suverană*, February 12, 1994, p. 3; "Să respectăm adevărul ştiinţific şi istoric," *Plus-Minus* 1994 (February): 8.

37. Ibid., "Pericolul aservirii politice a veşnicelor adevăruri."

38. William Crowther, "The Politics of Ethnic Confrontation in Moldova," paper presented at Woodrow Wilson Center conference on "High Conflict/Low Conflict: Six Case Studies," Washington, June 28–30, 1993.

39. "Poporul şi-a spus cuvîntul," *Moldova suverană*, March 12, 1994, p. 1. The results of the referendum were, however, highly suspect. The question as formulated made it difficult to give a clear affirmative/negative answer, and since it contained several subquestions within a single sentence, it was impossible to determine which portion of the general question the respondent might be answering

40. "Postanovlenie o gosudarstvennom gimne Respubliki Moldova," *Nezavisimaia Moldova*, June 9, 1994, p. 1.

41. *Constituţia Republicii Moldova* (Chisinau: Moldpres, 1994), p. 7.

42. Silviu Berejan, Anatol Ciobanu, and Nicolae Corlăteanu, "Adevărul nu se schimbă odată cu schimbările politicii," *Moldova suverană*, August 23, 1994, pp. 1, 3.

43. The party was prevented by law from using the name "Communist Party of Moldova," hence the unusual "Party of Communists" (*Partidul Comuniştilor*).

44. *Oxford Analytica East Europe Daily Brief*, March 27, 1998.

45. Address by Emil Constantinescu, President of Romania, at a joint meeting of the United States Congress, July 15, 1998.

46. "Memorandum," *România liberă*, August 21, 1991, p. 2.

47. *FBIS-EEU*, August 28, 1991, p. 28.

48. On this point, see Irina Livezeanu, "Moldavia, 1917–1990: Nationalism and Internationalism Then and Now," *Armenian Review* 43, no. 2 (1990): 153–93.

49. Alina Mungiu, "Sărutul mîntuirii," 22, September 1–8, 1991, p. 1.

50. "Trecerea Prutului cu buletinul în mînă," *România liberă*, September 31, 1991, p. 1.

51. Tatiana Popa, deputy director, Directorate for Romania's Relations with the Republic of Moldova, Romanian Ministry of Foreign Affairs, interview with the author, Bucharest, June 3, 1998.

52. Simion Bula, "Burse si manuale pentru fraţii de peste Prut," *România liberă*, September 11, 1991, p. 4.

53. Popa interview.

54. *Moldova: Economic Trends, Quarterly Issue, July–September 1998* (Brussels: European Commission, 1998), p. 102.

55. See Tom Gallagher, *Romania after Ceauşescu* (Edinburgh: Edinburgh University Press, 1996), pp. 185–88.

56. Gabriel Andreescu, Valentin Stan, and Renata Weber, "Raporturile României cu Republica Moldova," 22 (special supplement), January 1995.

CHAPTER 8

1. A. Bantoş, "Informaţie cu privire la activitatea Departamentului în perioada februarie–decembrie 1992," unpublished report, State Department of Languages, Chisinau.

2. For evidence of this orientation, see the responses by these and other parties to the questionnaire in "Expres-ancheta 'AP,'" *Arena politicii*, February 1997, pp. 17–19.

3. See "Report of the CSCE Human Dimension Mission to the Republic of Moldova," Warsaw, 1993; US Department of State, "Moldova Country Report on Human Rights Practices," 1998.

4. *Constituţia Republicii Moldova* (1994), Articles 1 and 2; *Constituţia României* (1991), Articles 1 and 4.

5. On ethnic attitudes, see William Crowther, "The Politics of Democratization in Postcommunist Moldova," in Karen Dawisha and Bruce Parrott, eds., *Democratic Changes and Authoritarian Reactions in Russia, Ukraine, Belarus, and Moldova* (Cambridge, Eng.: Cambridge University Press, 1997), pp. 282–329.

6. See Mihai Cimpoi, *O istorie dechisă a literaturii române din Basarabia* (Chisinau: Arc, 1997).

7. "Concepția politicii externe a Republicii Moldova," *Monitorul oficial al Republicii Moldova*, April 6, 1995, pp. 10–14.

8. *Itogi vsesoiuznoi perepisi naseleniia 1989 goda* (Minneapolis, Minn.: East View Publications, 1993), 7: Part 2, pp. 524–35.

9. Andrew Wilson, "The Ukrainians: Engaging the 'Eastern Diaspora,'" in Charles King and Neil J. Melvin, eds., *Nations Abroad: Diaspora Politics and International Relations in the Former Soviet Union* (Boulder, Colo.: Westview Press, 1998), pp. 121–25.

10. *RFE/RL Daily Report*, February 3, 1994.

11. See Bohdan Nahaylo, "Moldovan Conflict Creates New Dilemmas for Ukraine," *RFE/RL Research Report*, May 15, 1992, pp. 1–8.

12. Daria Fane, "Moldova: Breaking Loose from Moscow," in Ian Bremmer and Ray Taras, eds., *Nations and Politics in the Soviet Successor States* (Cambridge, Eng.: Cambridge University Press, 1993), p. 141.

13. "Priobshchenie k rodnomu iazyku," *Nezavisimaia Moldova*, November 9, 1993, p. 2.

14. "În apărarea limbii străbune," *Moldova suverană*, April 20, 1994, p. 2.

15. *Anuarul statistic al Republicii Moldova, 1992* (Chisinau: Universitaas, 1994), p. 170.

16. Chauncy D. Harris, "The New Russian Minorities: A Statistical Overview," *Post-Soviet Geography* 34, no. 1 (1993): 4–6.

17. Ibid., p. 7.

18. Ibid., p. 15.

19. Ibid., pp. 18–19.

20. Victor Pușcaș, "Dlui Prim-ministru Andrei Sangheli," *Materna* 1993 (March): 1.

21. Neil Melvin, *Russians Beyond Russia: The Politics of National Identity* (London: Pinter, 1995), pp. 68–73.

22. Jeff Chinn and Robert Kaiser, *Russians as the New Minority: Ethnicity and Nationalism in the Soviet Successor States* (Boulder, Colo.: Westview Press, 1996), p. 165.

23. *FBIS-SOV*, April 3, 1996, p. 2.

24. *Moldova: Economic Trends, Quarterly Issue, April–July 1998* (Brussels: European Commission, 1998), p. 23.

25. "În apărarea," p. 2; M. Dreizler, "Vsiak sushchii v nei iazyk," *Nezavisimaia Moldova*, October 5, 1993, p. 3.

26. Vladimir Socor, "Moldova," *RFE/RL Research Report*, April 22, 1994, p. 19.

27. *RFE/RL Daily Report*, July 13, 1994.

28. Stepan Serbinov, "Ochag bolgarizma," *Nezavisimaia Moldova*, August 26, 1993, p. 2.

29. Pavel Andreicenco, "Tsyganskie shatry na ploshchadi posle palatok volonterov?" *Nezavisimaia Moldova*, April 24, 1993, p. 3.

30. Ion Dron, "Tsygane Moldovy: Chislennost' i rasselenie," *Nezavisimaia Moldova*, July 7, 1993, p. 3.

31. Ibid.

32. "Dlia razvitiia kul'tury tsygan," *Nezavisimaia Moldova*, October 21, 1993, p. 6.

33. In late 1994, however, a standard Romany grammar was published in Bucharest, and the Romanian government introduced classes in the language in a small number of schools and at the University of Bucharest. Ion Dron, "Primul manual de limba ţigănească standardizată," *Moldova suverană*, September 29, 1994, p. 4.

CHAPTER 9

1. Vasile Nedelciuc, *The Republic of Moldova* (Chisinau: Parliament of the Republic of Moldova, 1992), p. 117; Helsinki Watch, *Human Rights in Moldova: The Turbulent Dniester* (New York: Human Rights Watch, 1993), pp. 6–7; information from International Organization for Migration at www.iom.int/iom/Publications/books_studies_surveys/Moldova.htm, accessed February 16, 1999.

2. The DMR also includes territory on the western bank of the Dnestr, around the city of Bender, and the central government also controls some territory on the eastern bank. The DMR is not therefore exactly coterminous with the region of Transnistria. The DMR authorities claim 4163 square kilometers under their control. See *Atlas of Dniester Moldavian Republic* (Tiraspol: Dniester State Corporative T. G. Shevchenko University, 1997).

3. Andrew Wilson, "The Ukrainians: Engaging the 'Eastern Diaspora,'" in Charles King and Neil J. Melvin, eds., *Nations Abroad: Diaspora Politics and International Relations in the Former Soviet Union* (Boulder, Colo.: Westview Press, 1998), p. 116.

4. Ion G. Pelivan, *La Bessarabie sous le régime russe (1812–1918)* (Paris: Imprimerie Générale Lahure, 1919), p. 16.

5. N. A. Troinitskii, ed., *Obshchii svod po imperii rezul'tatov razrabotki dannykh Pervoi vseobshchei perepisi naseleniia, proizvedennoi 28 ianvaria 1897 goda* (St. Petersburg: n.p., 1905), 2: 22.

6. See ANR-DAIC, f. Casa Şcoalelor, d. 562/1923, ff. 1–46.

7. Memorandum from N. Smochină, December 13, 1933, ANR-DAIC, f. Nichita Smochină, d. 7/1933, f. 5.

8. See N. P. Smochină, *Republica Moldovenească a Sovietelor* (Bucharest: Cartea Românească, n.d.); N. Popp, *Românii transnistrieni şi Republica Moldovenească* (Giurgiu: Tipografia Scrisul Românesc, 1935).

9. See Nicolae Titulescu, "Two Neighbours of Russia and Their Policies: (I) Roumania and Bessarabia," *Nineteenth Century and After* 95 (June 1924), pp. 791–803.

10. See Mihai Gribincea, *Basarabia în primii ani de ocupaţie sovietică, 1944–1950* (Cluj: Dacia, 1995), pp. 17–42.

11. John O'Loughlin, Vladimir Kolossov, and Andrei Tchepalyga, "National Construction, Territorial Separatism, and Post-Soviet Geopolitics in the Transdniester Moldovan Republic," *Post-Soviet Geography and Economics* 39, no. 6 (1998): 342.

12. Ibid.: 339.

13. *FBIS-SOV*, October 4, 1990, pp. 88–89.

14. See the collection of articles by the former Edinstvo leader, later to become president of a new Transnistrian university in Tiraspol, V. N. Iakovlev, *Terpistyi put' k spravedlivosti* (Tiraspol: n.p., 1993).

15. *FBIS-SOV*, January 30, 1990, pp. 55–56.

16. Idem, November 28, 1990, pp. 95–96.

17. Jean-Baptiste Naudet, "Nous ne serons jamais roumains," *Le Monde*, September 4, 1991, p. 4.

18. *FBIS-SOV*, August 29, 1991, p. 118.

19. "Declaraţia," *Moldova suverană*, March 20, 1991, p. 1.

20. "Telegramă a Preşedintelui Republicii Moldova," *Moldova suverană*, June 11, 1991, p. 1; "Implicarea Armatei a 14-a într-un conflict ar deveni o catastrofăa," *Curierul naţional*, April 4, 1992, pp. 1, 7; "Basarabia însîngerată," *România liberă*, April 4–5, 1992, p. 8.

21. Stephen Bowers, "The Crisis in Moldova," *Jane's Intelligence Review*, November 1992, p. 484.

22. Vladimir Socor, "Moldavia Builds a New State," *RFE/RL Research Report*, January 3, 1992, p. 44.

23. Helsinki Watch, *Human Rights in Moldova*, p. 19; "Bucarest et Moscou s'accusent d'armer les combattants," *Le Monde*, June 2, 1992, p. 4; "Tragediia na Dnestre," *Sovetskaia Rossiia*, July 7, 1992, p. 1.

24. Vladimir Socor, "Creeping Putsch in Eastern Moldova," *RFE/RL Research Report*, January 17, 1992, pp. 8–13.

25. *FBIS-SOV*, January 13, 1992, p. 55.

26. Jean-Baptiste Naudet, "Accord entre russophones et Moldaves sur le deploiement d'observateurs militaires," *Le Monde*, May 10–11, 1992, p. 3.

27. "Ruţkoi calomniază cu neruşinare," *România liberă*, June 23, 1992, p. 1.

28. Helsinki Watch, *Human Rights in Moldova*, pp. 19–21.

29. Ibid., p. 5, n. 5.

30. See David D. Laitin, *Identity in Formation: The Russian-Speaking Populations in the Near Abroad* (Ithaca, N.Y.: Cornell University Press, 1998).

31. Steven Erlanger, "Yeltsin Warns Moscow May Intervene in Ethnic Unrest," *International Herald Tribune*, June 22, 1992, p. 1.

32. Marc Champion, "Scale of Moldova Fighting Dashes Any Hope of Peace," *Independent*, June 24, 1992, p. 13.

33. Alexander Lebed, *My Life and My Country* (Washington: Regnery Publishing, 1997), p. 328. Apart from this episode, the memoirs of Lebed' do not deal with Transnistria, which he simply describes as "a little principality, where the wildest excesses reign supreme."

34. Charles King, "Moldova with a Russian Face," *Foreign Policy*, Winter 1994–95, p. 107.

35. N. V. Babilunga and V. G. Bomeshko, *Pagini din istoria plaiului natal* (Tiraspol: Transnistrian Institute of Continuing Education, 1997), p. 98.

36. Gerald B. Solomon, "Peacekeeping in the Transdniester Region: A Test Case for the OSCE," draft report by OSCE Special Rapporteur, November 1994.

37. Vladimir Atamaniuk, First Deputy Speaker of DMR Supreme Soviet, interview with the author, Tiraspol, August 1, 1997.

38. "Tragediia na Dnestre," p. 1.

39. "Eu sînt ofiţer rus," *Moldova suverană*, July 22, 1993, p. 2; John Kohan and Yuri Zarakhovich, "Awaiting His Nation's Call," *Time*, February 27, 1995, pp. 30–31; Sophie Shihab, "Alexandre Lebed, le général qui attend l'appel de la Russia," *Le Monde*, February 24, 1995, p. 2.

40. See Mihai Gribincea, "Challenging Moscow's Doctrine on Military Bases," *Transition*, October 20, 1995, pp. 4–8.

41. Mikhail Bergman, commander of Tiraspol garrison, interview with the author, Tiraspol, August 1, 1997.

42. *The Military Balance, 1997/98* (London: International Institute for Strategic Studies, 1997), p. 110.

43. *Moldova: Economic Trends, Quarterly Issue, April–June 1998* (Brussels: European Commission, 1998), p. 114.

44. *Moldova: Economic Trends, Quarterly Issue, January–March 1998* (Brussels: European Commission, 1998), p. 112.

45. See Neil J. Melvin, "The Russians: Diaspora and the End of Empire," in King and Melvin, *Nations Abroad*, pp. 27–57.

46. *The Military Balance, 1997/98*, p. 90.

47. See V. N. Iakovlev, ed., *Bessarabskii vopros i obrazovanie Pridnestrovskoi Moldavskoi Respubliki* (Tiraspol: RIO-PGKU, 1993).

48. World Bank, *Republic of Moldova: Economic Review of the Transnistria Region, June 1998* (Washington: World Bank, 1998), p. 27.

49. *Oxford Analytica East Europe Daily Brief*, January 11, 1999.

50. Valeriu Prudnicov, Moldovan police commissioner in Bender, interview with the author, Bender, August 1, 1997.

51. O'Loughlin et al., "National Construction, Territorial Separatism," p. 352.

52. Ibid., p. 340.

CHAPTER 10

1. Some estimates place the number of Gagauz outside the former Soviet Union at only around 15,000, although one authority contends that the number is significantly higher. I. D. Dron, *Gagauzskie geograficheskie nazvaniia* (Chisinau: Ştiinţa, 1992), p. 23.

2. *Itogi vsesoiuznoi perepisi naseleniia 1989 goda* (Minneapolis, Minn.: East View Publications, 1993), 7: Part 1, p. 10; Part 2, pp. 6, 524.

3. M. V. Marunevich, *Pravda o gagauzskom narode kak o samobytnom etnose i ego etnicheskoi territorii* (Comrat: Aydınnık, 1993).

4. Dron, *Gagauzskie*, p. 24.

5. V. A. Moshkov, "Turetskiia plemena na Balkanskom poluostrove," *Izvestiia imperatorskago russkago geograficheskago obshchestva* 40 (1904): 399–436; Wlodzimierz Zajaczkowski, "K etnogenezu gagauzov," *Folia Orientalia* 15 (1960): 77–86; Ernst Max Hoppe, "I Gagauzi, popolazione turco-cristiana della Bulgaria," *Oriente Moderno* 14 (1934): 132–43; Tadeusz Kowalski, *Les Turcs et la langue turque de la Bulgarie du nord-est* (Kraków: Polska Akademja Umiejętności, 1933), pp. 11–12.

6. Paul Wittek, "Les Gagaouzes: Les gens de Kaykaus," *Rocznik Orientalistyczny* 17 (1951–52): 12–24. For other views, see the extensive discussions in Ivan Gradeshliev, *Gagauzite* (Dobrich: Izdatelska kŭshta Liudmil Beshkov, 1994), pp. 76–84, and Nevzat Özkan, *Gagavuz Türkçesi grameri* (Ankara: Atatürk Kültür, Dil ve Tarih Yüksek Kurumu, 1996), pp. 7–39.

7. S. S. Kuroglo and M. V. Marunevich, *Sotsialisticheskie preobrazovaniia v byte i kul'ture gagauzskogo naseleniia MSSR* (Chisinau: Ştiinţa, 1983), p. 11.

8. A. Zashchuk, *Materialy dlia geografii i statistiki Rossii: Bessarabskaia oblast'* (St. Petersburg: n.p., 1862), p. 169.

9. Kuroglo and Marunevich, *Sotsialisticheskie*, p. 13.

10. Mihail Ciachir, *Dicţionar gagauzo (tiurco)-român pentru găgăuzii din Basarabia* (Chisinau: Tiparul Moldovenesc, 1938); idem, *Istoria găgăuzilor din Basarabia* (Chisinau: Tipografia Bancei Centrale Cooperative, 1933).

11. CPM Central Committee report on "Some Problems of the Development of Education in Taraclia, Comrat, Ciadîr-Lunga, Basarabeasca, and Vulcăneşti *Raions*," n.d., AOSPRM, n/c, l. 1.

12. D. G. Zidu, "On the Training of Specialists with Higher Eucation among the Gagauz," n.d., AOSPRM, n/c, l. 1.

13. CPM Central Committee Report on "Some Issues in the Development of Education among the Gagauz and Bulgarian Populations of the Republic," n.d., AOSPRM, n/c, l. 4.

14. F. A. Angheli, "Spravka of nekotorykh problemakh etnokul'turnogo i sotsial'no-ekonomicheskogo razvitiia natsii i narodov v iuzhnom regione Moldavskoi SSR," AOSPRM, n/c, l. 8.

15. Ibid., l. 12.

16. CPM Central Committee report on "Some Problems of the Development of Education," l. 6.

17. *Anuarul statistic al Republicii Moldova, 1992* (Chisinau: Universitas, 1994), pp. 64–65.

18. A. Romanov, "Puteshestvie v Gagauziu," *Izvestiia*, March 29, 1968, p. 4.

19. A. Pokrovskaia, *Grammatika gagauzskogo iazyka* (Chisinau: Lumina, 1990).

20. N. F. Arnaut, "Po zamknutomu krugu: Eshche raz o gagauzskom voprose," *Nezavisimaia Moldova*, August 3, 1993, p. 2.

21. Vladimir Socor, "Gagauz in Moldavia Demand Separate Republic," *RFE/RL Report on the USSR*, September 7, 1990, pp. 11–12.

22. Dionis Tanasoğlu, rector of Comrat University, interview with author, June 30, 1994.

23. *Anuarul, 1992*, p. 165.

24. D. Polozoglo, "Rozhdenie gagauzskogo kino," *Haberlär*, May 24, 1994, pp. 1–2.

25. Cassandra Cavanaugh, "Conflict in Moldova: The Gagauz Factor," *RFE/RL Research Report*, August 14, 1992, p. 12.

26. The two leaders, Stepan Topal and Mihail Kendigelian, were later released. "Arestări în Republic Moldova," *România liberă*, August 24–25, 1991, p. 1.

27. Stepan Topal, president of the Gagauz Republic, interview with the author, Comrat, June 30, 1994.

28. See R. Iuncu, *K voprosu o gagauzskoi avtonomii* (Chisinau: Cartea Moldovenească, 1990).

29. "Natsional'nyi sostav naselennykh punktov v raionakh kompaktnogo prozhivaniia gagauzov," manuscript from the State Department for National Relations, Chisinau, p. 1.

30. Ion Dron, "Găgăuzii în localităţile sud-vestului Republicii Moldova," *Moldova suverană*, February 24, 1994, p. 2.

31. "Lege privind statutul juridic special al Găgăuziei (Gagauz-Yeri)," *Monitorul oficial al Republicii Moldova*, January 14, 1995, pp. 46–49. For a discussion of the draft law in English, see Vladimir Socor, "Gagauz Autonomy in Moldova: A Precedent for Eastern Europe?" *RFE/RL Research Report*, August 26, 1994, pp. 20–28.

32. Charles King, "Gagauz Yeri and the Dilemmas of Self-Determination," *Transition*, October, 20, 1995, p. 25.

33. Information from International Foundation for Electoral Systems, Chisinau.

34. "Georgi Tabunşcik: Gagauzienın ilk başkanı," *Gagauz sesi*, June 30, 1995, p. 1.

35. "Gagauz-Ieri: Un act de trădare naţională finalizat," *Ţara*, July 28, 1995, p. 1.

36. Vasile Nedelciuc, "Va fi oare 'Găgăuzia' o Bosnie basarabeană?" *Mesagerul*, January 5, 1996, p. 6.

37. See the declaration of the Romanian government on the new Moldovan constitution. *SWB-EE*, August 3, 1994, pp. B/8–9.

38. Cristina Zarnescu, "Comuniştii moldoveni se tem de unirea republicii cu România," *Cotidianul*, November 14, 1998, p. 11.

39. "V nachale iunia sostoitsia vizit v Moldovu ofitsial'noi delegatsii Turtsii," *Grazhdanskii mir*, May 20, 1994, p. 1.

40. "Gagauzskaia administratsiia udovletvorena itogami vizita v Moldovu Prezidenta Turtsii," *Nezavisimaia Moldova*, June 9, 1994, p. 1.

41. "Dorim poporului găgăuz să devină o punte a prieteniei," *Moldova suverană*, June 1, 1994, p. 2; "Discursul Preşedintelui Republicii Turcia," *Moldova suverană*, June 4, 1994, p. 2.

42. Todur Zanet, "Neler yapıldı belli," *Ana sözü*, May 31, 1994, p. 2.

43. Ibid., pp. 2–3.

44. "Publicaţii în limba găgăuză," *Moldova suverană*, April 16, 1994, p. 3.

45. Harun Güngör and Mustafa Argunşah, *Gagauz Türkleri: Tarih, dil, folklor ve halk edebiyatı* (Ankara: Kültür Bakanlığı, 1991); idem, *Gagauzlar: Dünden bugüne* (Ankara: Elektronik İletişim Ajansı, 1993); Abdülmecit Doğru and Ismail Kaynak, *Gagauz türkçesini sözlüğü* (Ankara: Kültür Bakanlığı, 1991); Özkan, *Gagavuz Türkçesi grameri*.

CHAPTER 11

1. "Unirea nu se proclamă la mitinguri," *Dimineaţa*, November 27, 1991, pp. 1, 5.

2. Ion Ciocanu, "Călăuziţi de interesele neamului," *Materna* 1993 (March): 1, 4.

Glossary

The language from which foreign terms are derived is given in parentheses (Romanian, Russian, Gagauz). Unusual plurals are also indicated, as are alternative spellings for place names.

Bakannık Komitei (Gag.)   Executive committee of Gagauz Yeri

Başkan (Gag.)   Governor of Gagauz Yeri

Bessarabia   Historical region between Prut, Dnestr, and Danube Rivers and Black Sea

boiar (Rom.)   Romanian noble

Bugeac, Budjak   Extreme south of historical Bessarabia, currently in Republic of Moldova and Odessa region of Ukraine

Bukovina, Bucovina   Area straddling border of northeast Romania and Chernivtsi region of Ukraine

cămine culturale (Rom.)   Cultural hearths; literacy and educational centers in interwar Romania

Carabinieri (Rom.)   Interior Ministry troops in the Republic of Moldova

chiabur (Rom., pl. *chiaburi*)   Rich peasant; kulak

Descălecarea (Rom.)   Dismounting; term for the establishment of the first Moldovan state in the fourteenth century

Dobrogea, Dobrudja   Region between Danube River and Black Sea in southeast Romania and Bulgaria

domn, domnitor (Rom., pl. *domni*)   Prince of medieval and early modern Moldovan and Wallachian principalities

Gagauz Yeri (Gag.)   Autonomous district for Turkic Gagauz established in southern Moldova in 1995

guberniia (Rus.)   Imperial Russian administrative division (province)

Halk Toplușu (Gag.)   Legislative assembly of Gagauz Yeri

hospodar (Rom.)   Prince of Moldovan and Wallachian principalities, especially in period of Phanariot rule (1711–1821)

județ (Rom., pl. *județe*)   Romanian administrative division (county). Also used in Republic of Moldova after 1998.

khaty-chital'ni (Rus.)   Reading huts; local libraries established as part of Soviet literacy programs in the 1920s

knez (Rom.)   Local prince (before founding of larger Romanian principalities in fourteenth century)

Komsomol (Rus.)   Communist Youth League (*Kommunisticheskii Soiuz Molodezhi*)

korenizatsiia (Rus.)   Soviet policy of increasing the representation of non-Russians in state and party institutions

krasnye ugly (Rus.)   Red corners; sections in schools, factories, or other institutions dedicated to political propaganda in the early Soviet period

kulak (Rus.)   Rich peasant

kul'tarmeitsy (Rus.)   Cultural soldiers; propagandists and agents of mass mobilization in early Soviet period

latinizatory (Rus.)   Latinizers; teachers of the Latin alphabet during the alphabet reform campaign in the MASSR, 1932–38

Marea Adunare Națională (Rom.)   Grand National Assembly; mass gathering in Chisinau in August 1989 called to express support for new Moldovan language laws

Moldbrigadă (Rom., pl. *moldbrigăzi*)   Moldovanization brigade in MASSR

Narkompros (Rus.)   People's Commissariat of Enlightenment (Education) in early Soviet Union (*Narodnyi Komissariat Prosveshcheniia*)

narodnost' (Rus.)   Nationality; ethnic group

natsiia (Rus.)   Nation, in the sense of a distinct linguistic and cultural community

Obkom (Rus.)   Regional committee of the Communist Party of the Soviet Union; main party organization in MASSR, 1924–40 (*Oblastnoi Komitet*)

oblast' (Rus.)   Imperial Russian or Soviet administrative division (region) pan-Romanian, pan-Romanianism   Idea that all ethnic Romanians should be included in the same state

perestroika (Rus.)   Policy of economic restructuring launched by Mikhail Gorbachev

Phanariots   Greek or hellenized princes governing Romanian principalities, 1711–1821

Pioneers   Communist mass organization for young children

plemia (Rus.)   Loose ethnocultural group; tribe

Podul de Flori (Rom.)   Bridge of Flowers; demonstration in 1990 along the Prut River, when Romanians and Moldovans crossed previously closed border between the two states

Politburo (Rus.)   Political bureau; highest decision-making body of the Communist Party of the Soviet Union

raion (Rus.)   Soviet administrative division (district)

Regat (Rom.)   Old Kingdom; Romania before 1918 (Wallachia and Moldova)

romanization   Process of making Romanian, assimilating to Romanian culture

Sfatul Ţării (Rom.)   Bessarabian national council, 1917–18

Siguranţa (Rom.)   Romanian secret police in interwar period

sotsialisticheskaia natsiia (Rus.)   Socialist nation; highest form of ethnocultural development according to Soviet historians and ethnographers

Sovnarkom (Rus.)   Council of People's Commissars; main executive authority in early Soviet Union (*Sovet Narodnykh Komissarov*)

Ţara Românească (Rom.)   Romanian principality, also known as Wallachia, which united with western Moldova to form precursor of modern Romania in 1859

Transnistria   Area between Dnestr and Bug Rivers, governed by Romania from 1941 to 1944; area east of Dnestr River in present-day Moldova

uezd (Rus.)   Imperial Russian administrative division (district)

verst (Rus.)   Imperial Russian unit of measurement, equal to 3,500 feet

Vlah, Vlach, Wallach   General term for Romanian-speakers north and south of the Danube River until the rise of pan-Romanian nationalism in the eighteenth and nineteenth centuries; still used for Romance-speaking populations in Greece and Macedonia

voievod, *vodă* (Rom.)   Medieval Romanian prince

Wallachia   *See* Ţara Românească

zemstvo (Rus.)   System of elective district councils in prerevolution Russia

zhenotdel (Rus.)   Women's section; mass organization responsible for propaganda work among women after the Bolshevik Revolution (*zhenskii otdel*)

Bibliography

Research for this book relied heavily on archival and library resources in Romania and the Republic of Moldova. For the interwar period, the Central Historical Archive Division of the National Archives of Romania in Bucharest provided a treasury of documents on cultural policy and general political developments. The archive groups (*fonds*) of the presidency of the Council of Ministers, the Ministry of Education and Religion, and the Ministry of National Propaganda were important resources on the general policy direction pursued in Bessarabia, as well as on relations between Romanians and Soviets. The collection of the *Casa Şcoalelor*, the quasi-governmental organization charged with aiding local schools in Bessarabia and other parts of Greater Romania, contained extensive reports detailing the state of schools, literacy, and cultural propaganda. Several collections of private papers located in the National Archives were indispensable. These included the papers of the educator Onisifor Ghibu, the great historian of Bessarabia Alexandru Boldur, and Bessarabian writers and politicians Nichita Smochină, Ioan Pelivan, Pavel Gore, Gherman Pântea and, most importantly, Pantelimon Halippa. The extensive holdings of the library of the Romanian Academy included important periodicals, both from the interwar period and earlier, as well as major nineteenth-century works on Bessarabia published in both Romania and the Russian empire.

The former archive of the Communist Party of Moldova—now renamed the Archive of Social-Political Organizations of the Republic of Moldova—houses a remarkable collection of documents from the MASSR, even though one major Western guide to Soviet archives states mistakenly that this collection was destroyed during the Second World War. Among the *fonds* consulted were those of the Moldovan *oblast'* committee of the Communist Party of Ukraine (f. 49), the *oblast'* control commission (f. 52), and various *raion* and city party committees. From the period of the MSSR, the archive also contains the important *fonds* of the Central Committee of the Communist Party of Moldova (f. 51) and the Institute of Party History (f. 90). Copies of many of the post-1945 documents exist in Moscow and Kyiv, but by far the most important collection is in Chisinau.

Work in the National Archive of Moldova yielded documents from major state institutions, including the Tiraspol *uezd* council (f. P-656), which was the main governmental body in Transnistria before the establishment of the MASSR in 1924. From the interwar years, the archive also contained the records of the presidium of the MASSR Supreme Soviet (P-2947), the commissariat of enlightenment (P-1140), and the Moldovan Scientific Committee (P-1151). The National Library of Moldova, the Library of the Academy of Sciences, and the Palace of Books in Chisinau maintain almost complete runs of major newspapers and other periodicals, including *Plugarul roş*, *Krasnaia Bessarabiia*, *Moldova socialistă*, and others. Books from the period before the 1960s are scattered among these three libraries, with most concentrated in former "special groups" that even still have not been completely cataloged. Published books and periodicals from the twentieth century and earlier were also located at various libraries in Oxford, London, Munich and Washington.

For the later Soviet period, archival resources in Moldova are either not yet available or have not been properly cataloged, but the Radio Liberty/Radio Free Europe "Krasnyi Arkhiv" (formerly in Munich) held an array of clippings and reports on the MSSR from the 1960s to the 1980s. The newspaper collection at the Royal United Services Institute for Defence Studies in London was crucial for understanding the events of the late perestroika years. Frequent study visits to eastern Europe, interviews and conversations with Moldovan, Romanian, Russian, and other policymakers, and clippings from the local and international press were the major sources for the study of the contemporary period.

For every period under study, often the most important source—as any student of postcommunist Europe will understand—were street vendors in Bucharest and Chisinau, whose wares usually included indispensable works of history, literature, and political analysis unavailable in any library except, now, one's own. East European specialists have long had to build their own private research libraries by carting back suitcases stuffed with rare books. There is little sign that this is likely to change.

BOOKS AND ARTICLES

Romanian/Moldovan

10 ani de construire socialistă a RASSM (în ajutorul raporturilor). Tiraspol: Editura de Stat a Moldovei, 1934.

Actele legislative ale RSS Moldoveneşti cu privire la decretarea limbii moldoveneşti limbă de stat şi revenirea ei la grafia latină. Chisinau: Cartea Moldovenească, 1990.

Ancel, Jean. *Transnistria*. 3 vols. Bucharest: Editura Atlas, 1998.

Anuarul statistic al României, 1937 şi 1938. Bucharest: Editura Institutului Central de Statistică, 1939.

Arbore, Zamfir C. *Basarabia în secolul XIX*. Bucharest: Institutul de Arte Grafice, 1898.

Babilunga, N. V., and V. G. Bomeshko. *Pagini din istoria plaiului natal*. Tiraspol: Transnistrian Institute of Continuing Education, 1997.

Baluh, M. A. *Cu ce vine URSS: Cître animia Octiabrului a 15-a, şî RASSM în veţuiria de 8 ani*. Tiraspol: Editura de Stat a Moldovei, 1932.

Bobeică, Alexandru. *Sfatul Ţării: Stîndard al renaşterii naţionale*. Chisinau: Universitas, 1993.

Boldur, Alexandru. *Istoria Basarabiei*. Bucharest: Editura Victor Frunză, 1992.

Buciuşcanu, G. *Gramatica limbii moldoveneşti*. Balta: Editura de Stat a Moldovei, 1925.

———. *Slovar moldovo-rusesc*. Balta: Editura de Stat a Moldovei, 1926.

———. *Slovar ruso-moldovenesc*. Balta: Editura de Stat a Moldovei, 1926.

Bulat, G. I. *10 ani RASSM*. Tiraspol: Editura de Stat a Moldovei, 1934.

Cantemir, Dimitrie. *Descrierea Moldovei*. Chisinau: Hyperion, 1992.

Cazacu, P. *Moldova dintre Prut şi Nistru, 1812–1918*. Iaşi: Viaţa Românească, n.d.

———. *Zece ani dela unire: Moldova dintre Prut şi Nistru, 1918–1928*. Bucharest: Tipografia ziarului "Universul," 1928.

Chior, P. I. *Basarabia sub călcîiu boiresc*. Balta: Editura de Stat a Moldovei, 1928.

———. *Cîntece moldoveneşti (norodnice)*. Balta: Editura de Stat a Moldovei, 1927–28.

———. *Cuvîntelinic ruso-moldovnesc*. Tiraspol: Editura de Stat a Moldovei, 1930.

———. *Dispri orfografia lingii moldovineşti*. Bîrzula: Comitetul Ştiinţific Moldovenesc, 1929.

———. *Zîcătoarele moldoveneşti*. Balta: Editura de Stat a Moldovei, 1926.

Ciachir, Mihail. *Dicţionar găgăuzo (tiurco)-român pentru găgăuzii din Basarabia*. Chisinau: Tiparul Moldovenesc, 1938.

———. *Istoria găgăuzilor din Basarabia*. Chisinau: Tipografia Bancei Centrale Cooperative, 1933.

Ciachir, Nicolae. *Basarabia sub stăpînire ţaristă (1812–1917)*. Bucharest: Editura Didactică şi Pedagogică, 1992.

Cimpoi, Mihai. *O istorie deschisă a literaturii române din Basarabia*. Chisinau: Arc, 1997.

Cioban, I. D. *Cultura românească în Basarabia sub stăpînirea rusă*. Chisinau: Editura Enciclopedică "Gheorghe Asachi," 1992.

———. *Cuvîntelnic orfografic moldovenesc*. Tiraspol: Editura de Stat a Moldovei, 1940.

———. *Gramatica lindii moldoveneşti: Partia întîi (fonetica şi morfologhia)*. Tiraspol: Editura de Stat a Moldovei, 1939.

———. *Gramatica limbii moldoveneşti: Partia întîi, fonetica şi morfologia*. 3d ed. Chisinau: Editura de Stat a Moldovei, 1946.

Ciobanu, Ştefan. *Basarabia: Populaţia, istoria, cultura*. Chisinau: Ştiinţa, 1992.

———. *Unirea Basarabiei*. Chisinau: Universitas, 1993.

Constantin, Ioan. *România, Marile Puteri şi problema Basarabiei*. Bucharest: Editura Enciclopedică, 1995.

Corlăteanu, N. G. *Egale între egale: Limba moldovenească literară în perioada sovietică*. Chisinau: Secţia de redactare şi editare a AŞ din RSS Moldovenească, 1971.

———. *În constelaţie de limbi înfrăţite*. Chisinau: Lumina, 1982.

Craciun, P. I., and D. E. Grigorieva. *Abecedar*. Tiraspol: Editura de Stat a Moldovei, 1936.

Cuşmăunsă, Ia. *Gramatica lindii moldoveneşti: Partia a doua (sintacsisu)*. Tiraspol: Editura de Stat a Moldovei, 1939.

Dîmbul, A. P. *Gramatica, morfologia: Manual pentru şcoala medie, anul al cincilea de învăţămînt*. Tiraspol: Editura de Stat a Moldovei, 1933.

———. *Manual de limba moldovenească: Gramatica şi ortografia (clasă a 3-a şi a 4-a)*. Tiraspol: Editura de Stat a Moldovei, 1936.

Evdoşenco, Arcardie. *Comoara din străbuni*. Chisinau: Hyperion, 1992.

Fala, Porfirie. *Ce neam suntem? O lămurire pentru Moldovenii din Basarabia*. Chisinau: Glasul Ţării, 1920.

————. *Cugetările unui luptător moldovean în timpul revoluţiei ruseşti din 1917.* Bucharest: Editura Casei Şcoalelor, 1927.

Galopenţia, Anton. "Populaţia teritoriilor româneşti desprinse în 1940," *Geopolitica şi geoistoria: Revistă română pentru sudestul european* 1941, no. 3, pp. 3–17.

Ghibu, Onisifor. *De la Basarabia rusească la Basarabia românească.* Bucharest: Semne, 1997.

————. *În vîltoarea revoluţiei ruseşti: Însemnări din Basarabia anului 1917.* Bucharest: Editura Fundaţiei Culturale Române, 1993.

————. *Pe baricadele vieţii: În Basarabia revoluţionară (1917–1918).* Chisinau: Universitas, 1992.

————. *Trei ani pe frontul basarabean.* Bucharest: Fundaţia Culturală Română, 1996.

Goma, Paul. *Din calidor: O copilărie basarabeană.* Bucharest: Editura Albatros, 1990.

Gordinschi, G. C. *Dicţionarul terminologiei matematice.* Tiraspol: Editura de Stat a Moldovei, 1932.

Graur, Al. *Studii de lingvistică generală.* Bucharest: Editura Academiei Republicii Populare Romîne, 1960.

Gribincea, Mihai. *Basarabia în primii ani de ocupaţie sovietică, 1944–1950.* Cluj: Dacia, 1995.

————. *Trupele ruse în Republica Moldova: Factor stabilizator sau sursă de pericol?* Chisinau: Civitas, 1998.

Halippa, Pantelimon. *Basarabia noastră.* Bucharest: Universul, 1941.

Husărescu, Z. I. *Mişcarea subversivă în Basarabia.* Chisinau: Atelierele Imprimeriei Statului, 1925.

Împotriva falsificatorilor burgeji ai istoriei şi culturii poporului moldovenesc. Chisinau: Cartea Moldovenească, 1974.

Ioanid, Radu. *Evreii sub regimul Antonescu.* Bucharest: Hasefer, 1998.

Iorga, Nicolae. *Basarabia noastră: Scrisă după 100 ani de la răpirea ei de către Ruşi.* Valenii de Munte: Neamul Românesc, 1912.

Istoria RSS Moldoveneşti. 2 vols. Chisinau: Cartea Moldovenească, 1967, 1970.

Kogălniceanu, C. *Dragoş şi Bogdan seu întemeierea Principatului Moldova: Cercetare istorică.* Bucharest: Stabilimentul grafic Socecu şi Teclu, 1886.

Lupan, Ilie, ed. *Povară sau tezaur sfînt?* Chisinau: Cartea Moldovenească, 1989.

Madan, L. A. *Gramatica limbii moldoveneşti: Fonetica, morfologia şi sintaxa.* Tiraspol: Editura de Stat a Moldovei, 1932.

————. *Gramatica moldovniascî*. Tiraspol: Editura de Stat a Moldovei, 1929, 1930.

Mănuilă, Sabin. *Studiu etnografic asupra populaţiei României*. Bucharest: Editura Institutului Central de Statistică, 1940.

Marghiloman, Alexandru. *Reintrarea Basarabiei în sânul patriei-mume*. Bucharest: Institut de Arte Grafice, 1924.

Marx, Karl. *Însemnări despre români: Manuscrise inedite*. Edited by A. Oţetea and S. Schwann. Bucharest: Academia RPR, 1964.

Mâţu, Constantin. *O necesitate deconsiderată: Presa românească în Basarabia*. Chisinau: Cartea Românească, 1930.

Moldova: Materialile statistice. Balta: Moldavskoe Statisticheskoe Upravlenie, 1928.

Moldovan, Petre P. *Moldovenii în istorie*. Chisinau: Poligraf-Servis, 1993.

Moldoveanu, Petre. *Cum se falsifică istoria*. Baia Mare: Gutinul, 1991.

Munteanu, Cassian R. *Prin Basarabia românească: Însemnări de călătorie*. Lugoj: Tipografia Iosif Sidon, 1919.

Nedelea, Marin. *Prim-miniştrii României Mari*. Bucharest: Viaţa Românească, 1991.

Nistor, Ion. *Istoria Basarabiei*. Bucharest: Humanitas, 1991.

————. *Istoria Bucovinei*. Bucharest: Humanitas, 1991.

Pechenaia, L. *Două lageri—două politişi: Dispri zîdiria naţîonalo-culturnicî în RASSM şî staria în Basarabia ocupatî*. Tiraspol: Editura de Stat a Moldovei, 1931.

Pelivan, Ioan. *Ion Inculeţ şi conferinţa de pace dela Paris (1919–1920)*. Bucharest: Tipografia ziarului "Universul," 1920.

————. *Să vorbim româneşte*. Chisinau: Gazeta Basarabiei, 1938.

Pelivanu, Ioniţa. *Adunaria întemeetoare*. Chisinau: Tipografia Ocîrmuirei Guberniale, 1917.

Ploieşteanu, N. *Limba moldovenească: Gramatica şi ortografia (manual pentru şcolile de adulţi cu puţină ştiinţă de carte)*. Tiraspol: Editura de Stat a Moldovei, 1936.

Popovschi, Nicolae. *Mişcarea dela Balta sau Inochentizmul în Basarabia*. Chisinau: Cartea Românească, 1926.

————. *Problema naţionalizării în Basarabia*. Chisinau: Tipografia Societăţii de Editură Naţională "Luceafărul," 1922.

Popp, N. *Românii transnistrieni şi Republica Moldovenească*. Giurgiu: Scrisul Românesc, 1935.

Schina, M. C. *Pe marginea unirii: Basarabia, ianuarie 1918–iunie 1919*. Bucharest: Institut de Arte Grafice, 1938.

Scriban, August. *Gramatica limbii româneşti (morfologia) pentru folosinţa tuturor.* Iaşi: Institutu de Arte Grafice "Viaţa Românească," 1925.

Scurtu, Ioan. *Monarhia în România, 1866–1947.* Bucharest: Danubius, 1991.

Scurtu, Ioan, et al. *Istoria Basarabiei: De la începuturi până în 1998.* 2d ed. Bucharest: Semne, 1998.

Shemiakov, D. E., and V. P. Isak, eds. *Luptători pentru fericiria poporului.* Chisinau: Cartea Moldovenească, 1985.

Şişcanu, Ion. *Desţărănirea bolşevică în Basarabia.* Chisinau: Adrian, 1994.

Smochină, N. P. *Republica Moldovenească a Sovietelor.* Bucharest: Cartea Românească, n.d.

Stati, V. *Limba moldovenească şi răuvoitorii ei: Împotriva falsificatorilor burgeji ai dezvoltării limbii moldoveneşti.* Chisinau: Lumina, 1988.

Şuga, Alexandru. *Ştiinţă şi polemică: Istoricii ruşi, falsificatori ai istoriei.* Freiburg: Institutul Român de Cercetări, 1976.

Tătărescu, Gh. *Internaţională a III-a şi Basarabia.* Bucharest: Independenţa, 1925.

Titulescu, Nicolae. *Basarabia pămînt românesc.* Bucharest: Rum-Irina, 1992.

Trei Schini, A. *Dela regimul teocratic spre regimul democratic: Amintirile unui basarabean, 1870–1930.* Chisinau: Cartea Românească, 1930.

Verenca, Olivian. *Administraţia civilă română în Transnistria.* Chisinau: Universitas, 1993.

Vieru, Boris, ed. *O luptă, o suferinţă şi . . .* Chisinau: Literatura Artistică, 1989.

Weinberg, A. S. *Chişinăul în trecut şi prezent: Schiţă istorică.* Chisinau: Tipografia Carmen Silva, 1936.

Russian

Aleksandri, L. N. *Bessarabiia i bessarabskii vopros.* Moscow: Gosizdat, n.d.

Antoniuk, D. I., S. Ia. Afteniuk, A. S. Esaulenko, and M. B. Itkis. *Predatel'skaia rol' "Sfatul Tserii."* Chisinau: Cartea Moldovenească, 1969.

Batiushkov, R. N. *Bessarabiia: Istoricheskoe opisanie.* St. Petersburg: Obshchestvennaia Pol'za, 1892.

Berg, L. S. *Bessarabiia: Strana, liudi, khoziaistvo.* Petrograd: Ogni, 1918.

———. *Naselenie Bessarabii: Etnograficheskii sostav i chislennost'.* Petrograd: Rossiiskaia Akademiia Nauk, 1923.

Bochacher, M. N. *Moldaviia.* Moscow: Gosizdat, 1926.

Brezhnev, Leonid Il'ich. *Vospominaniia.* 2d ed. Moscow: Izdatel'stvo Politicheskoi Literatury, 1983.

Bromlei, Iu. V. *Etnosotsial'nye protsessy: Teoriia, istoriia, sovremennost'*. Moscow: Nauka, 1987.

Brysiakin, S. K., ed. *Kul'turnoe stroitel'stvo v Sovetskoi Moldavii*. Chisinau: Ştiinţa, 1974.

Ciachir, Mihail. *Russko-moldavskii slovar'*. Chisinau: Eparkhial'naia Tipografiia, 1907.

Dembo, V. *Bessarabskoe krest'ianstvo pod vlast'iu kulakov i pomeshchikov*. Moscow: Izdatel'stvo TsK MOPR SSSR, 1931.

———. *Nikogda ne zabyt'! Krovavaia letopis' Bessarabii*. Moscow: Krasnaia Nov', 1924.

———. *Sovetskaia Moldaviia i bessarabskii vopros*. Moscow: Izdatel'stvo Moskovskogo otdela Obshchestva bessarabtsev, 1925.

Derzhavin, K. N. "Literaturnoe stroitel'stvo v sotsialisticheskoi Moldavii." *Trudy Instituta slavianovedeniia Akademii Nauk SSSR*, 1932, no. 1, pp. 239–96.

Donchev, I. P. *Russko-rumynskie spravochnye razgovory*. St. Petersburg: Tipografiia V. Kandaurova, 1877.

Dron, I. D. *Gagauzskie geograficheskie nazvaniia*. Chisinau: Ştiinţa, 1992.

Garskii, Viktor. *Trudovaia Bessarabiia i sovetskaia vlast'*. Moscow: Gosizdat, 1921.

Ginkulov, Ia. *Nachertanie pravil' Valakho-moldavskoi grammatiki*. St. Petersburg: Tipografiia Imperatorskoi Akademii Nauk, 1840.

Grekul, A. *Rastsvet moldavksoi sotsialisticheskoi natsii*. Chisinau: Cartea Moldovenească, 1974.

Grosul, Ia. S., and N. A. Mokhov. *Istoricheskaia nauka Moldavskoi SSR*. Moscow: Nauka, 1970.

Guzun, G. K. *Protiv fal'sifikatsii sovetskogo natsional'no-gosudarstvennogo stroitel'stva v Moldavii (1924–1936 gg.) v burzhuaznoi ideologii*. Odessa: Odesskii Gosuniversitet imeni I. I. Mechnikova, 1974.

Iakovlev, V. N. *Terpisty put' k spravedlivosti*. Tiraspol: n.p., 1993.

Iakovlev, V. N., ed. *Bessarabskii vopros i obrazovanie Pridnestrovskoi Moldavskoi Respubliki*. Tiraspol: RIO-PGKU, 1993.

Il'iashenko, T. P. *Formirovanie romanskikh literaturnykh iazykov: Moldavskii iazyk*. Chisinau: Ştiinţa, 1983.

Isaev, M. I. *Iazykovoe stroitel'stvo v SSSR*. Moscow: Nauka, 1979.

———. *Sotsiolingvisticheskie problemy iazykov narodov SSSR*. Moscow: Vysshaia Shkola, 1982.

Istoriia Moldavskoi SSR. 2 vols. Chisinau: Cartea Moldovenească, 1987.

Itogi vsesoiuznoi perepisi naseleniia 1959 goda: Moldavskaia SSR. Moscow: Gostatizdat, 1962.

Itogi vsesoiuznoi perepisi naseleniia 1970 goda. Moscow: Statistika, 1973.

Itogi vsesoiuznoi perepisi naseleniia 1979 goda. Moscow: Goskomstat, 1989.

Itogi vsesoiuznoi perepisi naseleniia 1989 goda. Minneapolis, Minn.: East View Publications, 1993.

Iuncu, R. *K voprosu o gagauzskoi avtonomii.* Chisinau: Cartea Moldovenească, 1990.

Kholostenko, V. *3 goda natsional'nogo stroitel'stva v A.M.S.S.R., 10 let natsional'nogo ugneteniia v Bessarabii.* Balta: Gosizdat Moldavii, 1928.

Kopanskii, Ia. M. *Obshchestvo Bessarabtsev v SSSR i soiuzy bessarabskikh emigrantov (1924–1940).* Chisinau: Ştiinţa, 1978.

Krushevan, P. A. *Bessarabiia: Geograficheskii, istoricheskii, statisticheskii, ekonomicheskii, etnograficheskii, literaturnyi i spravochnyi sbornik.* Moscow: Bessarabtsa, 1903.

Kul'tura Moldavii za gody sovetskoi vlasti: Sbornik dokumentov. 1 vol. 2 parts. Chisinau: Ştiinţa, 1975.

Kul'turnoe stroitel'stvo v SSSR, 1917–1927: Dokumenty i materialy. Moscow: Nauka, 1989.

Kuroglo, S. S., and M. V. Marunevich. *Sotsialisticheskie preobrazovaniia v byte i kul'ture gagauzskogo naseleniia MSSR.* Chisinau: Ştiinţa, 1983.

Lashkov, N. V. *Stoletie prisoedineniia Bessarabii k Rossii, 1812–1912.* Chisinau: Tipografiia Bessarabskago Gubernskago Pravleniia, 1912.

Lazarev, A. M. *Moldavskaia sovetskaia gosudarstvennost' i bessarabskii vopros.* Chisinau: Cartea Moldovenească, 1974.

Lazo, E. S. *Moldavskaia partiinaia organizatsiia v gody stroitel'stva sotsializma (1924–1940).* Chisinau: Ştiinţa, 1981.

Lukianets, O. S. *Russkie issledovateli i moldavskaia etnograficheskaia nauka v XIX–nachale XX v.* Chisinau: Ştiinţa, 1986.

Martsell, Stepan. *Rossiisko-rumynskaia grammatika.* St. Petersburg: Tipografiia Departamenta Narodnago Prosveshcheniia, 1827.

Marunevich, M. V. *Pravda o gagauzskom narode kak o samobytnom etnose i ego etnicheskoi territorii.* Comrat: Aydınnık, 1993.

Mokhov, N. A. *Ocherki istorii formirovaniia moldavskogo naroda.* Chisinau: Cartea Moldovenească, 1978.

Moraru, A. G. *Obrazovanie i razvitie moldavskoi sotsialisticheskoi natsii v krivom zerkale burzhuaznoi istoriografii.* Chisinau: Znanie, 1973.

Moshkov, V. A. "Turetskiia plemena na Balkanskom poluostrove," *Izvestiia*

Imperatorskago russkago geograficheskago obshchestva 40 (1904): 399–436.

Nakko, Aleksei. *Istoriia Bessarabii s drevneishikh vremen.* 2 vols. Odessa: Tipografiia Ul'rikha i Shul'tse, 1875.

Narodnoe khoziaistvo Moldavskoi SSR, 1924–1984. Chisinau: Cartea Moldovenească, 1984.

Obrazovanie Moldavskoi SSR i sozdanie Kommunisticheskoi partii Moldavii: Sbornik dokumentov i materialov. Chisinau: Cartea Moldovenească, 1984.

Ocherki istorii Kommunisticheskoi partii Moldavii. 3d ed. Chisinau: Cartea Moldovenească, 1981.

Omelchuk, F. S. *Razvitie sotsialisticheskoi kul'tury v Moldavskoi SSSR.* Chisinau: Şcoala Sovietică, 1950.

Pervaia vseobshchaia perepis' naseleniia Rossiiskoi Imperii, 1897 g. St. Petersburg: Izdanie Tsentral'nago Statisticheskago Komiteta Ministerstva Vnutrennikh Del, 1905.

Pokrovskaia, A. *Grammatika gagauzskogo iazyka.* Chisinau: Lumina, 1990.

Repida, A. *Obrazovanie Moldavskoi ASSR.* Chisinau: Ştiinţa, 1974.

———. *Obrazovanie Moldavskoi SSR.* Chisinau: Cartea Moldovenească, 1983.

Semiriaga, M. I. *Tainy stalinskoi diplomatii, 1939–1941.* Moscow: Vysshaia Shkola, 1992.

Sergievskii, M. V. *Moldavo-slavianskie etiudy.* Moscow: Izdatel'stvo Akademii Nauk SSSR, 1959.

———. *Moldavskie etiudy.* Moscow: Izdatel'stvo Akademii Nauk SSSR, 1936.

Shemiakov, D. E., and Ia. S. Iatsenko. *Kul'turnaia revoliutsiia v Sovetskoi Moldavii (1924–1967 gody).* Chisinau: Cartea Moldovenească, 1969.

Skal'kovskii, A. A. "Istoricheskoe vvedenie v statisticheskoe opisanie Bessarabskoi oblasti'." *Zhurnal Ministerstva vnutrennikh del* 13 (1846): 169–98, 407–44.

Sovetskaia Bessarabiia i Sovetskaia Bukovina. Moscow: Gosudarstvennoe Izdatel'stvo Politicheskoi Literatury, 1940.

Stalin, I. V. *Sochineniia.* Moscow: Gosudarstvennoe Izdatel'stvo Politicheskoi Literatury, 1947.

Surilov, A. V., ed. *Gosudarstvenno-pravovye akty Moldavskoi SSR (1924–1941 gg.).* Chisinau: Cartea Moldovenească, 1963.

Syrku, Polikhronii. *Iz byta bessarabskikh rumyn.* Petrograd: Tipografiia V. D. Smirnova, 1914.

Sytnik, M. K., ed. *Stranitsy istorii Sovetskoi Moldavii.* Chisinau: Ştiinţa, 1973.

Tabak, I. V. *Russkoe naselenie Moldavii: Chislennost', rasselenie, mezhetnicheskie sviazi.* Chisinau: Ştiinţa, 1990.

Ţăran, A. M. *Golod v Moldove (1946–1947): Sbornik dokumentov.* Chisinau: Ştiinţa, 1993.

Tarasov, O. Iu. *Ocherki istorii organizatsii nauki v Sovetskoi Moldavii (1924–1961).* Chisinau: Ştiinţa, 1980.

Troinitskii, N. A., ed. *Obshchii svod po imperii rezul'tatov razrabotki dannykh pervoi vseobshchei perepisi naseleniia, proizvedennoi 28 ianvaria 1897 goda.* 2 vols. St. Petersburg: n.p., 1905.

Tsaranov, V. I., ed. *Istoricheskaia nauka Sovetskoi Moldavii: K 60-letiiu obrazovaniia Moldavskoi SSR i sozdaniia Kompartii respubliki.* Chisinau: Ştiinţa, 1984.

Ursul, D. T., and V. M. Topilina. *I. V. Ochinskii (1888–1970).* Chisinau: Ştiinţa, 1979.

Vne Rossii: Sbornik nauchnykh statei o russkikh i russkoi kul'ture Moldovei. Chisinau: Institute of National Minorities, Moldovan Academy of Sciences, 1997.

Voprosy moldavskogo iazykoznaniia. Moscow: Izdatel'stvo Akademii Nauk SSSR, 1953.

Vosstanavlivaia pravdu istorii. Chisinau: Cartea Moldovenească, 1989.

Vsesoiuznaia perepis' naseleniia 1926 goda. Moscow: Izdanie TsSU Soiuza SSR, 1929.

Zagorodnaia, E. M., and V. S. Zelenchuk. *Naselenie Moldavskoi SSR (sotsial'no-demograficheskie protsessy).* Chisinau: Cartea Moldovenească, 1987.

Zajaczkowski, Wlodzimierz. "K etnogenezu gagauzov." *Folia Orientalia* 15 (1960): 77–86.

Zashchuk, A. *Materialy dlia geografii i statistiki Rossii: Bessarabskaia guberniia.* St. Petersburg: n.p., 1862.

English

Anderson, Barbara, and Brian Silver. "Demographic Sources of the Changing Ethnic Composition of the Soviet Union," *Population and Development Review* 15, no. 4 (1989): 609–56.

Anderson, Benedict. *Imagined Communities.* Rev. ed. London: Verso, 1991.

Armstrong, Hamilton Fish. "The Bessarabian Dispute," *Foreign Affairs* 2, no. 4 (1924): 662–67.

———. *The New Balkans.* London: Harper and Brothers, 1926.

Atlas of Dniester Moldavian Republic. Tiraspol: Dniester State Corporative T. G. Shevchenko University, 1997.

Austin, Paul T. "Soviet Karelian: The Language That Failed," *Slavic Review* 51, no. 1 (1992): 16–35.

Bacon, Walter M., Jr. *Behind Closed Doors: Secret Papers on the Failure of Romanian-Soviet Negotiations, 1931–1932.* Stanford: Hoover Institution Press, 1979.

Baerlein, Henry. *Bessarabia and Beyond.* London: Methuen, 1935.

———. *In Old Romania.* London: Hutchinson, 1940.

Bibesco, Prince Antoine. *Redeeming Bessarabia.* New York: Society of the Friends of Roumania, 1921.

Blinkhoorn, Martin, ed. *Fascists and Conservatives: The Radical Right and the Establishment in Twentieth-Century Europe.* London: Unwin Hyman, 1990.

Bowers, Stephen. "The Crisis in Moldova," *Jane's Intelligence Review*, November 1992, pp. 483–86.

Bremmer, Ian, and Ray Taras, eds. *Nations and Politics in the Soviet Successor States.* Cambridge, Eng.: Cambridge University Press, 1993.

Brooks, Shirley. *The Russians of the South.* London: Longman, Brown, Green and Longmans, 1854.

Bruchis, Michael. "The Language Policy of the CPSU and the Linguistic Situation in Soviet Moldavia," *Soviet Studies* 36, no. 1 (1984): 108–26.

———. *Nations–Nationalities–People: A Study of the Nationalities Policy of the Communist Party in Soviet Moldavia.* Boulder, Colo.: East European Monographs, 1984.

———. *One Step Back, Two Steps Forward: On the Language Policy of the Communist Party of the Soviet Union in the National Republics (Moldavian: A Look Back, a Survey, and Perspectives, 1924–1980).* Boulder, Colo.: East European Monographs, 1982.

Cazacu, P. *The Truth about Bessarabia.* Bucharest: Cultura Naţională, 1926.

Chinn, Jeff, and Robert Kaiser. *Russians as the New Minority: Ethnicity and Nationalism in the Soviet Successor States.* Boulder, Colo.: Westview Press, 1996.

Chinn, Jeff, and Steven D. Roper. "Territorial Autonomy in Gagauzia," *Nationalities Papers* 26, no. 1 (1998): 87–101.

Ciorănesco, George. *Bessarabia: Disputed Land between East and West.* Munich: Editura Ion Dumitru, 1985.

Clark, Charles Upson. *Bessarabia: Russia and Roumania on the Black Sea.* New York: Dodd Mead, 1927.

———. *United Romania.* New York: Dodd Mead, 1932.

Clem, Ralph S., ed. *The Soviet West: Interplay between Nationality and Social Organization.* New York: Praeger, 1975.

Colley, Linda. *Britons: Forging the Nation, 1707–1837.* New Haven, Conn.: Yale University Press, 1992.

Cretzianu, Alexandre. *The Lost Opportunity.* London: Jonathan Cape, 1957.

Crowther, William. "Ethnic Politics and the Post-Communist Transition in Moldova," *Nationalities Papers* 26, no. 1 (1998): 147–64.

———. "Ethnicity and Participation in the Communist Party of Moldavia," *Journal of Soviet Nationalities* 1, no. 1 (1990): 148–49.

———. "The Politics of Ethno-National Mobilization: Nationalism and Reform in Soviet Moldavia," *Russian Review* 50 (April 1990): 183–202.

Dallin, Alexander. *Odessa, 1941–1944: A Case Study of Soviet Territory under Foreign Rule.* Rev. ed. Iaşi: Center for Romanian Studies, 1998.

Dawisha, Karen, and Bruce Parrott, eds. *Democratic Changes and Authoritarian Reactions in Russia, Ukraine, Belarus, and Moldova.* Cambridge, Eng.: Cambridge University Press, 1997.

Deletant, Dennis. "Genoese, Tatars and Rumanians at the Mouth of the Danube in the Fourteenth Century," *Slavonic and East European Review* 62, no. 4 (1981): 511–30.

———. "Moldavia between Hungary and Poland, 1347–1412," *Slavonic and East European Review* 64, no. 2 (1986): 187–211.

———. "Romania and the Moldavian SSR," *Soviet Analyst* 12, no. 1 (1983): 6–8.

———. "The Soviet View of Bessarabia," *Slavonic and East European Review* 56, no. 1 (1978): 115–18.

Demidov, Anatole de. *Travels in Southern Russia and the Crimea: Through Hungary, Wallachia, and Moldavia, during the Year 1837.* 2 vols. London: J. Mitchell, 1853.

Dima, Nicholas. *Bessarabia and Bukovina: The Soviet-Romanian Territorial Dispute.* Boulder, Colo.: East European Monographs, 1982.

———. *From Moldavia to Moldova: The Soviet-Romanian Territorial Dispute.* Boulder, Colo.: East European Monographs, 1991.

Diorditsa, A. F. *Moldavia: A Flourishing Orchard.* London: Soviet Booklets, 1960.

Dobrinescu, Valeriu Florin. *The Diplomatic Struggle over Bessarabia.* Iaşi: Center for Romanian Studies, 1996.

Dyer, Donald, ed. *Studies in Moldovan: The History, Culture, Language, and Contemporary Politics of the People of Moldova.* Boulder, Colo.: East European Monographs, 1996.

East, W. G. *The Union of Moldavia and Wallachia, 1859: An Episode in Diplomatic History.* Cambridge, Eng.: Cambridge University Press, 1929.

Elleman, Bruce A. "The 1925 Soviet-Japanese Secret Agreement on Bessarabia," *Diplomacy and Statecraft* 5, no. 2 (1994): 287–325.

Fierman, William. *Language Planning and National Development: The Uzbek Experience.* Berlin: Mouton, 1991.

Fischer, Louis. *Men and Politics: An Autobiography.* London: Jonathan Cape, 1941.

Fisher, Julius S. *Transnistria: The Forgotten Cemetery.* New York: Thomas Yoseloff, 1969.

Gafencu, Grigore. *Prelude to the Russian Campaign.* Translated by E. Fletcher-Allen. London: Frederick Muller, 1945.

Gallagher, Tom. *Romania after Ceauşescu.* Edinburgh: Edinburgh University Press, 1996.

Gellner, Ernest. *Thought and Change.* London: Weidenfeld and Nicolson, 1964.

Gleason, Abbott, Peter Kenez, and Richard Stites, eds., *Bolshevik Culture: Experiment and Order in the Russian Revolution.* Bloomington: Indiana University Press, 1985.

Gold, Jack. "Bessarabia: The Thorny 'Non-Existent' Problem,'" *East European Quarterly* 13, no. 1 (1974): 47–74.

Hall, D. J. *Romanian Furrow.* London: George G. Harrap, 1939.

Hamm, Michael F. "Kishinev: The Character and Development of a Tsarist Frontier Town," *Nationalities Papers* 26, no. 1 (1998): 19–37.

Harris, Chauncy. "The New Russian Minorities: A Statistical Overview," *Post-Soviet Geography* 34, no. 1 (1993): 1–27.

Helsinki Watch. *Human Rights in Moldova: The Turbulent Dniester.* New York: Human Rights Watch, 1993.

Hill, Ronald J. *Soviet Political Elites: The Case of Tiraspol.* New York: St. Martin's, 1977.

Hitchins, Keith. *The Romanians, 1774–1866.* Oxford: Clarendon Press, 1996.

———. *Rumania, 1866–1947.* Oxford: Clarendon Press, 1994.

Hobsbawm, Eric, and Terence Ranger, eds. *The Invention of Tradition.* Cambridge, Eng.: Cambridge University Press, 1983.

Iorga, Nicolae. *A History of Roumania.* Translated by Joseph McCabe. London: T. Fisher Unwin, 1925.

Jagendorf, Siegfried. *Jangendorf's Foundry.* New York: HarperCollins, 1991.

Jewsbury, George F. *The Russian Annexation of Bessarabia: 1774–1828.* Boulder, Colo.: East European Quarterly, 1976.

Karklins, Rasma. *Ethnic Relations in the USSR: The Perspective from Below.* Boston: Unwin Hyman, 1986.

Katz, Zev, ed. *Handbook of Major Soviet Nationalities.* London: Collier Macmillan, 1975.

Kaufman, Stuart J., and Stephen R. Bowers. "Transnational Dimensions of the Transnistrian Conflict," *Nationalities Papers* 26, no. 1 (1998): 129–46.

Kelley, Robert F. "Soviet Policy on the European Border," *Foreign Affairs* 3, no. 1 (1924): 91–98.

King, Charles. "Gagauz Yeri and the Dilemmas of Self-Determination," *Transition,* October 20, 1995, pp. 21–25.

———. "Moldova with a Russian Face," *Foreign Policy* (December 1994–95): 106–20.

King, Charles, and Neil J. Melvin, eds. *Nations Abroad: Diaspora Politics and International Relations in the Former Soviet Union.* Boulder, Colo.: Westview Press, 1998.

King, Robert R. *A History of the Romanian Communist Party.* Stanford: Hoover Institution Press, 1980.

———. *Minorities under Communism: Nationalities as a Source of Tension among Balkan Communist States.* Cambridge, Mass.: Harvard University Press, 1973.

Kirkwood, Michael, ed. *Language Planning in the Soviet Union.* London: Macmillan, 1989.

Kolstø, Pål, and Andrei Edemskiy, with Natalya Kalashnikova. "The Dniester Conflict: Between Irredentism and Separatism," *Europe-Asia Studies* 45, no. 6 (1993): 973–1000.

Kolstø, Pål, and Andrei Malgin. "The Transnistrian Republic: A Case of Politicized Regionalism," *Nationalities Papers* 26, no. 1 (1998): 104–27.

Kreindler, Isabelle, ed. *Sociolinguistic Perspectives on Soviet National Languages: Their Past, Present and Future.* Berlin: Mouton de Gruyter, 1985.

Kroupensky, A. N., and A. Ch. Schmidt. *The Bessarabian "Parliament" (1917–1918).* Paris: Imprimerie Lahure, n.d.

———. *What Is the "Bessarabian Question?"* Paris: Imprimerie Lahure, n.d.

Laitin, David D. *Identity in Formation: The Russian-Speaking Populations in the Near Abroad.* Ithaca, N.Y.: Cornell University Press, 1998.

Lebed, Alexander. *My Life and My Country.* Washington: Regnery Publishing, 1997.

Lewis, E. Glyn. *Multilingualism in the Soviet Union.* The Hague: Mouton, 1972.

Liber, George. *Soviet Nationality Policy, Urban Growth and Identity Change in the Ukrainian SSR, 1923–1934.* Cambridge, Eng.: Cambridge University Press, 1992.

Lithgow, William. *The Totall Discourse of the Rare Adventures and Painefull Peregrinations of Long Nineteene Yeares Travayles from Scotland to the Most Famous Kingdomes in Europe, Asia and Affrica.* Glasgow: James MacLehose and Sons, 1906 [1632].

Livezeanu, Irina. *Cultural Politics in Greater Romania: Regionalism, Nation-Building and Ethnic Struggle, 1918–1930.* Ithaca, N.Y.: Cornell University Press, 1995.

———. "Moldavia, 1917–1990: Nationalism and Internationalism Then and Now," *Armenian Review* 43, no. 2 (1990): 153–93.

———. "Urbanization in a Low Key and Linguistic Change in Soviet Moldavia, Part 1," *Soviet Studies* 33, no. 3 (1981): 327–51. Part 2," *Soviet Studies* 33, no. 4 (1981): 573–92.

Luckyj, George S. N. *Literary Politics in Soviet Ukraine, 1917–1934.* New York: Columbia University Press, 1956.

Lungu, Dov B. *Romania and the Great Powers, 1933–40.* Durham, N.C.: Duke University Press, 1989.

———. "Soviet-Romanian Relations and the Bessarabian Question in the 1920s," *Southeastern Europe/L'Europe du sud-est* 6, no. 1 (1979): 29–45.

Mace, James E. *Communism and the Dilemmas of National Liberation: National Communism in Soviet Ukraine, 1918–1933.* Cambridge, Mass.: Harvard University Press, 1983.

Martonne, Em. de. *What I Have Seen in Bessarabia.* Paris: Imprimerie des Arts et des Sports, 1919.

Marx, Anthony W. *Making Race and Nation: A Comparison of the United States, South Africa and Brazil.* Cambridge, Eng.: Cambridge University Press, 1998.

Melvin, Neil. *Russians beyond Russia: The Politics of National Identity.* London: Pinter, 1995.

Miliukov, Paul. *The Case for Bessarabia: A Collection of Documents.* 2d ed. London: Russian Liberation Committee, 1920.

Moldovan, Petre. *A. M. Lazarev: A Counterfeiter of History.* Milan: Nagard, 1976.

Mosley, Philip E. "Is Bessarabia Next?" *Foreign Affairs* 18, no. 3 (1940): 557–62.

Nandriş, Grigore. *Bessarabia and Bucovina: The Trojan Horse of Russian Colonial Expansion to the Mediterranean.* London: Editura Societăţii pentru Cultura, 1968.

Nedelciuc, Vasile. *The Republic of Moldova.* Chisinau: Parliament of the Republic of Moldova, 1992.

Nimigeanu, Dumitru. *Hell Moved Its Border.* London: Blandford Press, 1960.

O'Loughlin, John, Vladimir Kolossov, and Andrei Tchepalyga. "National Construction, Territorial Separatism, and Post-Soviet Geopolitics in the Transdniester Moldovan Republic," *Post-Soviet Geography and Economics* 39, no. 6 (1998): 332–58.

Pelivan, Ion G. *Chronology of the Most Important Events of the Life of Bessarabia.* Paris: Imprimerie des Arts et des Sports, 1920.

———. *The Right of the Roumanians to Bessarabia.* Idem.

———. *The Union of Bessarabia with Her Mother-Country Roumania.* Paris: Idem.

Popovici, Andrei. *The Political Status of Bessarabia.* Washington: Ransdell, 1931.

Rakovsky, C. G. *Roumania and Bessarabia.* London: W. Coates, 1925.

Seton-Watson, R. W. *A History of the Roumanians: From Roman Times to the Completion of Unity.* Cambridge, Eng.: Cambridge University Press, 1934.

Shlapentokh, Vladimir, Munir Senoich, and Emil Payin, eds. *The New Russian Diaspora: Russian Minorities in the Former Soviet Republics.* Armonk, N.Y.: M. E. Sharpe, 1994.

Skene, James Henry. *The Frontier Lands of the Christian and the Turk: Comprising Travels in the Regions of the Lower Danube in 1850 and 1851.* 2d ed. 2 vols. London: Richard Bentley, 1853.

Smith, Graham, ed. *The Nationalities Question in the Soviet Union.* London: Longman, 1990.

Sollors, Werner, ed. *The Invention of Ethnicity.* New York: Oxford University Press, 1989.

Spector, Sherman David. *Romania at the Paris Peace Conference.* Iaşi: Center for Romanian Studies, 1995.

Spencer, Edmund. *Travels in the Western Caucasus.* 2 vols. London: Henry Colburn, 1838.

Spinei, Victor. *Moldavia in the 11th–14th Centuries.* Bucharest: Editura Academiei Republicii Socialiste România, 1986.

Szajkowski, Bogdan, ed. *New Political Parties of Eastern Europe, Russia, and the Successor States.* London: Longman, 1995.

Titulescu, Nicolae. "Two Neighbours of Russia and Their Policies: (I) Roumania and Bessarabia," *Nineteenth Century and After 1924* (June): 791–803.

Todorova, Maria. *Imagining the Balkans.* New York: Oxford University Press, 1997.

Treaties of Peace with Italy, Romania, Bulgaria, Hungary and Finland. London: HMSO, 1947.

Urussov, Prince Serge Dmitriyevich. *Memoirs of a Russian Governor.* Translated by Herman Rosenthal. New York: Harper and Brothers, 1908.

Van Meurs, Wim. *The Bessarabian Question in Communist Historiography: Nationalist and Communist Politics and History-Writing.* Boulder, Colo.: East European Monographs, 1994.

Viola, Lynne. "Bab'i Bunty and Peasant Women's Protest during Collectivization," *Russian Review* 45, no. 1 (1986): 23–42.

———. *Peasant Rebels under Stalin.* Oxford: Oxford University Press, 1996.

Weber, Eugen. *Peasants into Frenchmen: The Modernization of Rural France, 1870–1914.* London: Chatto and Windus, 1977.

Wexler, Paul. *Purism and Language: A Study of Modern Ukrainian and Belorussian Nationalism (1840–1967).* Bloomington: Indiana University Press, 1974.

Wilkinson, William. *An Account of the Principalities of Wallachia and Moldavia.* London: Longman, Hurst, Rees, Orme, and Brown, 1820.

Winnifrith, T. J. *The Vlachs: The History of a Balkan People.* London: Duckworth, 1987.

Wolff, Larry. *Inventing Eastern Europe.* Stanford: Stanford University Press, 1994.

Other Languages

Alcuni documenti sulla unità della lingua romena. Florence: VIII Congresso Internazionale di Studi Romanzi, 1956.

Association "Pro Bessarabia" de France et de Grande-Bretagne, et al. *Pro Bassarabia: Mémoire.* Paris: Imprimerie Blanchard, 1955.

Babel, Antony. *La Bessarabie: Etude historique, ethnographique et économique.* Paris: Librairie Félix Alcan, 1926.

Cazacu, P. *Témoinages russes concernant le caractère roumain de la Bessarabie.* Bucharest: Institut d'Histoire Nationale de Bucarest, 1944.

Cioranesco, George, et al. *Aspects des relations russo-roumaines: Rétrospectives et orientations.* Paris: Minard, 1967.

Cioranesco, George, et al. *Aspects des relations soviéto-roumaines, 1967–1971: Sécurité européene.* Paris: Minard, 1971.

D'Hauterive, Le Comte. *Mémoire sur l'état ancien et actuel de la Moldavie en 1787.* Bucharest: Institutul de Arte Grafice "Carol Göbl," 1902.

Doğru, Abdülmecit, and Ismail Kaynak. *Gagauz türkçesini sözlüğü.* Ankara: Kültür Bakanlığı, 1991.

Gangloff, Sylvie. "L'émancipation politique des Gagaouzes, turcophones chrétiens de Moldavie," *Cahiers d'études sur la Méditerranée orientale et le monde turco-iranien* 1997, no. 23 (January–June): 231–57.

———. "Les Gagaouzes: Etat des recherches et bibliographie," *Turcica* 30 (1998): 13–61.

Gradeshliev, Ivan. *Gagauzite.* Dobrich: Izdatelska kŭshta Liudmil Beshkov, 1994.

Güngör, Harun, and Mustafa Argunşah. *Gagauz Türkleri: Tarih, dil, folklor ve halk edebiyatı.* Ankara: Kültür Bakanlığı, 1991.

———. *Gagauzlar: Dünden bugüne.* Ankara: Elektronik İletişim Ajansi, 1991.

Haarman, Harald. *Soziologie der kleinen Sprachen Europas.* 2 vols. Hamburg: Helmut Buske, 1973.

———. "Das Moldauische—eine eigenständige ostromanische Sprache?" *Südosteuropa-Mitteilungen* 27, no. 1 (1987): 56–62.

———. "Probleme der moldauischen Sprache in der Ära Gorbačev," *Südosteuropa* 38, no. 1 (1989): 28–53.

Heitmann, Klaus. "Rumänische Sprache und Literatur in Bessarabien und Transnistrien (die sogenannte moldauische Sprache und Literatur)," *Zeitschrift für romanische Philologie*, no. 81 (1965): 102–56.

Hoppe, Ernst Max. "I Gagauzi, popolazione turco-cristiana della Bulgaria," *Oriente Moderno* 14 (1934): 132–43.

Iorga, Nicolae. *Les roumains au-delà du Dniester: Pour éclarer le sens de la "République Moldave" des Soviets russes.* Paris: J. Gamber, 1925.

Kleess, Arnold. "Rumänisch und Moldauisch," *Osteuropa* 5 (1955): 281–84.

Kowalski, Tadeusz. *Les Turcs et la langue turque de la Bulgarie du nord-est.* Kraków: Polska Akademja Umiejętności, 1933.

Lozovan, Eugene. "La linguistique roumaine de 1952 à 1954," *Zeitschrift für romanische Philologie* 1955, no. 71, pp. 391–407.

Nistor, Ion. *La Bessarabie et la Bucovine.* Bucharest: Académie Roumaine, 1937.

Okhotnikov, J., and N. Batchinsky. *La Bessarabie et la paix européene.* Paris: Association des Emigrés Bessarabiens, 1927.

Özkan, Nevzat. *Gagavuz Türkçesi grameri.* Ankara: Atatürk Kültür, Dil ve Tarih Yüksek Kurumu, 1996.

Pelivan, Ion G. *La Bessarabie sous le régime russe (1812–1918).* Paris: Imprimerie Générale Lahure, 1919.

Şuga, Alexander. *Die völkerrechtliche Lage Bessarabiens in der geschichtlichen Entwicklung des Landes.* Bonn: n.p., 1958.

Tagliavini, Carlo. *Le origini delle lingue neolatine.* 6th ed. Bologna: Casa Editrice Prof. Riccardo Petron, 1969.

————. *Una nuova lingua letteraria romanza? Il moldavo.* Florence: Sansoni, 1956.

Tott, François de. *Mémoires du Baron de Tott sur les Turcs et les Tatares.* 2 vols. Amsterdam: n.p., 1784.

Weigand, Gustav. *Die Dialekte der Bukowina und Bessarabiens (mit einem Titelbilde und Musikbeilagen).* Leipzig: Johann Ambrosius Barth, 1904.

Wittek, Paul. "Les Gagaouzes: Les gens de Kaykaus," *Rocznik Orientalistyczny* 17 (1951–52): 12–24.

NEWSPAPERS AND OTHER PERIODICALS

22 (Bucharest)

Adevărul (Bucharest)

Ana sözü (Chisinau)

Analele Academiei Române (Bucharest)

Arena politicii (Chisinau)

Argumenty i fakty (Moscow)

Arhivele Basarabiei (Chisinau)

Arhivele totalitarismului (Bucharest)

Basarabia (Chisinau)

Basarabia economică (Chisinau)

Basarabia: Ziar săptămânal independent (Chisinau)

BBC Summary of World Broadcasts (London)

Contemporanul (Bucharest)

Cotidianul (Bucharest)

Cugetul (Chisinau)

Curierul național (Bucharest)

Cuvântul moldovenesc (Chisinau)

Demograficheskii ezhegodnik SSSR (Moscow)

Dimineața (Bucharest)

Dreptatea (Bucharest)

Economia națională a RSS Moldoveneşti/RSS Moldova/Republicii Moldova (Chisinau)

Flacăra (Bucharest)

Foreign Broadcast Information Service Daily Report (Washington)

Gagauz sesi (Comrat)

Grazhdanskii mir (Chisinau)

Haberlär (Comrat)

IMF Economic Reviews (Washington)

Independent (London)

International Herald Tribune (Paris)

Învăţămîntul public (Chisinau)

Izvestiia (Moscow)

Izvestiia Akademii Nauk Moldavskoi SSR, seriia obshchestvennykh nauk (Chisinau)

Kommunist (Moscow)

Kommunist Moldavii/Comunistul Moldovei (Chisinau)

Komsomol'skaia pravda (Moscow)

Krasnaia Bessarabiia (Moscow)

Kraznaia zvezda (Moscow)

Kul'tura/Cultura (Chisinau)

Le Figaro (Paris)

Le Monde (Paris)

Libertatea (Bucharest)

Limba şi literatura moldovenească (Chisinau)

Literatura şi arta (Chisinau)

Literaturnaia gazeta (Moscow)

Materna (Chisinau)

Mesagerul (Chisinau)

Mezhdunarodnaia zhizn' (Moscow)

Moldova: Economic Trends (Brussels/Chisinau)

Moldova nouă (Bucharest)

Moldova socialistă (Tiraspol/Chisinau)

Moldova suverană (Chisinau)

Monitorul oficial al Republicii Moldova (Chisinau)

Moscow News (Moscow)

Narodnoe khoziaistvo Moldavskoi SSR (Chisinau)

Nasha rech' (Bucharest)

Nezavisimaia Moldova (Chisinau)

Nistru (Chisinau)

Octiabriu/Octombrie/Oktiabr' (Tiraspol)

Oxford Analytica East Europe Daily Brief (Oxford)

Pămînt şi oameni (Chisinau)

Partiinaia zhizn' (Moscow)

Plugarul roş (Balta/Tiraspol)

Plus-Minus (Chisinau)

Pravda (Moscow)

Radio Free Europe/Radio Liberty Daily Report (Munich)

Radio Liberty Report on the USSR/Research Bulletin (Munich)

Revistă de istorie a Moldovei (Chisinau)

Revistă de lingvistică şi ştiinţă literară (Chisinau)

România liberă (Bucharest)

România nouă (Chisinau)

Sfatul Ţării (Chisinau)

Sovetskaia Moldaviia (Chisinau)

Sovetskaia Rossiia (Moscow)

Ţara (Chisinau)

Tineretul liber (Bucharest)

Tinerimia Moldovei (Chisinau)

Transition (Prague)

Tribuna (Chisinau)

Viaţa Basarabiei [newspaper and journal] (Chisinau)

Voprosy iazykoznaniia (Moscow)

Voprosy istorii (Moscow)

Index

Abkhazia, 179
Agrarian Democratic Party, 154, 157, 162, 187, 217
Akhromeev, Sergei, 129
Akkerman, 14, 94, 179
Albania, 36
Alecsandri, Vasile, 84
Alexander I, 19, 22–23
Alexandru cel Bun, 15
Alexei Mateevici Literary-Musical Club, 123, 127–28, 130, 186, 215
Alma Ata accords, 154
Ana sözü, 214
Andreeva, Nina, 187
Antisemitism, 24, 30, 44, 77, 93, 136, 174
Antonescu, Ion, 92, 94
Arbore, Ecaterina, 75–76
Association of Bessarabian Emigrés, 52
Association of Historians, 132
Atamaniuk, Vladimir, 197
August coup, 191, 205

Austrian empire: and Principality of Moldova, 16–18
Avars, 68
Azerbaijan, 79, 86

Bakannık Komiteti, 219
Balkan Entente, 91
Baltic republics, 127, 129, 133–34
Banat, 31, 37
Bănulescu-Bodoni, Gavril, 21–22
Basarab I, 14
Basarabia, 29, 32
Başkan, 219
Belarus, 70, 79, 184
Bender, 14, 51, 56, 179
Bender, battle of, 194–98
Berejan, Silviu, 133
Berg, L. S., 59
Bergman, Mikhail, 202
Berlin, Congress of, 22
Bessarabia: annexation of in 1812, 151; annexation of in 1940, 3, 91–93; au-

Bessarabia (*continued*)
tonomy, 33; church in, 23, 25, 30; code of 1829, 22; Germans in, 96; in Greater Romania, 41–51; independence, 33; literacy in, 23, 41; migration to, 23; minorities in, 44; name, 21; Moldovan Democratic Republic of, 33; negotiations over, 38, 82; population, 24, 41; reform movement in Russian empire, 28–32; Romanian cultural assistance to, 31; Romanian military intervention, 33; in Russian empire, 18–28; Russians in, 44; Soviet propaganda in, 51–52; statute of 1818, 21; union with Romania, 35; wine, 42

Bessarabian Countrymen (*Pământenia Basarabeană*), 28

Bessarabian Metropolitan Church, 165

Bessarabian question: in communist Romania, 103–106; in Romanian domestic politics, 166–67

Bessarabian Soviet Socialist Republic, 38

Bodiul, Ivan, 98–99, 100, 102, 104, 122, 139

Bogdan III, 15

Boğdan Saray, 17, 19 (illus.)

Bogdan, 14

Bogopol'skaia, Niunia, 75–76

Boiars, 16, 19, 22, 27

Bolgrad, 22

Bolshevik Revolution, 31, 32, 37

Bondarciuc, Nicolae, 133

Borodin, P. G., 100

Brătianu family, 37

Brătianu, Constantin, 94

Brătianu, Ionel, 36, 40

Brezhnev, Leonid, 95, 98, 100, 102, 104, 122

Bruchis, Michael, 113

Buburuz, Petru, 129

Bucharest, treaty of (1812), 19

Buciuşcanu, Gabriel, 65, 66, 87

Bugeac (Budjak), xxiii, 209

Bugeac Battalion, 216

Bukovina: annexation of in 1775, 18, 21, 151; annexation of in 1940, 2, 91–93

Bulgarian language, 175

Bulgarian minority, 175–76

Bulgars, 68

Buriat–Mongol autonomous republic, 55

Cahul, 22, 111, 135, 176

Callimachi family, 17

Cantemir, Dimitrie, 13, 16, 18, 20 (illus.)

Carabinieri, 192

Carol I, 40

Carol II, 36, 40–41, 50 (illus.), 83, 92, 94

Casa Noastră, 41

Catherine the Great, 18

Ceauşescu, Elena, 106, 148

Ceauşescu, Nicolae, 103–4, 106, 111, 113, 148

Ceauşescu, Nicu, 106

Charles XII, 179

Chechnya, 179

Chernenko, Konstantin, 98

Chernobyl, 103

Chervonyi orach. See Plugarul roş

Chichagov, Serafim, 29

Chior, Ion, 66

Chior, Pavel, 64–66, 67 (illus.), 68, 73, 80, 82, 85–87, 107

Chisinau: pogroms, 24, 30; population, 172; as provincial capital, 23

Chisinau Agricultural Institute, 134–35

Chisinau Pedagogical Institute, 175

Chisinau State University, 111, 134, 157, 174, 212, 230

Chiţac, Ştefan, 192

Christian Democratic Popular Front of Moldova. *See* Popular Front of Moldova

Ciachir, Mihail, 211

Cioban, I. D., 85–86, 108

Citizenship law, 169, 173

Ciubuc, Ion, 163

Civic Alliance (of Moldova), 155

Civic Alliance (of Romania), 164
Clark, Charles Upson, 44
Cobasna, 202
Committee for Moldovanization and
    Ukrainization, 70, 73, 78–79
Commonwealth of Independent States:
    Moldova and, 154, 197
Communist International, 52, 103
Communist Party of Moldova: creation
    of, 98; leadership, 100; leading role
    renounced, 148; membership, 99;
    Transnistrians in, 134–38
Communist Party of the Russian Federa-
    tion, 205
Congress of People's Deputies, 127,
    146, 215
Congress of the Intelligentsia, 154, 157.
    See also Party of Democratic Forces
Conservative Party (Romania), 37, 40,
    48
Constantinescu, Emil, 164, 167
Constantinople, 16–17
Constitution, 169, 159, 200
Constitutional Democrats (Russian em-
    pire), 30
Corlăteanu, Nicolae, 105, 108, 111
Cossacks: in Transnistrian conflict, 192,
    194
Costaş, Ion, 195
Council of Europe, 169, 222
Coval, N. G., 100
Cretzianu, Alexandre, 40
Crimea, 18
Crimean War, 22
Crişana, 37
Croitor, Dumitru, 222
Cumania, 14
Cumans, 13, 210
Cuvântul moldovenesc, 30, 32
Cuza, Alexandru Ioan, 27

Dabija, Nicolae, 127, 139
Dacii, 68
Danubian Principalities. *See* Moldova,
    Principality of; Wallachia; United
    Principalities
Deletant, Dennis, 113

Dembo, Vladimir, 59–61
Demirel, Süleyman, 221–22
Democratic Convention of Moldova,
    163
Descălecarea, 13
Devşirme, 15
D'Hauterive, Count, 17
Dima, Nicholas, 113
Dnestr Guards, 191, 197
Dnestr Moldovan Republic: creation of,
    147, 189. *See also* Transnistria
Dobrogea (Dobrudja), 37, 210–11
Dobrov, Leonid, 216
"Doina," 180
Dorpat (Tartu), University of, 28
Druc, Mircea, 151, 167, 216
Druţă, Ion, 115, 127, 138, 153, 155,
    224
Dubăsari: fighting in, 192
Duma, 28, 30, 200, 229

Edineţ, 43, 135
Edinstvo, 129–30, 140, 157, 188
Elections: for parliament (1994), 145,
    155–59; for parliament (1998), 162;
    for president (1996), 161; results since
    1991, 158; schedule, 161; for Su-
    preme Soviet (1990), 146
Electoral system, 160–61
Eminescu, Mihai, 84, 180
Engels, Friedrich, 105
Eremei, Grigore, 100, 191
Esperanto, 83
Ethnic identity: theories of, 1
Ethnic minorities. *See* Minorities
Evnevich, Evgenii, 202

Fala, Porfirie, 58
Ferdinand, 36–37, 40, 44, 50
Fifty-Ninth Guards Motorized Rifle Di-
    vision, 184
Finland, 33, 55, 92
First World War: peace settlement,
    36–38; Romania in, 31
Forty-Sixth Army, 184
Fourteenth Army: battle of Bender and,

Fourteenth Army (*continued*)
194; under Russian control, 192;
Transnistrian conflict and, 191–93;
withdrawal agreement, 200–2

Gagauz: demographics, 209, 218; ethnic
origins, 210–11; in Greater Romania,
211; independence movement,
215–17; linguistic assimilation, 213;
migration to Bessarabia, 211; social
problems, 212; in Soviet Union,
211–14; Turkey and, 221–22; vio-
lence, 215–16
Gagauz Halkı, 129, 138, 215–16
Gagauz language: alphabet, 213–14,
222; education and publishing,
211–15
Gagauz Yeri, 217–20
Gagauzia, Republic of: declaration of,
147. *See also* Gagauz; Gagauz Yeri
Galicia-Volhynia, 179
Gavriliță, Emanuil, 29–30
Gazprom, 203–4
Gellner, Ernest, 2
Getae, 68
Gheorghiu-Dej, Gheorghe, 103
Ghibu, Onisifor, 31–32, 165
Ghica family, 17
Gladkii, D. S., 100
Glasnost, 124
Glasul, 133
Goma, Paul, 19
Gorbachev, Mikhail, 121–22, 124, 136,
148, 150, 202, 205
Gorky, Maxim, 84
Goths, 68
Grachev, Pavel, 192, 195
Grand National Assembly. See *Marea
Adunare Naional*
Greater Romania Party, 166
Grossu, Semion, 98–100, 102, 121–24,
126, 136–37, 139, 148, 155
Guboglu, Mikhail, 222
Gülen, Fetullah, 222
Gurie, Metropolitan of Chisinau, 44
Gypsies, 93. *See also* Roma minority

Haarman, Harald, 113
Habsburg empire. *See* Austrian empire
Hadârcă, Ion, 128, 130, 153
Halippa, Pantelimon, 28–32, 35, 48, 58,
106
Halk Toplușu, 219
Heitmann, Klaus, 113
Herța, 92
Hohenzollern-Sigmaringen family, 40
Hotin, 14, 21, 51, 94, 179
Huns, 68

Iakovlev, Gennadii, 192
Iakovlev, Vasilii, 129
Ilașcu, Ilie, 206, 207 (illus.)
Iliescu, Ion, 148–49, 166
Inculeț, Ion, 32, 48, 50 (illus.), 65
Inochentism, 74
Institute for National Minorities, 169
Institute of Jewish Affairs, 174
Interdepartmental Commission for the
Study of the History and Problems of
the Development of Moldova, 125,
128
Interfront, 129, 162, 173
International Institute for Social His-
tory, 105
International Organization for Aiding
the Fighters of the Revolution, 52
Ion Vodă cel Viteaz, 18
Ionescu, Take, 39
Iorga, Nicolae, 32
Iron Guard, 38, 113
Ismail, 22, 94
Israeli Cultural Society, 174
Ivan III, 18

Jews: in Bessarabia, 23; in Moldova,
174–75
Jockey Club, 47
Johnson, Donald, 199
Joint Control Commission, 196

Kardașlık, 214
Karelia, 55, 81–82
Karpat, Kemal, 222

Kay-Kaus, Izz al-Din, 210
Kellogg–Briand pact, 39
Kendigelian, Mihail, 216
Kerensky, Alexander, 32, 48
Kharuzin, A. N., 29
Khaty–chital'ni, 78
Khrushchev, Nikita, 98, 104
Kievan Rus', 179
Kilia, 14, 179
Knezates, 13
Komsomol, 123
Korenizatsiia, 70, 72, 79
Krasnaia Bessarabiia, 52
Krasnye ugly, 78
Kravchuk, Leonid, 205
Kroupensky family, 24, 29
Krushevan, Pavalache, 30
Kuban, 18
Kuchma, Leonid, 205
Küçük Kaynarca, treaty of, 18
Kulaks, 51, 98

Language laws: changes after 1994, 159–60, 169. *See also* Moldovan language; MSSR
Lari, Leonida, 149, 154
Lazarev, Artiom, 105, 113
League of Nations, 38, 63
League of True Russians, 30
Lebed', Aleksei, 200
Lebed', Alexander, 178, 192, 195, 199 (illus.), 200, 202
Lebedev, Pavel, 25
Lenin, Vladimir, 23, 84
Liberal Democratic Party (Russia), 205
Liberal Party (Romania), 36, 40, 48, 94
"Limba noastră," 123, 159
Limba noastră holiday, 229
Literatura şi arta, 124, 127, 131–32, 139
Lithgow, William, 16
Litskai, Valerii, 197
Little Entente, 91
Local government, 175–76
Lozovan, Eugene, 113
Lubavitcher Hassidim, 174

Lucinschi, Petru, 100, 160–62, 163 (illus.), 167, 191
Ludovic I of Anjou, 14
Lupescu, Magda, 83
Lycostomium. *See* Kilia

Madan, Gheorghe, 29–30
Madan, Leonid, 66–67, 69, 72–73, 77, 80, 84, 86–88, 107–8, 112
Magyars, 13
Mahmud II, 19
Malai, I. A., 69
Mămăligă cu brânză, 28
Maniu, Iuliu, 49, 83, 94
Mao Tse-tung, 106
Maracuţa, Grigore, 197
Maramureş, 14, 37
Marea Adunare Naţională, 129, 134
Marghiloman, Alexandru, 48
Martonne, Emmanuel de, 11–12
Marx, Karl, 105
MASSR: creation of, 3, 52, 53–56; Cyrillic alphabet use, 84–86; education, 76–77; latinization campaign, 83; literacy, 78–79; population, 52, 54; publishing, 77–78; purges, 87–88; women in, 74–76
Mateevici, Alexei, 123, 159
Matei, Valeriu, 154
Maurocastro. *See* Akkerman
Mavrocordat family, 17
Michael VIII Palaeologus, 210
Mihai, 50 (illus.), 94
Milev, Dmitrii, 60–61
Military Unit 1045, 219
Minorities: laws relating to, 169–70; popular attitudes toward, 170. *See also entries by ethnic group*
Mircea cel Bătrân, 21
Mocanu, Alexandru, 133
Mokhov, N. A., 109
Moldova literarî, 77.
Moldova nouă, 181
Moldova socialistă, 77, 127, 132. See also *Plugarul ros.*
Moldova suverană, 173

Moldova, Principality of: 1821 revolution in, 22, 27; early history, 13–16; foundation myth, 13, 164; Ottoman empire and, 15–18; Russian occupation, 27. *See also* Bessarabia

Moldova: declaration of independence, 150–51; demographics, xxiii–xxiv; economy, xxiv; relations with Romania, 164–67; withdrawal of Russian troops, 200–2. *See also entries under individual topics*

Moldovan Autonomous Soviet Socialist Republic. *See* MASSR

Moldovan Academy of Sciences, 66, 105, 111, 114, 124, 131, 168–69, 213, 230

Moldovan Democratic Movement in Support of Restructuring, 123, 127–28, 186

Moldovan identity: development of, 49; future of, 229–30; in Middle Ages, 14–15; in nineteenth-century, 25–28; Romanian and Soviet views compared, 57–62; Soviet views on, 109–10; surveys, 159; Western views on, 112–14

Moldovan language: alphabet, 29–30, 45, 65–67, 77, 81–83, 107, 124–35; legal status in 1980s, 120–21, 127–31; legal status in 1990s, 159–60, 169; in MSSR, 106–8, 112; neologisms in, 69; Soviet construction of, 64–70; Western views on, 112–14. *See also* Romanian language

Moldovan leu, xxiv–xxv

Moldovan National Party, 30

Moldovan Scientific Committee, 66–67, 71 (illus.), 73, 79, 87–88

Moldovan Soviet Socialist Republic. See *MSSR*

Moldovan State Publishing House, 77

Moldovan Writers' Union, 131, 133, 157, 230

Moldovanization: of state and party apparat, 72–74; reversal of, 79–81. *See also* Moldovan identity

Moldovanul, 29

Molotov–Ribbentrop Pact, 91, 127, 129–30, 151

Mordovets, I. L., 96

Moşanu, Alexandru, 154

Movement for a Democratic and Prosperous Moldova, 162–63

MSSR: agriculture, 99; Bessarabian/Transnistrian divide, 119, 134–48; collectivization, 96; corruption, 102; creation of, 3, 94; demographic trends, 97, 100–3, 114–19; deportations, 96; intellectuals in, 106–112, 131–34; language laws, 120–21, 127–31; linguistic trends in, 115, 117–118; minorities, 115; name change, xv, 148, 150; national movement in, 121–31; relations with Romania, 148–49

Mungiu, Alina, 165

Nagorno-Karabakh, 179

Napoleon, 18

Năstase, Adrian, 150

National Christian Democratic Peasant Party (Romania), 164, 166

National identity, theories of, 1

National Liberal Party. *See* Liberal Party (Romania)

National Peasant Party (Romania), 48–49, 94

National Salvation Front, 150, 164

Nationalism, theories of, 1–2

Nazi–Soviet treaty. *See* Molotov–Ribbentrop Pact

Nedeliuc, Vasile, 154

Netkachev, Iurii, 194, 200

Nezavisimaia Moldova, 173

Nicholas I, 22

Nicholas II, 50

Ocinschi, Ivan, 80, 82–83, 85, 87

Octiabriu, 83

Octobrists, 20

Odessa military district, 184

Oğuz Turks, 210

Operation North, 96
Operation South, 96
Operational Group of Russian Forces. *See* Fourteenth Army
Organization for Security and Cooperation in Europe, 178–79, 198–204, 222
Our Home congress, 155–57

Party of Communists, 162, 173, 220
Party of Democratic Forces, 163
Party of Rebirth and Reconciliation, 163
Patzinakia, 13
Pechenegs, 13, 68, 210
Pelivan, Ion, 28–29, 58
Perestroika, 124–25, 151
Peter the Great, 18, 180
Phanariots, 16–17, 22, 27
Podolia, 180
Podul de Flori, 149
Political parties: fragmentation of, 162–63; growth of, 153–55. *See also individual parties*
Polovtsy, 68
Popovschi, Nicolae, 48
Popular Front of Moldova: creation of, 128; defections from, 153–55; and Gagauz, 215–16; in 1994 elections, 157; and Transnistria, 186–87; on union with Romania, 152–53
Protocols of the Learned Elders of Zion, 24
Purishkevich, V. M., 30
Pushkin, Alexander, 23

Radio Free Europe. *See* Radio Liberty
Radio Liberty, 104, 113
Rakovsky, Christian, 56–57, 59
Rareş, Petru, 15
Rasputin, 30
Regat, 36–37
Roma minority, 176–77. *See also* Gypsies; Romany language
Roman empire, 2, 13, 109–10
Romania: 1989 revolution, 4, 142, 148–49; constitution, 170; creation of, 27; Holocaust in, 93–94; minorities in, 38, 170; relations with Moldova, 164–67; relations with Soviet Union, 103–6
Romanian Academy, 105
Romanian Communist Party: Bessarabia and, 103, 105–6
Romanian identity. *See* Moldovan identity
Romanian language: in Bessarabia, 45–47; development of, 49; Soviet views on, 64–70; in Transnistria, 206. *See also* Moldovan language
Romany language, 176
Romii Moldovei, 176
Roşca, Iurie, 149, 152–53, 160
Russian empire: 1905 revolution, 28; February revolution, 31; and Moldova, early history, 18
Russian Federation: agreement on troop withdrawal, 200–202; relations with Moldova, 203–4; and Transnistrian conflict, 194–97
Russian language: legal status, 130, 173
Russian minority, 172–74; emigration and refugees, 173–74; and Transnistria, 187
Russian Revolution. *See* Bolshevik Revolution
Rutskoi, Alexander, 194

Salogor, N. I, 100
Sangheli, Andrei, 135, 153, 162, 218
Scînteiu leninist, 77
Second World War: Romania in, 91–95
Serdiuk, Z. T., 100
Serfs: emancipation of, 24
Sergievskii, M. V., 65
Seton-Watson, R. W., 36–37
Sfatul Ţării, 32–35, 43, 48, 57, 65, 93, 106, 147; Moldovan Bloc in, 33, 34 (illus.), 35; union with Romania, 35
Shevardnadze, Eduard, 148
Shevtsov, Vadim, 205
Shornikov, Petr, 129

Siguranţa, 42, 52
Skrypnyk, Mykola, 55, 87
Slavophiles, 26
Smirnov, Igor, 188, 181, 196 (illus.), 197, 206
Smochină, Nichita, 181
Snegur, Mircea, 130, 135–38, 141, 147, 150, 153, 156 (illus.), 161–62; and Gagauz, 217; and "Moldovanism," 4, 155, 166
Socialist Unity Bloc, 157, 173
Socialist Party of Moldova, 157
Socialist Revolutionary Party (Russia), 32, 48, 65
Society for Jewish Culture, 174
Society for Moldovan National Culture, 28, 30
Society of Bessarabians, 52
Solidarity, 133
Soroca, 176
Soviet Union: March 1991 referendum on union, 150; relations with Romania, 38, 51–57, 82, 103–6. *See also entries under individual topics*
Stalin, Joseph, 72, 79, 82, 84, 181
Stănileşti, battle of, 18
State Department for National Relations, 169, 213, 223
State Department of Languages, 159, 168–69
Ştefan cel Mare, 15–16, 18, 148
Stere, Constantin, 29, 31
Stroescu, Vasile, 30–31
Sturza, Ion, 163
Suceava, 15
Şuga, Alexandru, 113
Süleyman the Magnificent, 15
Suvorov, Alexander, 180

Tabunşcik, Georgi, 220
Tagliavini, Carlo, 112–13
Ţara Românească. *See* Wallachia
Taraclia, 175–76
Tatar Bunar, 51–52
Tatars, 13, 68
Ţâu, Nicolae, 135, 153

Tavşancı, Konstantin, 216
Teutonic Knights, 15
Three-Hundredth Guards Airborne Regiment (Russia), 200
Tighina. *See* Bender
Tiraspol Pedagogical Institute, 111
Titulescu, Nicolae, 38, 40, 53 (illus.), 56–57
Topal, Stepan, 191, 215, 216 (illus.), 217, 220
Tott, François de, 17
Transnistria: economy, 186, 205–6, 208; physical features, 178; population, 172–73, 183, 185, 208; refugees, 42, 51, 181; role in MSSR, 134–38; in Romanian history, 179–81; Romanian occupation, 93–94; Russian minority and, 173; in Soviet period, 181–84
Transnistrian conflict: 1997 memorandum on, 202–3; casualties, 178; chronology, 190; course of, 189–98; education and, 197; negotiations, 198–204; Odessa agreement on, 203; origins, 184–89; OSCE role, 198–204; peacekeeping, 196–97; Yeltsin–Snegur agreement, 196–97
Transylvania, 6, 35, 37, 220
Trianon, treaty of, 37
Turkey, 79, 91; and Gagauz, 221–22
Turkish Cooperation and Development Agency, 221
Turkish Language Society, 222

Ukraine: and Bessarabia, 33; relations with Moldova, 171
Ukrainian Self-Defense Forces, 171; and Transnistrian conflict, 197, 202, 205
Ukrainian minority, 170–72; emigration, 174
Ukrainian People's Republic, 33
Ungureanu, Ion, 149
Union of Russian People, 30
United Council of Work Collectives, 188–89
United Principalities: creation of, 27

Urussov, Sergei, 24, 26
Uzbekistan, 70, 79, 133

Vaslui, battle of, 15
Viaţa Basarabiei, 29
Vieru, Grigore, 127, 149, 154
Vlachs, 13–15, 180, 211
Voronin, Vladimir, 162
Voronovich, E. P., 75
Voronovich, Ekaterina, 75
Vorontsov, M. S., 22
Vŭzrazhdane, 175

Wallachia, 21, 36, 105; early history, 14; revolution of 1821, 22, 27; Russian occupation, 27

Wallachs. *See* Vlachs
Warsaw Pact, 103–4
Weigand, Gustav, 64
Wilson, Woodrow, 38
Wittek, Paul, 210
Women: in MASSR, 74–76
Women's Strike Committee, 187

Yeltsin, Boris, 194, 196, 205
Yugoslavia, 36, 91

Zatons'kyi, V. P., 81–82
Zemstvo system, 24, 42, 47
Zhenotdely, 75
Zhirinovsky, Vladimir, 205
Zyuganov, Gennadii, 205

ABOUT THE AUTHOR

CHARLES KING is an assistant professor in the School of Foreign Service and the Department of Government at Georgetown University, where he also holds the Ion Ratiu Chair of Romanian Studies. A former Marshall Scholar, he received a doctorate in political science from Oxford University. His publications include *Nations Abroad: Disapora Politics and International Relations in the Former Soviet Union* (as coeditor), as well as numerous articles in scholarly and policy journals.